AI-Driven Innovations in Electrochemical Technologies for Sustainable Energy Solutions

Edited by

Shreya Sharma, Peeyush Phogat
Ranjana Jha & Sukhvir Singh

Research Lab for Energy Systems
Department of Physics
Netaji Subhas University of Technology
Dwarka, New Delhi, India

AI-Driven Innovations in Electrochemical Technologies for Sustainable Energy Solutions

Editors: Shreya Sharma, Peeyush Phogat, Ranjana Jha & Sukhvir Singh

ISBN (Online): 979-8-89881-186-0

ISBN (Print): 979-8-89881-187-7

ISBN (Paperback): 979-8-89881-188-4

First published in 2026.

Bentham Science Publishers Pte. Ltd.
No. 9 Raffles Place
Office No. 26-01
Singapore 048619
Singapore
Email: subscriptions@benthamscience.net

BENTHAM
SCIENCE

CONTENTS

FOREWORD

In the quest for sustainable energy solutions, humanity stands at a pivotal crossroads. The urgency of climate change, the depletion of finite energy resources, and the relentless surge in global energy demand compel us to rethink our approach to energy innovation. Incremental advancements in existing technologies will no longer suffice; what we need are transformative breakthroughs that redefine the way we generate, store, and utilize energy. At the heart of this transformation lies electrochemical technology—a cornerstone of the future energy landscape. From batteries and fuel cells to supercapacitors, these technologies hold immense promise, yet their complexity demands innovative approaches to accelerate their development.

Enter Artificial Intelligence (AI), a revolutionary force that is transforming industries worldwide. By harnessing AI's unparalleled capabilities in pattern recognition, optimization, and predictive modelling, we can unlock new frontiers in electrochemical science. AI is not merely a tool; it is a catalyst that can propel the design of advanced materials, enhance device performance, and optimize system integration in ways previously unimaginable. The convergence of AI and electrochemistry represents a paradigm shift, offering unprecedented opportunities to address the pressing energy challenges of our time.

AI-Driven Innovations in Electrochemical Technologies for Sustainable Energy Solutions is a groundbreaking exploration of this transformative intersection. This book is a testament to the power of interdisciplinary collaboration, bridging the realms of AI, electrochemistry, and energy science. It delves into how AI can revolutionize the development and deployment of energy technologies, from optimizing energy storage systems to accelerating the discovery of next-generation materials for energy conversion. The potential of AI to streamline research processes, reduce development timelines, and enhance the efficiency of electrochemical devices is truly revolutionary.

What sets this book apart is its unique blend of theoretical rigor and practical relevance. It provides readers with a solid foundation in the principles of AI and electrochemistry while offering actionable insights through real-world applications. Topics such as machine learning-driven battery optimization, AI-guided material synthesis, and the modeling of complex electrochemical systems are explored in depth. The inclusion of case studies and examples from cutting-edge research ensures that readers gain a comprehensive understanding of how AI is already driving innovation in this field.

As someone deeply immersed in the research and development of energy technologies, I am convinced that this book is an indispensable resource for anyone committed to shaping the future of energy. The editors (Dr. Shreya, Dr. Peeyush Phogat, Prof. Ranjana Jha, and Prof. Sukhvir Singh) have curated a remarkable collection of insights from leading experts in the field. Their collective expertise and vision shine through in this meticulously crafted volume, which not only highlights the current state of AI-driven electrochemical research but also charts a course for future advancements.

The integration of AI into electrochemical research is not a fleeting trend; it is a fundamental evolution that will define the next generation of sustainable energy solutions. This book is a call to action for researchers, engineers, policymakers, and students alike. It challenges us to embrace the transformative potential of AI and to harness its power in the pursuit of a more sustainable and energy-efficient world. For anyone seeking to understand and contribute to this exciting frontier, "AI-Driven Innovations in Electrochemical Technologies for Sustainable Energy Solutions " is an essential read.

The journey toward a sustainable energy future is both a challenge and an opportunity. With AI as our ally and electrochemical technologies as our foundation, we are poised to make strides that were once thought impossible. This book serves as a beacon of inspiration, guiding us toward a future where innovation and sustainability are inextricably linked.

Ashok Kumar Nagawat
Delhi Skill and Entrepreneurship University
Delhi
India

PREFACE

The need for sustainable energy solutions has never been more pressing as the world grapples with the realities of climate change, resource depletion, and the imperative to reduce carbon emissions. Electrochemical technologies, especially those involved in energy storage, conversion, and utilization, play a pivotal role in the transition toward a cleaner and more sustainable energy future. The advent of Artificial Intelligence (AI) has brought a paradigm shift to this domain, offering unprecedented opportunities to enhance efficiency, optimize performance, and unlock innovative breakthroughs.

AI-Driven Innovations in Electrochemical Technologies for Sustainable Energy Solutions is an exploration of this transformative synergy between AI and electrochemical systems. This book explores the ways in which AI, machine learning, and advanced data analytics are transforming the design, development, and deployment of energy technologies. From optimizing battery systems to designing novel materials for energy storage and conversion, the integration of AI has the potential to accelerate innovation and efficiency in this field.

The chapters in this book offer insights into a wide range of topics, including the application of AI in the synthesis of advanced energy materials, optimization of energy storage devices such as batteries and supercapacitors, and the integration of renewable energy sources with grid storage. Drawing on both academic research and professional experience, the authors of this book aim to provide a comprehensive understanding of how AI can enhance electrochemical technologies while addressing the challenges associated with energy sustainability. This book is structured to present both fundamental and advanced concepts, making it suitable for a broad audience, including students, researchers, industry professionals, and policymakers. It provides an interdisciplinary perspective that connects the worlds of electrochemistry, AI, and sustainability. The inclusion of case studies and practical examples ensures that readers can appreciate not only the theoretical underpinnings but also the real-world applications of these technologies.

Throughout this journey, the authors have been fortunate to collaborate with numerous exceptional colleagues, mentors, and experts. All of the co-editors have contributed significantly to the development of this book. Their expertise, guidance, and unwavering commitment to advancing knowledge in their respective fields have been invaluable. This book also serves as a call to action, urging researchers, engineers, and policymakers to embrace AI-driven innovations as part of their efforts to solve the energy challenges of our time. The future of sustainable energy lies at the intersection of cutting-edge technologies and interdisciplinary collaboration, and AI is at the heart of this transformation.

We hope this work inspires readers to explore the vast potential of AI in the field of electrochemical technologies and to contribute to the development of solutions that will power a sustainable, energy-efficient future for generations to come.

Shreya Sharma, Peeyush Phogat
Ranjana Jha & Sukhvir Singh
Research Lab for Energy Systems
Department of Physics
Netaji Subhas University of Technology
Dwarka, New Delhi, India

DEDICATION

This book is dedicated to all the contributors, whose passion, insight, and dedication have made this work possible. Their unwavering commitment to advancing knowledge and innovation in the field of electrochemical technologies is a testament to their expertise and vision. I am deeply grateful for their collaboration and the collective effort that has brought this project to life.

To those who persist in their pursuit of progress, despite challenges and setbacks, this book stands as a testament to your resilience.

"Permanence, perseverance, and persistence in spite of all obstacles, discouragements, and impossibilities: It is this that in all things distinguishes the strong soul from the weak."

— Thomas Carlyle

List of Contributors

Aman Grewal	Academy of Scientific and Innovative Research (AcSIR), Ghaziabad-201002, India Advanced Materials & Instrumentation, CSIR-Central Scientific Instruments Organisation, Chandigarh-160030, India
Amandeep Kaur	Academy of Scientific and Innovative Research (AcSIR), Ghaziabad-201002, India Advanced Materials & Instrumentation, CSIR-Central Scientific Instruments Organisation, Chandigarh-160030, India
Anshi Pandey	Research Lab for Energy Systems, Department of Physics, Netaji Subhas University of Technology, Dwarka, New Delhi, India
Anuj Sharma	Advanced Materials & Instrumentation, CSIR-Central Scientific Instruments Organisation, Chandigarh-160030, India
Ashna Verma	Research Lab for Energy Systems, Department of Physics, Netaji Subhas University of Technology, Dwarka, New Delhi, India
Deepa Sharma	Department of Chemistry, Netaji Subhas University of Technology, Dwarka, New Delhi-110078, India
Dushyant Kumar	Department of Physics, Indian Institute of Technology Jodhpur, Rajasthan-342030, India
Jahanvi Thakur	Research Lab for Energy Systems, Department of Physics, Netaji Subhas University of Technology, Dwarka, New Delhi, India
Jyoti Jangra	Academy of Scientific and Innovative Research (AcSIR), Ghaziabad-201002, India Advanced Materials & Instrumentation, CSIR-Central Scientific Instruments Organisation, Chandigarh-160030, India
M.S. Sumitha	Centre for Advanced Materials Research, Department of Physics, Government College for Women, University of Kerala, Thiruvananthapuram, India
N. L. Singh	Department of Nanotechnology, Delhi Skill and Entrepreneurship University, Dwarka, New Delhi, India
Parneet Kaur	Advanced Materials & Instrumentation, CSIR-Central Scientific Instruments Organisation, Chandigarh-160030, India
Prashanth S. Adarakatti	Department of Chemistry, SVM Arts, Science and Commerce College, Ilkal, India
Priya Gupta	School of Basic and Applied Sciences, K.R. Mangalam University, Gurugram, Haryana, India
Purnima Jain	Department of Chemistry, Netaji Subhas University of Technology, Dwarka, New Delhi-110078, India
Ritika Khatri	School of Basic and Applied Sciences, K.R. Mangalam University, Gurugram, Haryana, India
Satyam Rawat	Research Lab for Energy Systems, Department of Physics, Netaji Subhas University of Technology, Dwarka, New Delhi, India
Shavita Salora	Academy of Scientific and Innovative Research (AcSIR), Ghaziabad-201002, India Advanced Materials & Instrumentation, CSIR-Central Scientific Instruments Organisation, Chandigarh-160030, India

Shilpi Sehrawat	Department of Chemistry, Netaji Subhas University of Technology, Dwarka, New Delhi-110078, India
Shubham Kumar Patial	Academy of Scientific and Innovative Research (AcSIR), Ghaziabad-201002, India Advanced Materials & Instrumentation, CSIR-Central Scientific Instruments Organisation, Chandigarh-160030, India
Soumya Rai	Research Lab for Energy Systems, Department of Physics, Netaji Subhas University of Technology, Dwarka, New Delhi, India
Suman Singh	Academy of Scientific and Innovative Research (AcSIR), Ghaziabad-201002, India Advanced Materials & Instrumentation, CSIR-Central Scientific Instruments Organisation, Chandigarh-160030, India
Suman Srivastava	Department of Chemistry, M.V. College Buxar (A Constituent Unit of Veer Kunwar Singh University Ara), Bihar, India
T.S Xavier	Centre for Advanced Materials Research, Department of Physics, Government College for Women, University of Kerala, Thiruvananthapuram, India
Tarun Kumar	Department of Physics, Indian Institute of Technology Jodhpur, Rajasthan-342030, India

CHAPTER 1

Introduction to AI-Driven Innovations in Electrochemical Technologies

Ashna Verma[1,*] and **N. L. Singh**[2]

[1] *Research Lab for Energy Systems, Department of Physics, Netaji Subhas University of Technology, Dwarka, New Delhi, India*

[2] *Department of Nanotechnology, Delhi Skill and Entrepreneurship University, Dwarka, New Delhi, India*

Abstract: Artificial Intelligence (AI) is revolutionizing electrochemical technologies, driving innovations in energy storage, conversion, and the discovery of advanced materials. This chapter delves into the transformative role of AI in the design, optimization, and enhancement of electrochemical systems, with a focus on applications such as batteries, fuel cells, supercapacitors, and electrolysis. By integrating AI-driven algorithms, researchers and engineers can rapidly analyze complex datasets, predict material properties, and optimize performance parameters, significantly reducing the time and cost of experimentation. Core AI techniques, including machine learning, neural networks, reinforcement learning, and predictive analytics, are explored in depth, highlighting their applications in electrochemistry. These techniques enable the prediction of reaction kinetics, modeling of complex electrochemical behaviors, optimization of energy storage and conversion systems, and data-driven decision-making for material discovery and process control. The chapter also examines emerging trends, including AI-enabled simulations, sustainable material design, and the integration of AI in next-generation systems. The interdisciplinary nature of these innovations is emphasized, showcasing collaboration across physics, chemistry, and data science. In addition to highlighting opportunities, the chapter also critically examines key challenges such as data scarcity, fragmentation, and the limited interpretability and transferability of AI models. These constraints pose significant hurdles to broader adoption and reliability, underscoring the need for standardized datasets, explainable AI, and domain-aware model development. Ultimately, the chapter underscores AI's pivotal role in accelerating advancements in electrochemical technologies, fostering sustainable energy solutions, and shaping the future of intelligent energy systems.

* **Corresponding author Ashna Verma:** Research Lab for Energy Systems, Department of Physics, Netaji Subhas University of Technology, Dwarka, New Delhi, India; E-mail: ashnaverma01@gmail.com

Shreya Sharma, Peeyush Phogat, Ranjana Jha & Sukhvir Singh (Eds.)

Keywords: Advanced material discovery, AI-enabled simulations, Artificial intelligence, Data scarcity, Data science, Energy storage, Interdisciplinary collaboration, Machine learning, Neural networks, Predictive analytics, Reinforcement learning.

INTRODUCTION

Electrochemical technologies serve as the cornerstone of numerous advancements in modern science and engineering, offering vital solutions to some of the most pressing global challenges in energy, sustainability, and industrial innovation. These technologies encompass a broad range of systems, including batteries, fuel cells, supercapacitors, and electrolysis units, which are integral to energy storage, energy conversion, and chemical production, as depicted in Fig. (**1**) [1]. From powering electric vehicles and storing renewable energy to producing green hydrogen and enabling portable electronics, electrochemical systems play a critical role in facilitating the global shift towards cleaner, more sustainable energy solutions. However, the development and optimization of such systems have historically faced significant challenges, including labor-intensive experimental methodologies, slow material discovery cycles, and the high costs associated with scaling up laboratory findings to real-world applications.

Fig. (1). Illustration of electrochemical technologies, which include **(a)** batteries, **(b)** fuel cells, **(c)** supercapacitors, and **(d)** electrolysis units, play a vital role in energy storage, conversion, and chemical production. The images have been created from ideogram.ai.

In recent years, the integration of Artificial Intelligence (AI) into the field of electrochemical technologies has revolutionized the way researchers approach these challenges, as shown in Fig. (**2**) [2]. AI, powered by Machine Learning (ML), Deep Learning (DL), and advanced data analytics, offers unprecedented capabilities in handling large, complex datasets. These algorithms can efficiently analyze experimental and computational data, identify hidden patterns, predict material properties, and optimize system-level parameters with a speed and precision unattainable through conventional approaches. This has accelerated the discovery of high-performance materials, improved energy efficiency, and enhanced the durability and reliability of electrochemical systems. For instance, AI-driven models are being used to identify novel electrode materials with superior energy density [3], predict electrochemical behaviour [4] under varying conditions, and simulate reaction mechanisms with remarkable accuracy. Furthermore, AI is enabling real-time monitoring and predictive maintenance of energy storage and conversion systems, significantly improving their safety and operational reliability. By reducing the time and cost required for experimentation, AI empowers researchers to shift their focus from trial-and-error methods to targeted, data-driven innovation.

Fig. (2). The image depicting the integration of Artificial Intelligence (AI) into the field of electrochemical technologies, showcasing their synergy and potential in advancing energy systems, has been created from ideogram.ai.

Despite these advancements, significant research gaps remain. Many AI-driven models and algorithms are yet to be fully validated in real-world applications, particularly in scaling up from laboratory conditions to industrial settings [5]. While AI has demonstrated remarkable predictive capabilities, many models—particularly those based on deep learning—operate as "black boxes," offering limited transparency into how inputs influence outputs. This lack of interpretability can hinder scientific understanding and reduce confidence in AI-assisted decision-making. However, it is important to recognize that not all AI methods are inherently opaque. For instance, decision trees, linear regression, and symbolic regression are inherently interpretable models. Post hoc explanation tools, such as SHAP (SHapley Additive exPlanations) and LIME (Local Interpretable Model-agnostic Explanations), have been successfully applied to interpret predictions from complex models in material discovery and battery diagnostics.

This chapter explores this intersection of AI and electrochemical systems, providing an overview of the fundamental principles of electrochemical technologies and discussing how AI is reshaping the landscape of research and development. Through examples and case studies, it delves into the groundbreaking applications of AI in materials discovery, process optimization, and sustainability [6]. By examining the challenges and future directions of this dynamic field, the chapter highlights how AI-driven innovations are paving the way for a smarter, more sustainable energy future.

FUNDAMENTALS OF ELECTROCHEMICAL TECHNOLOGIES

Electrochemical technologies are grounded in the principles of electrochemistry, which studies the interaction between electrical energy and chemical reactions. These technologies exploit the movement of ions and electrons to drive processes that enable energy storage, conversion, and chemical synthesis. The core components of an electrochemical system include electrodes (anode and cathode), an electrolyte, and an external circuit. When a chemical reaction occurs at the electrode surfaces, electrons are either released or absorbed, enabling the transfer of energy between chemical and electrical forms.

Electrochemical technologies are widely utilized in various devices, including batteries [7], fuel cells [8], supercapacitors [9], and electrolysis systems [10]. Batteries, such as lithium-ion cells, store energy in a chemical form and release it as electrical energy on demand, making them indispensable for portable electronics and electric vehicles [11]. Fuel cells convert chemical energy directly into electricity, offering clean and efficient energy solutions for transportation and stationary power applications. Supercapacitors, renowned for their rapid charging and discharging capabilities, are ideal for applications that require short bursts of high power. Electrolysis systems, such as water electrolyzers, use electricity to drive chemical reactions, enabling the production of hydrogen fuel and other valuable chemicals [12]. Despite their diverse applications, electrochemical systems face challenges such as limited efficiency, material degradation, and scalability. Innovations in electrode materials, reaction mechanisms, and system designs are critical to overcoming these limitations. By understanding these fundamentals, researchers and engineers can optimize electrochemical processes and develop technologies that meet the growing demands for clean, sustainable energy and industrial solutions.

Principles of Electrochemical Reactions

Electrochemical reactions form the foundation of electrochemical technologies, enabling the conversion of energy between chemical and electrical forms. Several key principles govern these reactions:

1. **Redox Reactions (Reduction- Oxidation):** Electrochemical reactions are based on redox processes, where oxidation (loss of electrons) occurs at the anode in which lithium atoms in the anode release electrons to form lithium ions ($Li \rightarrow Li^+ + e^-$), and reduction (gain of electrons) takes place at the cathode in which lithium ions migrate to the cathode during discharge and combine with electrons to form lithium atoms depicted in Fig. (**3a**) [13]. These reactions are the foundation of energy storage and conversion in electrochemical systems.
2. **Electrode-Electrolyte Interface:** Reactions occur at the interface between the electrodes, which are conductive materials (*e.g.*, metals, carbon, or semiconductors) and the electrolyte, which is a medium (liquid, solid, or gel), as in Fig. (**3b**). The electrodes facilitate electron transfer, while the electrolyte enables the movement of ions between them, ensuring charge balance within the system [14].
3. **Electrochemical Potential:** The driving force for an electrochemical reaction is the difference in electrochemical potential (often called the cell potential or voltage) between the anode and cathode shown in Fig. (**3c**). This potential difference arises from the inherent properties of the materials used and the chemical reactions that occur. The standard potential of the reactions is measured under standard conditions and determines the maximum voltage the system can produce or require. The higher the potential difference, the more energy the system can store or deliver, making material selection critical for high-performance electrochemical systems.

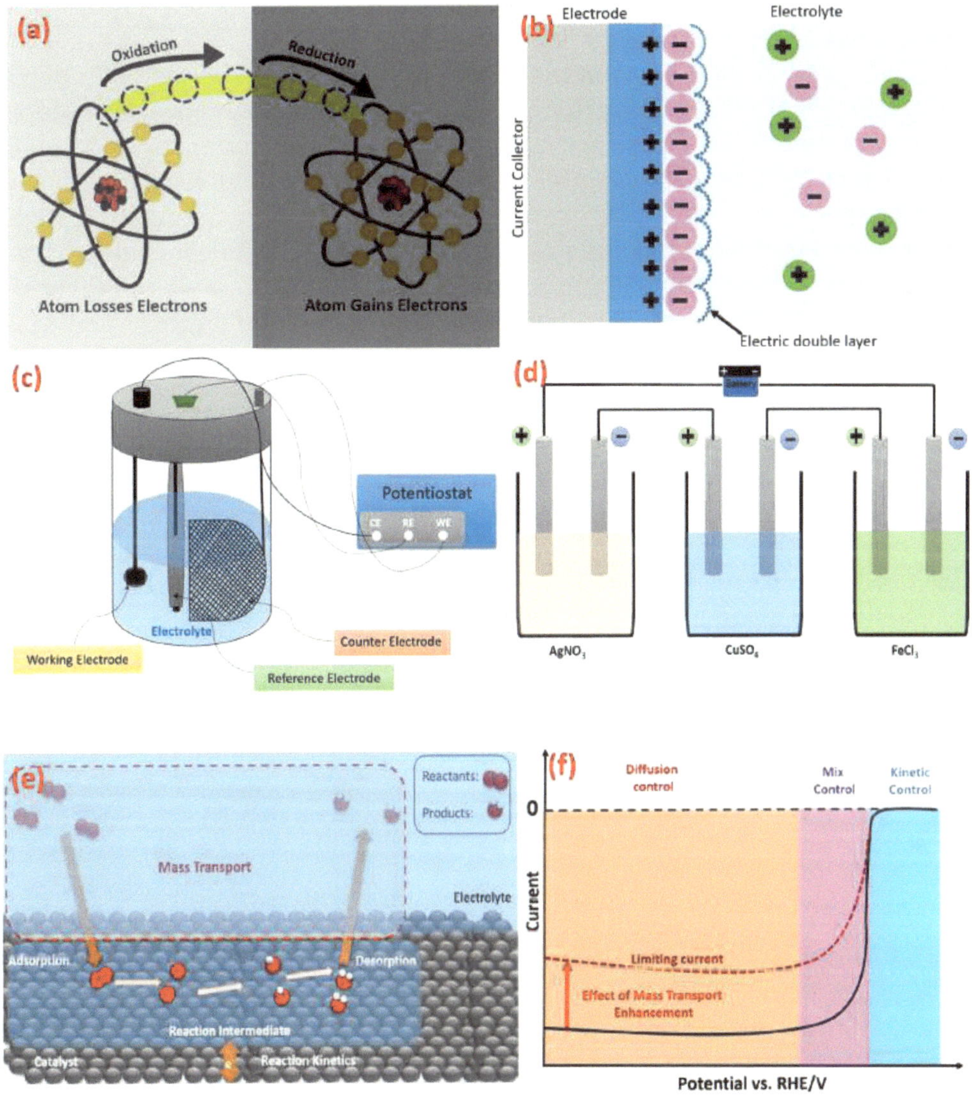

Fig. (3). Key Principles of Electrochemical Reactions including **(a)** Redox Reactions reproduced from reference [16] Copyright © 2021, Leverage Edu, **(b)** Electrode- Electrolyte Interface reproduced from reference [17] Copyright © 2008 - 2024 ResearchGate GmbH, **(c)** Electrochemical Potential reproduced from reference [18] Copyright © 2008 - 2024 ResearchGate GmbH, **(d)** Faraday's Laws of Electrolysis reproduced from reference [19] Copyright © 2024 (Chemistry Learner) **(e)** Kinetics and Mass Transport reproduced from reference [20] Copyright © 2008 - 2024 ResearchGate GmbH .

4. **Faraday's Laws of Electrolysis:** These laws relate the amount of substance transformed at the electrodes to the quantity of electric charge passed through the

system. Faraday's laws provide a quantitative framework for understanding electrochemical processes, as in Fig. (**3d**) [15].

5. **Kinetics and Mass Transport:** The rate of electrochemical reactions depends on the kinetics of electron transfer and the transport of reactants and products to and from the electrode surfaces shown in Fig. (**3e**). The current *versus* potential graph in electrochemical systems highlights three key regions: the activation-controlled region, dominated by reaction kinetics; the mixed region, where both kinetics and mass transport influence current; and the diffusion-limited region, where mass transport restricts current to a limiting value, as shown in Fig. (**3f**). It provides insights into reaction mechanisms, transport limitations, and system optimization.

Key Applications

Electrochemical technologies have found widespread applications across various domains, primarily in energy storage, energy conversion, and chemical production. These technologies play a pivotal role in addressing global challenges related to clean energy, sustainability, and industrial efficiency. Table **1** depicting the key applications of electrochemical technologies:

Table 1. Table highlighting the major applications of electrochemical technologies.

Application	Description	Examples
Batteries	Store energy in chemical form and release it as electrical energy when needed.	-**Lithium-Ion Batteries (LIBs):** Used in electric vehicles, portable electronics, and grid storage. -**Flow Batteries:** Scalable energy storage for renewable integration.
Fuel Cells	Convert chemical energy from fuels directly into electrical energy through redox reactions with minimal emissions.	-**PEMFCs:** Hydrogen-powered vehicles and portable power. -**SOFCs:** Stationary power generation using natural gas or hydrogen.
Supercapacitors	Store energy through electrostatic charge rather than chemical reactions, offering high power density and rapid charge-discharge capabilities.	- Regenerative braking in vehicles. - Grid stabilization. - Power backup systems for electronics.
Electrolysis Systems	Use electrical energy to drive chemical reactions, enabling the production of valuable fuels and chemicals.	-**Water Electrolysis:** Hydrogen fuel production. -**Chlor-Alkali Process:** Production of chlorine, hydrogen, and sodium hydroxide. - CO_2 reduction.

(Table 1) cont.....

Application	Description	Examples
Sensors and Diagnostics	Utilize electrochemical principles to detect gases, ions, and biological molecules for monitoring and analysis [21].	-**Biosensors:** Glucose monitoring for diabetes. -**Gas Sensors:** Detection of pollutants like CO. -**Impedance Spectroscopy:** Battery monitoring.
Industrial Processes	Leverage electrochemical systems for manufacturing and chemical production.	-**Electroplating:** Coating metals for corrosion resistance. -**Electrochemical Machining:** Shaping hard materials. -**Chemical Synthesis:** Ammonia production.

THE INTERSECTION OF AI AND ELECTROCHEMICAL TECHNOLOGIES

The integration of Artificial Intelligence (AI) with electrochemical technologies marks a transformative shift in how research, development, and optimization are approached in this field. Electrochemical systems often rely on complex processes involving material interactions, reaction mechanisms, and system-level performance parameters. Traditionally, the study and improvement of these systems have required extensive experimentation and simulations, which are time-intensive and resource-intensive. AI has emerged as a powerful tool to address these challenges by leveraging its ability to process vast datasets, uncover patterns, and make accurate predictions. By processing vast amounts of experimental and computational data, AI enables the rapid identification of trends and correlations that may not be apparent through conventional approaches. Machine Learning (ML) models, a subset of AI, can predict material properties, reaction kinetics, and system behavior based on existing datasets. This capability accelerates the discovery of novel materials, such as high-energy-density battery components or efficient catalysts for fuel cells and electrolyzers.

Moreover, AI excels in optimizing processes by analyzing operational data in real time [22]. For example, it can identify the most efficient operating conditions for a system, such as the optimal temperature, pressure, or current density, to enhance performance while minimizing energy losses. Beyond optimization, AI contributes to predictive maintenance [16], forecasting system failures [23], and diagnosing degradation in electrochemical systems [24]. By leveraging its predictive power, AI reduces downtime, enhances system safety, and extends the lifespan of devices. This convergence of AI and electrochemistry is reshaping the landscape of energy technologies, fostering innovation and efficiency.

Why AI? The Need for Data-Driven Insights

Electrochemical systems, including batteries, fuel cells, and electrolyzers, involve intricate processes such as electron and ion transport, electrochemical reactions, and material degradation. These systems operate in dynamic environments where multiple parameters, including temperature, pressure, current density, and voltage, can influence performance in complex ways. Traditional experimental techniques often rely on trial and error, empirical models, or computational methods that are either resource-intensive or lack the ability to handle the vast amounts of data generated in these systems [25]. Moreover, traditional models tend to oversimplify the complexities of these processes, which can limit their predictive power and applicability in real-world scenarios.

AI addresses these challenges by offering data-driven insights that significantly enhance the understanding, design, and optimization of electrochemical systems. Electrochemical devices, such as batteries or fuel cells, can benefit from AI's ability to monitor performance in real-time and adjust parameters dynamically to optimize efficiency and lifespan. For instance, AI can continuously adjust the charge/discharge cycles of a battery to optimize its energy storage capacity while minimizing degradation. In fuel cells, AI can regulate parameters such as pressure and temperature to ensure optimal reaction conditions and enhance overall efficiency. By continuously learning from feedback data, AI systems can make adjustments on the fly, which significantly reduces the need for human intervention and leads to more efficient system operation. Moreover, in electrochemical applications, the search for novel materials that can enhance the performance of energy storage devices or catalysis in fuel cells often involves testing a vast array of material combinations. AI can streamline this process by predicting the properties of new materials based on existing data, significantly reducing the time and cost required for experimental validation [26]. In electrochemistry, experiments often generate vast amounts of data from various sources, including spectroscopic measurements, microscopy images, and electrochemical tests [27]. AI models, particularly deep learning algorithms, are well-suited to process these large datasets and identify subtle patterns that may not be immediately apparent to human researchers. This ability to process and analyze data at scale makes AI indispensable for fields such as materials science, where new materials are continually being developed and tested. It empowers researchers to move beyond traditional methods, providing insights that would be difficult or impossible to obtain using conventional techniques. By leveraging AI, the field of electrochemistry is poised to achieve faster innovation, improved system performance, and more sustainable energy solutions.

Core AI Techniques in Electrochemistry

The application of Artificial Intelligence (AI) in electrochemistry hinges on various core techniques that enable significant advancements in the optimization of materials, processes, and systems. These techniques utilize advanced computational methods and data-driven approaches to enhance the performance, efficiency, and sustainability of electrochemical technologies. AI enables researchers to analyze complex datasets, identify patterns, and make predictions that would be challenging or time-consuming with traditional methods.

Key AI techniques used in electrochemistry include Machine Learning (ML), which helps in material discovery and process optimization by analysing large datasets to predict material properties and optimize system conditions [3]. Fig. (**4**) illustrates the overlap and interplay of core AI techniques in electrochemistry in the form of a Venn diagram. Deep Learning (DL), a more advanced subset of ML, can handle high-dimensional data, such as images and time-series data, making it particularly useful for analyzing electrode surfaces, predicting degradation, and enhancing simulations of electrochemical reactions. Reinforcement Learning (RL), on the other hand, allows for real-time optimization by continuously adjusting operating parameters in energy storage devices or fuel cells to maximize performance and longevity [28]. Together, these AI techniques provide transformative tools that are reshaping electrochemistry, driving innovation, and improving the efficiency and sustainability of energy systems.

Machine Learning (ML)

Machine Learning (ML) is a subset of Artificial Intelligence (AI) that focuses on developing algorithms that enable systems to learn from data, identify patterns, and make decisions without explicit programming. Instead of relying on predefined instructions, ML algorithms utilize statistical methods to derive insights from large datasets and continually improve their performance over time as they are exposed to more data. In its simplest form, machine learning involves training a model using input data and known outcomes, allowing the algorithm to recognize relationships and generalize from these examples to make predictions on unseen data.

ML can be broadly classified into three main types: supervised learning, unsupervised learning, and reinforcement learning. Supervised learning involves training a model on a labelled dataset, where the input data is paired with corresponding output labels [29]. This enables the model to learn the relationship between input and output, allowing it to predict the output for new, unseen data. Unsupervised learning, on the other hand, works with unlabelled data and focuses on identifying hidden patterns, such as clustering similar data points or reducing data dimensionality. Reinforcement learning involves training an agent to make a series of decisions by interacting with an environment and receiving feedback in the form of rewards or penalties. This type of learning is often employed in autonomous systems, where an agent must learn the optimal actions to take in order to maximize long-term success. In electrochemical technologies, machine learning plays a transformative role by analyzing complex and high-dimensional datasets that arise from experiments, simulations, and real-world operations. For example, in battery research, ML can be applied to predict the performance of new electrode materials or to optimize the charge-discharge cycles of existing battery systems. The algorithm learns from historical performance data to identify which material properties or operational conditions are most strongly correlated with performance metrics, such as energy density, efficiency, and lifespan.

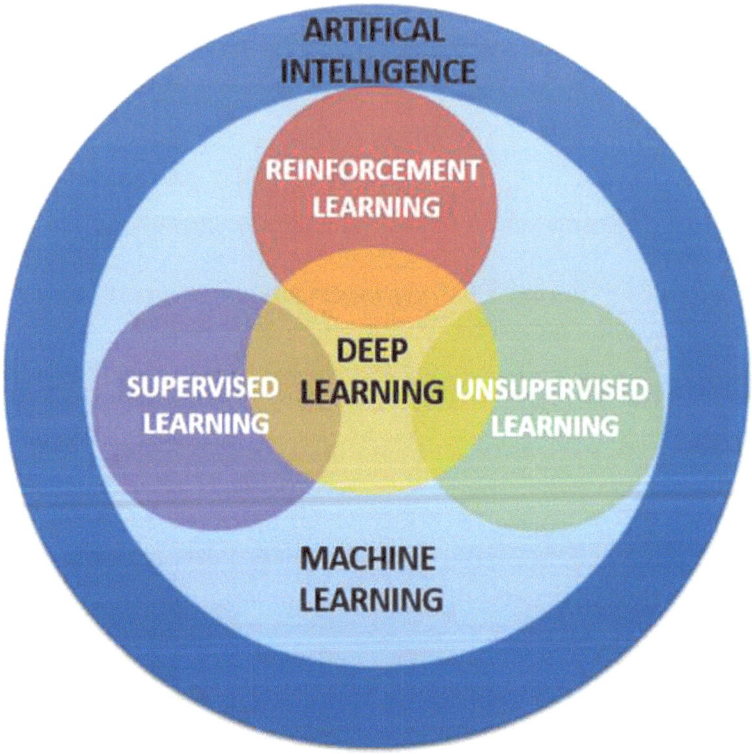

Fig. (4). Venn diagram illustrating the overlap and interplay of core AI techniques in electrochemistry.

Deep Learning

Deep learning, a specialized subset of machine learning, involves neural networks with multiple layers that process data hierarchically. These multilayered networks, also known as Deep Neural Networks (DNNs), can automatically extract complex patterns from large datasets without needing explicit feature extraction, making them particularly useful for tasks involving high-dimensional data [30]. The human brain's neural structure inspires deep learning models, which can recognize intricate relationships between input and output, making them ideal for applications that require complex pattern recognition. In electrochemistry, deep learning has found significant applications in several areas, particularly in the analysis and optimization of electrochemical systems. For example, deep learning is extensively used in material discovery, where it can predict the properties of novel materials by learning from vast databases of known compounds and their electrochemical characteristics. It can identify promising materials for battery electrodes, electrolytes, or fuel cell catalysts by analysing structural, electronic, and chemical data to predict their performance in real-world applications.

In addition to material discovery, deep learning is applied to process optimization in electrochemical systems. It can model and optimize the behavior of batteries, fuel cells, and electrolyzers by analyzing experimental data to determine the best operating conditions, such as voltage, temperature, or current density. Deep learning models can also enhance real-time monitoring, identifying degradation patterns in devices like batteries or fuel cells and predicting failures before they occur. Furthermore, deep learning aids in the analysis of microscopic images of electrode surfaces, enabling the detection of defects, corrosion, or other forms of degradation that could impact performance. By leveraging the power of deep learning, electrochemical technologies can be designed and operated more efficiently, leading to improved performance, longer lifespans, and more sustainable solutions.

Reinforcement Learning

Reinforcement Learning (RL) is a type of machine learning in which an agent learns to make decisions by interacting with an environment and receiving feedback in the form of rewards or penalties based on its actions. The goal of reinforcement learning is to maximize the cumulative reward over time, which requires the agent to explore different actions and learn from the consequences of those actions. Unlike supervised learning, where the model is trained on labeled data, RL is based on trial and error, allowing the agent to learn autonomously from its experience.

In the context of reinforcement learning, the agent operates within an environment, observing the current state, taking an action, and transitioning to a new state based on the action. The environment then provides feedback in the form of a reward signal, which quantifies how well or poorly the action aligns with achieving the agent's goal. The agent's objective is to find an optimal policy, which is a strategy that defines the best action to take in each state to maximize long-term rewards. This process is often modelled as a Markov Decision Process (MDP), where the environment's state, actions, and rewards are clearly defined [31].

In electrochemical technologies, Reinforcement Learning (RL) is applied to optimize processes and control systems. For instance, RL can be used to fine-tune the operating parameters of energy storage devices, such as batteries, fuel cells, and electrolyzers. By continuously adjusting factors such as temperature, current density, and voltage, an RL agent can learn the optimal settings that maximize energy output, minimize degradation, and extend the system's lifespan. RL also plays a key role in autonomous experimentation, guiding robotic systems or automated laboratories to explore various variables and material combinations to identify optimal conditions or new materials. Additionally, RL is utilized in predictive maintenance, helping to anticipate potential system failures or degradation, enabling proactive measures to ensure system stability and efficiency. Through these applications, reinforcement learning is driving advancements in the performance, efficiency, and sustainability of electrochemical technologies.

AI-DRIVEN ADVANCEMENTS IN ELECTROCHEMICAL SYSTEMS

The integration of Artificial Intelligence (AI) into electrochemical systems is revolutionizing the development, optimization, and maintenance of energy storage and conversion technologies. These systems, which include batteries, fuel cells, and electrolyzers, are vital for advancing sustainable energy solutions. However, their complexity poses significant challenges, as they involve intricate material interactions, chemical reactions, and system-level dynamics. Traditional methods of research and optimization often struggle to address these complexities effectively, requiring time-consuming experimentation and modeling. AI-driven approaches have emerged as a powerful solution to these challenges, offering innovative tools to accelerate progress and enhance system performance. By leveraging advanced computational techniques, AI enables researchers and engineers to analyze vast amounts of data generated from electrochemical experiments and operations. It can uncover hidden patterns and correlations that are difficult to identify using conventional methods, providing valuable insights for improving system efficiency and reliability. Furthermore, AI's ability to process complex datasets in real time facilitates dynamic adjustments to system operations, ensuring optimal performance under varying conditions.

This transformative approach also reduces the reliance on trial-and-error methods, significantly cutting down the time and resources needed for development. As a result, AI not only accelerates the pace of innovation but also enhances the sustainability and scalability of electrochemical technologies, making them more viable for widespread adoption in addressing global energy challenges. Key areas where AI excels include material discovery, process optimization, real-time monitoring, and predictive maintenance, as shown in Fig. (**5**).

AI IN MATERIAL DISCOVERY FOR ELECTROCHEMICAL SYSTEMS

Material discovery is a cornerstone of advancing electrochemical technologies, as the performance and efficiency of devices like batteries, fuel cells, and electrolyzers heavily depend on the materials used. Traditionally, identifying new materials involved trial-and-error experimentation and computational modeling, processes that are often time-consuming and resource-intensive. AI has transformed this field by providing data-driven tools to analyze material properties, predict performance, and accelerate the discovery of novel materials. AI algorithms, particularly Machine Learning (ML) models, analyze large datasets containing information on material compositions, structures, and properties [33]. Using these datasets, AI identifies patterns and relationships that humans might overlook, enabling the prediction of material behavior under specific electrochemical conditions. For example, AI can predict how a particular material will perform as an electrode in a lithium-ion battery or as a catalyst in a fuel cell, eliminating the need for exhaustive experimentation. These predictions facilitate the development of materials with desirable properties, such as higher conductivity, improved stability, or enhanced catalytic activity.

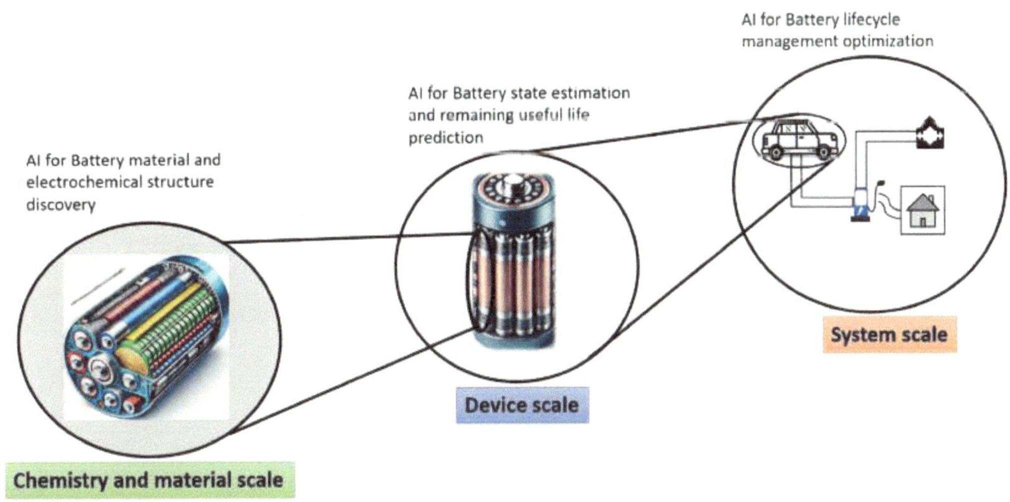

Fig. (5). The impact of AI on electrochemical energy storage: from designing materials to integrating systems. Reproduced from reference [32] Copyright © 2024 Elsevier Inc.

AI also aids in efficiently exploring vast chemical spaces. Advanced algorithms can simulate millions of potential material combinations and identify the most promising candidates for experimental validation. This approach significantly reduces the time and cost required for material discovery while increasing the likelihood of finding breakthrough materials. Table **2** shows the applications of AI in material discovery and their impact.

Table 2. The table illustrating the example Applications of AI in Material Discovery.

Applications	Role of AI	Impact
Electrode Material Design	Predicting properties like conductivity, stability, and energy density.	Faster development of high-performance electrodes.
Catalyst Optimization	Identifying catalysts with high activity and selectivity for fuel cells or electrolyzers.	Improved efficiency and reduced material costs.
Electrolyte Development	Analyzing ionic conductivity and stability for energy storage systems.	Enhanced safety and performance in batteries.
Material Screening	Exploring vast databases to identify potential materials for specific applications.	Accelerated material discovery process.

AI- Driven Optimization of Electrochemical Processes

The optimization of electrochemical processes is a cornerstone for improving the performance, scalability, and sustainability of energy storage and conversion technologies. These processes involve controlling multiple variables—such as temperature, pressure, current density, voltage, and material composition—to ensure that electrochemical devices, including batteries, fuel cells, and electrolyzers, operate at peak efficiency. Traditional optimization methods, which often rely on trial-and-error experimentation or oversimplified empirical models, can be both time-consuming and costly. Moreover, such approaches may not account for the complex, nonlinear interactions between the numerous factors that influence system performance. This is where AI-driven optimization comes into play, providing a transformative solution that can accelerate development and enhance performance through advanced algorithms and data-driven approaches [34].

AI-powered techniques, particularly Machine Learning (ML) and Reinforcement Learning (RL), are proving highly effective in optimizing electrochemical systems. ML models can process large amounts of experimental and operational data to identify hidden patterns and predict the outcomes of varying process conditions. For example, in battery technology, AI can analyze data from numerous charge/discharge cycles to determine the optimal charging rates and voltage levels that minimize degradation and maximize energy storage capacity.

Similarly, in fuel cells and electrolyzers, AI can fine-tune parameters such as pressure, temperature, and current density to enhance electrochemical reactions, improving efficiency and energy output. Reinforcement Learning (RL) takes optimization a step further by introducing a feedback-driven process. For instance, RL can be used to manage the charge/discharge cycles of batteries in real-time, thereby prolonging their lifespan while maximizing efficiency.

Moreover, AI-driven optimization models can play a significant role in scaling laboratory-scale systems to industrial-scale production. This is a critical factor in moving from prototype development to commercial manufacturing. AI algorithms can model reaction kinetics, material interactions, and flow dynamics in large-scale electrochemical processes, ensuring that production runs efficiently and consistently. By optimizing these processes, AI reduces energy consumption, minimizes material waste, and improves yield, which is vital for the economic and environmental sustainability of industrial production.

Additionally, AI models can be utilized to enhance operational decision-making in industrial settings. For instance, AI can assist in real-time quality control by identifying performance anomalies or degradation patterns, enabling timely interventions to avoid expensive repairs or replacements. With AI systems, manufacturers can predict issues before they occur, thereby reducing the risk of downtime and enhancing the reliability of electrochemical devices.

Real-time monitoring and predictive maintenance are crucial elements for ensuring the efficiency, longevity, and reliability of electrochemical systems, including batteries, fuel cells, and electrolyzers. These systems are subject to wear and degradation over time due to the constant cycling of charge/discharge processes, exposure to high temperatures, or chemical reactions within the cells. Traditional maintenance approaches are often reactive, requiring systems to fail before corrective actions are taken. However, AI-driven real-time monitoring and predictive maintenance allow for proactive management, reducing downtime, enhancing system performance, and minimizing costly repairs or replacements.

Real-Time Monitoring and Predictive Maintenance

Real-Time Monitoring involves the continuous collection and analysis of operational data from electrochemical devices. Sensors embedded in the system measure parameters such as voltage, current, temperature, pressure, and electrochemical impedance. AI algorithms, particularly Machine Learning (ML) and Deep Learning (DL), analyze this vast amount of data in real time to detect patterns, trends, and anomalies that could signal potential issues. For example, in batteries, AI can monitor voltage fluctuations and temperature changes to predict when cells are approaching failure or when energy efficiency begins to decline. In fuel cells, real-time data can be used to detect issues related to catalyst degradation, membrane failure, or fuel imbalance. These early warnings enable timely interventions to prevent catastrophic failures, reduce operational costs, and extend the system's lifespan.

Predictive Maintenance takes it a step further by utilizing both historical and real-time data to anticipate when maintenance will be required before a failure occurs. By analyzing the degradation patterns of various components, AI algorithms can forecast the optimal time for maintenance or part replacement. This helps avoid unplanned downtime, which can significantly impact productivity and performance in large-scale industrial operations. In the case of batteries, for instance, predictive maintenance algorithms can assess the cycle life of cells, identifying the point at which performance will begin to degrade [35]. This enables the optimization of charge/discharge cycles, ensuring the system operates efficiently throughout its lifespan.

Applications of Real-Time Monitoring and Predictive Maintenance in Electrochemical Systems:

1. **Batteries**: By monitoring voltage, temperature, and internal resistance, AI can accurately predict battery life and identify potential faults, such as short circuits or overcharging risks. Predictive models help extend battery lifespan by optimizing charging cycles and alerting users to potential failures before they happen.
2. **Fuel Cells**: Sensors in fuel cells monitor key performance indicators like fuel consumption, membrane integrity, and pressure. AI models predict when maintenance is needed to prevent efficiency losses due to degradation or contamination.
3. **Electrolyzers**: Electrolyzers, used for hydrogen production, require regular monitoring of electrode performance and cell efficiency. AI can detect early signs of reduced efficiency, corrosion, or clogging, triggering maintenance to restore performance.

CASE STUDIES

As the demand for clean, efficient, and sustainable energy solutions increases, the integration of AI into electrochemical technologies has proven to be a game-changer. From the optimization of energy storage systems, such as lithium-ion batteries and supercapacitors, to the advancement of hydrogen fuel cells and artificial photosynthesis, AI is enabling significant improvements in material discovery, process efficiency, and system reliability. By harnessing the power of machine learning, neural networks, and predictive analytics, researchers and engineers can analyze vast datasets, model complex electrochemical behaviors, and predict material properties —tasks that were previously time-consuming and costly. These case studies not only highlight the efficiency gains and cost reductions brought about by AI but also demonstrate its ability to uncover new insights, discover innovative materials, and optimize energy conversion and storage processes. Additionally, these examples highlight the importance of interdisciplinary collaboration, as AI-driven advancements often require expertise from multiple disciplines, including physics, chemistry, data science, and engineering. Through these case studies, we gain a deeper understanding of AI's potential to revolutionize electrochemical technologies and its pivotal role in shaping a more sustainable and intelligent energy landscape. The following case studies provide real-world examples of how AI is accelerating innovation, optimizing processes, and fostering sustainability in energy systems.

AI-Driven Optimization of Hydrogen Fuel Cells

Hydrogen fuel cells are a promising alternative to traditional combustion engines, offering clean energy for various applications. However, optimizing their efficiency and durability has been a complex challenge due to the intricacies of their chemical reactions and operating conditions. To address this, General Motors (GM) partnered with AI experts to apply Machine Learning (ML) models to optimize fuel cell performance [36, 37]. By integrating AI, they were able to simulate and predict the behavior of fuel cells under various conditions, such as temperature, pressure, and humidity. These AI-driven models analyzed large datasets from experiments and real-world data, identifying optimal parameters for catalyst materials, electrode configurations, and system management strategies. As a result, the performance of fuel cells was significantly enhanced, achieving higher efficiency and longer operational lifespans. The use of AI also streamlined the development cycle, reducing both time and costs associated with traditional trial-and-error methods. This case study demonstrates the potential of AI in enhancing the performance of energy conversion systems and highlights its capacity to address the challenges of real-world applications in sustainable energy technologies.

AI for Real-Time Monitoring and Predictive Maintenance in Supercapacitors

Supercapacitors are essential for applications that require rapid charge and discharge cycles, such as electric vehicles and renewable energy systems. However, ensuring their long-term reliability and efficiency remains a challenge due to the degradation of electrodes and electrolytes over time. Researchers at MIT developed an AI-based system to monitor supercapacitor performance in real-time and predict potential failures before they occur [38]. By integrating sensors with machine learning algorithms, the system continuously collected data on voltage, temperature, and current, which were then analyzed to detect early signs of degradation in the supercapacitor components. This predictive maintenance approach allowed for proactive intervention, extending the lifespan of the supercapacitors and preventing costly failures. The integration of AI also facilitated more efficient energy management by optimizing charge-discharge cycles, improving overall system performance. This case study demonstrates how AI can improve the reliability and efficiency of energy storage devices by providing real-time insights and predictive capabilities, resulting in significant cost savings and operational benefits.

AI in Green Hydrogen Production *via* Electrolysis

Green hydrogen, produced by splitting water molecules using renewable electricity in an electrolysis process, is considered a key component in sustainable energy systems. Siemens and TU Berlin collaborated to harness AI for optimizing water electrolysis systems, aiming to improve the efficiency of hydrogen production [39]. The team utilized AI-driven simulations to model the behavior of catalysts and electrolyzers under various conditions, allowing them to determine the optimal settings for maximizing hydrogen output while minimizing energy consumption. By integrating real-time data with AI models, the system continuously adjusted operational parameters to maintain optimal efficiency, reducing energy waste and increasing the sustainability of hydrogen production. The use of AI also accelerated the development of new, more efficient catalyst materials, further enhancing the overall performance of electrolysis systems. This case study highlights the role of AI in advancing clean energy technologies, particularly in improving the efficiency and scalability of green hydrogen production, which is essential for the global transition to a low-carbon economy.

AI in Material Discovery for Supercapacitors

IBM's AI platform, Deep Materials, was employed to identify sustainable, high-performance materials for supercapacitors, a critical technology for energy storage. Traditional methods of discovering new electrode materials for supercapacitors rely heavily on experimental trial and error, which can be both time-consuming and expensive. IBM's AI platform, however, used data-driven algorithms to analyze a wide range of material properties and predict the potential of bio-based materials as alternatives to conventional activated carbon [40]. The AI models identified several promising candidates that not only matched the performance of traditional materials but also offered a more sustainable and eco-friendly approach. These materials, derived from renewable resources, significantly reduced the environmental impact of supercapacitor production while maintaining high energy storage capacity and efficiency. This case study exemplifies how AI can drive innovation in material science, enabling the development of sustainable and high-performance materials for energy storage applications.

AI-Driven Simulation for Catalyst Design in Artificial Photosynthesis

Artificial photosynthesis, the process of mimicking natural photosynthesis to convert sunlight into chemical energy, is a promising solution for sustainable energy production. The U.S.-based Joint Center for Artificial Photosynthesis (JCAP) utilized AI to accelerate the design of efficient catalysts for artificial photosynthesis [41]. By combining machine learning algorithms with quantum chemistry models, the team was able to predict the behavior of various catalysts under different conditions, optimizing their performance for CO_2 conversion and hydrogen production. The AI models analyzed vast datasets from both computational and experimental studies, identifying key features that contributed to higher catalyst efficiency. This AI-driven approach not only reduced the time and cost of catalyst development but also led to the discovery of more efficient and durable catalysts. The interdisciplinary collaboration between physicists, chemists, and AI experts exemplifies the potential of AI to drive breakthroughs in complex energy systems and accelerate the transition to sustainable energy technologies.

FUTURE PRESPECTIVES

The future of AI-driven innovations in electrochemical technologies presents an exciting and transformative shift in the way energy systems are designed, optimized, and maintained. As the world increasingly pivots toward sustainable energy solutions, the demand for efficient, scalable, and durable electrochemical systems—such as batteries, fuel cells, and electrolyzers—continues to grow. These systems are crucial for various applications, including renewable energy storage, electric vehicles, and hydrogen production. However, the complexity of electrochemical processes, coupled with the need for higher efficiency, reliability, and cost-effectiveness, presents significant challenges. AI, with its advanced capabilities in data processing, pattern recognition, and predictive analytics, is poised to address these challenges in unprecedented ways.

As AI continues to evolve, its integration with emerging technologies, such as quantum computing, will unlock even greater potential, enabling more precise simulations and deeper insights into electrochemical processes. AI will enable more efficient scaling from laboratory research to commercial applications, optimizing both the material discovery process and large-scale production methods. Additionally, AI will contribute to sustainability efforts by promoting a circular economy in electrochemical technologies, optimizing resource use, minimizing waste, and improving the recyclability of materials used in batteries and fuel cells. Overall, AI-driven innovations in electrochemical technologies promise to enhance the performance, efficiency, and sustainability of energy systems. The continued advancements in AI, combined with breakthroughs in energy systems, will contribute to a more sustainable and resilient energy future, making AI a critical enabler of the global energy transition.

Emerging Trends in AI and Electrochemical Research

Emerging trends in AI and electrochemical research are reshaping the landscape of energy systems, offering innovative solutions for material development, process optimization, and system performance. As demand for cleaner and more efficient energy solutions grows, AI technologies are playing an increasingly vital role in advancing electrochemical technologies, including batteries, fuel cells, and electrolyzers. Table **3** summarizes the emerging trends in AI and electrochemical research.

Table 3. Table showcasing the emerging trends in AI.

Emerging Trend	Description
AI for Autonomous Design and Simulation	AI is integrated into the design and simulation of electrochemical systems, accelerating material discovery and optimizing system performance by predicting outcomes based on simulations.
AI-Powered Hybrid Models for Process Control	Combining AI with traditional models to improve process control. AI analyzes large datasets to optimize variables in real-time, including temperature, pressure, and reaction rates.
AI for Cross-Disciplinary Collaboration	AI fosters collaboration between various scientific disciplines by integrating diverse datasets and creating holistic models that address complex electrochemical phenomena.
AI in Smart Energy Networks and Grid Integration	AI optimizes the integration of electrochemical systems into smart grids by predicting energy demand, managing battery storage, and ensuring a stable energy supply through real-time adjustments.
AI for Personalization of Energy Storage Systems	AI customizes battery management systems for individual usage patterns, enhancing energy efficiency, lifespan, and reducing environmental impact.
Sustainability-Focused AI Applications	AI helps reduce the environmental impact of electrochemical systems by optimizing energy consumption, improving recyclability, and guiding the development of more durable components [42].
AI for Advanced Diagnostics and Fault Detection	AI-driven diagnostics continuously monitor system parameters to detect performance issues early, facilitating proactive maintenance and extending the system's lifespan.

Collaboration Across Domains: Physics, Chemistry, and Data Science

Collaboration across domains, such as physics, chemistry, and data science, is essential for advancing electrochemical technologies, particularly as the complexity of these systems increases. Electrochemical systems, including batteries, fuel cells, and electrolyzers, involve intricate interactions between materials, chemical reactions, and physical processes. To fully understand and optimize these systems, researchers must integrate knowledge from multiple disciplines, employing cross-disciplinary approaches to solve complex problems that cannot be addressed by a single field alone.

Physics and Chemistry Integration

Physics and chemistry have long been at the forefront of electrochemical research. Physics contributes essential insights into the fundamental principles of energy transfer, charge dynamics, and material properties at various scales. For example, the principles of thermodynamics, electromagnetism, and quantum mechanics are critical in understanding how electrochemical reactions occur, how electrons flow through materials, and how energy is stored and converted. On the other hand, chemistry plays a pivotal role in material selection, synthesis, and reaction mechanisms. The design of new catalysts, electrodes, and electrolytes—key components in fuel cells, batteries, and electrolyzers—is deeply rooted in chemical science [43]. By combining physics and chemistry, researchers can develop more efficient materials and systems that perform optimally in real-world applications.

Data Science and Electrochemical Research

As electrochemical systems become more complex, the need for advanced analytical tools to process large datasets is critical. This is where data science plays an indispensable role. Data science techniques such as Machine Learning (ML) and Artificial Intelligence (AI) can analyze vast quantities of data generated from experiments, simulations, and operational systems. In electrochemistry, this data can encompass a wide range of information, including material properties, reaction dynamics, process conditions, and system performance. By using data science tools, researchers can uncover hidden patterns, optimize system parameters, and predict material behaviors. This predictive capability helps identify optimal materials for energy storage, enhance battery management systems, and ensure more efficient and reliable operation of electrochemical systems.

Synergies between Domains

The integration of physics, chemistry, and data science enables researchers to approach electrochemical challenges from multiple angles. For example, AI can utilize physics-based models to simulate material behaviors at various scales or chemistry-driven experimental data to refine models and predict outcomes. The combination of these disciplines fosters the development of new materials, faster discovery cycles, and more efficient optimization processes. This cross-domain collaboration is accelerating advancements in electrochemical systems, particularly in the areas of energy storage and conversion.

CHALLENGES AND CONSTRAINTS IN AI-DRIVEN ELECTROCHEMICAL RESEARCH

The integration of Artificial Intelligence (AI) into electrochemical research has led to notable advances in energy storage, conversion, and material discovery. However, several critical challenges continue to limit the widespread adoption, scalability, and reliability of AI-driven approaches. These constraints span across technical, data-related, and methodological dimensions and must be addressed to realize the potential of AI in electrochemistry.

Data Scarcity, Fragmentation, and Quality Issues

Unlike more mature AI domains such as image recognition or natural language processing, electrochemical research lacks large, well-structured datasets that are essential for training robust machine learning models. Much of the available experimental data is scattered across individual research papers, lab notebooks, and proprietary databases, often with inconsistent formatting and missing metadata. This fragmentation makes it difficult to aggregate data across studies or reproduce results, significantly hindering the development of generalizable AI models. Furthermore, electrochemical systems are highly sensitive to experimental conditions, such as temperature, electrode composition, electrolyte concentration, and testing protocols; however, these variables are not always reported in a standardized manner. As a result, even datasets focused on similar materials or devices can differ substantially, limiting their utility for cross-comparative AI analysis. The problem is exacerbated by the lack of negative or null result data in publications, which introduces bias into the training process. Studies have shown that fewer than 25% of electrochemical publications include data in machine-readable formats, and even fewer provide open-access datasets suitable for direct use in AI workflows. For instance, in battery research, while initiatives like the Battery Archive and Stanford Battery Dataset have made progress, they still represent only a narrow subset of chemistries and operational conditions. This limited representation reduces the diversity of training data, resulting in models that may perform well under specific conditions but fail to generalize to new materials or devices.

Model Interpretability and Explainability

Another critical constraint in applying AI to electrochemical technologies is the lack of model interpretability and explainability, particularly in deep learning-based approaches. While these models can offer high predictive accuracy, they often function as "black boxes," providing little insight into how input features contribute to the output. This poses a significant problem in scientific disciplines such as electrochemistry, where understanding the underlying physical and chemical mechanisms is crucial for validating predictions and informing experimental design. Without interpretability, it becomes difficult to trust AI models in high-stakes applications such as battery degradation forecasting, fuel cell diagnostics, or catalyst performance prediction. Furthermore, the inability to explain model decisions hampers model generalization and reproducibility, two critical pillars of scientific research. It also limits the integration of AI tools into industry and regulatory settings, where decision-making must be transparent and auditable. While techniques such as SHAP (SHapley Additive Explanations) and LIME (Local Interpretable Model-agnostic Explanations) offer some interpretability, they are still underutilized in electrochemical applications and often lack domain-specific customization.

Generalization and Transferability Across Systems

Many AI models are trained on data collected under specific experimental setups or from a narrow class of materials, making them highly specialized and often unable to perform reliably outside their original domain. For instance, a model developed to predict cycle life or efficiency in lithium-ion batteries may perform poorly when applied to sodium-ion or solid-state batteries due to differences in material chemistry, reaction mechanisms, and degradation pathways. Similarly, models trained under controlled laboratory conditions may not accurately capture the complexities of real-world environments, where factors like temperature fluctuations, manufacturing variability, and long-term aging introduce additional uncertainties. This lack of generalization restricts the scalability of AI solutions and limits their usefulness in materials discovery or system optimization for emerging technologies. Moreover, transfer learning—an approach that has been widely successful in fields like computer vision—is still in its early stages in electrochemistry. Adapting pre-trained models to new datasets or related electrochemical systems remains difficult due to inconsistencies in data formats, feature representations, and domain-specific knowledge requirements. To overcome these limitations, there is a growing interest in developing more adaptable AI architectures, such as meta-learning and domain adaptation techniques, as well as incorporating domain knowledge through physics-informed models.

RELEVANCE OF SDGs TO CHALLENGES IN AI-DRIVEN ELECTROCHEMICAL RESEARCH

The challenges facing AI integration in electrochemical technologies extend beyond technical limitations—they are deeply intertwined with global sustainability goals, particularly those outlined in the United Nations Sustainable Development Goals (SDGs). These goals provide a strategic framework to align technological progress with the well-being of society and the environment.

One of the most pressing barriers is the lack of high-quality, standardized, and openly accessible datasets. This data deficiency obstructs the development and benchmarking of reliable AI models, thereby slowing innovation in clean energy technologies. This directly impacts **SDG 9 (Industry, Innovation and Infrastructure)**, which calls for building resilient infrastructure and fostering innovation. In electrochemical research, fragmented and inconsistent data prevent seamless collaboration across institutions, limit reproducibility, and delay the scaling of novel technologies from the lab to industrial applications [44]. Without standardized data protocols and centralized repositories, AI tools remain confined to narrow research domains, failing to translate into scalable solutions for energy systems.

Another critical issue is the interpretability and generalization of AI models. Many advanced models, particularly those based on deep learning, offer limited transparency into how predictions are made. This "black box" nature restricts trust among domain experts and decision-makers, complicating efforts to validate and implement AI-driven solutions in energy systems. Such limitations hinder progress toward **SDG 7 (Affordable and Clean Energy)**, which emphasizes universal access to reliable and modern energy services [45]. Interpretable and transferable AI models are crucial for optimizing the design and operation of energy storage and conversion systems, including batteries, supercapacitors, and fuel cells. Without trust and clarity in AI decision-making, the pathway to broader adoption and implementation in critical infrastructure remains uncertain.

Moreover, the absence of validated, high-fidelity AI models trained on diverse and representative data can lead to inefficiencies or errors in the design of electrochemical systems. This misalignment may result in suboptimal material use, increased energy consumption, and unintended environmental consequences—all of which run counter to the objectives of **SDG 13 (Climate Action)** [46]. As electrochemical technologies play a pivotal role in decarbonization strategies—particularly in the transition to renewable energy and electrified transport—the need for accurate, efficient, and transparent AI tools becomes even more urgent.

Addressing these interrelated challenges requires a multi-pronged approach that includes the development of open data ecosystems, cross-disciplinary collaboration, and the integration of domain knowledge into AI workflows. Furthermore, encouraging the use of explainable AI and physics-informed machine learning can bridge the gap between algorithmic predictions and electrochemical insight. By integrating sustainability considerations into the development of AI systems, the field can ensure that its innovations not only advance scientific frontiers but also make meaningful contributions to global development and climate resilience.

CONCLUSION

This book chapter explores the transformative impact of AI-driven innovations in electrochemical technologies, highlighting their potential to shape the future of energy storage, conversion, and management. The integration of AI techniques, including machine learning, deep learning, and reinforcement learning, with electrochemical systems provides unprecedented opportunities to accelerate material discovery, optimize complex processes, and enhance system performance in real-time. Through AI's ability to analyze vast datasets, uncover hidden patterns, predict outcomes, and dynamically adapt system parameters, researchers can significantly improve the efficiency, durability, and sustainability of energy technologies. The chapter highlights the significant impact of AI in the development of energy storage devices, including batteries, fuel cells, and electrolyzers, where it plays a crucial role in optimizing performance, mitigating degradation, and extending system lifespans. Moreover, real time monitoring and predictive maintenance powered by AI ensure continuous peak performance, minimizing downtime and enhancing operational longevity.

Looking to the future, the chapter explores how ongoing collaboration between AI, physics, chemistry, and data science will drive the next wave of breakthroughs in electrochemical systems. Such cross-disciplinary efforts will lead to the creation of more efficient materials, improved optimization strategies, and smarter, more resilient systems. AI's role in addressing global energy challenges, particularly in the integration of renewable energy sources, is emphasized as crucial to the transition toward a more sustainable energy future. Ultimately, this book chapter concludes that AI-driven innovations in electrochemical technologies are central to the evolution of more scalable, reliable, and sustainable energy systems. The integration of AI in this field holds immense potential for revolutionizing the energy sector, advancing toward a greener and more energy-efficient future.

ACKNOWLEGEMENTS

One of the authors, Ashna Verma, expresses their heartfelt gratitude to Prof. Anand Srivastava, Vice Chancellor, NSUT, for his invaluable guidance and unwavering support throughout the research work. The other author, N. L. Singh, extends their sincere thanks to Prof. Ashok Kumar Nagawat, Vice Chancellor of Delhi Skill Entrepreneurship University, for his encouragement and support, which greatly contributed to the successful completion of this study.

REFERENCES

[1] I.T. Bello, L.A. Jolaoso, R.A. Ahmed, and A. Bello, "Electrochemical energy conversion and Storage Systems: A perspective on the challenges and opportunities for sustainable energy in Africa", *Energy Reviews,* vol. 4, no. 1, p. 100109, 2025. [http://dx.doi.org/10.1016/j.enrev.2024.100109]

[2] A. Cernat, A. Groza, M. Tertis, B. Feier, O. Hosu-Stancioiu, and C. Cristea, "Where artificial intelligence stands in the development of electrochemical sensors for healthcare applications-A review", *Trends Analyt. Chem.,* vol. 181, p. 117999, 2024. [http://dx.doi.org/10.1016/j.trac.2024.117999]

[3] M. Soori, B. Arezoo, and R. Dastres, "Artificial intelligence, machine learning and deep learning in advanced robotics, a review", *Cognitive Robotics,* vol. 3, pp. 54-70, 2023. [http://dx.doi.org/10.1016/j.cogr.2023.04.001]

[4] H. Adamu, S.I. Abba, P.B. Anyin, Y. Sani, and M. Qamar, "Artificial intelligence-navigated development of high-performance electrochemical energy storage systems through feature engineering of multiple descriptor families of materials", *Energy Advances,* vol. 2, no. 5, pp. 615-645, 2023. [http://dx.doi.org/10.1039/D3YA00104K]

[5] S. Sinha, and Y.M. Lee, "Challenges with developing and deploying AI models and applications in industrial systems", *Discover Artificial Intelligence,* vol. 4, no. 1, p. 55, 2024. [http://dx.doi.org/10.1007/s44163-024-00151-2]

[6] I. Papadimitriou, I. Gialampoukidis, S. Vrochidis, and I. Kompatsiaris, "AI methods in materials design, discovery and manufacturing: A review", *Comput. Mater. Sci.,* vol. 235, p. 112793, 2024. [http://dx.doi.org/10.1016/j.commatsci.2024.112793]

[7] M. Wei, F. Zhang, W. Wang, P. Alexandridis, C. Zhou, and G. Wu, "3D direct writing fabrication of electrodes for electrochemical storage devices", *J. Power Sources,* vol. 354, pp. 134-147, 2017. [http://dx.doi.org/10.1016/j.jpowsour.2017.04.042]

[8] S.W. Perng, and H.W. Wu, "Effects of internal flow modification on the cell performance enhancement of a PEM fuel cell", *J. Power Sources,* vol. 175, no. 2, pp. 806-816, 2008. [http://dx.doi.org/10.1016/j.jpowsour.2007.09.095]

[9] M. I. A. Abdel Maksoud, "Advanced materials and technologies for supercapacitors used in energy conversion and storage: a review", *Environ. Chem. Lett.,* vol. 19, no. 1, pp. 375-439, 2020. [http://dx.doi.org/10.1007/S10311-020-01075-W]

[10] N. Xuan, C. Song, G. Cheng, and Z. Du, "Advanced triboelectric nanogenerator based self-powered electrochemical system", *Chem. Eng. J.,* vol. 481, p. 148640, 2024. [http://dx.doi.org/10.1016/j.cej.2024.148640]

[11] M. Gao, S.Y. Pan, W.C. Chen, and P.C. Chiang, "A cross-disciplinary overview of naturally derived materials for electrochemical energy storage", *Mater. Today Energy,* vol. 7, pp. 58-79, 2018. [http://dx.doi.org/10.1016/j.mtener.2017.12.005]

[12] I. Dincer, and A. A. AlZahrani, "Electrolyzers", *Compr. Energy Syst.,* vol. 4, pp. V4-985-V4-1025, 2018. [http://dx.doi.org/10.1016/B978-0-12-809597-3.00442-9]

[13] Maciej Serda, "Synteza i aktywność biologiczna nowych analogów tiosemikarbazonowych chelatorów żelaza", In: *Uniw. śląski* vol. 7. , 2013, no. 1, pp. 343-354. [http://dx.doi.org/10.2/JQUERY.MIN.JS]

[14] B. Narayanan, "Computational modeling of battery materials", *Encycl. Energy Storage,* vol. 1–4, pp. 278-290, 2022. [http://dx.doi.org/10.1016/B978-0-12-819723-3.00156-6]

[15] J.L. Patero, "Electromagnetic induction: Unraveling faraday's laws and their applications in generators and transformers", *International Journal of Advanced Research in Science, Communication and Technology,* no. Jul, pp. 814-819, 2023. [http://dx.doi.org/10.48175/IJARSCT-12376]

[16] "Leverage the full potential of AI to predictive maintenance." Accessed, 2024. Available from: https://vidyatec.com/blog/why-is-ai-so-crucial-for-predictive-maintenance/

[17] A. Velasco, Y.K. Ryu, A. Boscá, A. Ladrón-de-Guevara, E. Hunt, J. Zuo, J. Pedrós, F. Calle, and J. Martinez, "Recent trends in graphene supercapacitors: from large area to microsupercapacitors", *Sustain. Energy Fuels,* vol. 5, no. 5, pp. 1235-1254, 2021. [http://dx.doi.org/10.1039/D0SE01849J]

[18] S.B. Mujib, S. Mukherjee, Z. Ren, and G. Singh, "Assessing corrosion resistance of two-dimensional nanomaterial-based coatings on stainless steel substrates", *R. Soc. Open Sci.,* vol. 7, no. 4, p. 200214, 2020. [http://dx.doi.org/10.1098/rsos.200214] [PMID: 32431907]

[19] "Faraday's Laws of Electrolysis: First Law, Second Law & Formula" Accessed, 2024. Available from: https://www.chemistrylearner.com/faradays-laws-of-electrolysis.html

[20] P. Vensaus, Y. Liang, J.P. Ansermet, G.J.A.A. Soler-Illia, and M. Lingenfelder, "Enhancement of electrocatalysis through magnetic field effects on mass transport", *Nat. Commun.,* vol. 15, no. 1, p. 2867, 2024. [http://dx.doi.org/10.1038/s41467-024-46980-8] [PMID: 38570499]

[21] M. Giglio, A. Elefante, P. Patimisco, A. Sampaolo, and V. Spagnolo, "Quartz-enhanced photoacoustic sensors for environmental monitoring", *Encycl. Sensors Biosens.,* vol. 1–4, pp. 789-799, 2022. [http://dx.doi.org/10.1016/B978-0-12-822548-6.00126-6]

[22] M. Zahaib Nabeel, "AI-enhanced project management systems for optimizing resource allocation and risk mitigation", *Asian Journal of Multidisciplinary Research & Review,* vol. 5, no. 5, pp. 53-91, 2024. [http://dx.doi.org/10.55662/AJMRR.2024.5502]

[23] B. Dhyani, "Predicting equipment failure in manufacturing plants: An AI-driven maintenance strategy", *Mathematical Statistician and Engineering Applications,* vol. 70, no. 2, pp. 1326-1334, 2021. [http://dx.doi.org/10.17762/msea.v70i2.2324]

[24] S. Li, H. O. Gao, and F. You, *AI for science in electrochemical energy storage: a multiscale systems perspective on transportation electrification.,* 2024. [http://dx.doi.org/10.1016/j.ynexs.2024.100026]

[25] Y. Xu, X. Liu, X. Cao, C. Huang, E. Liu, S. Qian, X. Liu, Y. Wu, F. Dong, C.W. Qiu, J. Qiu, K. Hua, W. Su, J. Wu, H. Xu, Y. Han, C. Fu, Z. Yin, M. Liu, R. Roepman, S. Dietmann, M. Virta, F. Kengara, Z. Zhang, L. Zhang, T. Zhao, J. Dai, J. Yang, L. Lan, M. Luo, Z. Liu, T. An, B. Zhang, X. He, S.

Cong, X. Liu, W. Zhang, J.P. Lewis, J.M. Tiedje, Q. Wang, Z. An, F. Wang, L. Zhang, T. Huang, C. Lu, Z. Cai, F. Wang, and J. Zhang, "Artificial intelligence: A powerful paradigm for scientific research", *Innovation,* vol. 2, no. 4, p. 100179, 2021. [http://dx.doi.org/10.1016/j.xinn.2021.100179] [PMID: 34877560]

[26] S. Badini, S. Regondi, and R. Pugliese, "Unleashing the power of artificial intelligence in materials design", *Mater.,* vol. 16, no. 17, pp. 5927-5927, 2023. [http://dx.doi.org/10.3390/MA16175927]

[27] P.S. Nnamchi, and C.S. Obayi, "Electrochemical characterization of nanomaterials", *Charact. Nanomater. Adv. Key Technol.,* no. Jan, pp. 103-127, 2018. [http://dx.doi.org/10.1016/B978-0-08-101973-3.00004-3]

[28] S. Stavrev, and D. Ginchev, "Reinforcement learning techniques in optimizing energy systems", *Electron.,* vol. 13, no. 8, pp. 1459-1459, 2024. [http://dx.doi.org/10.3390/ELECTRONICS13081459]

[29] D. Sambyal, and A. Sarwar, "Recent developments in cervical cancer diagnosis using deep learning on whole slide images: An Overview of models, techniques, challenges and future directions", *Micron,* vol. 173, p. 103520, 2023. [http://dx.doi.org/10.1016/j.micron.2023.103520] [PMID: 37556898]

[30] I.H. Sarker, "Deep learning: A comprehensive overview on techniques, taxonomy, applications and research directions", *SN Computer Science,* vol. 2, no. 6, p. 420, 2021. [http://dx.doi.org/10.1007/s42979-021-00815-1] [PMID: 34426802]

[31] A.M.K. Adawadkar, and N. Kulkarni, "Cyber-security and reinforcement learning — A brief survey", *Eng. Appl. Artif. Intell.,* vol. 114, p. 105116, 2022. [http://dx.doi.org/10.1016/j.engappai.2022.105116]

[32] S. Li, H.O. Gao, and F. You, "AI for science in electrochemical energy storage: A multiscale systems perspective on transportation electrification", *Nexus,* vol. 1, no. 3, p. 100026, 2024. [http://dx.doi.org/10.1016/j.ynexs.2024.100026]

[33] "(PDF) Artificial Intelligence and Machine Learning in Materials Engineering." Accessed, 2024. Available from: https://www.researchgate.net/publication/384697846_Artificial_Intelligence_and_Machine_Learning_in_Materials_Engineering

[34] A. Obaigbena, "Exploring the potential of AI-driven optimization in enhancing network performance and efficiency", *Magna Scientia Advanced Research and Reviews,* vol. 10, no. 1, pp. 368-378, 2024. [http://dx.doi.org/10.30574/msarr.2024.10.1.0028]

[35] G. Patrizi, "A review of degradation models and remaining useful life prediction for testing design and predictive maintenance of lithium-ion batteries", *Sensors,* vol. 24, no. 11, pp. 3382-3382, 2024. [http://dx.doi.org/10.3390/S24113382]

[36] "GM Invests in AI and Battery Materials Innovator Mitra Chem | General Motors Company." Accessed, 2025. Available from: https://investor.gm.com/news-releases/news-release-details-gm-invests-ai-and-battery-materials-innovator-mitra-chem

[37] "Artificial Intelligence at General Motors | Emerj Artificial Intelligence Research." Accessed, 2025. Available from: https://emerj.com/artificial-intelligence-at-general-motors-two-use-cases/

[38] "MIT engineers create an energy-storing supercapacitor from ancient materials | MIT News | Massachusetts Institute of Technology." Accessed, 2025. Available from: https://news.mit.edu/2023/mit-engineers-create-supercapacitor-ancient-materials-0731

[39] "Siemens accelerates hydrogen ramp-up with generative artificial intelligence | Press | Company | Siemens." Accessed, 2025. Available from: https://press.siemens.com/global/en/pressrelease/siemens-accelerates-hydrogen-ramp-generative-artificial-intelligence

[40] "IBM open sources new AI models for materials discovery - IBM Research." Accessed, 2025.

Available from: https://research.ibm.com/blog/foundation-models-for-materials

[41] H.A. Atwater, "Artificial photosynthesis- Progress and prospects", *ECS Meet. Abstr.,* vol. MA2015-02, no. 50, pp. 1951-1951.

[42] S. Kaur, R. Kumar, K. Singh, and Y. Huang, "Leveraging artificial intelligence for enhanced sustainable energy management", *Journal of Sustainability for Energy,* vol. 3, no. 1, pp. 1-20, 2024. [http://dx.doi.org/10.56578/jse030101]

[43] P. Banoth, C. Kandula, and P. Kollu, "Introduction to electrocatalysts", *ACS Symp. Ser.,* vol. 1432, pp. 1-37, 2022.
[http://dx.doi.org/10.1021/bk-2022-1432.ch001]

[44] S. Küfeoğlu, *SDG-9: Industry.* Innovation and Infrastructure, 2022, pp. 349-369.
[http://dx.doi.org/10.1007/978-3-031-07127-0_11]

[45] A.N. Kay Lup, V. Soni, B. Keenan, J. Son, M.R. Taghartapeh, M.M. Morato, Y. Poya, and R.M. Montañés, "Sustainable energy technologies for the Global South: challenges and solutions toward achieving SDG 7", *Environmental Science: Advances,* vol. 2, no. 4, pp. 570-585, 2023.
[http://dx.doi.org/10.1039/D2VA00247G]

[46] D. Bodansky, "SDG 13: Take urgent action to combat climate change and its impacts", *Cambridge Handb. Sustain. Dev. Goals Int. Law,* no. Sep, pp. 328-353, 2022.
[http://dx.doi.org/10.1017/9781108769631.015]

CHAPTER 2

Optimization Techniques in Electrochemical Devices Using AI

Priya Gupta[1], **Suman Srivastava**[2,*] and **Ritika Khatri**[1,*]

[1] *School of Basic and Applied Sciences, K.R. Mangalam University, Gurugram, Haryana, India*

[2] *Department of Chemistry, M.V. College Buxar (A Constituent Unit of Veer Kunwar Singh University Ara), Bihar, India*

Abstract: The development of electrochemical devices has long been identified as a promising area for applications such as energy storage and conversion due to their environment-friendly, high-efficiency, and portable nature. There has been much focus on various electrochemical devices for over a century, including batteries, fuel cells, sensors, electrolyzers, and supercapacitors. A systematic approach to designing materials for electrochemical devices is necessary, which typically involves the design of electrodes, electrolytes, catalysts, and other components. In the modern era, the introduction of AI (Artificial Intelligence) has marked the beginning of a new phase in the progress of electrochemical devices. Various approaches, including neural networks, genetic algorithms, and machine learning models, are employed to optimize electrochemical devices. For example, the efficacy of AI in active chlorine production, battery management systems, and solid oxide fuel cells is remarkable. AI helps predict material properties and behaviors with greater accuracy, optimizes electrochemical machining parameters, and significantly reduces reliance on costly and time-consuming experiments and computational methods. This chapter will examine the impact of AI on the advancement of electrochemical devices, facilitating material discovery, enhancing sensor technology, and optimizing manufacturing processes. The recent technological advancements significantly align with several United Nations Sustainable Development Goals (SDGs), notably SDG 7, which focuses on affordable and clean energy, SDG 9, emphasizing industry, innovation, and infrastructure, and SDG 13, dedicated to Climate Action. By facilitating the development of cleaner energy technologies and enhancing production efficiency, AI-driven electrochemical devices are essential in promoting sustainable industrial growth and addressing the challenges posed by climate change.

* **Corresponding authors Suman Srivastava and Ritika Khatri:** Department of Chemistry, M.V. College Buxar (A Constituent Unit of Veer Kunwar Singh University Ara), Bihar, India; School of Basic and Applied Sciences, K.R. Mangalam University, Gurugram, Haryana, India;
E-mails: sumansamiran@gmail.com; khatriritika1992@gmail.com

Shreya Sharma, Peeyush Phogat, Ranjana Jha & Sukhvir Singh (Eds.)

Keywords: Artificial intelligence, Algorithm, Anode, Cathode, Electrochemical devices, Energy storage, Fuel cell, Machine learning, Nanomaterials, Optimization, Sensors, Supercapacitor.

INTRODUCTION

An electrochemical device functions based on electrochemical principles, utilizing electrical energy to initiate chemical reactions or generate electrical energy through them. These devices are essential in various technologies that significantly impact sectors such as energy storage, conversion, environmental monitoring, healthcare, and more [1]. They facilitate the movement of electrons between electrodes and electrolytes, promoting redox (reduction-oxidation) reactions that produce or consume electrical energy. Fig. (**1**) provides a comprehensive overview of the chapter.

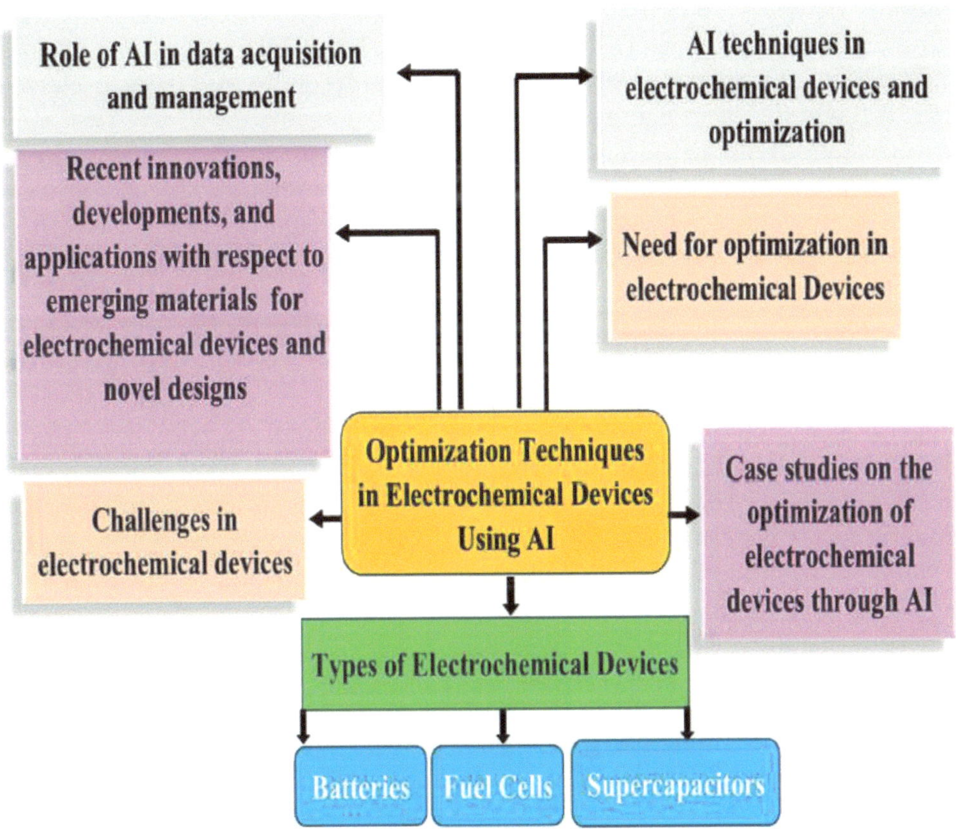

Fig. (1). Schematic diagram for a complete overview of the chapter.

Instances of such devices include batteries, supercapacitors, fuel cells, biosensors, electrolysis cells, and environmental sensors [2, 3]. A battery functions as a device that accumulates and transforms chemical energy into electrical energy, serving as a portable and dependable power source for various uses. The fundamental operational mechanism of a battery is based on electrochemical reactions occurring between two electrodes: the anode, which is negatively charged, and the cathode, which is positively charged. These electrodes are divided by an electrolyte. When a battery is connected to an external circuit, electrons migrate from the anode to the cathode through the circuit, producing an electric current that can power electronic devices, vehicles, or other machinery. The electrolyte facilitates ions' movement between the electrodes, thereby sustaining the reaction [4]. Their capacity to convert chemical energy into electrical energy makes them vital for numerous modern technologies, particularly in electric automobiles, sustainable energy solutions, and mobile electronic devices. Whereas a supercapacitor, commonly known as an ultracapacitor or an Electric Double-Layer Capacitor (EDLC), is a type of energy storage device characterized by its ability to rapidly store and release electrical energy, it functions as an energy storage device that accumulates electrical energy *via* electrostatic fields [5]. These devices are notable for their rapid charging and discharging capabilities, rendering them ideal for applications that demand swift power delivery. Supercapacitors offer high power density and extended cycle life, although they generally have a lower energy storage capacity compared to traditional batteries. A fuel cell, conversely, is an electrochemical device that generates electricity by converting the chemical energy stored in a fuel, typically hydrogen, into electrical energy through a chemical reaction with oxygen. In contrast to conventional combustion engines, fuel cells generate electricity without the combustion process, leading to enhanced efficiency and the elimination of harmful emissions, with water being the sole byproduct [1]. These devices are employed in numerous applications, such as Electric Vehicles (EVs), stationary power generation, and portable electronic devices, presenting a viable alternative to traditional energy sources due to their ecological advantages and sustainable functionality.

There has been a notable surge in interest in electrochemical devices in the current scenario, driven by global concerns regarding sustainable energy, environmental conservation, and technological advancements [6]. As the world confronts climate change, the demand for efficient, sustainable, and clean energy solutions is crucial. These devices facilitate the accumulation of energy produced from sources such as wind, solar, and hydropower, ensuring its accessibility when required and addressing the sporadic nature of these energy sources. For example, Fuel cells are considered an attractive option for clean transportation and industrial applications [7]. Concurrently, modernization in battery technology—particularly in lithium-ion, sodium-ion, and solid-state batteries is continually expanding the potential of energy storage, leading to more lasting and robust devices for multiple applications [8].

Conversely, supercapacitors are ideal in areas that demand quick energy bursts, such as hybrid EVs, grid stabilization, and some consumer electronics [9]. Furthermore, advancements in materials science, particularly with the incorporation of graphene and carbon nanotubes, have led to significant improvements in the energy density and efficiency of supercapacitors, thereby promoting their application in both the automotive and renewable energy sectors. While energy conversion and storage are the most recognized functions of electrochemical devices, electrochemistry is also essential in a variety of other applications. In the field of sensing, electrochemical sensors are utilized across various industries, ranging from healthcare to environmental monitoring. These sensors identify specific chemical compounds, often at very low levels, translating this chemical data into a quantifiable electrical signal. For instance, glucose sensors used by individuals managing diabetes operate on electrochemical principles to track blood glucose levels. In contrast, environmental sensors are capable of identifying pollutants such as heavy metals or harmful gases in air and water [10]. The high sensitivity and specificity of electrochemical sensors, combined with their relatively low cost and ease of integration into portable devices, have made them important tools in medical diagnostics and environmental conservation.

A major advantage of electrochemical techniques is their capacity to operate right at the site of contamination and address a wide range of pollutants that are difficult to remove using conventional approaches [11]. Furthermore, electrochemical methods can be tailored to target particular pollutants, resulting in more efficient and cost-effective remediation approaches. In addition to their applications in energy production, sensing, and environmental cleansing, electrochemical devices also hold great potential for emerging fields such as bioelectronics, medical testing, and wearable technology. Combining electrochemical devices with biological systems opens up new possibilities for health surveillance, medication delivery, and customized healthcare. For example, researchers are developing electrochemical biosensors to monitor biomarkers in the human body, providing immediate information on a person's health status [12]. These devices could enable the early identification of illnesses, continuous health evaluations, and more precise therapies customized to meet each patient's individual requirements. Additionally, electrochemical technology might lead to the advancement of implantable devices that harness bioelectric signals to address problems such as neurological conditions or chronic pain. Besides their applications in energy, sensing, and environmental cleanup, electrochemical devices are also playing a crucial role in advancing emerging areas such as bioelectronics, medical diagnostics, and wearable technologies [13]. The integration of electrochemical devices with biological systems presents promising opportunities for health monitoring, drug delivery, and personalized healthcare. Scientists are developing electrochemical biosensors that monitor biomarkers in the body, providing real-time data regarding a person's health status. These tools could enable early detection of diseases, continuous health evaluations, and treatments that are more precise and tailored to the unique requirements of patients. Furthermore, electrochemical technologies could pave the way for the advancement of implantable devices that utilize bioelectric signals to tackle problems such as neurological disorders or chronic pain. The rapid advancement of electrochemical technologies is also due to ongoing research in fields such as materials science, nanotechnology, and electrochemical engineering.

The efficacy of electrochemical devices is significantly determined by the characteristics of the materials incorporated into their construction, particularly the electrodes and electrolytes. Progress in nanomaterials, such as nanoparticles, nanowires, and graphene-derived materials, has led to visible improvements in the efficiency of these devices [14]. These materials enhance surface areas, improve conductivity, and increase stability, resulting in higher energy densities, longer lifespans, and more efficient performance. Additionally, the development of solid-state electrolytes and adaptable electrodes is laying the foundation for future generations of electrochemical devices that promise to be not only more influential but also lighter, more compact, and appropriate for various uses, including wearable technology, flexible displays, and autonomous systems.

Optimization is crucial for improving the efficiency of electrochemical devices, which are key in energy storage, conversion, and sensing applications. The efficiency, power density, stability, and lifespan of these devices, including batteries, fuel cells, supercapacitors, and electrochemical sensors, are heavily influenced by numerous factors such as materials, design, and operating conditions [15]. For instance, choosing the appropriate materials is essential. This encompasses selecting electrode materials for batteries and fuel cells, as well as finding suitable catalysts to enhance reaction efficiency. By fine-tuning these materials to optimize their conductivity, stability, and electrochemical properties, substantial improvements in device performance can be achieved. Likewise, refining electrolytes, which facilitate the movement of ions between the electrodes, is crucial for ensuring proper functionality. The composition of the electrolyte, along with its ionic conductivity and compatibility with surrounding materials, can significantly impact factors such as cycle life and energy density in devices like lithium-ion batteries or fuel cells.

The design of electrodes plays a typical role in the effectiveness of devices, with enhancement typically focused on maximizing the active surface area and facilitating even ion transport. For instance, in supercapacitors, utilizing nanostructured electrodes can expand the surface area, resulting in quicker charge and discharge cycles [16]. Likewise, the efficiency of catalysts in fuel cells can be enhanced through optimization, concentrating on improving their effectiveness and reducing long-term degradation. In this scenario, catalysts such as platinum-based materials or alternative non-precious metals are fine-tuned to achieve the highest catalytic activity while keeping costs low and minimizing degradation. The configuration of the device and its thermal management are also essential; the design of the device, including elements like current collectors, separators, and the overall cell architecture, needs to be constructed to reduce internal resistance and promote even current distribution [17]. Additionally, proper thermal management plays a key role in preventing overheating, which can negatively impact performance.

Optimization methods primarily include computational modeling, high-throughput screening, Machine Learning (ML), and experimental validation [19]. Computational models simulate ion transport, reaction kinetics, and various performance metrics, providing valuable insights that aid in material selection and design prior to physical experimentation [18]. Particularly, ML is emerging as a critical resource, allowing researchers to predict the influence of various factors on the performance of devices and facilitating the discovery of novel materials. These optimization strategies can lead to notable advancements in energy storage systems, such as lithium-ion batteries, by enhancing energy density, cycle life, and safety [21]. It is essential to optimize devices not just for their performance but also for their recyclability and minimized environmental impact to guarantee the sustainability of electrochemical technologies in the long run [19].

As a significant development in electrochemical devices, AI has surfaced as an innovative resource for the improvement and study of modern electrochemical devices, greatly enhancing the efficiency of material exploration, design, and performance prediction. In electrochemical systems, batteries, fuel cells, and supercapacitors, AI techniques such as Deep Learning (DL) and ML are being employed to analyze large datasets produced from experiments and simulations, uncovering patterns and relationships that may be difficult to discern using conventional approaches [20]. A major domain in which AI is making a notable impact is in the identification of new materials. By utilizing algorithms trained on vast datasets of material properties, AI can forecast the effectiveness of novel electrode materials, electrolytes, and catalysts, thus accelerating the materials design workflow [21]. This strategy reduces dependence on lengthy and costly trial-and-error experiments, enabling a more focused examination of advanced materials suitable for electrochemical applications. AI can play a crucial role in enhancing device performance by predicting how various elements—such as temperature, current density, and electrode configuration—impact device efficiency, durability, and reliability. For instance, AI algorithms can simulate the behaviour of electrochemical reactions in real-time, providing an understanding of how variations in material properties or device configurations will affect performance under various operating conditions. In the case of batteries, AI helps optimize charging and discharging processes, predicts electrode and electrolyte degradation, and notifies users of potential failure modes beforehand. Similarly, in fuel cells, AI models can aid in enhancing catalyst design and improving reaction kinetics, leading to increased energy conversion efficiency and enhanced durability [22].

Another area where AI is making strides is in automating electrochemical testing and high-throughput screening. AI-driven robots and automation systems can rapidly evaluate and analyse a vast array of samples across different conditions. It will generate high-quality data that can be used to train models and improve design iterations. This significantly accelerates the research and development process, allowing for faster progress in next-generation electrochemical technologies. Furthermore, AI applications are being utilized for real-time monitoring and predictive maintenance of operational electrochemical devices, which promotes proactive optimization and management of energy storage systems and fuel cells in active settings [23].

In this chapter, we will focus on how AI can contribute to the improvement of electrochemical devices, with a particular emphasis on the various techniques that have been enhanced to improve their effectiveness, efficiency, and longevity. This chapter seeks to illustrate how ML, DL, and predictive modelling aid in advancing device design and enhancing real-time management and upkeep. Furthermore, it aims to determine the transformative impact of AI on the advancement of energy storage technologies, including batteries, fuel cells, supercapacitors, and sensors, by identifying the most suitable materials and enhancing efficiency. We will gain a deeper understanding of how AI can significantly aid in advancing electrochemical technologies, making them more efficient, sustainable, and economically viable. This chapter not only offers technical insights but also aligns with the global sustainability agenda by addressing key aspects of the SDGs. By enhancing the design and efficiency of energy storage and conversion technologies, it directly supports SDG 7, Affordable and Clean Energy, ensuring greater access to reliable and renewable energy solutions. Furthermore, the incorporation of artificial intelligence into industrial processes and energy systems advances SDG 9, Industry, Innovation and Infrastructure, fostering sustainable industrial practices and innovation in clean technologies. Additionally, the strategies outlined here contribute to SDG 13, Climate Action, by minimizing energy losses, extending device lifespans, and promoting the use of environmentally friendly materials, thereby mitigating environmental impacts and bolstering climate change initiatives. Overall, this chapter highlights the role of AI in electrochemical technology while situating these advancements within the framework of a sustainable and resilient future. Table **1** provides an overview of various AI-driven methods used in the optimization of electrochemical devices. It features the technique, its benefits, common applications, and the types of electrochemical devices involved.

Table 1. Various AI techniques with their advantages, applications, and uses.

S. No.	AI Techniques	Advantage	Typical Application	Electrochemical Device based on AI Techniques
1.	ML	Prediction of complex nonlinear behaviour	Materials properties predictions	Batteries, Fuel Cells, Supercapacitors
2.	Genetic Algorithms	Optimize the complex high-dimensional problems	Electrode design optimization	Batteries, electrolyzers
3.	DL	Providing large data sets with high accuracy	Charge/discharge cycle optimization	Fuel Cells, Lithium-ion batteries
4.	Reinforcement learning (RL)	Real-time learning and adaptive optimization	Controlled process and real-time decision-making	Electrolysis system, Fuel Cells
5.	Artificial Neural Networks (ANN)	Nonlinear relationship modelling	Simulation and electrochemical modelling	Fuel Cells, Supercapacitor
6.	Support Vector Machines (ANN)	Perfect for small datasets	Electrode materials classification	Fuel Cell, Batteries

TYPES OF ELECTROCHEMICAL DEVICES

Electrochemical devices play a crucial role in numerous applications, such as energy storage, energy conversion, and sensing. These devices utilize electrochemical reactions to either store or generate electrical energy. There are various kinds of electrochemical devices, each tailored for specific functions. Yet, all operate based on the basic principles of electron transfer and ion movement between electrodes through an electrolyte. The most prevalent types of electrochemical devices include batteries, fuel cells, and supercapacitors.

Batteries

Batteries represent one of the most widely employed electrochemical systems for energy storage. They convert chemical energy into electrical energy *via* oxidation-reduction reactions that take place at the electrode [24]. The most commonly used battery types today include lithium-ion (Li-ion), lithium-polymer, and sodium-ion batteries, which are frequently found in portable electronics, EVs, and systems for storing renewable energy. During the discharge process, electrons flow from the anode, which serves as the negative electrode, to the cathode, the positive electrode, through an external circuit, thereby providing energy to the device. The electrolyte within the battery facilitates the transfer of ions between the two electrodes. The power performance of a battery is influenced by aspects such as energy density, cycle life, and safety. Developments in battery technology aim to enhance these features, with solid-state and sodium-ion batteries developing as promising alternatives to lithium-based options [25].

AI has recently become a significant asset in battery research and development. Techniques such as ML, neural networks, and predictive modeling are being employed to expedite the identification of new electrode and electrolyte materials, enhance charging and discharging processes, and more accurately forecast battery degradation and lifespan [26]. AI-driven models can sift through extensive datasets from experimental and simulation studies, uncovering patterns and correlations that traditional methods may overlook. This capability fosters quicker innovation, lowers development costs, and enhances both the safety and efficiency of batteries.

The integration of AI in battery technology plays a crucial role in advancing multiple SDGs. By improving the efficiency and sustainability of batteries, AI facilitates the achievement of Affordable and Clean Energy, thereby enhancing the accessibility of energy storage solutions [27]. Furthermore, the incorporation of AI in battery manufacturing and lifecycle management aligns with advancements in Industry, Innovation, and Infrastructure, fostering advancements in smart manufacturing practices. Additionally, AI's ability to prolong battery life and optimize resource utilization led to responsible Consumption and Production. The development of cleaner, more durable energy storage systems directly contributes to climate action, aiding in the reduction of greenhouse gas emissions and minimizing environmental impact [28].

Fuel Cells

Fuel cells are systems that convert chemical energy into electrical energy *via* electrochemical processes involving a fuel (typically hydrogen) and an oxidizer (like oxygen from the atmosphere [29]. In these cells, the cathode and anode are divided by an electrolyte membrane that facilitates ion conduction while preventing the direct combination of the fuel and oxidizer. The Proton Exchange Membrane Fuel Cell (PEMFC) is the most prevalent type, utilizing hydrogen as fuel, and is commonly applied in transportation (hydrogen-fueled vehicles) and stationary energy production [33]. Other varieties, including Solid Oxide Fuel Cells (SOFCs) and Alkaline Fuel Cells (AFCs), are employed in industrial and large-scale energy contexts. Fuel cells are considered more efficient than internal combustion engines because they generate electricity through a chemical reaction that occurs at lower temperatures, resulting in water and heat as the sole byproducts, thereby offering a cleaner alternative for energy production [34].

AI is increasingly advancing the research, development, and operation of fuel cells. By employing ML and data-driven algorithms, researchers can enhance the design of fuel cell systems, forecast their performance across different operational scenarios, and track degradation and failure mechanisms. Additionally, AI facilitates real-time diagnostics and predictive maintenance, thereby boosting the reliability and longevity of these systems. Moreover, AI models are instrumental in the creation of innovative materials for membranes, electrodes, and catalysts, as they expedite the analysis of extensive experimental datasets and simulations [30, 31].

Incorporating AI into fuel cell technology is crucial in advancing several SDGs. By improving the efficiency and dependability of hydrogen energy systems, the application of intelligent control and automation in the production and implementation of fuel cells promotes the achievement of the SDGs. AI-enhanced fuel cells significantly contribute to SDG 13, which addresses climate action, by lowering pollutant emissions and fostering cleaner transportation and industrial processes, ultimately reducing reliance on fossil fuels and mitigating the impacts of climate change [32].

Supercapacitors

Supercapacitors, commonly referred to as ultracapacitors, are devices used for energy storage that retain energy electrostatically rather than chemically. The structure consists of two electrodes separated by an electrolyte, with energy being stored through the buildup of charge on the electrodes. In comparison to batteries, which store energy through reversible chemical processes, supercapacitors capture energy in an electric field, allowing for rapid charging and discharging. This characteristic makes supercapacitors suitable for uses that demand high power density and swift energy bursts, such as regenerative braking systems utilized in EVs, backup power systems, and consumer electronics. Nevertheless, Supercapacitors demonstrate a lower energy density compared to batteries, indicating that they store less energy per unit of mass or volume [33]. Researchers continually strive to enhance the cycle life and energy density of supercapacitors by developing new materials, such as graphene and carbon nanotubes, to improve their efficiency.

The integration of AI has proven instrumental in supercapacitor research, particularly in areas such as material selection, structural optimization, and performance forecasting. ML algorithms analyze extensive datasets to predict electrochemical behaviors, capacitance values, and degradation trends under varying conditions. This technology accelerates the identification of advanced nanomaterials with superior surface areas and conductivity, including optimized graphene forms and hybrid nanocomposites. Furthermore, AI-driven control systems are being designed for intelligent energy management, particularly in hybrid setups that combine supercapacitors with batteries or fuel cells [34]. The application of AI in supercapacitor innovation significantly advances the SDGs by enhancing the efficiency and affordability of high-power energy storage. Focusing on material innovation and device optimization aligns with various SDGs. Supercapacitors also contribute to energy-efficient transportation and sustainable energy systems, Sustainable Cities and Climate Action by facilitating technologies that minimize carbon emissions and energy waste [35]. Fig. (**2**) shows the types of electrochemical devices.

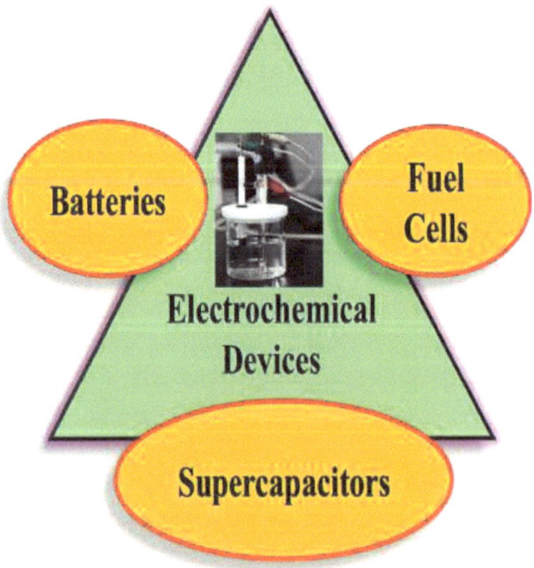

Fig. (2). Some types of electrochemical devices.

In addition to fuel cells, batteries, and supercapacitors, a variety of other electrochemical devices are making visible contributions to the evolution of energy storage, conversion, and utilization technologies. These devices play a crucial role in defining the future framework of clean energy and energy-efficient technologies. For example, flow batteries represent a category of rechargeable batteries that utilize liquid electrolytes for energy storage, enabling scalable solutions with the capability for extended durations and enhanced energy capacities relative to conventional batteries. Among these, Redox Flow Batteries (RFBs) stand out as particularly advantageous for large-scale stationary energy storage applications. Electrolyzers, a process that enables the electrochemical dissociation of water into hydrogen and oxygen, are crucial for hydrogen production, thereby fostering the advancement of hydrogen-based energy solutions and contributing to the sustainability of clean energy cycles. Additionally, metal-air batteries, which utilize atmospheric oxygen as the cathode reactant, have high energy density and are drawing significant attention for potential applications in EVs and grid energy storage. Another innovative device is the electrochemical capacitive deionization (CDI) system, which employs an electrochemical mechanism to extract salts and impurities from water, presenting a viable option for desalination and water purification. Moreover, bioelectrochemical systems, such as Microbial Fuel Cells (MFCs), utilize microbial processes to generate electricity from organic materials, offering promising prospects for sustainable waste management and energy production. At the same time, Electrochemical sensors are instruments that identify particular chemical or biological compounds by measuring the electrical signals produced during redox reactions at the sensor's electrode surface. These sensors are broadly used in environmental monitoring, medical diagnostics, and various industrial applications. For example, glucose biosensors, which utilize enzymes in electrochemical processes, measure blood glucose levels by monitoring the electric current produced from glucose oxidation at the electrode interface. Additional applications include the detection of gases such as carbon monoxide, oxygen, and nitrogen dioxide, as well as heavy metals and other contaminants.

Electrochemical devices exhibit a shared characteristic of providing cleaner and more sustainable alternatives for energy generation, storage, and conversion. As advancements in electrochemical technologies continue, these devices are poised to become instrumental in addressing global energy issues, particularly in reducing reliance on fossil fuels and facilitating the transition to renewable, low-carbon energy sources. Continuous innovations in materials, efficiency, and scalability are expected to enhance the versatility of these devices across numerous industries, thereby contributing to a more sustainable and energy-efficient future.

RECENT INNOVATIONS, DEVELOPMENTS, AND APPLICATIONS WITH RESPECT TO EMERGING MATERIALS FOR ELECTROCHEMICAL DEVICES

New developments in advanced materials and innovative designs for electrochemical devices, including batteries, supercapacitors, fuel cells, and sensors, are shaping the future of energy storage, conversion, and sensor technologies. These advancements are motivated by the demand for improved efficiency, extended lifespans, enhanced environmental sustainability, and affordability. These advancements significantly contribute to the achievement of the SDGs by facilitating more efficient and accessible energy solutions. They also align with SDGs through the promotion of cutting-edge technological development and support by mitigating greenhouse gas emissions. The development of emerging materials is crucial for constructing cleaner, smarter, and more sustainable energy systems that are essential for achieving a low-carbon future. Some of the advancements are given below:

Advanced Battery Materials

a. Solid-State Batteries (SSBs): Solid electrolytes, like ceramics (*e.g.*, garnet-type $Li_7La_3Zr_2O_{12}$) and polymer-based electrolytes (*e.g.*, PEO composites), are becoming more popular due to their capability to achieve greater energy densities, enhanced safety (as they are not flammable), and extended cycle life when compared to conventional lithium-ion batteries that utilize liquid electrolytes [36].
b. Lithium-Sulfur (Li-S) Batteries: Sulfur is being considered as a cathode material due to its impressive theoretical energy density (1672 Wh/kg). Research is directed at addressing challenges such as low conductivity and the dissolution of polysulfides. Carbon-based materials (*e.g.*, graphene and carbon nanotubes) are utilized to support sulfur cathodes and boost their performance [37].
c. Sodium-Ion Batteries (SIBs): SIBs are increasingly recognized as a more affordable and eco-friendlier substitute for lithium-ion batteries. Researchers are working on enhancing the anode materials (*e.g.*, hard carbon and tin-based compounds) and electrolytes (*e.g.*, sodium-based salts) to enhance the efficiency and stability of these batteries [38].
d. Next-generation anode materials (*e.g.*, Silicon, Tin): The advancement of next-generation anode materials is crucial for the evolution of electrochemical devices, particularly within the field of energy storage technologies. These innovative materials address existing challenges, such as limited capacity, inadequate cycling stability, and sluggish charge/discharge rates [39].

i. Silicon-based anodes: Silicon demonstrates a markedly greater capacity than graphite. Current research is investigating various approaches, including silicon-carbon composites, nanostructured silicon, and silicon alloys such as silicon-germanium, to enhance both cycle longevity and overall performance [45].
ii. Lithium Metal Anodes: Lithium metal is considered one of the most promising options for anode materials because of its remarkably high theoretical capacity. Nowadays, there is a focus on developing protective coatings, solid-state electrolytes, and innovative current collectors to address the issue of dendrite proliferation [40].
iii. Sodium-ion anodes: Sodium-ion batteries are increasingly being recognized as a feasible alternative to lithium-ion batteries, utilizing the plentiful and economically favourable sodium resource. Experiments are being conducted on various materials, including hard carbon, titanate, and metal oxide-based anodes, to assess their efficacy in larger-scale applications, specifically in the context of grid energy storage [41].
iv. Alloy-based anodes: Research is underway on materials like tin, antimony, and germanium that form alloys with lithium or sodium to mitigate challenges associated with capacity degradation and volumetric expansion. These alloy systems are anticipated to deliver enhanced energy densities through innovative structural configurations that can effectively manage expansion [42].

Advanced Materials for Supercapacitors and Energy Storage: In the realm of energy storage, the integration of supercapacitors with renewable energy systems is becoming increasingly prevalent. This integration is particularly significant in applications such as wind and solar energy storage, where supercapacitors facilitate the management of rapid charge and discharge cycles, thereby mitigating fluctuations in power generation [43]. By capturing surplus energy during periods of peak production and discharging it during times of low generation, supercapacitors play a crucial role in enhancing the stability and efficiency of renewable energy grids. Furthermore, emerging energy storage technologies are combining supercapacitors with batteries and solid-state solutions, which provide both high energy density and swift charge/discharge capabilities. These advancements are poised to enhance the performance, sustainability, and durability of energy storage systems across a wide range of sectors, including consumer electronics and extensive renewable energy initiatives [44]. Due to their excellent electrical conductivity and large surface area, materials based on graphene and Graphene Oxide (GO) remain a key area of focus for enhancing the performance of supercapacitors. Graphene aerogels and composites made from graphene (in combination with carbon nanotubes, conductive polymers, or metal oxides) are contributing to the enhancement of both energy density and charge/discharge rates [45]. On the other hand, Hybrid Supercapacitors, which integrate batteries and supercapacitors (such as lithium-ion capacitors or asymmetric supercapacitors), enable the combination of high power density with high energy density. Researchers are exploring advanced electrode materials, such as Metal-Organic Frameworks (MOFs) and carbon-rich substances, that promise improved performance [46].

Advanced Materials in Electrocatalysts for Fuel Cells: Electrolytes play an essential role in fuel cells by allowing the movement of ions between the anode and cathode, which is vital for the electrochemical reactions that produce electricity. The selection of an appropriate electrolyte has a significant influence on the efficiency, temperature range, and overall functionality of the fuel cell [47]. Proton Exchange Membrane (PEM) electrolytes are widely utilized in low-temperature fuel cells, where they facilitate proton conduction in a hydrated state. While they demonstrate high efficiency, they necessitate the use of pure hydrogen fuel [48]. In contrast, Phosphoric Acid (PA) is employed in Phosphoric Acid Fuel Cells (PAFCs), which operate at elevated temperatures and exhibit greater tolerance to fuel impurities, albeit with a lower power density [55]. Solid SOFCs incorporate ceramic materials, such as Yttria-Stabilized Zirconia (YSZ), as electrolytes, providing high efficiency and versatility in fuel types. However, their operation at high temperatures (ranging from 600 to 1000°C) restricts their applicability in mobile settings [56]. Alkaline Fuel Cells (AFCs) utilize potassium hydroxide as the electrolyte, effectively conducting hydroxide ions and operating efficiently with hydrogen, though they are vulnerable to contamination from Carbon dioxide (CO_2) [49]. Molten Carbonate Fuel Cells (MCFCs) utilize molten carbonate salts as electrolytes, making them suitable for large-scale power generation and capable of operating with a variety of fuels; however, they require high temperatures and specialized materials [58]. Anion Exchange Membranes (AEMs) represent a newer category of electrolytes that conduct hydroxide ions, offering the potential for lower operating temperatures and more economical materials [50].

Advanced Materials for Sensors and Energy Harvesting: Innovations in flexible, stretchable, and printable materials, such as carbon nanotube-based inks, conductive polymers, and graphene oxide, have enabled the creation of lightweight, wearable, and adaptable sensors and energy-harvesting devices that can be applied to various surfaces [51]. There are substances such as quantum dots, nanowires, carbon nanomaterials, and MOFs that are being combined with sensors for use in environmental monitoring, health diagnostics, and wearable electronics. These materials enhance the sensitivity, selectivity, and stability of electrochemical sensors [52]. Here, Fig. (**3**) shows the diagrammatic view of materials and innovations in electrochemical devices.

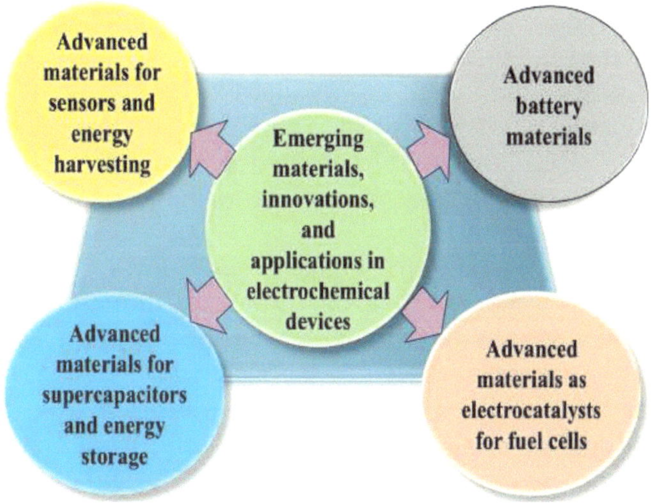

Fig. (3). Schematic representation of emerging materials and innovations in electrochemical devices.

The incorporation of sensors alongside energy-harvesting technologies presents new opportunities for the development of sustainable and autonomous systems that function independently of regular battery changes or external power sources. Progress in low-power electronic components, energy storage solutions, and energy-efficient sensor architectures, coupled with advancements in energy harvesting materials such as high-efficiency photovoltaic cells and flexible piezoelectric substances, is facilitating a broader and more effective application of these technologies. Such innovations are anticipated to propel the emergence of the next generation of self-sustaining, maintenance-free devices, which will find utility in areas such as environmental monitoring, health tracking, smart city infrastructure, and industrial automation.

CHALLENGES IN ELECTROCHEMICAL DEVICES

Electrochemical devices encounter various challenges that affect their performance, efficiency, durability, and scalability. There are the following challenges in electrochemical devices [53, 54]:

a. Energy density Constraints: Electrochemical devices, particularly batteries, encounter significant obstacles in enhancing energy density without adversely affecting dimensions, mass, or safety. This challenge is particularly pertinent for applications such as EVs and portable electronics, where spatial and weight limitations are critical.
b. Material degradation: The materials utilized in electrochemical devices experience degradation over time due to repeated charge and discharge cycles, resulting in diminished capacity and efficiency. Factors such as electrode wear,

catalyst deterioration, and electrolyte instability are pivotal in constraining the operational lifespan of these devices.

c. Economic factors and material availability: The production of high-performance devices often relies on rare and expensive materials, including lithium, cobalt, and platinum. The limited availability and elevated costs of these materials present significant hurdles for large-scale manufacturing and commercial feasibility.
d. Thermal management and safety: The generation of excessive heat during operation can lead to thermal runaway or device failure. Effectively managing heat and ensuring the safety of electrochemical devices, particularly in high-power applications, remains a significant challenge.
e. Scalability and production Challenges: The transition from laboratory-scale development to mass production is fraught with difficulties due to intricate manufacturing processes, elevated production costs, and challenges associated with scaling high-performance materials, which impede widespread implementation.

NEED FOR OPTIMIZATION IN ELECTROCHEMICAL DEVICES

The optimization of electrochemical devices is crucial for enhancing their performance, efficiency, and durability. As the demand for energy storage and conversion technologies continues to rise, the optimization of these devices plays a vital role in increasing energy density, power output, and overall system reliability, thereby making them more applicable across a range of sectors, including EVs and renewable energy systems [55]. By fine-tuning factors such as material selection, electrode architecture, electrolyte formulation, and operational parameters, the efficacy and efficiency of devices like batteries, fuel cells, and supercapacitors can be significantly enhanced. Traditional optimization strategies, including experimental trial-and-error and parameter adjustment, tend to be labour-intensive and often yield suboptimal outcomes [56]. These conventional methods are constrained by their inability to harness the complexities inherent in electrochemical systems and are limited in their capacity to navigate extensive parameter landscapes. In this context, AI-driven optimization techniques emerge as a transformative solution, providing opportunities for more accurate, data-informed optimization. AI can process large datasets from experiments to determine optimal configurations, forecast material behaviours, and model device performance across diverse conditions. Additionally, AI can facilitate real-time optimization, adaptive control, and predictive maintenance, thereby enhancing the operational efficiency and lifespan of electrochemical devices. By utilizing AI, researchers and engineers can transcend the limitations of traditional optimization approaches, paving the way for the development of more sophisticated, cost-effective, and sustainable electrochemical technologies [57]. This methodology is essential for addressing the dynamic requirements of the energy storage and conversion sectors.

AI TECHNIQUES IN OPTIMIZATION OF ELECTROCHEMICAL DEVICES

Electrochemical devices are considered very efficient in modern energy storage, conversion, and management technologies. The demand for more efficient, durable, and environmentally sustainable solutions has led to substantial advancements in these devices. In this context, AI has become a valuable tool for enhancing the design, operation, and life-cycle management of electrochemical systems. This chapter examines the application of AI methodologies in electrochemical devices, highlighting their contributions to performance enhancement, the automation of optimization processes, and the facilitation of sustainable progress. We will analyse the principal AI techniques, their practical applications, and their implications for the future development of electrochemical technologies. Table **2** presents a brief analysis of AI-driven optimization techniques in comparison to conventional methods, highlighting their respective impacts on the diverse design parameters of electrochemical devices.

Table 2. Comparative Study of traditional and AI-driven methods.

Optimization Aspect	AI-Driven Methods	Traditional Methods
Speed of Optimization	Fast due to parallel processing and automation.	Slow, often requires manual iteration.
Accuracy of Predictions	High, especially with large datasets.	Less accuracy due to simplified models.
Adaptability to New Data	Can adapt in real-time, improving over time.	Limited adaptability and fixed optimization strategies.
Scalability	Easily scalable for large and complex systems.	Struggle with high high-dimensional system.
Design Flexibility	High flexibility, capable of accommodating complex systems.	Limited flexibility, predefined constraints.

In Material Discovery and Design

The advancement of electrochemical devices significantly depends on the development of high-performance materials. Historically, the process of discovering new materials has been characterized by its slow pace and high resource demands, often relying on a trial-and-error method. AI has revolutionized this domain by enabling rapid identification and optimization of materials with desired electrochemical properties.

a. **ML for Material Screening:** ML methodologies, including regression analysis and Support Vector Machines (SVMs), are employed to forecast material characteristics (such as conductivity, capacity, and stability) utilizing existing datasets. The application of these models can significantly reduce the time and expenses associated with the material selection process [58].
b. **Generative Models for Novel Material Development**: Generative AI frameworks, such as variational autoencoders (VAEs) and Generative Adversarial Networks (GANs), are utilized to create new materials exhibiting superior electrochemical characteristics. These models analyse the underlying features of current materials and produce innovative material candidates that have the potential to surpass conventional alternatives [59].
c. **High-Throughput Screening**: AI enhances the process of high-throughput screening for materials by examining extensive datasets derived from experimental databases, uncovering correlations, and proposing potential candidates for additional study. ML models can combine experimental data with simulation outcomes to forecast the performance of materials in various electrochemical devices [60]. For example, AI has been employed to predict the performance of numerous transition metal oxide compounds, leading to the discovery of promising new candidates that exhibit enhanced energy densities.

Modelling and Simulation of Electrochemical Processes

The simulation of electrochemical processes in devices such as batteries and fuel cells presents significant computational challenges. Models utilizing AI are a valuable tool for simulating these processes and predicting device performance under various conditions [61]. These processes are characterized by intricate interactions among electrochemical reactions, mass transport phenomena, and electric fields, all of which are described by fundamental equations including the Nernst equation for electrode potential, the Butler-Volmer equation for reaction kinetics, and Fick's laws governing diffusion. Models can vary significantly, from straightforward zero-dimensional (0D) representations that capture the overall behavior of the system, to more sophisticated one-dimensional (1D), two-dimensional (2D), or even three-dimensional (3D) models that account for spatial variations in concentration, temperature, and electric potential. In the context of batteries, models like the Pseudo 2-Dimensional (P2D) model effectively represent the diffusion of ions within both the electrodes and the electrolyte, as well as the electrochemical reactions occurring at the interfaces. It is crucial to integrate electrochemical processes with thermal dynamics and mechanical stress, particularly in battery systems where volumetric changes during charge and discharge cycles may lead to mechanical deformation. Multiscale modeling techniques merge atomic-level interactions with the behavior of macroscopic systems, thereby enhancing the accuracy of performance predictions. Simulation tools such as COMSOL Multiphysics, CFD-ACE+, MATLAB/Simulink, and various open-source platforms dedicated to corrosion and battery modeling are crucial in the design of effective electrochemical devices. These simulation methodologies are instrumental not only in enhancing the performance of current technologies but also in facilitating the development of novel materials and augmenting the overall efficiency of electrochemical systems employed in energy storage, energy conversion, and corrosion mitigation. Some of the processes are given below:

Surrogate Models for Electrochemical Simulations

Surrogate models serve as ML approaches that aim to imitate the results of costly and complex physical simulations. Utilizing these models allows for a substantial decrease in both the computational cost and the time required to analyse the performance of electrochemical systems [62].

Deep Learning for Nonlinear Process Modelling

Deep learning techniques, such as Convolutional Neural Networks (CNNs) and Recurrent Neural Networks (RNNs), are notably efficient at detecting the complex, nonlinear relationships between input variables (such as temperature, pressure, and concentration) and performance metrics (like voltage and current). This ability is especially important in dynamic situations, such as the charging and discharging cycles seen in batteries and fuel cells [63].

For example, AI-powered Surrogate models have been utilized to mimic the voltage behaviours of lithium-ion batteries during the charging and discharging phases. This method enables a quicker evaluation of different battery chemistries, eliminating the need for time-consuming full-scale simulations.

Electrochemical Process Modelling

Electrochemical process modelling, particularly when augmented by AI, can encompass the simulation of charge transfer, ion diffusion, and reaction kinetics within systems dedicated to energy storage and conversion. The incorporation of AI enhances predictive accuracy by refining the integration of physical, chemical, and thermodynamic principles, thereby allowing for a comprehensive modelling of system behaviour across diverse operational scenarios. Critical parameters, including electrochemical potential, current density, ion concentration gradients, and reaction rates, are scrutinized through AI algorithms to optimize device performance. Advanced computational methods, such as ML and DL, support real-time optimization of systems, facilitate material discovery, and contribute to performance improvements. Furthermore, multi-scale modelling, bolstered by AI, bridges atomic-level simulations with the behaviour of macroscopic systems, leading to more accurate predictions. The implementation of AI-driven models can promote ongoing adaptation, thereby enhancing the efficiency, longevity, and reliability of electrochemical devices in fluctuating environments. Here, Fig. (**4**) depicts various AI techniques used for electrochemical devices.

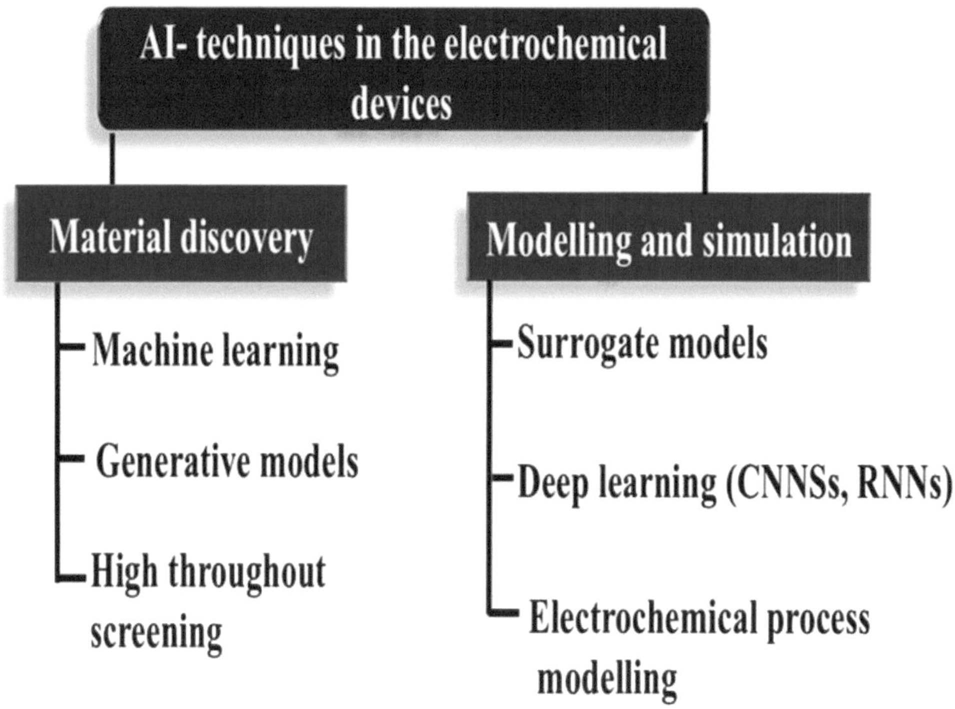

Fig. (4). Various AI- techniques in electrochemical devices.

OPTIMIZATION OF ELECTROCHEMICAL DEVICE

The enhancement of electrochemical devices involves carefully fine-tuning multiple factors to improve efficiency, power production, longevity, and safety. The incorporation of AI is transforming the techniques used in these optimization efforts, making them faster and more precise.

Genetic Algorithms for Multi-Objective Optimization

Genetic Algorithms (GAs) serve as a method for enhancing the design of electrochemical devices by developing solutions that simultaneously address multiple objectives. For example, in battery design, GAs can successfully balance energy density, cycle life, and thermal stability [64].

RL for Adaptive Control

RL is employed to develop optimal control strategies for electrochemical devices, such as Battery Management Systems (BMS). By continuously interacting with the system, RL agents improve their decision-making skills over time, thereby optimizing charging and discharging processes to maximize longevity and efficiency [74].

Bayesian Optimization for Hyperparameter Tuning

Bayesian optimization is a probabilistic method designed to discover improved hyperparameters in electrochemical systems, all while reducing the number of experiments needed. This method is especially beneficial for improving the production processes of electrochemical cells, as each experimental trial can lead to considerable expenses [65].

For example, In the progress of SOFCs, optimization techniques powered by AI were employed to identify the optimal operating conditions, such as temperature and fuel mixture, leading to improved efficiency and lifespan.

REAL-TIME MONITORING AND REGULATION OF ELECTROCHEMICAL SYSTEMS

The use of AI techniques in electrochemical systems is on the rise, enabling real-time monitoring of performance and the modification of operational settings to improve both efficiency and lifespan [66].

Predictive Maintenance

ML algorithms are utilized to predict possible failures in the parts of electrochemical systems. By analysing sensor data and identifying early signs of deterioration, these algorithms facilitate proactive maintenance approaches, helping to reduce the likelihood of unexpected failures.

Fault Detection and Anomaly Identification

AI-driven adaptive control systems possess the ability to alter the operational settings of electrochemical devices, such as fuel cells and batteries, to maintain peak performance. Agents utilizing reinforcement learning are especially skilled at flexibly modifying factors such as charge and discharge rates or fuel supply levels [67].

Adaptive Control Utilizing RL

AI-powered adaptive control systems can adjust the operational settings of electrochemical systems, such as fuel cells and batteries, in order to maintain peak performance. RL algorithms are especially skilled at flexibly adjusting factors such as charge and discharge rates or fuel supply [68].

For example, in lithium-ion batteries, AI algorithms help assess the State Of Charge (SOC) and State Of Health (SOH), allowing for real-time monitoring and enhancing charging cycles, which aids in extending the battery's lifespan.

ENVIRONMENTAL SUSTAINABILITY AND THE IMPACT OF ELECTROCHEMICAL DEVICES

AI plays a crucial role in enhancing the environmental sustainability of electrochemical devices by optimizing material usage, reducing energy consumption, and promoting recyclability [69].

Selection of Sustainable Materials

AI algorithms aid in identifying more eco-friendly materials, highlighting options that are not harmful and more readily accessible than conventional battery elements like lithium and cobalt [70].

Life Cycle Assessment (LCA)

AI technologies have the potential to enhance life cycle assessment by providing important information regarding the Ecological consequences of electrochemical devices throughout their entire lifespan, beginning with the removal of raw materials and continuing through to the recycling stage [71].

For example, Life cycle assessment powered by AI has been utilized to evaluate the environmental conditions and effects of lithium-ion battery manufacturing, aiding in pinpointing chances for reducing emissions and improving recycling techniques. Fig. (**5**) shows the different optimizations of electrochemical devices.

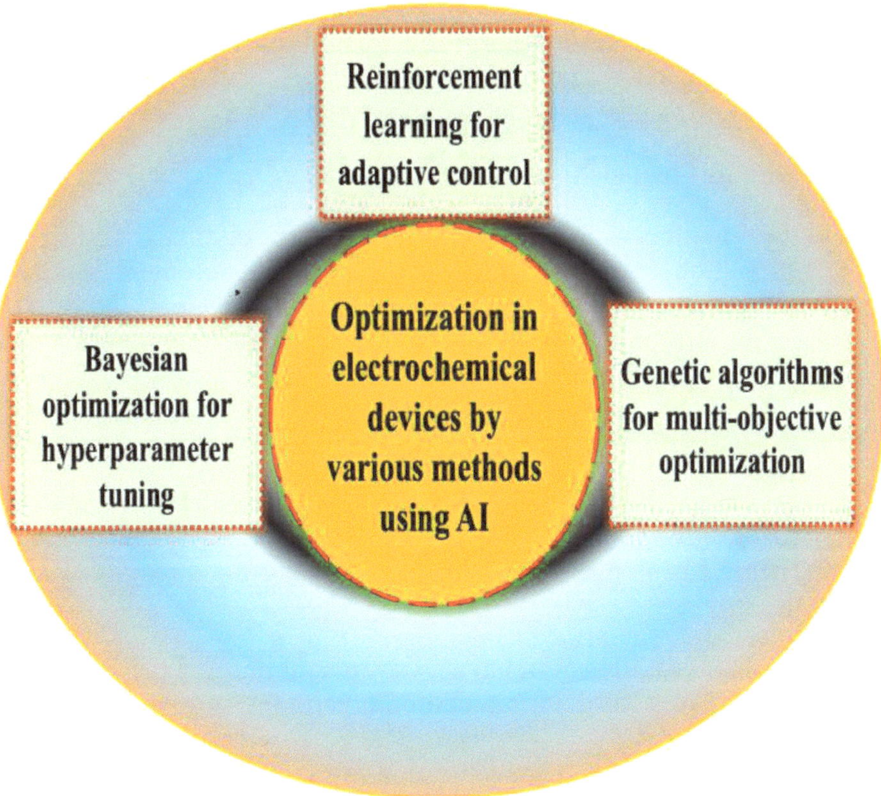

Fig. (5). Optimization of electrochemical devices by various methods using AI.

Thus, AI is transforming the field of electrochemical devices by providing advanced techniques for discovering materials, enhancing systems, enabling real-time monitoring, and promoting sustainability [72]. As these methods develop, they have the potential to accelerate progress in energy storage and conversion technologies, paving the way for next-generation electrochemical devices that demonstrate enhanced efficiency, extended lifespan, and greater environmental sustainability.

ROLL OF AI IN DATA ACQUISITION AND MANAGEMENT

In electrochemical systems such as batteries, fuel cells, supercapacitors, and electrolysers, the ability to collect, analyze, and understand a large volume of data is crucial for enhancing performance, ensuring reliability, and improving overall efficiency [73]. AI is gaining prominence in this domain, as it enhances data collection systems, optimizes data processing, and enables advanced analytical techniques that facilitate informed decision-making and device optimization. AI plays a typical role in the acquisition and management of data within electrochemical systems, highlighting the integration of sensor data, real-time monitoring features, data preprocessing strategies, and the utilization of AI approaches for the management and analysis of extensive datasets.

Data Collection in Electrochemical Devices

The data collection process in electrochemical devices involves acquiring various types of information from multiple sensors and measurement systems. This information is necessary for evaluating the performance, status, and efficiency of the devices, especially in contexts that require predictive maintenance, real-time monitoring, and optimization strategies.

Sensor Integration and IoT in Electrochemical Devices

Contemporary electrochemical systems frequently incorporate integrated sensor data that pertains to the collection of information regarding essential performance indicators. These sensors play a crucial role in monitoring a range of parameters, which include:

1. Voltage, current, and power output, as seen in batteries and fuel cells.
2. Temperature and humidity, for maintaining thermal stability in devices such as batteries and fuel cells.
3. Electrolyte composition and concentration, important for the operation of fuel cells, electrolysers, and supercapacitors.
4. Electrode potential and impedance, vital for assessing degradation in batteries.
5. Gas composition, significant for the functioning of fuel cells and electrolysers.

The emergence of the Internet of Things (IoT) has enabled the immediate transmission of data from sensors to centralized systems, cloud infrastructures, or edge devices. IoT-enabled sensors support remote monitoring and real-time diagnostics, thereby allowing AI to process and analyse large quantities of data effectively [74].

For example, the incorporation of sensor data pertaining to voltage, current, and temperature in lithium-ion batteries, facilitated by ML algorithms, significantly improves the precision of monitoring SOC and SOH. This development plays a significant role in enhancing the BMS employed in EVs.

Data Management in Electrochemical Devices

The effective management of data collected from sensors is crucial to sustain the accessibility, security, and suitability of the data for subsequent analysis [75]. The application of AI methodologies is crucial for processing extensive and complex datasets, which often originate from diverse sources and are available in various formats.

Data Preprocessing and Cleaning

The raw data obtained from electrochemical devices frequently encounter issues such as noise, incompleteness, or corruption. To improve and preprocess this data for further analysis, AI-based techniques, including autoencoders and outlier detection algorithms, are employed. This enhancement process encompasses [76]:

1. **Noise Mitigation**: Reducing the electrical noise effect or signal interference during real-time measurements.
2. **Outlier Detection**: Identifying and eliminating data points that diverge from expected patterns, which may indicate sensor malfunctions or atypical occurrences.
3. **Data Standardization**: Adjusting data to a consistent range, thus facilitating the effective implementation of ML models for optimization purposes.
   a. Data storage and access

The management of substantial amounts of data collection over time presents a considerable challenge in electrochemical systems. AI can contribute in several ways [77]:

1. **Optimized Data Storage**: AI can enhance data storage solutions (such as cloud-based systems or edge devices) by compressing and structuring data in efficient formats.
2. **Data Organization and Indexing**: ML algorithms can differentiate and index data according to parameters such as time, device type, or operational conditions, for more efficient and rapid retrieval during analysis.
3. **Data Protection**: AI-driven systems can pinpoint anomalous access patterns, thereby safeguarding the security and integrity of sensitive information related to electrochemical devices.

Real-time Data Processing and Analytics

Electrochemical systems, especially those utilized in dynamic environments like EVs and grid energy storage, require the collection of real-time data processing [78]. The application of AI techniques, such as streaming analytics, enables the continuous monitoring of data and facilitates prompt decision-making. This functionality offers numerous benefits:

1. **Anomaly Detection**: Algorithms powered by AI possess the ability to independently recognize unusual patterns or deviations in performance,

including abrupt rises in temperature, drops in voltage, or variations in current, which could indicate possible malfunctions or suboptimal functioning [79].
2. **Dynamic Data Filtering**: Techniques evolved from ML can proficiently assess and prioritize the most relevant data for examination, effectively eliminating less significant information to improve overall processing efficiency [80].

For example, in fuel cell systems, algorithms powered by AI can analyse real-time sensor data to evaluate the condition of components such as membranes and catalysts. This capability enables the anticipation of issues such as membrane degradation or catalyst poisoning. Consequently, such predictive analytics support proactive maintenance and operational adjustments, reducing the likelihood of system failures.

AI-enhanced Data Analysis and Optimization

AI exhibits remarkable capabilities in examining large datasets, enabling the derivation of insights and the development of predictive models. Within electrochemical devices, AI-driven data analysis provides essential data that can be leveraged to enhance performance, prolong operational longevity, and promote autonomous operation.

Predictive Analytics for Performance and Degradation

A common utilization of AI in electrochemical devices is predictive analytics. Techniques in ML are capable of analyzing historical data sets to identify patterns that can anticipate the future performance of these devices, which include [81, 82]:

1. **Estimation of Cycle Life**: ML techniques, Such as SVMs and random forests, demonstrate efficacy in predicting the number of charge and discharge cycles a battery can withstand before significant performance decline.
2. **Assessment of Health**: Neural networks and Long Short-Term Memory (LSTM) architectures possess the ability to project the future state SOH of batteries or fuel cells by examining degradation patterns extracted from historical datasets.
3. **Prediction of Failures**: Models driven by AI can foresee potential failures in devices by analysing real-time sensor information, including fluctuations in voltage, temperature anomalies, and various other performance indicators. In this way, AI plays a crucial role in data acquisition and management for electrochemical devices. Through the integration of advanced ML algorithms, real-time data processing, and predictive analytics, AI is transforming how these devices are monitored, controlled, and optimized. As electrochemical technologies continue to evolve, AI-driven data management and optimization

will be crucial to enhancing performance, reliability, and sustainability across a broad range of energy storage and conversion applications.

CASE STUDIES ON THE OPTIMIZATION OF ELECTROCHEMICAL DEVICES THROUGH AI

Incorporating artificial into electrochemical devices is increasingly common, intending to improve performance, extend operational lifespans, and enable new functionalities. The use of AI methodologies, such as ML, DL, and RL, has led to significant progress in the design, functioning, and management of a range of electrochemical systems, including batteries, fuel cells, supercapacitors, and electrolysers. The subsequent case studies offer a detailed analysis of the effects of AI optimization on various electrochemical devices.

Case 1. AI Optimization in Lithium-Ion Batteries (LIBs) by Enhancement of BMS by Predictive Battery Management for EVs: Lithium-Ion Batteries (LIBs) are extensively utilized in sectors such as EVs, energy storage for grids, and portable electronic devices. The safety, operational efficiency, and longevity of LIBs are significantly affected by their management and usage. AI has been significantly employed to enhance multiple facets of LIB functionality, encompassing the optimization of charging and discharging cycles, as well as the calculation of SOC and SOH.

The primary aim is to improve the longevity and operational capability of lithium-ion batteries utilized in EVs by refining the charging and discharging processes, reducing degradation, and forecasting potential battery failure. These two ways are proposed:

1. Advanced RL algorithms, powered by AI, were employed to develop an optimized charging protocol for EV batteries. By engaging with the battery system, RL agents learned the most efficient charging techniques, adjusting variables such as charge rate and cut-off voltage to enhance energy retention and reduce degradation.
2. Deep Neural Networks (DNNs) have been employed to deliver real-time assessments of the SOH and SOC of batteries, significantly improving the accuracy of battery monitoring systems. The training of these models utilized historical data that included voltage, temperature, and current profiles to predict future battery performance and deterioration.

The outcome of this approach will be an increased battery lifespan, characterized by a notable reduction in capacity degradation and the likelihood of thermal runaway, resulting in a 20–30% enhancement in battery longevity. Conversely, the optimization of battery performance, achieved through accurate assessments of SOC and SOH, has enabled better management of charge and discharge cycles, thus improving battery efficiency throughout both vehicle operation and charging activities [83, 84].

Case 2: AI Optimization in Fuel Cells by Enhancing Fuel Cell Performance by Real-Time Monitoring and Optimization of Fuel Cells

Fuel cells facilitate the direct conversion of chemical energy into electrical energy *via* electrochemical processes, serving a variety of applications including hydrogen-powered vehicles and stationary energy systems [85]. Improving the performance and capability of fuel cells is crucial for their economic viability. The integration of AI has been utilized to optimize fuel cell operations, improve catalyst performance, and reduce energy losses. The primary target is to enhance the performance and longevity of PEM fuel cells used in transportation sectors, such as hydrogen-fueled vehicles, through the optimization of operational parameters and the proactive detection of potential failures. This resulted in a 10–15% increase in overall fuel efficiency, achieved by improving hydrogen utilization and reducing waste heat production. By persistently adjusting operational parameters to reduce stress on the essential components of the fuel cell, especially the membrane and catalyst, AI has contributed to extending the life cycle of PEM fuel cells by up to 25%.

Case 3: AI Optimization in Supercapacitors by Energy Storage Enhancement through Optimization of Hybrid Energy Storage Systems (HESS)

Supercapacitors function as energy storage devices, distinguished by their high power density and rapid charge and discharge capabilities, making them ideal for applications that require an immediate energy supply. The application of AI optimization methods is improving the efficiency, cycle life, and durability of supercapacitors, particularly in Hybrid Energy Storage Systems (HESS) that combine them with batteries.

This will enhance the energy allocation in hybrid energy systems that combine batteries and supercapacitors, thereby improving overall performance, energy efficiency, and longevity. In this configuration, SVMs are used to predict the optimal power allocation between the battery and supercapacitor. The SVM model was formed using data from the system, which encompassed power demand, the SOC of both energy storage elements, and temperature variations. Conversely, Model Predictive Control (MPC) was employed to facilitate real-time modifications to the power distribution between the battery and supercapacitor, based on projected energy requirements. This optimization strategy, powered by AI, effectively allocated the battery for long-term energy storage, while the supercapacitor catered to immediate, short-term energy requirements. This dual approach resulted in an overall energy efficiency enhancement of 15–20%, achieved through the minimization of energy losses and the optimal utilization of the supercapacitor for high-power demands. Additionally, the overall lifespan of the system was improved, resulting in a decrease in battery degradation rates of up to 30% [86].

Case 4: AI Optimization in Electrolysers by Enhancing Electrolysis Efficiency by Optimization of Proton Exchange Membrane (PEM) Electrolysers

Electrolysers serve as devices that convert electrical energy into chemical energy by facilitating the electrolysis of water, resulting in the separation of hydrogen and oxygen. These systems are crucial for producing green hydrogen, a key component in sustainable energy systems. The incorporation of AI is being utilized to enhance the efficiency of electrolysers, increase hydrogen production, and lower operational costs. To improve the operational efficiency and energy consumption of PEM electrolysers utilized in large-scale hydrogen production, it is essential to optimize critical Operational variables, including voltage, current, and temperature. The application of deep RL algorithms has enhanced the optimization of PEM electrolyser functions by determining the most efficient operational parameters. This approach enabled real-time adjustments to variables such as applied voltage and flow rates, ultimately increasing hydrogen production while minimizing energy consumption. Neural networks were employed to predict the electrochemical behaviour of the electrolyser across different operational scenarios. These 1. Predictive models were developed using historical data that included voltage, temperature, and gas flow rates, facilitating the development of strategies for real-time optimization. Thc adjustments made to voltage and current resulted in a 10–15% reduction in energy consumption, optimizing these parameters to their most effective levels for hydrogen production. Consequently, the enhanced operational settings resulted in a 12–18% increase in the hydrogen production rate, significantly improving the economic viability and efficiency of the electrolyser system.

The integration of AI-driven optimization within various electrochemical devices has led to significant improvements in their performance and longevity. Specifically, in the realm of EV batteries, AI has enabled the development of adaptive charging techniques, real-time monitoring frameworks, and predictive maintenance approaches. These advancements work in concert to enhance battery efficiency and markedly extend its operational lifespan. In Proton-Exchange Membrane (PEM) fuel cells, AI approaches, such as real-time monitoring and RL, have been instrumental in refining operational parameters. This optimization allows these fuel cells to operate at peak efficiency while simultaneously improving their durability. Similarly, in hybrid energy storage systems, AI methods, including SVMs and Model Predictive Control (MPC), have been utilized to enhance power management, which reduces degradation and prolongs the lifespan of both batteries and supercapacitors. Furthermore, the integration of deep RL and neural networks in PEM electrolysers has resulted in decreased energy usage alongside improved hydrogen production efficiency, thus fostering a more sustainable and economically viable approach to hydrogen generation. In summary, AI has become an essential element in optimizing the efficiency, safety, and longevity of electrochemical devices, facilitating the exploration of more sustainable and cost-efficient methods in the realms of energy storage, conversion, and production [87, 88].

Case 5: AI-assisted Optimization in Direct Methanol Fuel Cells (DMFCs) using Response Surface Methodology (RSM)

DMFCs are highly regarded for both portable and stationary power applications, primarily due to their impressive energy density, straightforward system architecture, and the capability to utilize liquid methanol directly as fuel. Nevertheless, the efficiency of DMFCs is significantly influenced by various operating conditions, including methanol concentration, catalyst loading, and temperature. Therefore, optimizing these factors is crucial for enhancing power output and fuel efficiency while also reducing methanol crossover and degradation.

This case study examines the application of RSM, a statistical technique compatible with AI, to model and optimize the essential operating conditions of DMFCs. RSM serves as an effective tool for developing mathematical models that predict system performance using limited experimental data, thereby facilitating the identification of optimal operating conditions while minimizing the need for extensive trial-and-error experimentation.

The research explores two primary optimization strategies:

1. Design of Experiments (DoE) and regression modeling: A Central Composite Design (CCD) is employed to methodically adjust critical parameters, including methanol concentration (ranging from 0.5 to 2.0 M), catalyst loading (from 1 to 5 mg/cm^2), and temperature (between 40 and 80 °C). Based on the experimental data, a second-order polynomial regression model is constructed to depict the relationship between these variables and the resulting power output. The model's validity is confirmed through ANOVA, ensuring both statistical significance and precision.
2. Multi-objective optimization utilizing RSM and AI techniques: The RSM is enhanced through the integration of optimization algorithms, including genetic

algorithms and desirability functions. This led to the achievement of the dual goals of maximizing power output and efficiency while minimizing methanol crossover and fuel loss concurrently. This hybrid approach, which combines AI with statistical methods, provides a more comprehensive and accurate optimization strategy than conventional techniques.

The results of this method indicate a significant enhancement in power density, achieving increases of 25–35% under optimal conditions, alongside a decrease in methanol consumption and greater stability of the fuel cells over time. These improvements render DMFCs more suitable for use in compact energy systems and remote applications. This case aligns with the SDGs by optimizing renewable energy systems for cleaner fuel use. Additionally, it fosters the SDGs through the incorporation of advanced modeling techniques in industrial energy systems, while also contributing to the goals by improving the efficiency of low-emission technologies and decreasing reliance on fossil fuels [89, 90].

CONCLUDING REMARKS

The incorporation of AI into electrochemical systems has led to a significant evolution in the design, optimization, and management of devices, including batteries, fuel cells, supercapacitors, electrolyzers, and sensors. Sophisticated AI techniques such as ML, DL, RL, and evolutionary algorithms have greatly improved the comprehension and operational oversight of these systems. By utilizing data-driven strategies, AI facilitates the rapid identification of electrode, electrolyte, and catalyst materials, predictive modeling of electrochemical performance, and real-time monitoring and management of State-Of-Charge (SOC) and State-Of-Health (SOH) within Battery Management Systems (BMS). Furthermore, AI plays a vital role in dynamic system-level optimization, operating parameters, and intelligent power distribution in hybrid energy storage systems.

As we approach 2030, AI is poised to become a key driver of intelligent, sustainable, and adaptive electrochemical energy systems. Anticipated advancements include autonomous AI-driven platforms for material discovery, digital twins for electrochemical devices, and self-healing systems that enable real-time optimization and fault correction. These innovations promise to significantly decrease development timelines, operational expenses, and environmental footprints while bolstering system resilience. In line with global sustainability initiatives, these technological strides will directly support the United Nations SDGs. Nationally, programs like India's National Electric Mobility Mission Plan, the National Green Hydrogen Mission, and the Production-Linked Incentive Scheme for advanced chemistry cell batteries will leverage AI-enhanced energy storage technologies to enhance energy security, promote green transportation, and reduce reliance on fossil fuels. Furthermore, AI will play a crucial role in advancing the recycling and circularity of electrochemical devices, a vital step toward achieving a net-zero carbon economy. By 2030, the integration of AI in electrochemical systems is expected to not only expedite the shift to clean energy but also foster climate resilience, industrial innovation, and inclusive economic growth on both global and regional levels.

While significant advancements have been made, several fundamental research obstacles continue to exist. These challenges encompass the scarcity of high-quality, application-specific datasets. These AI models are both explainable and informed by physical principles, as well as the intricacies involved in integrating AI frameworks with existing electrochemical systems. Additionally, areas such as AI-enhanced recycling methods, real-time modeling of material degradation, and the enhancement of hydrogen production through electrolysis are still inadequately investigated. To overcome these deficiencies, collaborative efforts that integrate electrochemistry, materials science, and computational intelligence will be essential. Moving forward, the creation of scalable, interpretable, and energy-efficient AI technologies will be crucial for the progression of next-generation, self-optimizing energy systems that can fulfill the requirements of a low-carbon future.

So, we can conclude that the incorporation of AI will enhance not only technical efficiency but also facilitate inclusive, resilient, and low-carbon energy transitions globally by the end of this decade.

ACKNOWLEDGEMENTS

Authors RK and Priya are highly obliged to K. R. Mangalam University for promoting research and providing the necessary infrastructure and facilities. Authors RK and SS would like to acknowledge the seed research grant (KRMU/ADMIN/SEED/2024-25/4331(A)), and RK would also like to acknowledge the seed research grant (KRMU/ADMIN/SEED/2023-24/3910(4)) received from K. R. Mangalam University. The author SS gratefully acknowledges the Department of Chemistry, M.V. College, Buxar, for providing the necessary facilities and a supportive research environment.

ABBREVIATIONS USED

AEM	Anion Exchange Membranes
AI	Artificial Intelligence
AFCs	Alkaline Fuel Cells
BMS	Battery Management Systems

CDI	Capacitive Deionization
CO_2	Carbon Dioxide
CNN	Convolutional Neural Networks
DL	Deep Learning
EDLCElectric	Double-Layer Capacitor
EVs	Electric Vehicles
GANs	Generative Adversarial Networks
GAs	Genetic Algorithms
GO	Graphene Oxide
LCA	Life Cycle Assessment
Li-ion	Lithium-ion
Li-poly	Lithium-polymer
MFCs	Microbial Fuel Cells
ML	Machine Learning
MOFs	Metal-Organic Frameworks
PEMFCProton Exchange	Membrane Fuel Cell
PAFCsPhosphoric	Acid Fuel Cells
PEO	Polyethylene Oxide
RFBs	Redox Flow Batteries
RL	Reinforcement Learning
RNNs	Recurrent Neural Networks
SIBs	Sodium-Ion Batteries
SOFCsSolid	Oxide Fuel Cells
SSBs	Solid-State Batteries
SOC	State of Charge
SOH	State of Health
SVMs	Support Vector Machines
VAEs	Variational Autoencoders
YSZ	Yttria-Stabilized Zirconia

REFERENCES

[1] Q. Abbas, M. Mirzaeian, M.R.C. Hunt, P. Hall, and R. Raza, "Current state and future prospects for electrochemical energy storage and conversion systems", *Energies,* vol. 13, no. 21, p. 5847, 2020. [http://dx.doi.org/10.3390/en13215847]

[2] D. Ohayon, and S. Inal, "Organic bioelectronics: from functional materials to next- generation devices and power sources", *Adv. Mater.,* vol. 32, no. 36, p. 2001439, 2020. [http://dx.doi.org/10.1002/adma.202001439] [PMID: 32691880]

[3] A. G., "A comprehensive review on supercapacitors: Their promise to flexibility, high temperature, materials, design, and challenges", *Energy,* p. 131043, 2024.

[4] G.G. Njema, R.B.O. Ouma, and J.K. Kibet, "A review on the recent advances in battery development and energy storage technologies", *J. Renew. Energy,* no. 1, pp. 1-35, 2024. [http://dx.doi.org/10.1155/2024/2329261]

[5] S. Tumma, D. Velpula, U.K. Adapa, S. Konda, R.K. Thida, M. Sakaray, S.C. Chidurala, B.N. Tumma, and K. Srilatha, *An overview of fuel cells and supercapacitors.* Energy Harvesting and Storage Devices, 2023, pp. 25-46. [http://dx.doi.org/10.1201/9781003340539-2]

[6] I.T. Bello, L.A. Jolaoso, R.A. Ahmed, and A. Bello, "Electrochemical energy conversion and storage systems: A perspective on the challenges and opportunities for sustainable energy in Africa", In: *Energy Rev,* 2024, p. 100109.

[7] M. Ehsani, Y. Gao, S. Longo, and K. Ebrahimi, *Modern Electric, Hybrid Electric, and Fuel Cell Vehicles.* CRC Press, 2018.

[8] K. Shi, B. Guan, Z. Zhuang, J. Chen, Y. Chen, Z. Ma, C. Zhu, X. Hu, S. Zhao, H. Dang, J. Guo, L. Chen, K. Shu, Y. Li, Z. Guo, C. Yi, J. Hu, and Z. Huang, "Recent progress and prospects on sodium-ion battery and all-solid-state sodium battery: A promising choice of future batteries for energy storage", *Energy Fuels,* vol. 38, no. 11, pp. 9280-9319, 2024. [http://dx.doi.org/10.1021/acs.energyfuels.4c00980]

[9] R.T. Yadlapalli, R.R. Alla, R. Kandipati, and A. Kotapati, "Super capacitors for energy storage: Progress, applications and challenges", *J. Energy Storage,* vol. 49, p. 104194, 2022. [http://dx.doi.org/10.1016/j.est.2022.104194]

[10] J. Baranwal, B. Barse, G. Gatto, G. Broncova, and A. Kumar, "Electrochemical sensors and their applications: A review", *Chemosensors (Basel),* vol. 10, no. 9, p. 363, 2022. [http://dx.doi.org/10.3390/chemosensors10090363]

[11] S. Manikandan, S.R. Deena, R. Subbaiya, D.S. Vijayan, S. Vickram, B. Preethi, and N. Karmegam, "Waves of change: Electrochemical innovations for environmental management and resource recovery from water – A review", *J. Environ. Manage.,* vol. 366, p. 121879, 2024. [http://dx.doi.org/10.1016/j.jenvman.2024.121879] [PMID: 39043086]

[12] A. Barhoum, S. Hamimed, H. Slimi, A. Othmani, F.M. Abdel-Haleem, and M. Bechelany, "Modern designs of electrochemical sensor platforms for environmental analyses: Principles, nanofabrication opportunities, and challenges", *Trends in Environmental Analytical Chemistry,* vol. 38, p. e00199, 2023. [http://dx.doi.org/10.1016/j.teac.2023.e00199]

[13] K. Nemčeková, and J. Labuda, "Advanced materials-integrated electrochemical sensors as promising medical diagnostics tools: A review", *Mater. Sci. Eng. C,* vol. 120, p. 111751, 2021. [http://dx.doi.org/10.1016/j.msec.2020.111751] [PMID: 33545892]

[14] H.M. Saleh, and A.I. Hassan, "Synthesis and characterization of nanomaterials for application in cost-effective electrochemical devices", *Sustainability (Basel),* vol. 15, no. 14, p. 10891, 2023. [http://dx.doi.org/10.3390/su151410891]

[15] M. Tawalbeh, A. Farooq, R. Martis, and A. Al-Othman, "Optimization techniques for electrochemical devices for hydrogen production and energy storage applications", *Int. J. Hydrogen Energy,* vol. 52, pp. 1058-1092, 2024. [http://dx.doi.org/10.1016/j.ijhydene.2023.06.264]

[16] M.D. Reale Batista, S. Chandrasekaran, B.D. Moran, M. Salazar de Troya, A. Pinongcos, Z. Wang, R. Hensleigh, A. Carleton, M. Zeng, T. Roy, D. Lin, X. Xue, V.A. Beck, D.A. Tortorelli, M. Stadermann, R. Zheng, Y. Li, and M.A. Worsley, "Design and additive manufacturing of optimized electrodes for energy storage applications", *Carbon,* vol. 205, pp. 262-269, 2023.

[http://dx.doi.org/10.1016/j.carbon.2023.01.044]

[17] Y. Ma, J. Peng, J. Tian, W. Gao, J. Xu, F. Li, P. Tieu, H. Hu, Y. Wu, W. Chen, L. Pan, W. Shang, P. Tao, C. Song, H. Zhu, X. Pan, T. Deng, and J. Wu, "Highly stable and active catalyst in fuel cells through surface atomic ordering", *Sci. Adv.,* vol. 10, no. 42, p. eado4935, 2024. [http://dx.doi.org/10.1126/sciadv.ado4935] [PMID: 39423264]

[18] D. Grazioli, M. Magri, and A. Salvadori, "Computational modeling of Li-ion batteries", *Comput. Mech.,* vol. 58, no. 6, pp. 889-909, 2016. [http://dx.doi.org/10.1007/s00466-016-1325-8]

[19] K. Dissanayake, and D. Kularatna-Abeywardana, "A review of supercapacitors: Materials, technology, challenges, and renewable energy applications", *J. Energy Storage,* vol. 96, p. 112563, 2024. [http://dx.doi.org/10.1016/j.est.2024.112563]

[20] P. Radanliev, "Artificial intelligence: reflecting on the past and looking towards the next paradigm shift", *J. Exp. Theor. Artif. Intell.,* pp. 1-18, 2024. [http://dx.doi.org/10.1080/0952813X.2024.2323042]

[21] X. Liu, K. Fan, X. Huang, J. Ge, Y. Liu, and H. Kang, "Recent advances in artificial intelligence boosting materials design for electrochemical energy storage", *Chem. Eng. J.,* vol. 490, p. 151625, 2024. [http://dx.doi.org/10.1016/j.cej.2024.151625]

[22] S. Li, O. Gao, and F. You, *AI for Science in Electrochemical Energy Storage: A Multi-Scale Systems Perspective on Transportation Electrification.* Nexus, 2024.

[23] H. Adamu, S.I. Abba, P.B. Anyin, Y. Sani, and M. Qamar, "Artificial intelligence-navigated development of high-performance electrochemical energy storage systems through feature engineering of multiple descriptor families of materials", *Energy Advances,* vol. 2, no. 5, pp. 615-645, 2023. [http://dx.doi.org/10.1039/D3YA00104K]

[24] K. Schmidt-Rohr, "How batteries store and release energy: explaining basic electrochemistry", *J. Chem. Educ.,* vol. 95, no. 10, pp. 1801-1810, 2018. [http://dx.doi.org/10.1021/acs.jchemed.8b00479]

[25] T. Wulandari, D. Fawcett, S.B. Majumder, and G.E.J. Poinern, "Lithium-based batteries, history, current status, challenges, and future perspectives", *Battery Energy,* vol. 2, no. 6, p. 20230030, 2023. [http://dx.doi.org/10.1002/bte2.20230030]

[26] A. Valizadeh, and M.H. Amirhosseini, "Machine learning in lithium-ion battery: Applications, challenges, and future trends", *SN Computer Science,* vol. 5, no. 6, p. 717, 2024. [http://dx.doi.org/10.1007/s42979-024-03046-2]

[27] M. Cavus, D. Dissanayake, and M. Bell, "Next generation of electric vehicles: AI-driven approaches for predictive maintenance and battery management", *Energies,* vol. 18, no. 5, p. 1041, 2025. [http://dx.doi.org/10.3390/en18051041]

[28] M.V. Gowrishankar, "Sustainable manufacturing practices for EV battery packs: Lowering the environmental impacts and increasing recyclability", *Future Batteries,* vol. 6, p. 100061, 2025. [http://dx.doi.org/10.1016/j.fub.2025.100061]

[29] J. Lindorfer, D.C. Rosenfeld, and H. Böhm, "Fuel cells: Energy conversion technology", In: *In Future Energy.* Elsevier, 2020, pp. 495-517. [http://dx.doi.org/10.1016/B978-0-08-102886-5.00023-2]

[30] S.G. Nnabuife, C. Udemu, A.K. Hamzat, C.K. Darko, and K.A. Quainoo, "Smart monitoring and control systems for hydrogen fuel cells using AI", *Int. J. Hydrogen Energy,* vol. 110, pp. 704-726, 2024. [http://dx.doi.org/10.1016/j.ijhydene.2025.02.232]

[31] M. Batool, O. Sanumi, and J. Jankovic, "Application of artificial intelligence in the materials science, with a special focus on fuel cells and electrolyzers", *Energy and AI,* vol. 18, p. 100424, 2024.

[http://dx.doi.org/10.1016/j.egyai.2024.100424]

[32] Z. Fan, Z. Yan, and S. Wen, "Deep learning and artificial intelligence in sustainability: a review of SDGs, renewable energy, and environmental health", *Sustainability (Basel),* vol. 15, no. 18, p. 13493, 2023.
[http://dx.doi.org/10.3390/su151813493]

[33] P. Mehra, S. Saxena, and S. Bhullar, "A comprehensive analysis of supercapacitors and their equivalent circuits—A review", *World Electric Vehicle Journal,* vol. 15, no. 8, p. 332, 2024.
[http://dx.doi.org/10.3390/wevj15080332]

[34] H. Sharma, A.D. Pathak, S. Mohanty, K. Chatterjee, P. Kekarjawlekar, P. Viswesh, A. Nazir, and K.K. Sahu, *A holistic treatise on artificial intelligence (AI) and machine learning (ML) tools for green supercapacitors,* 2023.
[http://dx.doi.org/10.1039/BK9781837672479-00376]

[35] K. Kasinathan, R. Ladchumananandasivam, S.B. Mohamed, Ed., *New Technologies for Energy Transition Based on Sustainable Development Goals: Factors Contributing to Global Warming.* Springer Nature, 2024.
[http://dx.doi.org/10.1007/978-981-97-2527-4]

[36] A. Machín, C. Morant, and F. Márquez, "Advancements and challenges in solid-state battery technology: An in-depth review of solid electrolytes and anode innovations", *Batteries,* vol. 10, no. 1, p. 29, 2024.
[http://dx.doi.org/10.3390/batteries10010029]

[37] Y. Li, J.G. Shapter, H. Cheng, G. Xu, and G. Gao, "Recent progress in sulfur cathodes for application to lithium–sulfur batteries", *Particuology,* vol. 58, pp. 1-15, 2021.
[http://dx.doi.org/10.1016/j.partic.2021.01.008]

[38] F. Xie, Z. Xu, Z. Guo, and M.M. Titirici, "Hard carbons for sodium-ion batteries and beyond", *Progress in Energy,* vol. 2, no. 4, p. 042002, 2020.
[http://dx.doi.org/10.1088/2516-1083/aba5f5]

[39] C. Zhang, F. Wang, J. Han, S. Bai, J. Tan, J. Liu, and F. Li, "Challenges and recent progress on silicon-based anode materials for next-generation lithium-ion batteries", *Small Struct.,* vol. 2, no. 6, p. 2100009, 2021.
[http://dx.doi.org/10.1002/sstr.202100009]

[40] B. Acebedo, M.C. Morant-Miñana, E. Gonzalo, I. Ruiz de Larramendi, A. Villaverde, J. Rikarte, and L. Fallarino, "Current status and future perspective on lithium metal anode production methods", *Adv. Energy Mater.,* vol. 13, no. 13, p. 2203744, 2023.
[http://dx.doi.org/10.1002/aenm.202203744]

[41] S. Qiao, Q. Zhou, M. Ma, H.K. Liu, S.X. Dou, and S. Chong, "Advanced anode materials for rechargeable sodium-ion batteries", *ACS Nano,* vol. 17, no. 12, pp. 11220-11252, 2023.
[http://dx.doi.org/10.1021/acsnano.3c02892] [PMID: 37289640]

[42] C.R. Sun, and J.H. Kim, "Development of bismuth alloy-based anode material for lithium-ion battery", *Cleanroom Technol.,* vol. 30, no. 1, pp. 23-27, 2024.

[43] N. A., Mohamed Ansari, M. N., M. Nomanbhay, S., A. Hamid, N., Tan, N. M. L., Yahya, Z., & Abdullah, I. Nordin, "Integrating Photovoltaic (PV) solar cells and supercapacitors for sustainable energy devices: A review", *Energies,* vol. 14, no. 21, p. 7211, 2021.
[http://dx.doi.org/10.3390/en14217211]

[44] A. Shuja, H.R. Khan, I. Murtaza, S. Ashraf, Y. Abid, F. Farid, and F. Sajid, "Supercapacitors for energy storage applications: Materials, devices and future directions: A comprehensive review", *J. Alloys Compd.,* vol. 1009, p. 176924, 2024.
[http://dx.doi.org/10.1016/j.jallcom.2024.176924]

[45] Q. Ke, and J. Wang, "Graphene-based materials for supercapacitor electrodes – A review", *Journal of*

Materiomics, vol. 2, no. 1, pp. 37-54, 2016.
[http://dx.doi.org/10.1016/j.jmat.2016.01.001]

[46] S. Alam, M.I. Khan, F. Fiaz, M.Z. Iqbal, F. Alam, Z. Ahmad, and H.H. Hegazy, "Advancements in asymmetric supercapacitors: Material selection, mechanisms, and breakthroughs with metallic oxides, sulfides, and phosphates", *J. Energy Storage,* vol. 72, p. 108208, 2023.
[http://dx.doi.org/10.1016/j.est.2023.108208]

[47] F.S. Nanadegani, and B. Sunden, "Review of exergy and energy analysis of fuel cells", *Int. J. Hydrogen Energy,* vol. 48, no. 84, pp. 32875-32942, 2023.
[http://dx.doi.org/10.1016/j.ijhydene.2023.05.052]

[48] Y. Zhou, and B. Chen, "Investigation of optimization and evaluation criteria for flow field in proton exchange membrane fuel cell: A critical review", *Renew. Sustain. Energy Rev.,* vol. 185, p. 113584, 2023.
[http://dx.doi.org/10.1016/j.rser.2023.113584]

[49] A.T. Hamada, M.F. Orhan, and A.M. Kannan, "Alkaline fuel cells: Status and prospects", *Energy Rep.,* vol. 9, pp. 6396-6418, 2023.
[http://dx.doi.org/10.1016/j.egyr.2023.05.276]

[50] J. Hyun, and H.T. Kim, "Powering the hydrogen future: current status and challenges of anion exchange membrane fuel cells", *Energy Environ. Sci.,* vol. 16, no. 12, pp. 5633-5662, 2023.
[http://dx.doi.org/10.1039/D3EE01768K]

[51] Q. Li, J. Zhang, Q. Li, G. Li, X. Tian, Z. Luo, F. Qiao, X. Wu, and J. Zhang, "Review of printed electrodes for flexible devices", *Front. Mater.,* vol. 5, p. 77, 2019.
[http://dx.doi.org/10.3389/fmats.2018.00077]

[52] B. Hu, W. Chen, and J. Zhou, "High performance flexible sensor based on inorganic nanomaterials", *Sens. Actuators B Chem.,* vol. 176, pp. 522-533, 2013.
[http://dx.doi.org/10.1016/j.snb.2012.09.036]

[53] R. Sharma, H. Kumar, G. Kumar, S. Sharma, R. Aneja, A.K. Sharma, R. Kumar, and P. Kumar, "Progress and challenges in electrochemical energy storage devices: Fabrication, electrode material, and economic aspects", *Chem. Eng. J.,* vol. 468, p. 143706, 2023.
[http://dx.doi.org/10.1016/j.cej.2023.143706]

[54] B.H. Xiao, K. Xiao, J.X. Li, C.F. Xiao, S. Cao, and Z.Q. Liu, "Flexible electrochemical energy storage devices and related applications: recent progress and challenges", *Chem. Sci. (Camb.),* vol. 15, no. 29, pp. 11229-11266, 2024.
[http://dx.doi.org/10.1039/D4SC02139H] [PMID: 39055032]

[55] D.A. Elalfy, E. Gouda, M.F. Kotb, V. Bureš, and B.E. Sedhom, "Comprehensive review of energy storage systems technologies, objectives, challenges, and future trends", *Energy Strategy Reviews,* vol. 54, p. 101482, 2024.
[http://dx.doi.org/10.1016/j.esr.2024.101482]

[56] X. Fu, W. Cheng, G. Wan, Z. Yang, and B.C.K. Tee, "Toward an AI era: Advances in electronic skins", *Chem. Rev.,* vol. 124, no. 17, pp. 9899-9948, 2024.
[http://dx.doi.org/10.1021/acs.chemrev.4c00049] [PMID: 39198214]

[57] I.T. Bello, R. Taiwo, O.C. Esan, A.H. Adegoke, A.O. Ijaola, Z. Li, S. Zhao, C. Wang, Z. Shao, and M. Ni, "AI-enabled materials discovery for advanced ceramic electrochemical cells", *Energy and AI,* vol. 15, p. 100317, 2024.
[http://dx.doi.org/10.1016/j.egyai.2023.100317]

[58] Y. Liu, O.C. Esan, Z. Pan, and L. An, "Machine learning for advanced energy materials", *Energy and AI,* vol. 3, p. 100049, 2021.
[http://dx.doi.org/10.1016/j.egyai.2021.100049]

[59] M. Aghaei Meibodi, *"Generative design exploration: Computation and material practice"*, Ph.D.

dissertation, KTH Royal Inst. Technol, 2016.

[60] I. Wallach, D. Bernard, K. Nguyen, G. Ho, A. Morrison, A. Stecula, A. Rosnik, A.M. O'Sullivan, A. Davtyan, B. Samudio, B. Thomas, B. Worley, B. Butler, C. Laggner, D. Thayer, E. Moharreri, G. Friedland, H. Truong, H. van den Bedem, H.L. Ng, K. Stafford, K. Sarangapani, K. Giesler, L. Ngo, M. Mysinger, M. Ahmed, N.J. Anthis, N. Henriksen, P. Gniewek, S. Eckert, S. de Oliveira, S. Suterwala, S.V.K. PrasadPrasad, S. Shek, S. Contreras, S. Hare, T. Palazzo, T.E. O'Brien, T. Van Grack, T. Williams, T-R. Chern, V. Kenyon, A.H. Lee, A.B. Cann, B. Bergman, B.M. Anderson, B.D. Cox, J.M. Warrington, J.M. Sorenson, J.M. Goldenberg, M.A. Young, N. DeHaan, R.P. Pemberton, S. Schroedl, T.M. Abramyan, T. Gupta, V. Mysore, A.G. Presser, A.A. Ferrando, A.D. Andricopulo, A. Ghosh, A.G. Ayachi, A. Mushtaq, A.M. Shaqra, A.K.L. Toh, A.V. Smrcka, A. Ciccia, A.S. de Oliveira, A. Sverzhinsky, A.M. de Sousa, A.I. Agoulnik, A. Kushnir, A.N. Freiberg, A.V. Statsyuk, A.R. Gingras, A. Degterev, A. Tomilov, A. Vrielink, A.A. Garaeva, A. Bryant-Friedrich, A. Caflisch, A.K. Patel, A.V. Rangarajan, A. Matheeussen, A. Battistoni, A. Caporali, A. Chini, A. Ilari, A. Mattevi, A.T. Foote, A. Trabocchi, A. Stahl, A.B. Herr, A. Berti, A. Freywald, A.G. Reidenbach, A. Lam, A.R. Cuddihy, A. White, A. Taglialatela, A.K. Ojha, A.M. Cathcart, A.A.L. Motyl, A. Borowska, A. D'Antuono, A.K.H. Hirsch, A.M. Porcelli, A. Minakova, A. Montanaro, A. Müller, A. Fiorillo, A. Virtanen, A.J. O'Donoghue, A. Del Rio Flores, A.E. Garmendia, A. Pineda-Lucena, A.T. Panganiban, A. Samantha, A.K. Chatterjee, A.L. Haas, A.S. Paparella, A.L.S. John, A. Prince, A. ElSheikh, A.M. Apfel, A. Colomba, A. O'Dea, B.N. Diallo, B.M.R.M. Ribeiro, B.A. Bailey-Elkin, B.L. Edelman, B. Liou, B. Perry, B.S.K. Chua, B. Kováts, B. Englinger, B. Balakrishnan, B. Gong, B. Agianian, B. Pressly, B.P.M. Salas, B.M. Duggan, B.V. Geisbrecht, B.W. Dymock, B.C. Morten, B.D. Hammock, B.E.F. Mota, B.C. Dickinson, C. Fraser, C. Lempicki, C.D. Novina, C. Torner, C. Ballatore, C. Bon, C.J. Chapman, C.L. Partch, C.T. Chaton, C. Huang, C-Y. Yang, C.M. Kahler, C. Karan, C. Keller, C.L. Dieck, C. Huimei, C. Liu, C. Peltier, C.K. Mantri, C.M. Kemet, C.E. Müller, C. Weber, C.M. Zeina, C.S. Muli, C. Morisseau, C. Alkan, C. Reglero, C.A. Loy, C.M. Wilson, C. Myhr, C. Arrigoni, C. Paulino, C. Santiago, D. Luo, D.J. Tumes, D.A. Keedy, D.A. Lawrence, D. Chen, D. Manor, D.J. Trader, D.A. Hildeman, D.H. Drewry, D.J. Dowling, D.J. Hosfield, D.M. Smith, D. Moreira, D.P. Siderovski, D. Shum, D.T. Krist, D.W.H. Riches, D.M. Ferraris, D.H. Anderson, D.R. Coombe, D.S. Welsbie, D. Hu, D. Ortiz, D. Alramadhani, D. Zhang, D. Chaudhuri, D.J. Slotboom, D.R. Ronning, D. Lee, D. Dirksen, D.A. Shoue, D.W. Zochodne, D. Krishnamurthy, D. Duncan, D.M. Glubb, E.L.M. Gelardi, E.C. Hsiao, E.G. Lynn, E.B. Silva, E. Aguilera, E. Lenci, E.T. Abraham, E. Lama, E. Mameli, E. Leung, E.M. Christensen, E.R. Mason, E. Petretto, E.F. Trakhtenberg, E.J. Rubin, E. Strauss, E.W. Thompson, E. Cione, E.M. Lisabeth, E. Fan, E.G. Kroon, E. Jo, E.M. García-Cuesta, E. Glukhov, E. Gavathiotis, F. Yu, F. Xiang, F. Leng, F. Wang, F. Ingoglia, F. van den Akker, F. Borriello, F.J. Vizeacoumar, F. Luh, F.S. Buckner, F.S. Vizeacoumar, F.B. Bdira, F. Svensson, G.M. Rodriguez, G. Bognár, G. Lembo, G. Zhang, G. Dempsey, G. Eitzen, G. Mayer, G.L. Greene, G.A. Garcia, G.L. Lukacs, G. Prikler, G.C.G. Parico, G. Colotti, G. De Keulenaer, G. Cortopassi, G. Roti, G. Girolimetti, G. Fiermonte, G. Gasparre, G. Leuzzi, G. Dahal, G. Michlewski, G.L. Conn, G.D. Stuchbury, G.R. Bowman, G.M. Popowicz, G. Veit, G.E. de Souza, G. Akk, G. Caljon, G. Alvarez, G. Rucinski, G. Lee, G. Cildir, H. Li, H.E. Breton, H. Jafar-Nejad, H. Zhou, H.P. Moore, H. Tilford, H. Yuan, H. Shim, H. Wulff, H. Hoppe, H. Chaytow, H-K. Tam, H. Van Remmen, H. Xu, H.M. Debonsi, H.B. Lieberman, H. Jung, H-Y. Fan, H. Feng, H. Zhou, H.J. Kim, I.R. Greig, I. Caliandro, I. Corvo, I. Arozarena, I.N. Mungrue, I.M. Verhamme, I.A. Qureshi, I. Lotsaris, I. Cakir, J.J.P. Perry, J. Kwiatkowski, J. Boorman, J. Ferreira, J. Fries, J.M. Kratz, J. Miner, J.L. Siqueira-Neto, J.G. Granneman, J. Ng, J. Shorter, J.H. Voss, J.M. Gebauer, J. Chuah, J.J. Mousa, J.T. Maynes, J.D. Evans, J. Dickhout, J.P. MacKeigan, J.N. Jossart, J. Zhou, J. Lin, J. Xu, J. Wang, J. Zhu, J. Liao, J. Xu, J. Zhao, J. Lin, J. Lee, J. Reis, J. Stetefeld, J.B. Bruning, J.B. Bruning, J.G. Coles, J.J. Tanner, J.M. Pascal, J. So, J.L. Pederick, J.A. Costoya, J.B. Rayman, J.J. Maciag, J.A. Nasburg, J.J. Gruber, J.M. Finkelstein, J. Watkins, J.M. Rodríguez-Frade, J.A.S. Arias, J.J. Lasarte, J. Oyarzabal, J. Milosavljevic, J. Cools, J. Lescar, J. Bogomolovas, J. Wang, J-M. Kee, J-M. Kee, J. Liao, J.C. Sistla, J.S. Abrahão, K. Sishtla, K.R. Francisco, K.B. Hansen, K.A. Molyneaux, K.A. Cunningham, K.R. Martin, K. Gadar, K.K. Ojo, K.S. Wong, K.L. Wentworth, K. Lai, K.A. Lobb, K.M. Hopkins, K. Parang, K. Machaca, K. Pham, K. Ghilarducci, K.S. Sugamori, K.J. McManus, K. Musta, K.M.E. Faller, K. Nagamori, K.J. Mostert, K.V. Korotkov, K. Liu, K.S. Smith, K. Sarosiek, K.H. Rohde, K.K. Kim, K.H. Lee, L. Pusztai, L. Lehtiö, L.M. Haupt, L.E. Cowen, L.J. Byrne, L. Su, L. Wert-Lamas, L.

Puchades-Carrasco, L. Chen, L.H. Malkas, L. Zhuo, L. Hedstrom, L. Hedstrom, L.D. Walensky, L. Antonelli, L. Iommarini, L. Whitesell, L.M. Randall, M.D. Fathallah, M.H. Nagai, M.L. Kilkenny, M. Ben-Johny, M.P. Lussier, M.P. Windisch, M. Lolicato, M.L. Lolli, M. Vleminckx, M.C. Caroleo, M.J. Macias, M. Valli, M.M. Barghash, M. Mellado, M.A. Tye, M.A. Wilson, M. Hannink, M.R. Ashton, M.V.C. Cerna, M. Giorgis, M.K. Safo, M.S. Maurice, M.A. McDowell, M. Pasquali, M. Mehedi, M.S.M. Serafim, M.B. Soellner, M.G. Alteen, M.M. Champion, M. Skorodinsky, M.L. O'Mara, M. Bedi, M. Rizzi, M. Levin, M. Mowat, M.R. Jackson, M. Paige, M. Al-Yozbaki, M.A. Giardini, M.M. Maksimainen, M. De Luise, M.S. Hussain, M. Christodoulides, N. Stec, N. Zelinskaya, N. Van Pelt, N.M. Merrill, N. Singh, N.A. Kootstra, N. Singh, N.S. Gandhi, N-L. Chan, N.M. Trinh, N.O. Schneider, N. Matovic, N. Horstmann, N. Longo, N. Bharambe, N. Rouzbeh, N. Mahmoodi, N.J. Gumede, N.C. Anastasio, N.B. Khalaf, O. Rabal, O. Kandror, O. Escaffre, O. Silvennoinen, O.T. Bishop, P. Iglesias, P. Sobrado, P. Chuong, P. O'Connell, P. Martin-Malpartida, P. Mellor, P.V. Fish, P.O.L. Moreira, P. Zhou, P. Liu, P. Liu, P. Wu, P. Agogo-Mawuli, P.L. Jones, P. Ngoi, P. Toogood, P. Ip, P. von Hundelshausen, P.H. Lee, R.B. Rowswell-Turner, R. Balaña-Fouce, R.E.O. Rocha, R.V.C. Guido, R.S. Ferreira, R.K. Agrawal, R.K. Harijan, R. Ramachandran, R. Verma, R.K. Singh, R.K. Tiwari, R. Mazitschek, R.K. Koppisetti, R.T. Dame, R.N. Douville, R.C. Austin, R.E. Taylor, R.G. Moore, R.H. Ebright, R.M. Angell, R. Yan, R. Kejriwal, R.A. Batey, R. Blelloch, R.J. Vandenberg, R.J. Hickey, R.J. Kelm Jr, R.J. Lake, R.K. Bradley, R.M. Blumenthal, R. Solano, R.M. Gierse, R.E. Viola, R.R. McCarthy, R.M. Reguera, R.V. Uribe, R.L. do Monte-Neto, R. Gorgoglione, R.T. Cullinane, S. Katyal, S. Hossain, S. Phadke, S.A. Shelburne, S.E. Geden, S. Johannsen, S. Wazir, S. Legare, S.M. Landfear, S.K. Radhakrishnan, S. Ammendola, S. Dzhumaev, S-Y. Seo, S. Li, S. Zhou, S. Chu, S. Chauhan, S. Maruta, S.R. Ashkar, S-L. Shyng, S.G. Conticello, S. Buroni, S. Garavaglia, S.J. White, S. Zhu, S. Tsimbalyuk, S.H. Chadni, S.Y. Byun, S. Park, S.Q. Xu, S. Banerjee, S. Zahler, S. Espinoza, S. Gustincich, S. Sainas, S.L. Celano, S.J. Capuzzi, S.N. Waggoner, S. Poirier, S.H. Olson, S.O. Marx, S.R. Van Doren, S. Sarilla, S.M. Brady-Kalnay, S. Dallman, S.M. Azeem, T. Teramoto, T. Mehlman, T. Swart, T. Abaffy, T. Akopian, T. Haikarainen, T.L. Moreda, T. Ikegami, T.R. Teixeira, T.D. Jayasinghe, T.H. Gillingwater, T. Kampourakis, T.I. Richardson, T.J. Herdendorf, T.J. Kotzé, T.R. O'Meara, T.W. Corson, T. Hermle, T.H. Ogunwa, T. Lan, T. Su, T. Banjo, T.A. O'Mara, T. Chou, T-F. Chou, U. Baumann, U.R. Desai, V.P. Pai, V.C. Thai, V. Tandon, V. Banerji, V.L. Robinson, V. Gunasekharan, V. Namasivayam, V.F.M. Segers, V. Maranda, V. Dolce, V.G. Maltarollo, V.C. Scoffone, V.A. Woods, V.P. Ronchi, V. Van Hung Le, W.B. Clayton, W.T. Lowther, W.A. Houry, W. Li, W. Tang, W. Zhang, W.C. Van Voorhis, W.A. Donaldson, W.C. Hahn, W.G. Kerr, W.H. Gerwick, W.J. Bradshaw, W.E. Foong, X. Blanchet, X. Wu, X. Lu, X. Qi, X. Xu, X. Yu, X. Qin, X. Wang, X. Yuan, X. Zhang, Y.J. Zhang, Y. Hu, Y.A. Aldhamen, Y. Chen, Y. Li, Y. Sun, Y. Zhu, Y.K. Gupta, Y. Pérez-Pertejo, Y. Li, Y. Tang, Y. He, Y-C. Tse-Dinh, Y.A. Sidorova, Y. Yen, Y. Li, Z.J. Frangos, Z. Chung, Z. Su, Z. Wang, Z. Zhang, Z. Liu, Z. Inde, Z. Artía, A. Heifets, and E. Giles, "Author Correction: AI is a viable alternative to high throughput screening: a 318-target study", *Sci. Rep.*, vol. 14, no. 1, p. 21579, 2024.
[http://dx.doi.org/10.1038/s41598-024-70321-w] [PMID: 39284864]

[61] F.F. Rivera, T. Pérez, L.F. Castañeda, and J.L. Nava, "Mathematical modeling and simulation of electrochemical reactors: A critical review", *Chem. Eng. Sci.*, vol. 239, p. 116622, 2021.
[http://dx.doi.org/10.1016/j.ces.2021.116622]

[62] W. Du, N. Xue, W. Shyy, and J.R.R.A. Martins, "A surrogate-based multi-scale model for mass transport and electrochemical kinetics in lithium-ion battery electrodes", *J. Electrochem. Soc.*, vol. 161, no. 8, pp. E3086-E3096, 2014.
[http://dx.doi.org/10.1149/2.013408jes]

[63] S. Lucia, and B. Karg, "A deep learning-based approach to robust nonlinear model predictive control", *IFAC-PapersOnLine,* vol. 51, no. 20, pp. 511-516, 2018.
[http://dx.doi.org/10.1016/j.ifacol.2018.11.038]

[64] A. Konak, D.W. Coit, and A.E. Smith, "Multi-objective optimization using genetic algorithms: A tutorial", *Reliab. Eng. Syst. Saf.*, vol. 91, no. 9, pp. 992-1007, 2006.
[http://dx.doi.org/10.1016/j.ress.2005.11.018]

[65] M. Santos, "Bayesian optimization for hyperparameter tuning", *J. Bioinformatics Artif. Intell.*, vol. 2,

no. 2, pp. 1-13, 2022.

[66] J. Wang, "Real-time electrochemical monitoring: toward green analytical chemistry", *Acc. Chem. Res.,* vol. 35, no. 9, pp. 811-816, 2002. [http://dx.doi.org/10.1021/ar010066e] [PMID: 12234211]

[67] J. Zhao, X. Feng, Q. Pang, M. Fowler, Y. Lian, M. Ouyang, and A.F. Burke, "Battery safety: Machine learning-based prognostics", *Pror. Energy Combust. Sci.,* vol. 102, p. 101142, 2024. [http://dx.doi.org/10.1016/j.pecs.2023.101142]

[68] W. Pinthurat, T. Surinkaew, and B. Hredzak, "An overview of reinforcement learning-based approaches for smart home energy management systems with energy storages", *Renew. Sustain. Energy Rev.,* vol. 202, p. 114648, 2024. [http://dx.doi.org/10.1016/j.rser.2024.114648]

[69] I. Sultana, Y. Chen, S. Huang, and M.M. Rahman, "Recycled value-added circular energy materials for new battery application: Recycling strategies, challenges, and sustainability-a comprehensive review", *J. Environ. Chem. Eng.,* vol. 10, no. 6, p. 108728, 2022. [http://dx.doi.org/10.1016/j.jece.2022.108728]

[70] B. Ramasubramanian, R.P. Rao, V. Chellappan, and S. Ramakrishna, "Towards sustainable fuel cells and batteries with an AI perspective", *Sustainability (Basel),* vol. 14, no. 23, p. 16001, 2022. [http://dx.doi.org/10.3390/su142316001]

[71] "Enhanced Electrochemical Performance and Charge-Transfer Dynamics of 2D MoS2/WO3 Nanocomposites for Futuristic Energy Applications; Shreya, Peeyush Phogat, Ranjana Jha, and Sukhvir Singh", In: *ACS Applied Nano Materials* vol. 7. , 2024, no. 8, p. 8593-8611. [http://dx.doi.org/10.1021/acsanm.3c06017]

[72] N.H. Vasoya, "Revolutionizing nanomaterials processing through IoT-AI integration: opportunities and challenges", *J. Mater. Sci. Res. Rev.,* vol. 6, no. 3, pp. 294-328, 2023.

[73] M. Batool, O. Sanumi, and J. Jankovic, "Application of artificial intelligence in the materials science, with a special focus on fuel cells and electrolyzers", *Energy and AI,* vol. 18, p. 100424, 2024. [http://dx.doi.org/10.1016/j.egyai.2024.100424]

[74] R. Bocu, "Extended review concerning the integration of electrochemical biosensors into modern IoT and wearable devices", *Biosensors (Basel),* vol. 14, no. 5, p. 214, 2024. [http://dx.doi.org/10.3390/bios14050214] [PMID: 38785688]

[75] A. Gharaibeh, M.A. Salahuddin, S.J. Hussini, A. Khreishah, I. Khalil, M. Guizani, and A. Al-Fuqaha, "Smart cities: A survey on data management, security, and enabling technologies", *IEEE Commun. Surv. Tutor.,* vol. 19, no. 4, pp. 2456-2501, 2017. [http://dx.doi.org/10.1109/COMST.2017.2736886]

[76] R. Krishnamurthi, A. Kumar, D. Gopinathan, A. Nayyar, and B. Qureshi, "R. K rishnamurthi, A. Kumar, D. Gopinathan, A. Nayyar, and B. Qureshi, "An overview of IoT sensor data processing, fusion, and analysis techniques,"", *Sensors (Basel),* vol. 20, no. 21, p. 6076, 2020. [http://dx.doi.org/10.3390/s20216076] [PMID: 33114594]

[77] Y. Roh, G. Heo, and S.E. Whang, "A survey on data collection for machine learning: a big data-AI integration perspective", *IEEE Trans. Knowl. Data Eng.,* vol. 33, no. 4, pp. 1328-1347, 2021. [http://dx.doi.org/10.1109/TKDE.2019.2946162]

[78] E. Chemali, M. Preindl, P. Malysz, and A. Emadi, "Electrochemical and electrostatic energy storage and management systems for electric drive vehicles: State-of-the-art review and future trends", *IEEE J. Emerg. Sel. Top. Power Electron.,* vol. 4, no. 3, pp. 1117-1134, 2016. [http://dx.doi.org/10.1109/JESTPE.2016.2566583]

[79] D. Sathya, G. Saravanan, K. Senthilvadivu, S.B. Jeniffer, R. Thangamani, and M.S. Kruthika, "Demand response management using artificial intelligence-empowered electric vehicles", In: *in Artificial Intelligence-Empowered Modern Electric Vehicles in Smart Grid Systems.* Elsevier, 2024,

pp. 115-151.

[80] A. Diez-Olivan, J. Del Ser, D. Galar, and B. Sierra, "Data fusion and machine learning for industrial prognosis: Trends and perspectives towards Industry 4.0", *Inf. Fusion,* vol. 50, pp. 92-111, 2019. [http://dx.doi.org/10.1016/j.inffus.2018.10.005]

[81] S. Liu, J. Han, Y. Shen, S.Y. Khan, W. Ji, H. Jin, and M. Kumar, "The contribution of artificial intelligence to phase change materials in thermal energy storage: From prediction to optimization", In: *Renewable Energy* vol. Vol. 121973. , 2024.

[82] T. Batu, H.G. Lemu, and H. Shimels, "Application of artificial intelligence for surface roughness prediction of additively manufactured components", *Materials (Basel),* vol. 16, no. 18, p. 6266, 2023. [http://dx.doi.org/10.3390/ma16186266] [PMID: 37763543]

[83] M.S.H. Lipu, M.S. Miah, T. Jamal, T. Rahman, S. Ansari, M.S. Rahman, R.H. Ashique, A.S.M. Shihavuddin, and M.N. Shakib, "Artificial intelligence approaches for advanced battery management system in electric vehicle applications: A statistical analysis towards future research opportunities", *Vehicles,* vol. 6, no. 1, pp. 22-70, 2023. [http://dx.doi.org/10.3390/vehicles6010002]

[84] M. Ghalkhani, and S. Habibi, "Review of the Li-ion battery, thermal management, and AI-based battery management system for EV application", *Energies,* vol. 16, no. 1, p. 185, 2022. [http://dx.doi.org/10.3390/en16010185]

[85] J. Hasikos, H. Sarimveis, P.L. Zervas, and N.C. Markatos, "Operational optimization and real-time control of fuel-cell systems", *J. Power Sources,* vol. 193, no. 1, pp. 258-268, 2009. [http://dx.doi.org/10.1016/j.jpowsour.2009.01.048]

[86] S. R, and M. Kowsalya, "HESS-based microgrid control techniques empowered by artificial intelligence: A systematic review of grid-connected and standalone systems", *J. Energy Storage,* vol. 84, p. 111012, 2024. [http://dx.doi.org/10.1016/j.est.2024.111012]

[87] A. Mohamed, H. Ibrahem, R. Yang, and K. Kim, "Optimization of proton exchange membrane electrolyzer cell design using machine learning", *Energies,* vol. 15, no. 18, p. 6657, 2022. [http://dx.doi.org/10.3390/en15186657]

[88] J. Mao, Z. Li, J. Xuan, X. Du, M. Ni, and L. Xing, "A review of control strategies for proton exchange membrane (PEM) fuel cells and water electrolyser: from automation to autonomy", In: *Energy and AI,* 2024, p. 100406.

[89] N. Magama, M.O. Ojemaye, N.C. Manene, O.O. Okoh, and A.I. Okoh, "Global research progression on electro-catalysts for direct methanol fuel cells between 1992 and 2023 using bibliometric indicators", *Ionics,* vol. 30, no. 10, pp. 5951-5968, 2024. [http://dx.doi.org/10.1007/s11581-024-05666-3]

[90] D. Zhang, Y. Liu, and Z. Zhao, "Adaptive joint multiobjective operating parameters' optimization for active direct methanol fuel cells", *Energy Technol. (Weinheim),* vol. 12, no. 4, p. 2300897, 2024. [http://dx.doi.org/10.1002/ente.202300897]

CHAPTER 3

Real-Time Monitoring and Predictive Maintenance in Electrochemical Systems

Shavita Salora[1,2], Jyoti Jangra[1,2], Shubham Kumar Patial[1,2], Anuj Sharma[2], Amandeep Kaur[1,2], Aman Grewal[1,2], Parneet Kaur[2] and **Suman Singh[1,2,*]**

[1] *Academy of Scientific and Innovative Research (AcSIR), Ghaziabad-201002, India*

[2] *Advanced Materials & Instrumentation, CSIR-Central Scientific Instruments Organisation, Chandigarh-160030, India*

Abstract: Electrochemical systems such as batteries, fuel cells, and supercapacitors have become more crucial due to the global push towards environmentally friendly and energy-efficient technologies. These electrochemical systems are used in various applications, ranging from portable electronics to large-scale devices, and hence, there is an urgent need for advanced maintenance and monitoring methods. The integration of real-time monitoring and predictive maintenance technologies within electrochemical systems can play a crucial role in advancing sustainable energy solutions. This chapter will discuss the fundamental principles of electrochemical systems, the importance of real-time data acquisition for the systems, the challenges faced in managing energy consumption, the need for technological advancements, and the technologies that facilitate the transition towards more sustainable energy systems—highlighting the ongoing research and innovations required to overcome the challenges related to such systems and potential research areas and emerging technologies including IoT, ML, or energy harvesting technologies. Overall, this comprehensive detail could contribute to the ongoing technological advancements in smart cities and the future possibilities in the field. Integrating real-time monitoring and predictive maintenance technologies is essential for unlocking the full potential of such systems.

Keywords: Electrochemical systems, Predictive maintenance, Real-time monitoring, Sustainable energy, Technological advancements.

INTRODUCTION

Recent advances in battery and electrochemical energy storage have dramatically changed the outlook for electric vehicles. Stiffening the demand for further elec-

* **Corresponding author Suman Singh:** Academy of Scientific and Innovative Research (AcSIR), Ghaziabad-201002, India; Advanced Materials and Instrumentation, CSIR-Central Scientific Instruments Organisation, Chandigarh-160030, India; E-mail: ssingh@csio.res.in

Shreya Sharma, Peeyush Phogat, Ranjana Jha & Sukhvir Singh (Eds.)

trification in transportation modes is fundamentally premised on environmental and economic factors. The energy density of batteries has improved significantly, from approximately 100 Wh/kg in the early 2000s to nearly 280 Wh/kg as of 2023, thereby enhancing the range and efficiency of EVs [1, 2]. However, lithium-ion batteries, which electric vehicles rely on, cost 89% less now than they did in 2010-2020. In simple terms, electric vehicles meet all the requirements for regular use, with the average range per charge approximately 220 miles; however, this remains inferior to the mileage of conventional gasoline-powered vehicles [3]. This highlights the need for continually innovative development in batteries and electrochemical storage systems, aiming for longer travel distances with reduced recharge times and the use of greener materials. These developments will make electric cars much more viable and attractive as the primary mode of transportation for society in general. Transport electrification is at the centre of this shift, with renewed spurts driven by improvements in battery technology that are advancing in this area. More widespread penetration in the market and increasing sales of electric vehicles help bridge the gap between battery technology and the green revolution [4]. Electric vehicles rely heavily on the significant advancements that have been made in battery and electrochemical energy storage technologies. The future of batteries is built around six key characteristics: increased energy density, fast charging capabilities, longer life, low cost, sustainability, and safety [5]. The range anxiety associated with electric vehicles must be addressed in the context of greater energy density, thereby avoiding the need for these vehicles to be built larger or heavier than their corresponding traditional gasoline vehicles. Moreover, rapid charging capability is intrinsic to today's mainstream battery technologies [6]. The objective is to reduce the charging duration to a level comparable to, or sufficiently close to, that of conventional refueling, thereby addressing one of the most significant obstacles to the widespread adoption of electric vehicles [6, 7]. Essential components in this endeavor include longevity and affordability; enhanced longevity extends the life cycles of batteries, facilitating waste reduction and sustainability [8, 9]. Future developments in battery technology should ensure increased energy density while remaining environmentally friendly with greater operation lifetimes and user safety. Sustainable practices for the development of batteries include using materials whose sourcing and production have the least negative impact on the environment, energy-efficient methods of production, and secured mechanisms for recycling and proper disposal of batteries [10, 11]. Design vehicle batteries to optimize safety and prevent overheating, fires, and explosions. The application of AI (Artificial Intelligence) has brought about tremendous changes to many scientific and technological aspects of human life. These primarily transformed to make them advance fast. It can analyse large data sets, identify trends, and develop predictive models. It has hastened the methodology and opened up new avenues for innovation and discovery. This has dramatically improved the identification of new compounds and reaction pathways in chemistry, significantly reducing the time and cost associated with more traditional experimental approaches [12, 13]. Likewise, AI is revolutionizing the field of materials science for predicting and simulating material properties, thereby supporting the creation of advanced materials for energy storage, electronics, biomedicine, and other applications. AI, through its predictive analytics and optimization algorithms, has significantly contributed to the transformation of renewable energy systems in the energy sector, bringing intelligent management to smart grids [14, 15]. Its widespread application signals all the possibilities within it: not only the potential through advanced research and development but across the many disciplines that further facilitate it. Yet another area in which the GenAI (Generative Artificial Intelligence) models have made an important contribution is science and engineering. GenAI models can generate new data, whether images, text, or simulations of phenomena, which are close enough approximations to the real patterns and distributions [16]. Applications of the models in research, coupled with the simultaneous creation of complex molecular structures and materials, speed up the innovation process in this area of materials science and structural discovery. For instance, electrochemists make use of GenAI to simulate design options. In this way, a concept can be quickly generated and evaluated in a virtual world. Designing will save time and reduce costs and resources. Contributing to environmental science, GenAI can allow for the modelling of ecological systems and predicting the effects of climate change: this will help with conservation and policy orientation. This extraordinary characteristic of creating novel, high-quality data revolutionises the approach toward problems in science and engineering by allowing for creative and unprecedented paths of discovery and innovation. It particularly applies to using AI and Generative AI for research into battery technology and the electrochemical energy storage system. In these circumstances, artificial intelligence plays a significant role in the developmental process by revealing new opportunities for enhanced performance, safety, and sustainability in battery technology. This subsequently influences the efficiency and viability of electric vehicles and solutions for renewable energy storage.

Types of Sensors Used for Real-time Monitoring of Composites

Strain Sensors

Composite materials can be monitored in real-time using strain sensors, thus giving information on the loads and stresses imposed on them. The most common uses of strain sensors in composite materials include electrical resistance strain gauges, optical strain sensors, and piezoelectric sensors [17]. Electrical resistance strain gauges operate on the principle that a conductive material changes its electrical resistance when stretched or compressed, providing high sensitivity and accuracy [18]. Optical strain sensors operate based on the optical deformation principle, measuring the strain in composite materials. These are noncontact devices, therefore reducing the chances of causing any damage. On the other hand, piezoelectric sensors work based on the piezoelectric effect, wherein mechanical deformation is converted into electrical signals and is highly sensitive to high frequencies. A critical attribute of strain sensors for composites is their elevated sensitivity, outstanding precision, and capability for real-time monitoring. However, the disadvantages include cost, material damage, and technological complexity, which require careful planning before implementation. In general, these drawbacks aside, this strain sensor development is invaluable for the real-time monitoring of composites in situations that can contribute to a critical understanding of how the material behaves under varied loads.

Temperature Sensors

Real-time observation of composite materials should be performed using temperature sensors, as they provide information about temperature distribution and evaluate the thermal properties of these materials, including thermal conductivity, stability, resistance to heat, and coefficient of thermal expansion. The three main types of temperature sensors employed for composite materials are thermocouples, Resistance Temperature Detectors (RTDs), and infrared temperature sensors. These sensors operate on the principle that when the temperature of a metallic conductor changes, so does its resistance. RTDs are more accurate than thermocouples; however, their response time is longer, making them less useful in most real-time monitoring applications. Infrared temperature sensors measure the temperature of an object without contact using infrared radiation, thus substantially minimizing the likelihood of damaging the testing material [19]. The main features of composite temperature sensors include real-time response, precision, and noncontact measurement. Such constraints include the cost, the potential for material damage during installation, and the intricacies that require expertise and specialized training. An area critical for making a live evaluation of composite materials is the integration of temperature sensors. Therefore, such sensors' information about thermal behaviour is a necessary outcome. However, deploying such sensors requires some careful strategy, considering the specific limitations of these sensors and the potential impacts on the materials being monitored [20]. However, temperature sensors have become necessary for maintenance purposes with composite material applications. As the authors pointed out, temperature monitoring becomes integral to assessing the performance of composite structures. The review encompasses and elaborates on various temperature sensor technologies, including resistance-based sensors, thermocouples, infrared sensors, fibre-optic sensors, and wireless sensors, as well as their principles of operation, advantages, limitations, and suitability for specific maintenance situations involving composites.

Humidity Sensors

Real-time observation of the moisture content in composites was conducted using humidity sensors. The two primary types of humidity sensors available for this purpose are capacitive and resistive. In capacitive humidity sensors, the working principle is based on the change in capacitance due to changes in humidity levels, providing instantaneous and accurate information. The basic mechanism of the resistive type of humidity sensor features a resistive component whose resistance changes with changes in humidity, making it an economical and accessible choice [21]. Its ability to provide instantaneous data on moisture content in composite materials makes it instrumental in the early detection of potential problems, thereby enhancing predictive maintenance strategies while ensuring accurate measurements of a material's moisture content. However, some kinds of humidity sensors are expensive to acquire and install. The mechanism may also be complex, requiring specialised knowledge and skills that limit usage. Consequently, humidity sensors are necessary for real-time monitoring of composites, as they provide critical data related to the material's moisture content. However, these technologies require detailed planning and thought regarding their limitations and potential impact on the observed object [22].

Optical Sensors

The optical sensors form the backbone of real-time composite material assessment, providing an evaluation mechanism for crucial properties such as temperature, strain, and deformation. Among these, thermographic cameras and strain gauges are the primary types of optical sensors used to monitor composites. Thermographic cameras utilize high-end infrared technology to capture and record temperature differences in materials, thereby providing critical information on their thermal behavior [23]. Thermographic cameras are used to identify temperature differences and assess thermal performance, as they provide real-time thermal details. However, using optical fibres or waveguides measures strain or deformation by observing changes in the light transmission properties due to the applied strain. Optical sensing offers several advantages, including higher sensitivity and continuous, real-time condition monitoring. The advantage of strain gauges is their non-invasive nature, which enables the retention of composite materials' mechanical properties, making them suitable for continuous monitoring. This also enables the early detection of potential problems through improved predictive maintenance techniques. The advantages of optical sensors applied in composite monitoring include their non-invasiveness and, thus, minimal disturbance to the material's integrity. Real-time tracking enables quick data acquisition and analysis, allowing for immediate decision-making and efficient risk management. Additionally, the high sensitivity of optical sensors enables the accurate monitoring and quantification of material characteristics. On the other hand, optical sensors do have limitations or constraints. The deployment costs and complexities may be challenging, involving expert and technical skills to ensure proper functionality.

Fundamentals of AI in Electrochemical Systems

Traditionally, intelligence has been defined based on the capabilities of advanced biological entities, particularly humans. As a result, research in AI has mainly focused on developing machines that can perceive, learn, and reason. The ultimate goal is to create an AI system capable of emulating human intelligence, often referred to as a Turing-powerful system. Given this objective, it is not surprising that scientists, mathematicians, and philosophers working in AI have drawn inspiration from the brain's mechanical, structural, and functional characteristics.

Various AI methods are employed for modeling, optimizing, and improving hybrid systems [24]. Key approaches include neural networks, fuzzy logic control, and concurrent computation algorithms. This research evaluates the performance of four popular heuristic algorithms to minimize the size of a photovoltaic (PV), wind, and Fuel Cell (FC) hybrid system. The goal is to meet the demand consistently while reducing the total annual cost. The article presents an economic analysis of renewable energy, aiming to enhance the functionality of hybrid system components and provide more economical and reliable electricity, while also utilizing clean energy sources. Parameters such as performance, infrastructure, resource availability, and mathematical models can limit the development and implementation of design and optimisation strategies. Recent computational science developments have facilitated the solution of optimization problems using various optimization and simulation methods. The role of AI algorithms in modeling, sizing, controlling, and estimating the output of renewable energy, specifically photovoltaic (PV) systems, is investigated. Energy storage is a crucial and regulated utility in the grid that significantly supports the adoption of renewable energy, optimal power grid control, and safe and economical grid services. Applications of AI encompass various aspects of energy storage integration with renewable energy, including parameter estimation, optimal design, and control operation. The development of self-powered intelligent systems has led to advances in innovative robotic systems, digital health monitoring tools, intelligent security systems, and sustainable energy production, resulting in a significant revolution in the modern era. Also, the amount of information sensors produce is high, and their real-time data analysis is also one of the challenges of sensor networks.

Algorithms Used in Electrochemical Monitoring

Fourier Transform or Fast Fourier Transform

Fourier Transforms (FT) are often used to study frequency-domain data in Electrochemical Impedance Spectroscopy (EIS). EIS is a non-destructive technique for studying the properties of materials and electrochemical systems [25]. The mixed-signal FT method for EIS measurement has been developed to minimize both memory usage and computation time in computer-aided FT analysis. In the traditional approach, FT is performed separately on both the voltage and current signals. In contrast, the proposed method combines these signals into a single data set, which is then Fourier-transformed to obtain a spectral function. The electrochemical impedance is extracted from this spectral function. EIS measurements were conducted on a polymer electrolyte membrane fuel cell using both the proposed method and a commercial impedance analyzer to validate the proposed method. The results obtained showed good agreement in both the magnitude and phase of the impedance [26 - 28].

In real-time monitoring, FFT enables continuous tracking of frequency-domain signatures, which indicate any deviation from normal operating conditions. Such a function enables the early detection of internal faults that can be linked to specific degradation mechanisms. Therefore, FFT becomes a vital tool for planning predictive maintenance.

Numerical Simulations

Numerical simulations of various forms are employed in electrochemical systems, for instance, Finite Element Analysis (FEA), Molecular Dynamics (MD), Monte Carlo simulations, *etc*. FEA multiphysics modelling method to simulate EIS responses of SPEs modified by self-assembled monolayers of 11-Mercaptoundecanoic acid (MUA). Simulations were conducted on a detailed 3D multiphysics model constructed using COMSOL Multiphysics®, specifically tailored for screen-printed electrodes. To make the model suitable for strong predictions of experimental results, the model was calibrated through a series of Cyclic Voltammetry (CV) and EIS measurements on different concentrations of the Self-Assembled Monolayer (SAM) on the electrode surface. The model is also validated by simulating a new set of EIS curves at different concentrations of MUA. COMSOL Multiphysics® utilises the finite element method, allowing for the integrating of various equations that govern different physical phenomena.

Molecular Dynamics (MD) simulations are now a crucial tool for studying Electrical Double Layers (EDLs), which play a pivotal role in various electrochemical devices. The atomic structure of the EDL in the interfacial region at various potentials can be precisely represented by MD simulations. Essential features of this structure, such as the orientation of interfacial water, hydrogen bonding (H-bonds), and the solvation structure, significantly influence interfacial reaction properties. For example, the orientation of interfacial water and the connectivity of H-bond networks can affect both the electron transfer from the electrode to water and proton transfer in the interfacial region. Therefore, obtaining detailed information about interfacial structures is crucial for understanding the mechanisms that govern interface regulation, which in turn facilitates the design of batteries with enhanced performance. In addition to the selectivity of anions, the selectivity of cations is also a concern and has been investigated using MD simulations. Furthermore, MD simulations are employed to study the salt removal capacity of porous electrodes, such as Carbon Nanotubes (CNTs). Research using MD simulations has shown that charged CNTs are hydrophilic, allowing water molecules to penetrate ion pairs or clusters. This interaction disrupts the pair or cluster structure, making ion separation easier and ultimately enhancing ion adsorption capacity and water purification. Moreover, the polarisation of water molecules increases the dielectric constant and improves the availability of hydrogen bonding sites, which accelerates the dielectric response [29 - 32].

Lattice Kinetic Monte Carlo (KMC) simulations connect microscopic jump processes to macroscopic transport properties by tracking the statistical motion of mobile ions along available migration paths, each of which typically has varying energies. Such energies can be calculated using ab initio methods, such as Density Functional Theory (DFT). The system dynamics are simplified by ignoring the vibrations of ions around their lattice positions. The model focuses instead on the transitions between these fixed lattice sites, with the jump rate being controlled by a pre-specified attempt frequency. This facilitates simulations of thousands to millions of ions over microseconds-long time scales, which is sufficient for studying the effects of composition and temperature on ionic transport. In recent years, such simulations have been conducted for doped ceria and other fluorite-structured oxides using various energy models [33, 34]. Our ability to provide input structures for our workflows limits the exploration of computational materials. Although structure identification is achievable, it is often computationally intensive, and we currently lack design rules to guide our searches in high-throughput setups. To overcome this issue, it is necessary to develop tools that can suggest promising candidates, allowing for automated implementation and enhanced efficiency. Using machine learning models for these tasks helps to solve these problems. However, current methods usually rely on hand-crafted inputs. This means that their performance is limited by the intuitions encapsulated in the selected inputs. We introduce a new approach to casting the machine learning problem as a set regression problem over the components of a material. We demonstrate that our method has higher sample efficiency than other well-established composition-based methods.

Computational simulations, such as Finite Element Analysis (FEA), Molecular Dynamics (MD), and Kinetic Monte Carlo (KMC), are powerful predictive tools for understanding how electrochemical systems respond to mechanical, thermal, and chemical stresses. Such simulations enable us to model key degradation mechanisms, such as dendrite growth in batteries, thermal hotspots in fuel cells, or dissolution of catalyst particles in electrolysis systems, at high spatial and temporal resolutions.

With integrated real-time sensor inputs, these simulations enable the creation of digital twins—virtual models that continually update themselves in real-time from live operational data. With this integration, the system can compare simulated behavior against real sensor readings, enabling the detection of aberrant trends early on before they become visible through a fault.

Machine Learning and VAE Modeling

Most machine learning models are "black box" systems, which give classification outcomes without providing insights into the underlying physical descriptors. VAEs are another method to analyze EIS data. This approach integrates classification, parameter prediction, and visualization of physical descriptors. The VAE model demonstrated strong classification performance, achieving accuracy rates ranging from 82.0% to 92.4%. It achieves a high R-squared for parameter prediction for the Randles circuit. Furthermore, the VAE effectively maps physical descriptors into the latent space, which can then be transformed into the property space; this is a critical feature in optimizing and exploring novel materials during research. The VAE can be implemented using a Python framework. Such frameworks are pre-installed with TensorFlow and Keras libraries [35]. The core component of the VAE is a dense, fully connected layer that acts as the operational layer. There are two components of the architecture: an encoder, which is used for compressing features, and a decoder for reconstructing features. It, therefore, enhances the extraction of features while carrying out these subtasks. As a generative model, the autoencoder compresses data from a large dimension into lower dimensions of some latent variable before decompressing it to produce the original input data. However, in this extension, enforcing a normal distribution on the latent variable and jointly minimizing reconstruction loss, such as mean squared error on the original input data and their reconstructions by the

VAE, collectively referred to as VAE loss, comes to be jointly minimized with the Kullback-Leibler divergence. This design ensures a continuous latent space distribution, which enables precise reconstructions. The structured latent space also supports unsupervised data clustering, which can be applied to reconstruct and classify EIS circuit data. Since unsupervised models typically produce lower accuracy than supervised ones, a supervised classifier neural network was introduced [16]. This framework utilizes a latent variable representation to predict the equivalent circuit, as illustrated in Fig. (**1**).

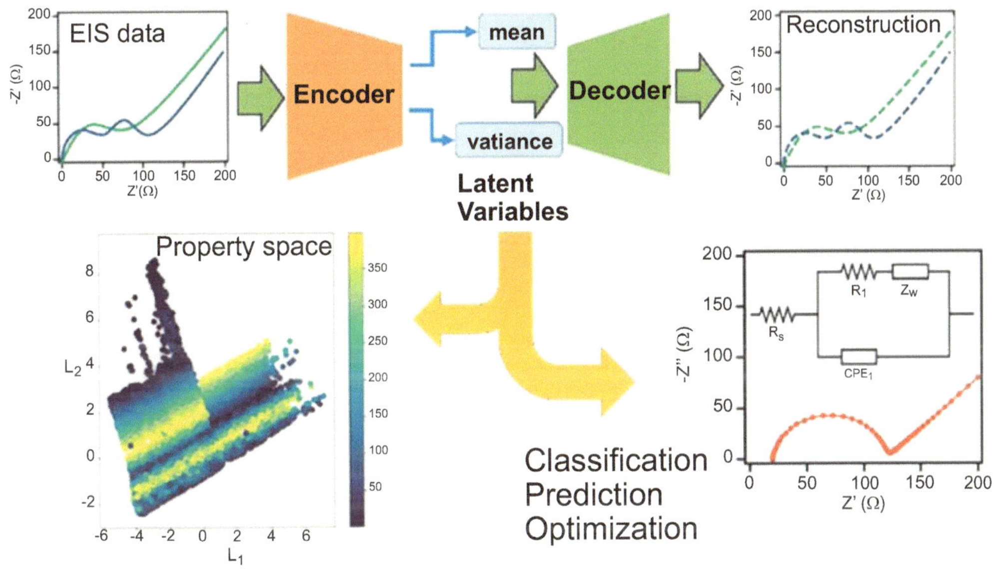

Fig. (1). This picture illustrates a supervised Variational Autoencoder (VAE) model designed for the classification of Electrochemical Impedance Spectroscopy (EIS) data. Reprinted with permission, Copyright 2023, Published by Elsevier [16].

Machine learning, particularly deep learning models such as VAEs, is crucial for real-time monitoring and predictive maintenance of electrochemical systems. VAEs are unsupervised models that learn compact, low-dimensional representations of complex sensor data during normal operating conditions. By repeatedly reconstructing real-time arriving signals, these models are able to identify anomalies as a function of deviations in reconstruction error.

In electrochemical devices, certain anomalies may indicate the early stages of electrode deterioration, electrolyte exhaustion, or thermal instability, often before any visible system malfunction occurs. This makes VAEs very suitable for predictive maintenance, enabling on-time interventions. When implemented on embedded or edge platforms, VAEs provide low-latency diagnostics, making them a crucial tool in real-time health monitoring and the prediction of failures.

Real-Time Monitoring and Predictive Maintenance in Electrochemical Systems

Electrochemical systems are crucial to various technologies, including energy storage, environmental monitoring, and industrial processes. Real-time monitoring and predictive maintenance have become vital strategies for ensuring these systems work efficiently and safely over time. By providing ongoing insights into electrochemical processes, these methods enable timely interventions that enhance reliability and effectiveness [36, 37].

Importance of Real-Time Monitoring

Traditionally, analysing electrochemical systems involves periodic offline testing, often missing transient changes or early signs of problems. Real-time monitoring addresses this limitation by continuously tracking key parameters, such as voltage, current, impedance, and temperature. This constant data collection is essential when failures can have serious consequences, such as in large battery systems or water treatment facilities [38]. Moreover, real-time monitoring enhances predictive maintenance strategies, allowing for the analysis of trends and unusual patterns to anticipate potential issues. This proactive approach minimises downtime, lowers maintenance costs, and prolongs the lifespan of electrochemical devices [39, 40].

Key Techniques for Real-Time Monitoring

Electrochemical Impedance Spectroscopy (EIS)

EIS is a popular technique used in battery and fuel cell research. It involves applying an Alternating Current (AC) signal and observing how the system responds, offering valuable insights into charge transfer dynamics, diffusion processes, and interface stability. EIS has proven effective in spotting the early stages of degradation in lithium-ion batteries, facilitating timely maintenance actions [41].

Cyclic Voltammetry (CV)

In CV, the current response is measured as the voltage is changed linearly, yielding information about redox reactions and the stability of materials. This technique is beneficial for detecting side reactions and capacity loss in batteries and electrochemical sensors [42].

Chronoamperometry and Chronopotentiometry

These methods involve applying a constant voltage or current while monitoring the system's response over time, providing insights into deposition processes and the stability of reactions. For example, chronoamperometry has been used effectively to track real-time performance related to hydrogen evolution in electrocatalysis [43].

In-Situ Spectroscopic Techniques

Researchers can monitor structural changes during operation by merging electrochemistry with spectroscopic techniques like Raman [43], FTIR [44], and UV-Vis [45] spectroscopy. *In-situ* Raman spectroscopy has been particularly useful for observing phase transitions in battery electrodes, leading to a deeper understanding of degradation mechanisms and enhanced material performance [43].

Quartz Crystal Microbalance (QCM)

QCM is a sensitive method that measures changes in mass on electrode surfaces, making it perfect for monitoring adsorption processes and forming thin films. Real-time QCM studies are crucial in corrosion monitoring and electrodeposition research [46].

Electrochemical Scanning Probe Techniques

Using techniques such as Scanning Electrochemical Microscopy (SECM), researchers can gather detailed spatial data on local electrochemical activity at surfaces. This information is invaluable for identifying localized corrosion sites, which informs predictive maintenance strategies [46].

Online Mass Spectrometry (OEMS)

OEMS is particularly effective in analysing gas evolution in batteries and fuel cells. Collecting real-time data can identify side reactions and thermal runaway conditions, significantly enhancing system safety [47].

Challenges and Solutions for Real-Time Data in Electrochemical Systems

While real-time data collection and analysis in electrochemical systems present significant advantages, they also pose several challenges to navigate. These issues span technical, operational, and analytical aspects. Here's a closer look at some key challenges and their potential solutions.

Challenges

Electrochemical sensors often suffer from calibration drift due to harsh operating conditions, chemical fouling, and material degradation, leading to unreliable readings. Signal interference from electrical noise, environmental factors, or sensor cross-talk complicates detecting subtle system changes [48]. Additionally, real-time monitoring generates vast amounts of data, creating challenges in processing, storing, and analysing information, particularly in large-scale systems [49]. Continuous sensor operation in harsh environments reduces lifespan, requiring frequent maintenance or replacements, which can be costly. Raw electrochemical data often require complex analysis, making real-time interpretation and decision-making difficult. Integrating modern monitoring systems into existing infrastructure, especially in older facilities, can be complex and expensive [49]. Data security and privacy also pose significant challenges, as connected systems are vulnerable to cyber-attacks. Managing the overwhelming data volume while maintaining sensor performance in varying environmental conditions adds another layer of complexity, especially when scaling systems across large facilities [50].

Solutions

Implementing automatic or semi-automatic recalibration protocols and utilising self-calibrating sensors with built-in standards can maintain data accuracy. Advanced signal processing techniques, such as digital filtering and the wavelet transform, combined with optimized sensor placement and shielding, can mitigate noise. Leveraging cloud-based data storage and edge computing facilitates scalable and efficient data management, while AI and machine learning models streamline data interpretation and highlight critical information. Enhancing sensor durability with advanced materials, such as graphene coatings, and incorporating self-diagnostic features supports predictive maintenance, thereby extending sensor lifespan. Modular sensor systems and IoT-enabled technologies simplify integration with existing infrastructure, while robust cybersecurity measures safeguard data integrity, including encryption and regular audits. Anomaly detection algorithms and hierarchical processing systems help filter critical insights from routine data, reducing overload. Protective sensor encasements and temperature compensation ensure consistent performance under varying environmental conditions. Cost-effective sensor deployment strategies and open-source analysis tools enable scalable, budget-friendly solutions for comprehensive real-time monitoring in electrochemical systems. By tackling these challenges with innovative solutions, we can enhance the accuracy, efficiency, and reliability of real-time monitoring in electrochemical systems. This ensures that devices used in energy storage, environmental monitoring, or biomedical applications operate safely and effectively over extended periods.

Applications of AI in Electrochemical Technologies

Electrochemical technologies encompass a range of techniques, from sensing to energy production and energy storage. This section summarises the use of artificial intelligence in automating the electrochemical technologies.

Energy Storage Systems

Electric Double-Layer Capacitors (EDLC) are used in energy storage for electric vehicles and battery applications. EDLCs have garnered significant interest due to their energy storage potential, high cycling efficiency, long maintenance-free life, and high power density [51 - 53].

The traditional idea of increasing the specific surface area of the electrode to enhance capacitance requires materials with a porous structure for charge storage. However, many reports have suggested that in some instances, porous structures may lead to a decrease in power density and capacitance of the EDLC [54, 55]. Low energy density is a limiting factor for the commercialisation of supercapacitors, and a potential solution lies in the use of Machine Learning (ML) practices for the development of new capacitor materials [56 - 58]. Zhou *et al.* employed AI and machine learning to correlate structural characteristics with the power densities of EDLC [59]. In their work, they proposed an ML method that studies the influence of structural characteristics using four ML algorithms: generalised linear regression, generalised linear classifier, decision tree, and neural network. They deduced that although each ML algorithm can work and identify the correct trend, their efficiencies in representing the experimental data differ.

A similar pattern was observed with battery materials, from discovery to application; each material takes months or even years for evaluation. This limits the growth and introduction of new materials in battery technology. The application of AI and ML methods addresses the time issue by automating optimization processes and simulating results for a better understanding of the material [60 - 62]. Attia *et al.* reported using ML algorithms to reduce the time consumption in the optimisation process of a new material by up to 90% [63]. Their procedure required data on only the initial 100 cycles of battery performance for learning purposes. The collected data was then fed to a Bayesian Optimisation (BO) algorithm for further testing, and the learning curve continued for each cycle. Once the learning curve was refined, the testing time for the batteries was reduced, with fewer experiments required for material testing. The

CLO system can identify and rectify material characterisation and testing mistakes *via* a feedback loop and validation protocols [64, 65]. The ML methods can accelerate most of the stages in battery development and can be used to reduce cost and time for new material testing [66, 67].

Fuel Cells and Electrolyzers

Fuel cells and electrolysers are devices that produce green energy and have the potential to contribute towards carbon reduction and emission globally [68, 69]. Electrolysers are devices that electrochemically split water to generate hydrogen [70, 71]. Fuel cells can convert the chemical energy of electrochemical redox reactions into electricity and water vapour as a result [72, 73]. The electrochemical reactions for fuel cells and electrolyzers occur in the Membrane Electrode Assemblies (MEAs) [74]. These assemblies constitute the cathode and anode electrodes separated by a proton exchange membrane [75]. MEAs contain additional layers for water and heat management, including a microporous layer and a porous transport layer [76]. The materials used in electrode applications often consist of porous structures and are electroactive in nature [77]. The development and testing of these materials are in high demand to meet energy demands [78]. Various circuit models are used to electrochemically characterize the electrode materials, such as the Rint, Randles, and Thevenin hysteresis models [79 - 82]. The major drawback of using these models is that they are either too idealistic or too complex. Once functional, some sensors collect data from these devices on several operating parameters [83]. The application of artificial intelligence can be applied to data handling and curation [84].

Artificial intelligence models rely on the availability of vast amounts of data and a learning curve to follow [85]. The data from the sensors is fed to the AI models, and machine learning algorithms help these models understand and interpret the data [86]. AI is a powerful tool that can be used to monitor and control the parameters for material testing [87]. This can be achieved by feeding the data collected by the sensors to the AI model and initiating the ML process [88]. Most ML algorithms work with built-in feedback loops or backpropagation to adjust the model for better results [89]. The ability of AI models to continually improve at data curation makes them the most suitable candidates for material design and selection. Some notable examples of AI models include neural networks, fuzzy logic, and neural fuzzy [90, 91]. Khajeh-Hosseini *et al.* employed an artificial neural network model to investigate the impact of structural parameters on the performance of catalyst layers in fuel cells [92]. The group developed a model for research on the influence of structural parameters on the catalyst layer, including Fick's law of diffusion and electrochemical reactions at the catalyst surface. They used ML algorithms like ANN, KNN, Random forest, support vector machine and logistic regression, to name a few. The model developed by the authors is illustrated in Fig. (2), which shows the layout of neural nodes in relation to hidden layers and weights.

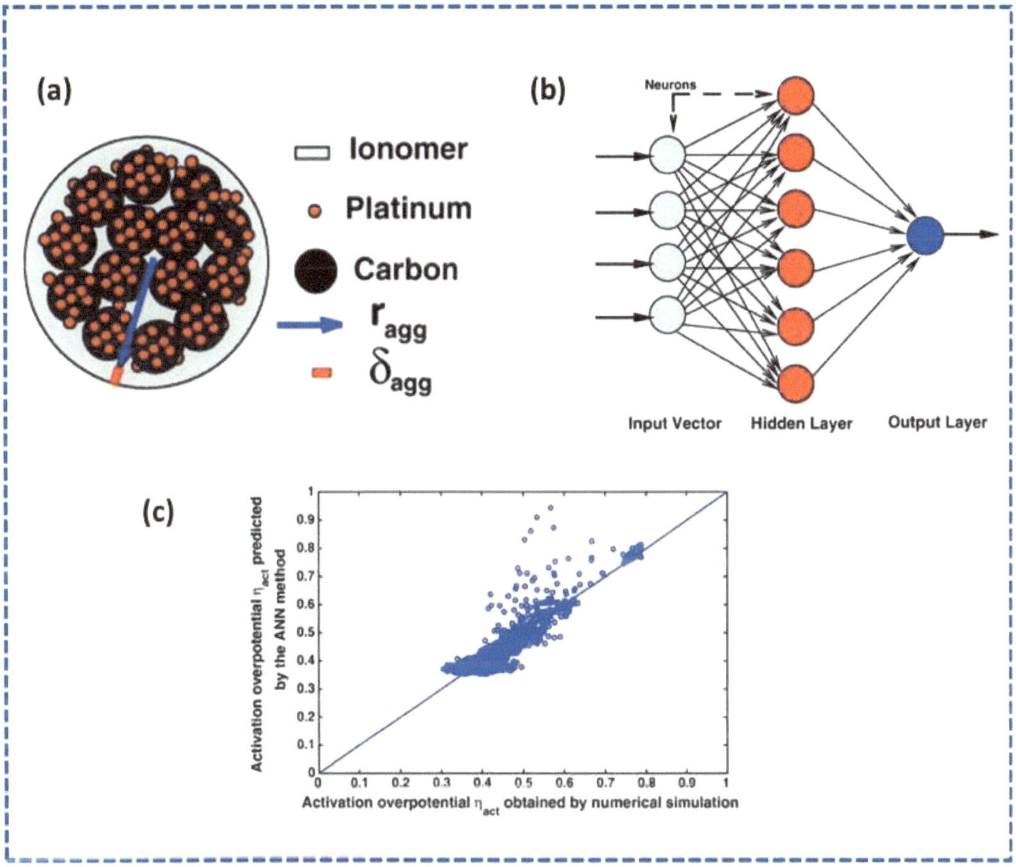

Fig. (2). **(a)** Agglomerate model design, **(b)** schematic representation of ANN, **(c)** Predicted activation overpotential *versus* actual activation potential from numerical simulation. Reprinted with permission, Copyright 2011, Published by Elsevier [92].

Direct Methanol Fuel Cells (DMFCs) are a type of fuel cell that utilizes energy-dense methanol as fuel. In DMFCs, methanol (CH_3OH) is directly oxidized to carbon dioxide (CO_2) at the anode, a process that also generates protons and electrons. The produced protons then selectively pass through the highly selective Proton exchange membrane towards the cathode, where they react with oxygen (O_2) to form water [93]. Currently, DMFCs are a major research focus because methanol is much cheaper and also has a higher octane value compared to fossil fuels like gasoline. Additionally, storing methanol is much easier compared to other counterparts, such as hydrogen [94].

The efficiency and productivity of DMFCs are primarily influenced by several factors, including methanol concentration, fuel and air flow rates, operating temperature, and others. Hence, numerous operating variables need to be optimized to find the most optimal working condition of DMFCs [93]. These optimizations require performing numerous experiments; therefore, the use of statistical tools and Design of Experiment (DOE) is essential. The most commonly used methods for DOE include Response Surface Methodology (RSM), Taguchi Orthogonal arrays, full factorial methods, and many others [95]. Out of these methods, the RSM method is one of the best ways to design experiments, especially for DMFCs, as RSM comprises statistical tools that are useful for modeling and optimizing operating parameters, and most importantly, the detection of parameter interactions based on the design of experiments. RSM helps in understanding the effect of operating parameters and the relationship between them based on the response. Therefore, RSM is one of the best methods to find the optimal condition of internal variables, ultimately leading to the highest possible power density.

Imdat *et al.* used quadratic RSM methodology to determine the optimal cell working conditions and also the relationship between the internal parameters. These parameters include methanol flow rate, oxygen flow rate, fuel temperature, humidification temperature, and cell temperature. The optimal parameters obtained from the quadratic model were found to be in good agreement with the experimental values [96].

Shima *et al.* also used RSM methods to optimize the cell temperature, inlet methanol concentration, and inlet oxygen flow to yield maximum power density in parallel serpentine channels based DMFCs. They checked these parameters within the operating range: cell temperature (50-75 °C), Methanol concentration (0.5-2 M), and oxygen flow rate (300–1000 ml/min). According to the statistical analysis, the optimal working conditions were a cell temperature of 70 °C, a methanol concentration of 1 M, and an oxygen flow Rate of 300ml/min. These statistical optimizations were found to be in good agreement with the experimental values [97].

Corrosion Monitoring and Prevention

Corrosion affects the structural integrity of metallic materials, and monitoring of this process is crucial for its prevention. This section examines the application of artificial intelligence in predicting and monitoring corrosion. As stated earlier, artificial intelligence operates on a test dataset and a learning curve; the larger the test dataset, the more effective the learning process. Various methods and algorithms have been tested using both supervised and unsupervised learning approaches. Kamarunnhar *et al.* utilized Neural Networks (NN) with supervised learning for predicting the corrosion behavior of steel alloys by mapping the alloy composition, tensile strength, environmental factors, and stress [98]. The test dataset was derived by producing corrosion data on various alloys and then fed to the NN. They reported high accuracy of the NN across different corrosion metrics, including polarisation resistance, corrosion current density, corrosion potential, and log (current density). They also mentioned the advantage of larger datasets, which improve generalization. Similar to this study, Jiménez *et al.* applied ANNs for the prediction of AISI 316L stainless steel based on environmental factors and breakdown potential values [99]. They reported high classification accuracy by combining Bayesian algorithms with this method, achieving a precision of up to 0.996 and a recall of 0.989. They also concluded that the presence of large datasets would have given better control over the learning curve and generalisation of the datasets. Pei *et al.* reported a comparative analysis of various machine-learning methods for predicting atmospheric corrosion of carbon steel [100]. Among the models, Random Forest (RF) demonstrated the best results, with an accuracy of 0.940. The study concluded the presence and effect of environmental factors on corrosion rates and intensity. Fig. (**3**) illustrates the general model adaptation and application of the ML model in simulating the crossing process. The evaluation of different models for monitoring environmental factors normally includes relative humidity and temperature variation, which have the most significant impact on corrosion rates.

The reported studies suggest that optimizing input features is an effective approach to improving the efficiency of AI models. Diao *et al.* used Gradient-Boosting Decision Trees (GBDT) and Principal Component Analysis (PCA) to predict the corrosion rate of low-alloy steel [102]. The model employed feature reduction methods to eliminate outliers, achieving an accuracy of 0.92. The group deduced a similar pattern to many others working in automation research: the availability of large datasets that can help better generalise data. A Building Information Modelling (BIM) approach has been extensively used to overcome the issue of large datasets. A BIM includes all the sensors built for machinery or buildings, and providing the output feed of the BIM to an AI model can enable the model to work for many iterations without losing data. For this, Tsai *et al.* proposed an approach for combining BIM and AI models for corrosion rate analysis and prediction in the petrochemical industry [103]. The BIM approach reduces time and inspection efforts as the idea is to optimise the process by focusing on data-driven monitoring and prediction. Although the approach will work faster and has the potential to reduce workload, it encountered a few limitations, such as the use of idealized conditions and the validation of diverse alloy materials. There are some challenges associated with the use of AI and constraints that come with the use of AI, which will be discussed in the upcoming sections.

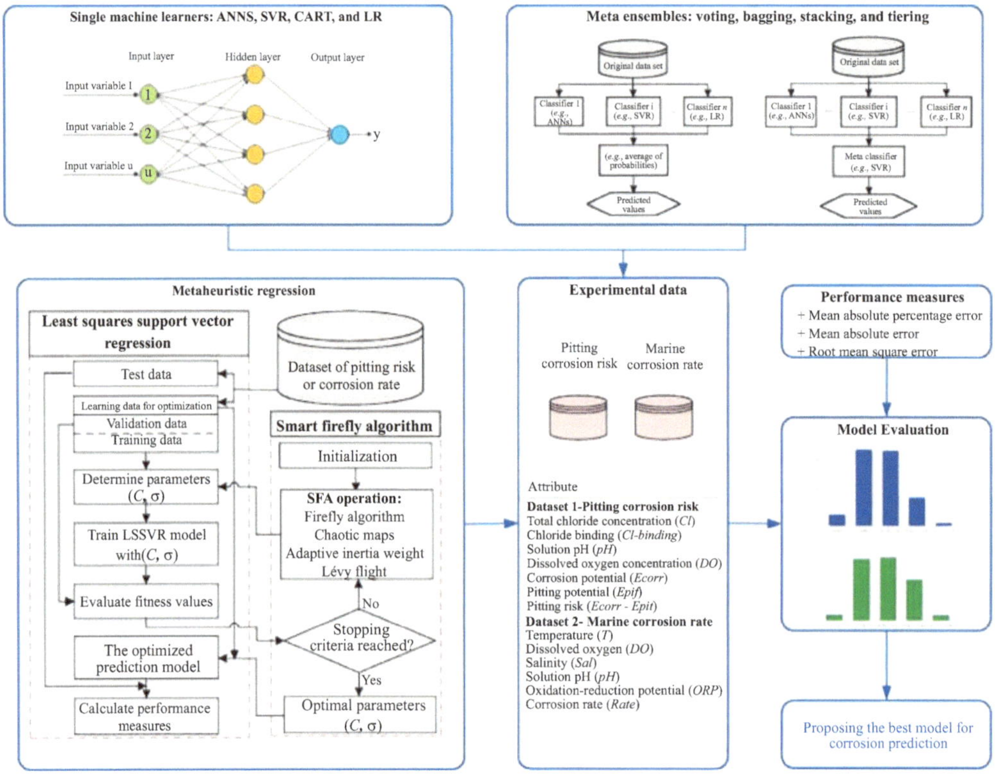

Fig. (3). General schematic for the application of AI in Corrosion monitoring systems. The use of AI/ML methods, such as ANN and closed-loop optimisation, encourages the better normalisation of data and provides good accuracy to these monitoring systems. Reprinted with permission, Copyright 2011, Published by Elsevier [101].

CONCLUSION AND FUTURE TRENDS IN AI AND ELECTROCHEMICAL TECHNOLOGIES

The literature review shows that techniques of artificial intelligence have been established for performance prediction and electrochemical process optimization. However, the use of AI has become more global in many electrochemical processes. The techniques of data augmentation have been demonstrated in deep learning across several disciplines, specifically in speech recognition and image processing, and should be applied cautiously with respect to regressing experimental work on limited data. This is because the output's behavior in an experimental context may be complicated rather than being used for predetermined functions. Hence, regulating the parameters of an AI model and using techniques to overcome fitting problems, the principal parts focus on: The

ANNs are a preferred methodology for electrochemical processes. The reason might be due to the inherent ability to find relationships between outputs and inputs in nonlinear processes. Neural networks with back-propagation training have been the most common application in treatment applications. The optimization of AI models' hyperparameters and process outputs has thus used metaheuristic optimization algorithms. In the literature, both multi-objective and single-objective approaches to optimization have been employed to determine the optimal process conditions. Although the ANNs are of a black-box-type nature, some efforts have still been made to interpret the process investigation regarding the importance of input variables that are independent of the desired output.

The techniques of AI are alternatives to linear parametric methods for modelling in various areas of research. As in ANNs, the network parameters, such as the number of neurons in hidden layers, the number of hidden layers, the momentum factor, and the learning algorithm, are basic tasks in the case of ANN modelling. Until now, only a few studies have utilized optimization techniques, such as PSO, for optimizing the ANN model. The reviewed work predicted the performance of their systems using single neural networks. However, this approach has the disadvantage that neural networks are very sensitive to the training data. Hence, leading to predictions that differ every time. To overcome this challenge, the ensemble modelling approach is used, in which multiple models are trained and combined to make predictions, rather than relying on a single model. In the reviewed papers, very few studies applied an ensemble modelling approach, such as stacked neural networks, and they showed good performance. However, the developments related to the BP-MLP networks with traditional functions are not the best choice. Further work is needed for different activation functions (*e.g.*, ReLU or rectified linear activation function), different algorithms such as SVM, or different networks such as ANFIS, GRNN, for the monitoring of electrochemical processes.

CREDIT AUTHORSHIP CONTRIBUTION STATEMENT

Shavita: Writing – original draft, Investigation, Jyoti Jangra: Writing – original draft, Investigation, Shubham Patial: Writing – original draft, Investigation, Anuj Sharma: Writing – original draft, Investigation, Amandeep Kaur: Writing – original draft, Investigation, Aman Grewal: Writing – original draft, Investigation, Formal analysis, Parneet Kaur: Writing – original draft, Investigation. Suman Singh: Idea conceptualisation, Supervision, Investigation, Writing – review and editing, Discussion.

ACKNOWLEDGEMENTS

The authors are grateful to the Director of CSIR-CSIO, Chandigarh, India, for his constant support and encouragement throughout this work.

REFERENCES

[1] S. Li, O. Gao, and F. You, *AI for Science in Electrochemical Energy Storage: A Multi-Scale Systems Perspective on Transportation Electrification.* Nexus, 2024.

[2] A. García, J. Monsalve-Serrano, S. Martinez-Boggio, and D. Golke, "Energy assessment of the ageing phenomenon in Li-Ion batteries and its impact on the vehicle range efficiency", *Energy Convers. Manage.,* vol. 276, p. 116530, 2023. [http://dx.doi.org/10.1016/j.enconman.2022.116530]

[3] Y. Ding, Z.P. Cano, A. Yu, J. Lu, and Z. Chen, "Automotive Li-ion batteries: current status and future perspectives", *Electrochemical Energy Reviews,* vol. 2, no. 1, pp. 1-28, 2019. [http://dx.doi.org/10.1007/s41918-018-0022-z]

[4] H. Bajolle, M. Lagadic, and N. Louvet, "The future of lithium-ion batteries: Exploring expert conceptions, market trends, and price scenarios", *Energy Res. Soc. Sci.,* vol. 93, p. 102850, 2022. [http://dx.doi.org/10.1016/j.erss.2022.102850]

[5] M. Waseem, M. Ahmad, A. Parveen, and M. Suhaib, "Battery technologies and functionality of battery management system for EVs: Current status, key challenges, and future prospectives", *J. Power Sources,* vol. 580, p. 233349, 2023. [http://dx.doi.org/10.1016/j.jpowsour.2023.233349]

[6] C. Zhang, J. Yan, and F. You, "Critical metal requirement for clean energy transition: A quantitative review on the case of transportation electrification", *Advances in Applied Energy,* vol. 9, p. 100116, 2023. [http://dx.doi.org/10.1016/j.adapen.2022.100116]

[7] N. Wassiliadis, J. Schneider, A. Frank, L. Wildfeuer, X. Lin, A. Jossen, and M. Lienkamp, "Review of fast charging strategies for lithium-ion battery systems and their applicability for battery electric vehicles", *J. Energy Storage,* vol. 44, p. 103306, 2021. [http://dx.doi.org/10.1016/j.est.2021.103306]

[8] A. Khatua, R. Ranjan Kumar, and S. Kumar De, "Institutional enablers of electric vehicle market: Evidence from 30 countries", *Transp. Res. Part A Policy Pract.,* vol. 170, p. 103612, 2023. [http://dx.doi.org/10.1016/j.tra.2023.103612]

[9] G.N. Newton, L.R. Johnson, D.A. Walsh, B.J. Hwang, and H. Han, *Sustainability of battery technologies: today and tomorrow.,* A.C.S. Publications, Ed., vol. 9. , 2021, pp. 6507-6509.

[10] Y. Xu, X. Liu, X. Cao, C. Huang, E. Liu, and S. Qian, *Artificial intelligence: A powerful paradigm for scientific research.* vol. 2. The Innovation, 2021.

[11] S.E. Bibri, J. Krogstie, A. Kaboli, and A. Alahi, "Smarter eco-cities and their leading-edge artificial intelligence of things solutions for environmental sustainability: A comprehensive systematic review", *Environmental Science and Ecotechnology,* vol. 19, p. 100330, 2024. [http://dx.doi.org/10.1016/j.ese.2023.100330] [PMID: 38021367]

[12] K.M. Jablonka, D. Ongari, S.M. Moosavi, and B. Smit, "Big-data science in porous materials: materials genomics and machine learning", *Chem. Rev.,* vol. 120, no. 16, pp. 8066-8129, 2020. [http://dx.doi.org/10.1021/acs.chemrev.0c00004] [PMID: 32520531]

[13] S. Badini, S. Regondi, and R. Pugliese, "Unleashing the power of artificial intelligence in materials design", *Materials (Basel),* vol. 16, no. 17, p. 5927, 2023. [http://dx.doi.org/10.3390/ma16175927] [PMID: 37687620]

[14] M.E.E. Alahi, A. Sukkuea, F.W. Tina, A. Nag, W. Kurdthongmee, K. Suwannarat, and S.C. Mukhopadhyay, "Integration of IoT-enabled technologies and artificial intelligence (AI) for smart city scenario: recent advancements and future trends", *Sensors (Basel),* vol. 23, no. 11, p. 5206, 2023. [http://dx.doi.org/10.3390/s23115206] [PMID: 37299934]

[15] E. Brynjolfsson, D. Li, and L.R. Raymond, *Generative AI at work.* National Bureau of Economic Research, 2023. [http://dx.doi.org/10.3386/w31161]

[16] D. Doonyapisut, B. Kim, J.K. Kim, E. Lee, and C.H. Chung, "Deep generative learning for exploration in large electrochemical impedance dataset", *Eng. Appl. Artif. Intell.,* vol. 126, p. 107027, 2023. [http://dx.doi.org/10.1016/j.engappai.2023.107027]

[17] P. Rao, S. Bukkapatnam, O. Beyca, Z.J. Kong, and R. Komanduri, "Real-time identification of incipient surface morphology variations in ultraprecision machining process", *J. Manuf. Sci. Eng.,* vol. 136, no. 2, p. 021008, 2014. [http://dx.doi.org/10.1115/1.4026210]

[18] M. Tomás, S. Jalali, and A. Silva de Vargas, "Creep evaluation and temperature dependence in self-sensing micro carbon polymer-based composites for further development as an Internet of Things Sensor device", *J. Compos. Mater.,* vol. 56, no. 6, pp. 961-973, 2022. [http://dx.doi.org/10.1177/00219983211058805]

[19] X. Jin, X. Qi, Y. Wang, J. Yang, H. Li, Z. Zhou, and Y. Wang, "Polypyrrole/helical carbon nanotube composite with marvelous photothermoelectric performance for longevous and intelligent internet of things application", *ACS Appl. Mater. Interfaces,* vol. 13, no. 7, pp. 8808-8822, 2021. [http://dx.doi.org/10.1021/acsami.0c22123] [PMID: 33565860]

[20] Y. Yang, G. Chiesura, B. Plovie, T. Vervust, G. Luyckx, J. Degrieck, T. Sekitani, and J. Vanfleteren, Design and integration of flexible sensor matrix for *in situ* monitoring of polymer composites., *ACS Sens.,* vol. 3, no. 9, pp. 1698-1705, 2018. [http://dx.doi.org/10.1021/acssensors.8b00425] [PMID: 30010319]

[21] X. Guo, D. Kuang, Z. Zhu, Y. Ding, L. Ge, Z. Wu, B. Du, C. Liang, G. Meng, and Y. He, "Humidity sensing by graphitic carbon nitride nanosheet/TiO2 nanoparticle/Ti3C2Tx nanosheet composites for monitoring respiration and evaluating the waxing of fruits", *ACS Appl. Nano Mater.,* vol. 4, no. 10, pp. 11159-11167, 2021. [http://dx.doi.org/10.1021/acsanm.1c02625]

[22] S. Tachibana, Y.F. Wang, T. Sekine, Y. Takeda, J. Hong, A. Yoshida, M. Abe, R. Miura, Y. Watanabe, D. Kumaki, and S. Tokito, "A printed flexible humidity sensor with high sensitivity and fast response using a cellulose nanofiber/carbon black composite", *ACS Appl. Mater. Interfaces,* vol. 14, no. 4, pp. 5721-5728, 2022. [http://dx.doi.org/10.1021/acsami.1c20918] [PMID: 35067045]

[23] M.J. Sousa, A. Moutinho, and M. Almeida, "Thermal infrared sensing for near real-time data-driven fire detection and monitoring systems", *Sensors (Basel),* vol. 20, no. 23, p. 6803, 2020. [http://dx.doi.org/10.3390/s20236803] [PMID: 33260498]

[24] S.M. Zahraee, M. Khalaji Assadi, and R. Saidur, "Application of artificial intelligence methods for hybrid energy system optimization", *Renew. Sustain. Energy Rev.,* vol. 66, pp. 617-630, 2016. [http://dx.doi.org/10.1016/j.rser.2016.08.028]

[25] S.M.M. Alavi, C.R. Birkl, and D.A. Howey, "Time-domain fitting of battery electrochemical impedance models", *J. Power Sources,* vol. 288, pp. 345-352, 2015. [http://dx.doi.org/10.1016/j.jpowsour.2015.04.099]

[26] N. Katayama, and S. Kogoshi, "Mixed-signal fourier transform for electrochemical impedance spectroscopy", *J. Fuel Cell Sci. Technol.,* vol. 10, no. 1, p. 011006, 2013. [http://dx.doi.org/10.1115/1.4023219]

[27] Y. Zhu, H. Wu, W. Zhang, and Z. Wang, "A modeling method for lithium-ion batteries based on EIS and FFRLS", *Electronic and Automation Control Conference (ITNEC)* 2024, pp. 317-321. [http://dx.doi.org/10.1109/ITNEC60942.2024.10733023]

[28] B.A. Boukamp, "Fourier transform distribution function of relaxation times; application and limitations", *Electrochim. Acta,* vol. 154, pp. 35-46, 2015. [http://dx.doi.org/10.1016/j.electacta.2014.12.059]

[29] Y. Mabrouk, N. Safaei, F. Hanke, J.M. Carlsson, D. Diddens, and A. Heuer, "Reactive molecular dynamics simulations of lithium-ion battery electrolyte degradation", *Sci. Rep.,* vol. 14, no. 1, p. 10281, 2024. [http://dx.doi.org/10.1038/s41598-024-60063-0] [PMID: 38704444]

[30] L. Zeng, J. Peng, J. Zhang, X. Tan, X. Ji, and S. Li, "Molecular dynamics simulations of electrochemical interfaces", *J. Chem. Phys.,* vol. 159, 2023.

[31] X. Tan, M. Chen, J. Zhang, S. Li, H. Zhang, L. Yang, T. Sun, X. Qian, and G. Feng, "Decoding Electrochemical Processes of Lithium-Ion Batteries by Classical Molecular Dynamics Simulations", *Adv. Energy Mater.,* vol. 14, no. 22, p. 2400564, 2024. [http://dx.doi.org/10.1002/aenm.202400564]

[32] M.G. Shirkoohi, R.D. Tyagi, P.A. Vanrolleghem, and P. Drogui, "Artificial intelligence techniques in electrochemical processes for water and wastewater treatment: a review", *J. Environ. Health Sci. Eng.,* vol. 20, no. 2, pp. 1089-1109, 2022. [http://dx.doi.org/10.1007/s40201-022-00835-w] [PMID: 36406623]

[33] P. Hein, B.O.H. Grope, J. Koettgen, S. Grieshammer, and M. Martin, "Kinetic Monte Carlo simulations of ionic conductivity in oxygen ion conductors", *Mater. Chem. Phys.,* vol. 257, p. 123767, 2021. [http://dx.doi.org/10.1016/j.matchemphys.2020.123767]

[34] J. Koettgen, P.C. Schmidt, T. Bučko, and M. Martin, "Ab initio calculation of the migration free energy of oxygen diffusion in pure and samarium-doped ceria", *Phys. Rev. B,* vol. 97, no. 2, p. 024305, 2018. [http://dx.doi.org/10.1103/PhysRevB.97.024305]

[35] A. Gulli, and S. Pal, *Deep learning with Keras.* Packt Publishing Ltd, 2017.

[36] Z.B. Zhou, B.S. He, L.D. Feng, and N.C. Cai, "Multi-sensor technique and solid-state electrochemical sensor system for real-time and dynamic monitoring of multi-component gases", *Sens. Actuators B Chem.,* vol. 108, no. 1-2, pp. 379-383, 2005. [http://dx.doi.org/10.1016/j.snb.2005.01.053]

[37] J. Wang, "Real-time electrochemical monitoring: toward green analytical chemistry", *Acc. Chem. Res.,* vol. 35, no. 9, pp. 811-816, 2002. [PMID: 12234211]

[38] T. Defever, M. Druet, M. Rochelet-Dequaire, M. Joannes, C. Grossiord, B. Limoges, and D. Marchal, "Real-time electrochemical monitoring of the polymerase chain reaction by mediated redox catalysis", *J. Am. Chem. Soc.,* vol. 131, no. 32, pp. 11433-11441, 2009. [PMID: 19722651]

[39] P. Khanipour, M. Löffler, A.M. Reichert, F.T. Haase, K.J.J. Mayrhofer, and I. Katsounaros, "Electrochemical real-time mass spectrometry (EC-RTMS): monitoring electrochemical reaction products in real time", *Angew. Chem. Int. Ed.,* vol. 58, no. 22, pp. 7273-7277, 2019. [http://dx.doi.org/10.1002/anie.201901923] [PMID: 30882984]

[40] C. Parolo, A. Idili, G. Ortega, A. Csordas, A. Hsu, N. Arroyo-Currás, Q. Yang, B.S. Ferguson, J. Wang, and K.W. Plaxco, "Real-time monitoring of a protein biomarker", *ACS Sens.,* vol. 5, no. 7, pp. 1877-1881, 2020. [http://dx.doi.org/10.1021/acssensors.0c01085] [PMID: 32619092]

[41] E.C. Yang, S.T. Wang, K.L. Liu, W.H. Juang, M.H. Sheu, and H.C. Wu, "Fast measurement of impedance calculation for electrochemical impedance spectroscopy", presented at the 2023 20th International Soc Design Donference, ISOCC, 2023. [http://dx.doi.org/10.1109/ISOCC59558.2023.10396167]

[42] H. Yamada, K. Yoshii, M. Asahi, M. Chiku, and Y. Kitazumi, *Cyclic Voltammetry Part 1: Fundamentals.* vol. 90. ELECTROCHEMISTRY, 2022.

[43] S.S. Gavande, A.S. Salunkhe, Y.H. Navale, S. Gavande, P.S. Kulkarni, and B.R. Karche, "Comparative analysis of electrodeposited cobalt oxide thin films by chronoamperometry and chronopotentiometry modes for supercapacitor application", *DAE SOLID STATE PHYSICS SYMPOSIUM 2019,* 2020 [http://dx.doi.org/10.1063/5.0017211]

[44] G. Trettenhahn, and A. Köberl, Anodic decomposition of citric acid on gold and stainless steel electrodes: An *in situ*-FTIR-spectroscopic investigation., *Electrochim. Acta,* vol. 52, no. 7, pp. 2716-2722, 2007. [http://dx.doi.org/10.1016/j.electacta.2006.09.028]

[45] J. Gamby, A. Pailleret, C.B. Clodic, C.M. Pradier, and B. Tribollet, *in situ* detection and characterization of potable water biofilms on materials by microscopic, spectroscopic and electrochemistry methods., *Electrochim. Acta,* vol. 54, no. 1, pp. 66-73, 2008. [http://dx.doi.org/10.1016/j.electacta.2008.07.018]

[46] M.J.M. Jafeen, M.A. Careem, and S. Skaarup, "A novel method for the determination of membrane hydration numbers of cations in conducting polymers", *J. Solid State Electrochem.,* vol. 16, no. 5, pp. 1753-1759, 2012. [http://dx.doi.org/10.1007/s10008-011-1594-2]

[47] J. Scharf, and F.M. Matysik, "Study of the response characteristics of an online electrochemical mass spectrometry system for gas analysis of lithium-ion cells using chronoamperometry", *Monatsh. Chem.,* vol. 154, no. 9, pp. 1025-1033, 2023. [http://dx.doi.org/10.1007/s00706-023-03094-z]

[48] M.M. Shrestha, and L. Wei, "Review-perspectives on the roles of real time nitrogen sensing and IoT integration in smart agriculture", *J. Electrochem. Soc.,* vol. 171, no. 2, p. 027526, 2024. [http://dx.doi.org/10.1149/1945-7111/ad22d8]

[49] J.R. Camargo, L.O. Orzari, J. de Souza Rodrigues, L. Felipe de Lima, T.R. Longo Cesar Paixão, L.F. Fraccto, and B.C. Janegitz, "Advancements in disposable electrochemical systems for sustainable agriculture monitoring: Trends, gaps, and applied examples", *Trends Analyt. Chem.,* vol. 180, p. 117968, 2024. [http://dx.doi.org/10.1016/j.trac.2024.117968]

[50] J.M. Stine, L.A. Beardslee, S. Chu, S. Liu, D. Motabar, W.E. Bentley, and R. Ghodssi, "Wireless sensor-integrated platform for localized dissolved oxygen sensing in bioreactors", *J. Microelectromech. Syst.,* vol. 29, no. 5, pp. 713-719, 2020. [http://dx.doi.org/10.1109/JMEMS.2020.2999089]

[51] M.D. Stoller, and R.S. Ruoff, "Best practice methods for determining an electrode material's performance for ultracapacitors", *Energy Environ. Sci.,* vol. 3, no. 9, pp. 1294-1301, 2010. [http://dx.doi.org/10.1039/c0ee00074d]

[52] A. Berrueta, A. Ursua, I.S. Martin, A. Eftekhari, and P. Sanchis, "Supercapacitors: electrical characteristics, modeling, applications, and future trends", *IEEE Access,* vol. 7, pp. 50869-50896, 2019. [http://dx.doi.org/10.1109/ACCESS.2019.2908558]

[53] K. Song, X. Wang, J. Li, B. Zhang, R. Yang, P. Liu, and J. Wang, "3D hierarchical CoFe2O4/CoOOH nanowire arrays on Ni-Sponge for high-performance flexible supercapacitors", *Electrochim. Acta,* vol. 340, p. 135892, 2020.

[http://dx.doi.org/10.1016/j.electacta.2020.135892]

[54] A. Ghosh, and Y.H. Lee, "Carbon-based electrochemical capacitors", *ChemSusChem,* vol. 5, no. 3, pp. 480-499, 2012.
[http://dx.doi.org/10.1002/cssc.201100645] [PMID: 22389329]

[55] G. Hasegawa, K. Kanamori, K. Nakanishi, and T. Abe, "New insights into the relationship between micropore properties, ionic sizes, and electric double-layer capacitance in monolithic carbon electrodes", *J. Phys. Chem. C,* vol. 116, no. 50, pp. 26197-26203, 2012.
[http://dx.doi.org/10.1021/jp309010p]

[56] K. Ajay, and M. Dinesh, "Influence of various activated carbon based electrode materials in the performance of super capacitor".*IOP Conference Series.* Materials Science and Engineering, 2018, p. 012083.
[http://dx.doi.org/10.1088/1757-899X/310/1/012083]

[57] Q.Z. Zhang, D. Zhang, Z.C. Miao, X.L. Zhang, and S.L. Chou, "Research progress in MnO 2 –carbon based supercapacitor electrode materials", *Small,* vol. 14, no. 24, p. 1702883, 2018.
[http://dx.doi.org/10.1002/smll.201702883]

[58] H. Su, S. Lin, S. Deng, C. Lian, Y. Shang, and H. Liu, "Predicting the capacitance of carbon-based electric double layer capacitors by machine learning", *Nanoscale Adv.,* vol. 1, no. 6, pp. 2162-2166, 2019.
[http://dx.doi.org/10.1039/C9NA00105K] [PMID: 36131961]

[59] M. Zhou, A. Gallegos, K. Liu, S. Dai, and J. Wu, "Insights from machine learning of carbon electrodes for electric double layer capacitors", *Carbon,* vol. 157, pp. 147-152, 2020.
[http://dx.doi.org/10.1016/j.carbon.2019.08.090]

[60] T. Du, A. Li, J. Ma, and F. Liu, "Research progress of SOC estimation of power battery", *Chinese Journal of Power Source,* vol. 39, pp. 844-845, 2015.

[61] E. Flamand, D. Rossi, F. Conti, I. Loi, A. Pullini, and F. Rotenberg, "GAP-8: A RISC-V SoC for AI at the Edge of the IoT",
[http://dx.doi.org/10.1109/ASAP.2018.8445101]

[62] S. Li, H. He, and J. Li, "Big data driven lithium-ion battery modeling method based on SDAE-ELM algorithm and data pre-processing technology", *Appl. Energy,* vol. 242, pp. 1259-1273, 2019.
[http://dx.doi.org/10.1016/j.apenergy.2019.03.154]

[63] P.M. Attia, A. Grover, N. Jin, K.A. Severson, T.M. Markov, Y.H. Liao, M.H. Chen, B. Cheong, N. Perkins, Z. Yang, P.K. Herring, M. Aykol, S.J. Harris, R.D. Braatz, S. Ermon, and W.C. Chueh, "Closed-loop optimization of fast-charging protocols for batteries with machine learning", *Nature,* vol. 578, no. 7795, pp. 397-402, 2020.
[http://dx.doi.org/10.1038/s41586-020-1994-5] [PMID: 32076218]

[64] P.H.L. Notten, J.H.G.O. Veld, and J.R.G. Beek, "Boostcharging Li-ion batteries: A challenging new charging concept", *J. Power Sources,* vol. 145, no. 1, pp. 89-94, 2005.
[http://dx.doi.org/10.1016/j.jpowsour.2004.12.038]

[65] V.H. Mehta, and J.B. Straubel, *Fast charging with negative ramped current profile.,* G. Patents, Ed., , 2014.

[66] A. Paryani, *Low temperature charging of Li-ion cells.,* G. Patents, Ed., , 2013.

[67] L. Myoung-Seok, S-B. Song, J-S. Jung, and D. Golovanov, *Battery charging method and battery pack using the same.,* G. Patents, Ed., , 2018.

[68] J.N. de Figueiredo, and M.F. Guillén, *Green Power: Perspectives on sustainable electricity generation.* CRC Press, 2014.
[http://dx.doi.org/10.1201/b16492]

[69] M.H. de Sá, "Electrochemical devices to power a sustainable energy transition—an overview of green

hydrogen contribution", *Appl. Sci. (Basel),* vol. 14, no. 5, p. 2168, 2024. [http://dx.doi.org/10.3390/app14052168]

[70] J. Newman, and N.P. Balsara, *Electrochemical systems.* John Wiley & Sons, 2021.

[71] T. Smolinka, and J. Garche, *Electrochemical power sources: fundamentals, systems, and applications: hydrogen production by water electrolysis.* Elsevier, 2021.

[72] J..J. Larminie, A. Dicks, and M.S. McDonald, *Fuel cell systems explained.* vol. 2: J. Wiley Chichester, UK, 2003.

[73] X. Li, *Principles of fuel cells.* CRC press, 2005. [http://dx.doi.org/10.1201/9780203942338]

[74] A. Bennagi, O. AlHousrya, D.T. Cotfas, and P.A. Cotfas, "Comprehensive study of the artificial intelligence applied in renewable energy", *Energy Strategy Reviews,* vol. 54, p. 101446, 2024. [http://dx.doi.org/10.1016/j.esr.2024.101446]

[75] A. Al-Othman, M. Tawalbeh, R. Martis, S. Dhou, M. Orhan, M. Qasim, and A. Ghani Olabi, "Artificial intelligence and numerical models in hybrid renewable energy systems with fuel cells: Advances and prospects", *Energy Convers. Manage.,* vol. 253, p. 115154, 2022. [http://dx.doi.org/10.1016/j.enconman.2021.115154]

[76] S. Grigoriev, V. Fateev, D. Bessarabov, and P. Millet, "Current status, research trends, and challenges in water electrolysis science and technology", *Int. J. Hydrogen Energy,* vol. 45, pp. 26036-26058, 2020.

[77] T.L. Oladosu, J. Pasupuleti, T.S. Kiong, S.P.J. Koh, and T. Yusaf, "Energy management strategies, control systems, and artificial intelligence-based algorithms development for hydrogen fuel cell-powered vehicles: A review", *Int. J. Hydrogen Energy,* vol. 61, pp. 1380-1404, 2024. [http://dx.doi.org/10.1016/j.ijhydene.2024.02.284]

[78] Z. Feng, J. Huang, S. Jin, G. Wang, and Y. Chen, "Artificial intelligence-based multi-objective optimisation for proton exchange membrane fuel cell: A literature review", *J. Power Sources,* vol. 520, p. 230808, 2022. [http://dx.doi.org/10.1016/j.jpowsour.2021.230808]

[79] A.J. Fairweather, M.P. Foster, and D.A. Stone, "Modelling of VRLA batteries over operational temperature range using Pseudo Random Binary Sequences", *J. Power Sources,* vol. 207, pp. 56-59, 2012. [http://dx.doi.org/10.1016/j.jpowsour.2012.02.024]

[80] T. Huria, G. Ludovici, and G. Lutzemberger, "State of charge estimation of high power lithium iron phosphate cells", *J. Power Sources,* vol. 249, pp. 92-102, 2014. [http://dx.doi.org/10.1016/j.jpowsour.2013.10.079]

[81] C.R. Gould, C.M. Bingham, D.A. Stone, and P. Bentley, "New battery model and state-of-health determination through subspace parameter estimation and state-observer techniques", *IEEE Trans. Vehicular Technol.,* vol. 58, no. 8, pp. 3905-3916, 2009. [http://dx.doi.org/10.1109/TVT.2009.2028348]

[82] V.H. Johnson, "Battery performance models in ADVISOR", *J. Power Sources,* vol. 110, no. 2, pp. 321-329, 2002. [http://dx.doi.org/10.1016/S0378-7753(02)00194-5]

[83] K.T. Butler, D.W. Davies, H. Cartwright, O. Isayev, and A. Walsh, "Machine learning for molecular and materials science", *Nature,* vol. 559, no. 7715, pp. 547-555, 2018. [http://dx.doi.org/10.1038/s41586-018-0337-2] [PMID: 30046072]

[84] R. Ramprasad, R. Batra, G. Pilania, A. Mannodi-Kanakkithodi, and C. Kim, "Machine learning in materials informatics: recent applications and prospects", *npj Comput. Mater.,* vol. 3, p. 54, 2017.

[85] M. Abadi, A. Agarwal, P. Barham, E. Brevdo, Z. Chen, and C. Citro, "Tensorflow: Large-scale

machine learning on heterogeneous distributed systems", .

[86] P. Jienkulsawad, K. Wiranarongkorn, Y.S. Chen, and A. Arpornwichanop, "Identifying catalyst layer compositions of proton exchange membrane fuel cells through machine-learning-based approach", *Int. J. Hydrogen Energy,* vol. 47, no. 75, pp. 32303-32314, 2022. [http://dx.doi.org/10.1016/j.ijhydene.2022.07.126]

[87] X. Liu, K. Park, M. So, S. Ishikawa, T. Terao, K. Shinohara, C. Komori, N. Kimura, G. Inoue, and Y. Tsuge, "3D generation and reconstruction of the fuel cell catalyst layer using 2D images based on deep learning", *Journal of Power Sources Advances,* vol. 14, p. 100084, 2022. [http://dx.doi.org/10.1016/j.powera.2022.100084]

[88] Y. Lou, M. Hao, and Y. Li, "Machine-learning-assisted insight into the cathode catalyst layer in proton exchange membrane fuel cells", *J. Power Sources,* vol. 543, p. 231827, 2022. [http://dx.doi.org/10.1016/j.jpowsour.2022.231827]

[89] B. Wang, B. Xie, J. Xuan, and K. Jiao, AI-based optimization of PEM fuel cell catalyst layers for maximum power density *via* data-driven surrogate modeling., *Energy Convers. Manage.,* vol. 205, p. 112460, 2020.

[90] M. Fayyazi, P. Sardar, S.I. Thomas, R. Daghigh, A. Jamali, T. Esch, H. Kemper, R. Langari, and H. Khayyam, "Artificial intelligence/machine learning in energy management systems, control, and optimization of hydrogen fuel cell vehicles", *Sustainability (Basel),* vol. 15, no. 6, p. 5249, 2023. [http://dx.doi.org/10.3390/su15065249]

[91] A. Jayakumar, M. Ramos, and A. Al-Jumaily, "A Novel fuzzy schema to control the temperature and humidification of PEM fuel cell system", *International Conference on Fuel Cell Science, Engineering and Technology,* 2015 [http://dx.doi.org/10.1115/FUELCELL2015-49623]

[92] N. Khajeh-Hosseini-Dalasm, S. Ahadian, K. Fushinobu, K. Okazaki, and Y. Kawazoe, "Prediction and analysis of the cathode catalyst layer performance of proton exchange membrane fuel cells using artificial neural network and statistical methods", *J. Power Sources,* vol. 196, no. 8, pp. 3750-3756, 2011. [http://dx.doi.org/10.1016/j.jpowsour.2010.12.061]

[93] M.S. Alias, S.K. Kamarudin, A.M. Zainoodin, and M.S. Masdar, "Active direct methanol fuel cell: An overview", *Int. J. Hydrogen Energy,* vol. 45, no. 38, pp. 19620-19641, 2020. [http://dx.doi.org/10.1016/j.ijhydene.2020.04.202]

[94] P. Joghee, J.N. Malik, S. Pylypenko, and R. O'Hayre, "A review on direct methanol fuel cells–In the perspective of energy and sustainability", *MRS Energy & Sustainability,* vol. 2, no. 1, p. 3, 2015. [http://dx.doi.org/10.1557/mre.2015.4]

[95] S. Sharifi, R. Rahimi, D. Mohebbi-Kalhori, and C.O. Colpan, "Optimization and experimental approaches to the direct methanol fuel cell stack using a response surface methodology", *Journal of Renewable Energy and Environment,* vol. 6, pp. 22-29, 2019.

[96] I. Taymaz, F. Akgun, and M. Benli, "Application of response surface methodology to optimize and investigate the effects of operating conditions on the performance of DMFC", *Energy,* vol. 36, no. 2, pp. 1155-1160, 2011. [http://dx.doi.org/10.1016/j.energy.2010.11.034]

[97] S. Sharifi, R. Rahimi, D. Mohebbi-Kalhori, and C.O. Colpan, "Coupled computational fluid dynamics-response surface methodology to optimize direct methanol fuel cell performance for greener energy generation", *Energy,* vol. 198, p. 117293, 2020. [http://dx.doi.org/10.1016/j.energy.2020.117293]

[98] M. Kamrunnahar, and M. Urquidi-Macdonald, "Prediction of corrosion behavior using neural network as a data mining tool", *Corros. Sci.,* vol. 52, pp. 669-677, 2010. [http://dx.doi.org/10.1016/j.corsci.2009.10.024]

[99] M.J. Jiménez-Come, I.J. Turias, J.J. Ruiz-Aguilar, and F.J. Trujillo, "Characterization of pitting corrosion of stainless steel using artificial neural networks", *Mater. Corros.*, vol. 66, no. 10, pp. 1084-1091, 2015.
[http://dx.doi.org/10.1002/maco.201408173]

[100] Z. Pei, D. Zhang, Y. Zhi, T. Yang, L. Jin, and D. Fu, Towards understanding and prediction of atmospheric corrosion of an Fe/Cu corrosion sensor *via* machine learning., *Corros. Sci.*, vol. 170, p. 108697, 2020.
[http://dx.doi.org/10.1016/j.corsci.2020.108697]

[101] J.-S. Chou, N.-T. Ngo, and W. K. Chong, "The use of artificial intelligence combiners for modeling steel pitting risk and corrosion rate", *Eng. Appl. Artif. Intell.*, vol. 65, pp. 471-483, 2017.
[http://dx.doi.org/10.1016/j.engappai.2016.09.008]

[102] Y. Diao, L. Yan, and K. Gao, "Improvement of the machine learning-based corrosion rate prediction model through the optimization of input features", *Mater. Des.*, vol. 198, p. 109326, 2021.
[http://dx.doi.org/10.1016/j.matdes.2020.109326]

[103] Y.-H. Tsai, J. Wang, W.-T. Chien, C.-Y. Wei, X. Wang, and S.-H. Hsieh, "A BIM-based approach for predicting corrosion under insulation", *Autom. Constr.*, vol. 107, p. 102923, 2019.
[http://dx.doi.org/10.1016/j.autcon.2019.102923]

CHAPTER 4

Artificial Intelligence in Energy Systems: Applications, Challenges, and Future Directions

Satyam Rawat[1,*] and **N. L. Singh**[2]

[1] *Research Lab for Energy Systems, Department of Physics, Netaji Subhas University of Technology, Dwarka, New Delhi, India*

[2] *Department of Nanotechnology, Delhi Skill and Entrepreneurship University, Dwarka, New Delhi, India*

Abstract: Artificial Intelligence (AI) is transforming energy conversion and storage technologies by enhancing efficiency, scalability, and reliability. This chapter examines AI-driven innovations in electrochemical processes, including battery design, fuel cell optimization, and supercapacitor operation. Advanced algorithms, such as Machine Learning (ML) and Deep Learning (DL), enable precise modeling, real-time diagnostics, and predictive analytics, thereby accelerating material discovery and improving energy storage efficiency. Key developments are highlighted in charge-discharge optimization, energy loss reduction, and lifecycle extension for lithium-ion, solid-state, and flow batteries. The chapter also examines AI's impact on dynamic energy management, fault detection, and predictive maintenance in large-scale energy systems, such as solar and wind. Case studies demonstrate the transition from trial-an--error to data-driven approaches, resulting in reduced costs and enhanced sustainability. Further discussions include algorithmic frameworks, digital twins, and hybrid modeling for enhanced energy conversion. Challenges such as data scarcity, model generalization, and ethical considerations are addressed, along with insights into future trends. This work envisions a sustainable energy landscape driven by AI and advanced computational intelligence.

Keywords: Artificial intelligence, Digital twin technology, Energy conversion, Energy storage, Fuel cells, Machine learning, Material discovery, Neural networks, Photovoltaic cells, Predictive maintenance, Renewable energy systems, Smart grids, Supercapacitors, Sustainable energy.

INTRODUCTION

AI has become a cornerstone of innovation across various domains, with sustainable energy technologies standing out as one of the most impactful areas.

* **Corresponding author Satyam Rawat:** Research Lab for Energy Systems, Department of Physics, Netaji Subhas University of Technology, Dwarka, New Delhi, India; E-mail: rawatsatyam2802@gmail.com

Shreya Sharma, Peeyush Phogat, Ranjana Jha & Sukhvir Singh (Eds.)

As the world grapples with the dual challenges of rising energy demands and the pressing need to reduce carbon emissions, AI has emerged as a transformative tool to enhance the efficiency, reliability, and scalability of sustainable energy systems. By leveraging vast datasets and advanced computational algorithms, AI enables data-driven decision-making that optimizes energy generation, storage, and distribution processes. The integration of AI into sustainable energy technologies involves the use of Machine Learning (ML), Deep Learning (DL), and other advanced computational methods to analyze and predict system behaviors. These techniques help uncover patterns in energy consumption, improve resource allocation, and enhance the operational efficiency of renewable energy systems. For instance, AI algorithms can predict solar irradiance with high precision, enabling photovoltaic systems to operate at optimal performance. Similarly, in wind energy systems, AI models can analyze historical weather data to forecast wind speeds, ensuring efficient turbine operation and energy output. AI has also revolutionized the development and optimization of energy storage technologies, a critical component of sustainable energy systems [1, 2].

The unpredictable output of renewable energy sources, such as solar and wind power, requires sophisticated storage solutions. AI facilitates the development of cutting-edge materials for high-performance batteries through expedited simulations and predictive analysis. Moreover, AI is crucial for the continuous monitoring and control of energy storage systems, enabling the detection of potential issues before they cause system breakdowns and maximizing charge-discharge cycles to prolong battery lifespan. AI's most notable contribution to sustainable energy technologies is its capacity to enable dynamic energy management. For instance, smart grids utilize AI to equilibrate energy supply and demand instantaneously. By examining data from various sensors and user profiles, AI algorithms ensure efficient electricity distribution while minimizing energy waste. Furthermore, AI-driven systems can adjust to fluctuating energy demands and smoothly integrate renewable energy sources into the grid, thereby decreasing dependence on fossil fuels and enhancing grid resilience. Digital twin technology, a rapidly expanding AI application, has further improved the dependability of sustainable energy systems. Digital twins generate virtual replicas of physical systems, allowing real-time simulation and optimization of energy processes. In the realm of renewable energy, digital twins enable operators to forecast system performance under various conditions, identify inefficiencies, and implement corrective measures without physical interventions. This not only reduces operational expenses but also enhances the longevity and reliability of energy systems. Despite its transformative potential, integrating AI into sustainable energy technologies presents challenges. Data quality and availability remain significant obstacles, as AI models require extensive datasets for training and validation. Ensuring the interpretability and transparency of AI algorithms is another crucial concern, particularly in safety-critical applications such as energy storage and grid management. Additionally, the energy consumption of AI systems themselves must be addressed to align with broader sustainability goals. Looking forward, the future of AI in sustainable energy technologies appears promising. Emerging advancements in AI, such as federated learning and edge computing, offer new opportunities to address existing challenges. Federated learning protects data privacy and enhances scalability by enabling cooperative model training across distributed data sources. In the meantime, edge computing enhances real-time energy management by reducing the latency and energy consumption associated with cloud-based AI systems [3].

The importance of AI in energy conversion and storage lies in its unparalleled ability to address the complexities and inefficiencies inherent in traditional energy systems. Energy conversion, which involves transforming energy from one form to another—such as solar radiation into electricity or chemical energy into mechanical energy—requires precision and optimization to maximize efficiency. Energy storage, on the other hand, ensures the availability of energy when it is needed, thereby overcoming the intermittency of renewable sources such as solar and wind. AI offers transformative solutions in both domains, enabling the development of more efficient, reliable, and sustainable energy systems. AI improves the efficiency of renewable energy technology in energy conversion by using adaptive control systems and predictive analytics. To forecast energy output and improve panel orientation in real time, for example, AI systems examine enormous volumes of data from solar panels, including temperature, shading, and irradiance. In wind energy systems, AI models process meteorological data to forecast wind speeds and adjust turbine parameters, ensuring maximum power generation. These data-driven approaches not only increase energy conversion efficiency but also reduce operational costs and minimize downtime. When it comes to energy storage, AI plays a crucial role in advancing battery technology, a cornerstone of modern energy systems. AI-driven simulations accelerate the discovery of new materials with enhanced storage capacities, thermal stability, and charge-discharge efficiencies. Machine learning models identify optimal electrode compositions and electrolyte formulations, significantly reducing the time and cost associated with experimental trials [4]. Moreover, AI enables real-time monitoring of batteries, detecting anomalies such as overheating or capacity loss before they escalate into critical failures. This predictive capability extends battery lifespans and enhances safety, addressing one of the primary concerns in energy storage technologies. AI also facilitates the integration of energy storage with smart grid systems, creating a dynamic ecosystem where energy supply and demand are balanced seamlessly. AI systems optimize the timing of energy storage and release by examining consumption patterns and grid data. This ensures that excess energy generated during periods of peak production is effectively stored and utilized during periods of high demand. This not only stabilizes the grid but also reduces energy wastage, contributing to greater overall sustainability. Furthermore, the role of AI extends beyond individual systems to encompass the broader energy infrastructure. Digital twin technology, a cutting-edge AI application, creates virtual replicas of energy storage systems, enabling real-time simulations and predictive maintenance. These digital twins offer insights into system performance under various conditions, enabling proactive measures that enhance reliability and efficiency. The growing reliance on AI in energy conversion and storage underscores its critical role in achieving global energy sustainability goals. By addressing inefficiencies, reducing costs, and enabling the development of innovative technologies, AI not only enhances the feasibility of renewable energy adoption but also accelerates the transition toward a low-carbon future. As research and development continue to expand the horizons of AI, its applications in energy systems are expected to become even more sophisticated, unlocking new possibilities for sustainable energy solutions [5].

This chapter aims to provide a comprehensive exploration of the transformative role of AI in energy conversion and storage technologies. The scope of the chapter encompasses both theoretical and practical dimensions of AI applications, focusing on how advanced computational methods are revolutionizing renewable energy systems. By addressing key aspects such as optimization, material discovery, and system integration, the chapter seeks to highlight AI's potential to enhance the efficiency, reliability, and scalability of sustainable energy solutions. The primary objective is to provide readers with a detailed understanding of how AI is enabling breakthroughs in energy conversion—from optimizing photovoltaic and wind energy systems to enhancing bioenergy processes. Similarly, the chapter delves into AI's contributions to energy storage technologies, including advanced battery management, predictive maintenance, and the discovery of novel materials. Additionally, the chapter examines the integration of AI with smart grid technologies and digital twin applications, illustrating their collective impact on real-time energy management and fault diagnostics. By presenting state-of-the-art research, practical applications, and real-world case studies, the chapter aims to equip researchers, engineers, and policymakers with insights into leveraging AI for a sustainable energy future. Ultimately, it underscores AI's pivotal role in addressing global energy challenges and advancing renewable energy technologies [6].

ARTIFICIAL INTELLIGENCE FUNDAMENTALS

AI combines ML, DL, and advanced algorithms to analyze data, recognize patterns, and optimize processes. It enables systems to learn and make decisions autonomously. In energy technologies, AI enhances predictive analytics, system optimization, and real-time management by processing complex datasets. This foundational capability drives innovations in energy conversion, storage, and smart grid integration, making AI a crucial tool for advancing efficiency and sustainability in renewable energy systems.

FOUNDATIONAL AI TECHNOLOGIES

ML, DL, and neural networks form the backbone of AI, each contributing uniquely to its capabilities.

Machine Learning

A branch of AI called ML aims to create systems that can recognize patterns and make judgments or predictions without explicit programming. It is classified into supervised, unsupervised, and reinforcement learning, with applications in energy forecasting, anomaly detection, and system optimization [7].

Deep Learning

DL, a subfield of machine learning, models intricate data interactions using Artificial Neural Networks (ANNs). These neural networks, composed of layers of interconnected nodes or neurons, resemble the organization of the human brain. DL excels in tasks requiring hierarchical feature extraction, such as image recognition, time-series analysis, and large-scale data modeling, making it indispensable for renewable energy systems [8].

Neural Networks

Neural networks are computer models that process and learn from data, and they are modeled after biological neurons. An input layer, one or more hidden layers, and an output layer are commonly found in neural networks. To generate an output, each neuron uses activation functions and weighted connections to process inputs. Recurrent neural networks (RNNs) and Convolutional Neural Networks (CNNs) are examples of advanced designs designed for purposes such as sequential data processing and spatial data analysis, respectively [9].

In energy technologies, ML and DL, powered by neural networks, facilitate predictive maintenance, energy demand forecasting, and material discovery. For instance, DL models optimize solar and wind energy systems by analyzing meteorological data and improving efficiency. Neural networks also enable the real-time monitoring of energy storage systems, allowing for the detection of anomalies and the extension of lifespans. These key concepts underpin AI's transformative role, driving innovation and efficiency in sustainable energy technologies.

AI ALGORITHMS RELEVANT TO ENERGY APPLICATIONS

In energy applications, AI algorithms are essential for solving problems and streamlining procedures. These algorithms utilize cutting-edge computer methods to analyze vast datasets, identify trends, and refine judgment. Supervised learning methods, such as decision trees and Support Vector Machines (SVMs), are frequently employed in the energy industry for problem identification, system optimization, and energy demand forecasting. Principal Component Analysis (PCA) and k-means clustering are two examples of unsupervised learning algorithms that excel at identifying hidden patterns in energy consumption data, enabling more effective resource allocation [10].

Reinforcement learning algorithms are particularly relevant for dynamic and adaptive energy systems, such as smart grids and autonomous energy management. These algorithms learn optimal actions by interacting with the environment, enabling real-time energy distribution and grid balancing. DL architectures, like CNNs and RNNs, provide exceptional capabilities for analyzing time-series data, meteorological inputs, and spatial energy patterns, which are critical for optimizing renewable energy systems. Additionally, optimization techniques such as particle swarm optimization and genetic algorithms aid in the design of effective energy storage systems, thereby enhancing the functionality of renewable energy technology. When considered as a whole, these AI algorithms facilitate the development of intelligent, effective, and sustainable energy systems that address global energy challenges and accelerate the transition to greener energy sources [11].

TOOLS AND PLATFORMS FOR AI IMPLEMENTATION

The implementation of AI in energy systems relies on a variety of tools and platforms that provide robust environments for developing, training, and deploying AI models. Programming languages like Python and R are widely used due to their extensive libraries, such as TensorFlow, PyTorch, and Scikit-learn, which facilitate ML and DL model development. Platforms like MATLAB are also popular for energy-focused AI applications, offering tools for data analysis, algorithm design, and simulation. Cloud computing platforms, including AWS, Google Cloud, and Microsoft Azure, offer scalable resources for processing large datasets and training complex AI models, which are essential for tasks such as energy demand forecasting and grid optimization. Additionally, specialized tools like IBM Watson and H2O.ai streamline AI deployment in industrial energy applications. For real-time energy management, edge computing frameworks such as NVIDIA Jetson and Intel OpenVINO enable AI processing closer to data sources, reducing latency and energy consumption. These tools and platforms are instrumental in integrating AI into energy conversion, storage, and distribution systems, driving advancements in efficiency and sustainability [12].

AI IN ENERGY CONVERSION TECHNOLOGIES

The following section explores the application of AI in optimizing energy conversion processes across various sectors. It covers the enhancement of photovoltaic cell efficiency through AI-driven optimization, forecasting solar irradiance, and improving wind power generation with AI models for turbine efficiency and forecasting. Additionally, the section highlights the role of AI in optimizing biomass conversion processes, contributing to more efficient and sustainable energy conversion from renewable sources [13].

SOLAR ENERGY CONVERSION

It focuses on utilizing AI to enhance the efficiency of solar energy systems. By adjusting operating factors such as temperature, irradiance, and ambient conditions based on real-time data, AI plays a crucial role in optimizing the performance of photovoltaic (PV) cells. ML algorithms can predict and correct performance degradation, enabling systems to operate at their peak efficiency. Additionally, AI is used to predict solar irradiance patterns, which are crucial for enhancing energy yield forecasting and facilitating grid integration management. By utilizing AI models, solar power systems can dynamically adjust to changing environmental conditions, reduce energy losses, and increase the overall reliability and sustainability of solar energy conversion [14 - 16].

Optimization of Photovoltaic Cell Efficiency

It examines how AI can significantly improve the efficiency of PV cells. PV systems convert sunlight into electricity, but various factors, including temperature, shading, and material properties, influence their efficiency. AI, particularly ML, can optimize PV performance by analyzing large datasets collected from environmental sensors, historical performance data, and real-time system conditions. Through algorithms like supervised learning, ML models can identify patterns and predict the optimal operating conditions for PV cells, adjusting parameters such as voltage and current to minimize energy losses. AI can also facilitate the detection of faults or degradation in solar panels, enabling proactive maintenance and reducing downtime. Additionally, advanced AI techniques, such as DL, can model the complex interactions within PV systems, helping to design more efficient materials and structures for solar cells. By continuously learning from data, AI ensures that PV cells operate at peak efficiency, contributing to a more reliable and sustainable solar energy infrastructure [17]. Fig. (**1**) illustrates how AI optimizes PV systems by analyzing environmental factors, including irradiance, temperature, and shading. AI models dynamically adjust operational parameters, minimizing energy losses and ensuring peak efficiency. The visualization highlights the interplay between AI-driven predictions and real-time adjustments, showcasing AI's potential in sustainable solar energy systems.

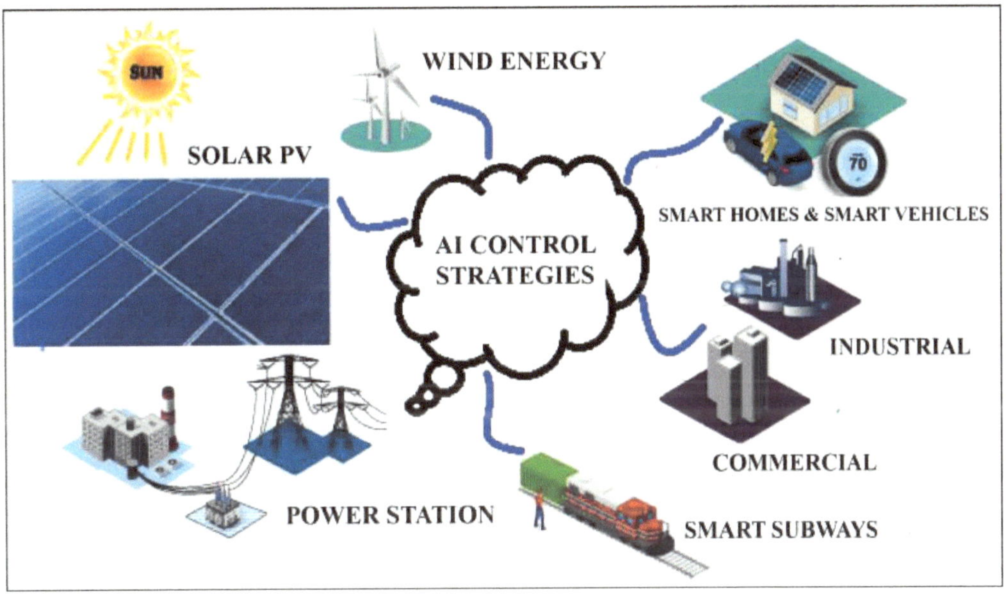

Fig. (1). AI-Driven Optimization of PV Systems for Enhanced Efficiency under Variable Environmental Conditions. Reprinted with permission from ref [18]. © 2023 by the authors. Licensee MDPI, Basel, Switzerland.

AI Models for Solar Irradiance Prediction

It focuses on the application of AI to predict solar irradiance, a critical factor in optimizing solar energy generation. Solar irradiance—the amount of solar power received per unit area—fluctuates due to weather conditions, geographical location, and time of day. Accurate prediction of irradiance allows for better energy yield forecasting, grid management, and system optimization. To accurately predict solar irradiance, AI models—particularly machine learning algorithms—can analyze past data on weather trends, atmospheric conditions, and satellite imagery. Complex, non-linear interactions between environmental conditions and irradiance levels are often modeled using methods such as time-series forecasting, regression analysis, and neural networks. DL, a subset of ML, can be used to handle large datasets and improve prediction accuracy by learning complex patterns in data. These AI-driven models continuously improve through feedback loops, refining their predictions over time. Real-time modifications to solar power systems are made possible through AI-driven solar irradiance prediction, which helps maximize energy output and minimize inefficiencies. Additionally, precise irradiance forecasting facilitates the grid's integration of solar energy, aiding in the transition to a more reliable and sustainable renewable energy infrastructure [19].

WIND ENERGY CONVERSION

It explores the role of AI in enhancing the efficiency and performance of wind energy systems. AI models are applied to optimize the operation of wind turbines by analyzing real-time data from sensors that measure wind speed, direction, and other environmental factors. ML algorithms can predict wind patterns, allowing for more accurate power generation forecasts and improved turbine performance. Additionally, AI can optimize turbine positioning and operational parameters, such as blade angle, to maximize energy capture from variable wind conditions. AI-driven predictive maintenance models are also employed to detect wear and tear in turbine components, reducing downtime and increasing the overall lifespan of wind energy systems. These models analyze sensor data to predict potential failures and recommend maintenance actions before costly breakdowns occur. By utilizing AI for wind energy conversion, power systems can become more adaptable to changing weather patterns, thus enhancing the stability, efficiency, and sustainability of wind energy generation. AI's contribution to wind energy also facilitates better integration with energy grids, helping to balance supply and demand and ensuring a reliable renewable energy source [20 - 22].

AI for Wind Power Forecasting and Turbine Efficiency

It discusses how AI is used to enhance the forecasting of wind power generation and optimize the efficiency of wind turbines. Accurate wind power forecasting is crucial for integrating wind energy into the grid, as it enables the anticipation of energy production and the management of grid stability. AI algorithms, particularly ML models, analyze historical wind data, weather forecasts, and environmental conditions to predict wind power output with greater precision. These AI models can identify complex, non-linear relationships between factors such as wind speed, direction, temperature, and turbine performance, resulting in improved forecasting accuracy compared to traditional methods. Moreover, AI contributes to optimizing turbine efficiency by dynamically adjusting operational parameters, such as blade pitch and rotational speed, to suit changing wind conditions. ML algorithms continuously learn from sensor data collected from turbines, enabling real-time adjustments that maximize power output while minimizing wear and tear. Predictive models also monitor turbine health, detecting anomalies and forecasting maintenance needs, thus reducing downtime and extending the life of the turbines. Overall, AI not only improves the prediction of wind power but also enhances turbine operation, making wind energy generation more efficient, reliable, and integrated into the broader energy grid [23, 24].

BIOENERGY AND THERMAL ENERGY CONVERSION

It examines the application of AI in optimizing the conversion of biomass into energy and enhancing thermal energy systems. In bioenergy, AI algorithms analyze complex datasets, including feedstock characteristics, environmental conditions, and conversion processes, to optimize the efficiency of bioenergy production. Machine learning models are used to predict biomass degradation rates, enhance the design of bio-conversion systems, and improve the yields of biofuels. In thermal energy systems, AI is utilized to enhance heat generation and distribution, ensuring optimal performance in processes such as combustion, cogeneration, and heat recovery. In addition to detecting potential maintenance issues before they lead to failures, AI-driven predictive models can optimize thermal plant operating parameters, including fuel consumption and temperature management. AI is essential to the development of renewable energy technologies and the mitigation of environmental impacts, as it enhances the sustainability and efficiency of thermal energy conversion and bioenergy [25 - 27].

Enhancing Biomass Conversion Processes Using AI

It focuses on the application of AI to optimize the conversion of biomass into bioenergy, a key renewable energy source. Biomass conversion involves complex biochemical and thermochemical processes, including combustion, fermentation, and gasification, which are influenced by numerous factors such as feedstock properties, environmental conditions, and process parameters. AI plays a pivotal role in improving the efficiency of these conversion processes by analyzing large datasets from sensors and operational systems. ML algorithms are employed to predict the behavior of different biomass types, optimize process parameters, and enhance the conversion efficiency. For instance, AI can identify the most suitable feedstock for specific conversion methods by analyzing factors like moisture content, particle size, and chemical composition. Furthermore, AI models can optimize reaction conditions, such as temperature and pressure, to maximize the yield of biofuels or biogas while minimizing the generation of by-products. AI also supports the real-time monitoring of biomass conversion systems, detecting anomalies or inefficiencies that could lead to energy loss or equipment degradation. Predictive maintenance models, powered by ML, enable early detection of potential failures, reducing downtime and operational costs. Additionally, AI-driven process optimization helps to improve energy balance and sustainability by fine-tuning resource utilization. By enhancing biomass conversion processes, AI not only boosts energy output but also contributes to reducing greenhouse gas emissions, making biomass a more viable and sustainable energy source in the transition to a renewable energy future [28].

AI IN ENERGY STORAGE TECHNOLOGIES

AI revolutionizes energy storage technologies by enhancing performance, reliability, and lifespan. Machine learning models accelerate the discovery of advanced materials for batteries, optimizing properties such as capacity and thermal stability. AI-driven analytics enable real-time monitoring of storage systems, predicting faults and optimizing charge-discharge cycles to maximize efficiency. Additionally, AI integrates storage systems with renewable energy sources and smart grids, ensuring seamless energy flow and reducing wastage. These innovations make AI pivotal in addressing energy storage challenges and advancing sustainable energy systems [29].

AI FOR BATTERY TECHNOLOGY

AI is transforming battery technology by optimizing material discovery, manufacturing processes, and real-time performance management. Batteries are central to energy storage systems, particularly in the integration of renewable energy, Electric Vehicles (EVs), and portable electronics. AI accelerates advancements in battery technology by analyzing complex datasets to uncover insights that traditional methods may overlook [30].

In material discovery, ML algorithms predict the properties of potential battery materials, such as electrode compositions and electrolyte formulations, reducing the time and cost of experimental trials. AI-driven simulations enable researchers to identify materials with high energy density, improved thermal stability, and longer lifespans, fostering innovations in lithium-ion, solid-state, and emerging battery technologies. AI also enhances manufacturing processes by optimizing quality control and resource utilization. Real-time production line monitoring by sophisticated models ensures consistent performance by identifying irregularities. By streamlining production, cutting waste, and increasing cost effectiveness, next-generation batteries become more widely available.

Real-time battery management is another critical application of AI. Algorithms monitor key parameters such as temperature, charge-discharge rates, and capacity degradation to optimize battery performance and prevent failures. AI-powered systems enable predictive maintenance by identifying potential issues before they escalate, thereby extending battery life and enhancing safety. Furthermore, AI facilitates the integration of batteries with renewable energy systems and smart grids, optimizing energy storage and release based on demand patterns. This dynamic management reduces energy wastage and stabilizes power supply, addressing the intermittency of renewable sources. As battery technology continues to evolve, AI remains at the forefront, driving innovation and ensuring the development of sustainable energy solutions [31].

Material Discovery for High-Performance Batteries

Material discovery is a cornerstone of advancing high-performance batteries, and AI plays a transformative role in this domain. By leveraging ML and predictive modeling, AI accelerates the identification and optimization of materials with desirable properties such as high energy density, improved thermal stability, and enhanced charge-discharge efficiency. Traditional trial-and-error methods in material science are time-intensive and resource-heavy, but AI-driven simulations drastically reduce development timelines by exploring vast chemical spaces. AI algorithms analyze datasets from experimental and computational studies to predict the performance of novel electrode and electrolyte materials. For example, ML models can screen for materials with fast ion conductivity or high structural stability, which are crucial for next-generation battery systems, such as solid-state and lithium-sulfur batteries. Additionally, AI aids in understanding degradation mechanisms, enabling the design of materials that mitigate capacity loss and improve cycle life. The integration of AI with quantum chemistry simulations and high-throughput screening further enhances material discovery, allowing researchers to predict molecular behaviors and optimize compositions at the atomic scale. This synergy of AI and material science accelerates breakthroughs in battery technology, paving the way for sustainable and high-performance energy storage systems critical to renewable energy integration and electric mobility [32, 33].

Predictive Maintenance of Lithium-Ion Batteries (LIBs)

Predictive maintenance of LIBs is a critical application of AI that enhances safety, performance, and lifespan of these batteries. By utilizing machine learning algorithms and advanced analytics, AI monitors key battery parameters, such as voltage, temperature, and charge-discharge cycles, in real-time. This data-driven approach identifies early signs of degradation, overheating, or capacity loss, enabling preemptive actions to mitigate failures. AI models predict the Remaining Useful Life (RUL) of batteries by analyzing both historical and real-time data, providing precise estimates of when maintenance is required. This reduces unexpected downtime and prevents catastrophic failures in applications like EVs and renewable energy systems. Furthermore, AI optimizes battery usage by dynamically adjusting charging protocols to minimize stress on the cells, extending their operational life. By improving reliability and safety, AI-driven predictive maintenance supports the broader adoption of lithium-ion batteries in sustainable energy systems and advanced technologies. Fig. (**2**) showcases how AI predicts and prevents faults in lithium-ion batteries. By monitoring key parameters such as temperature and voltage in real-time, AI identifies potential failures early. These insights optimize maintenance schedules, reduce downtime, and enhance safety, illustrating AI's critical role in advancing energy storage reliability [34, 35].

FUEL CELLS AND SUPERCAPACITORS

AI is revolutionizing fuel cells and supercapacitors by optimizing their design, performance, and integration. For fuel cells, AI accelerates the discovery of materials for catalysts, enhancing efficiency and reducing costs. It also improves operational control by monitoring and predicting system behaviors, ensuring optimal performance. In supercapacitors, AI facilitates the development of advanced electrode materials and predicts energy storage capabilities. By enabling real-time diagnostics and predictive maintenance, AI ensures the reliability and scalability of these technologies, advancing sustainable energy storage solutions [37, 38].

AI in Fuel Cell Optimization and Durability

AI plays a pivotal role in enhancing the optimization and durability of fuel cells, which are critical for clean energy applications. AI-driven algorithms analyze complex data sets from fuel cell operations to optimize system performance, including fuel utilization, power output, and thermal management. By identifying inefficiencies in real-time, AI enables dynamic control of operating parameters, thereby maximizing energy conversion efficiency. In material development, AI accelerates the discovery of advanced catalysts and membranes, essential for improving fuel cell durability and reducing costs. Machine learning models predict the properties and performance of materials, allowing researchers to design catalysts with higher activity and resilience to degradation. Furthermore, AI enhances durability by monitoring key metrics such as temperature, pressure, and reactant flow rates. Predictive analytics identify early signs of wear or failure, enabling preemptive maintenance and extending system life. These advancements ensure that fuel cells remain reliable and cost-effective, supporting their integration into sustainable energy systems, such asydrogen-powered vehicles and stationary power applications [39, 40]. Hydrogen (H_2) reaches the anode side of a Proton Exchange Membrane Fuel Cell (PEMFC) system, where it separates into

H^+ and e^- as shown in Fig. (**3**). While the electrons move through an external circuit to produce electricity, the protons move through the proton exchange membrane. Airborne oxygen (O_2) reacts with protons and electrons at the cathode to create water and emit heat. The system also features catalytic layers and gas diffusion layers, which enhance reaction efficiency and sustainability. This process highlights the clean energy potential of fuel cells by producing water as a byproduct.

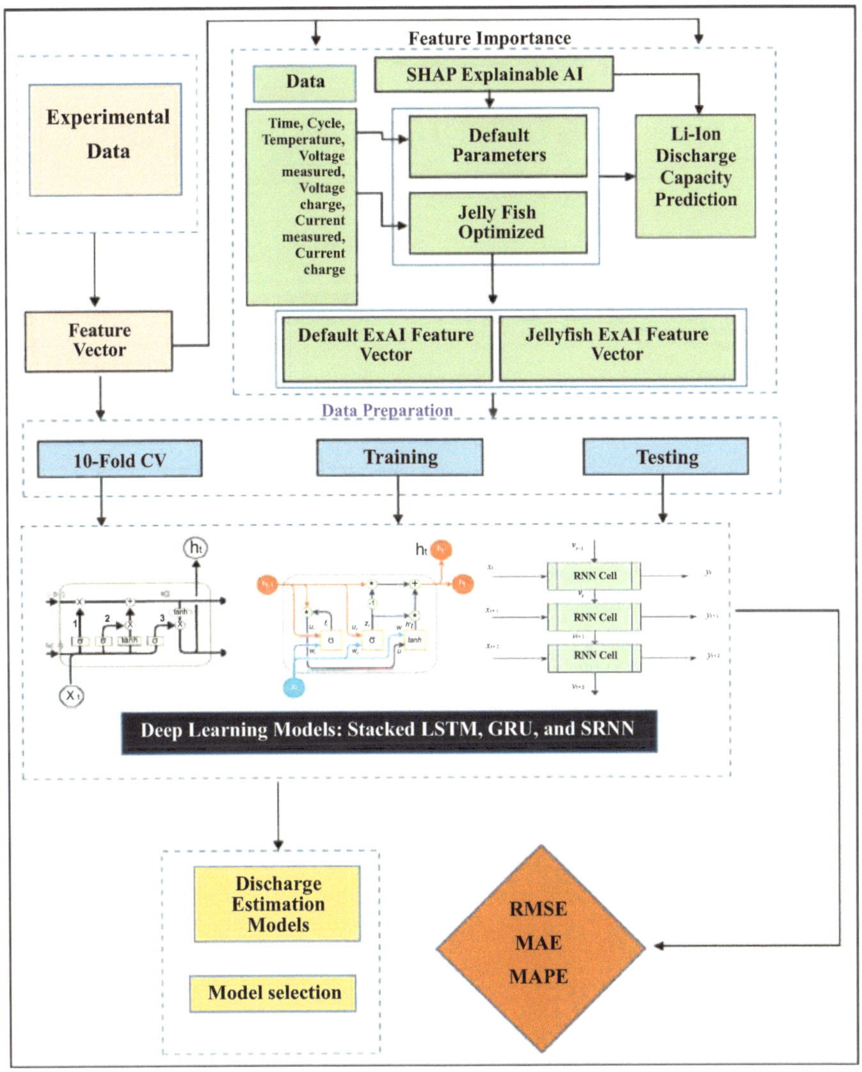

Fig. (2). AI-Enabled Predictive Maintenance in Lithium-Ion Battery Systems for Extended Lifespan. Reprinted with permission from ref [36]. © 2023 by the authors. Licensee MDPI, Basel, Switzerland.

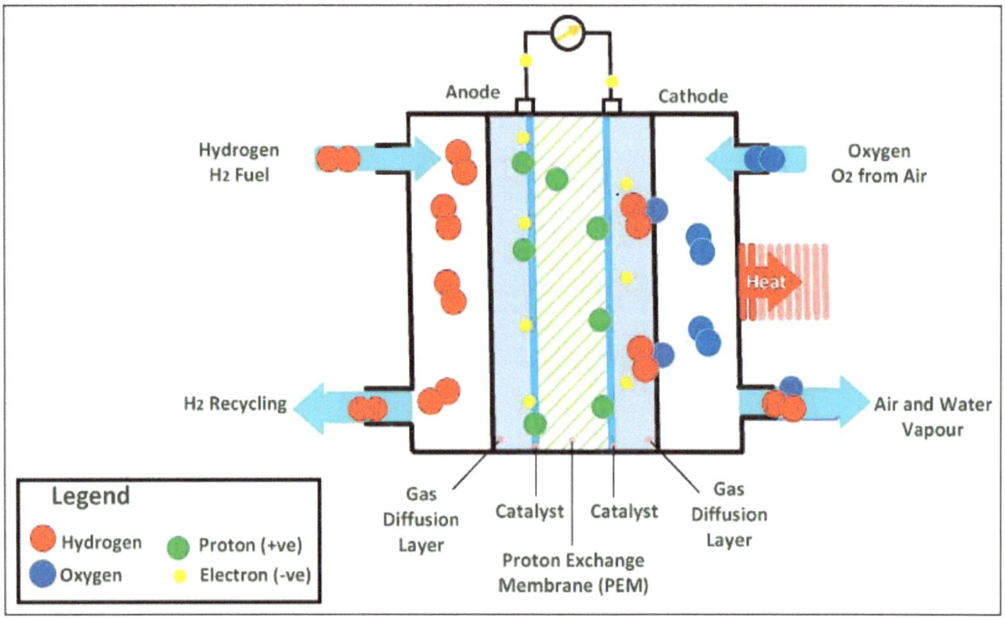

Fig. (3). Schematic Representation of a PEMFC: An illustration of hydrogen and oxygen reactions, showcasing electron and proton flow, catalytic layers, gas diffusion layers, and energy conversion processes resulting in heat, water, and electrical energy. Reprinted with permission from ref [41]. © 2023 by the authors. Licensee MDPI, Basel, Switzerland.

Real-Time Diagnostics for Supercapacitors

Real-time diagnostics for supercapacitors, powered by AI, significantly enhance their performance, safety, and lifespan. Supercapacitors are energy storage devices that are essential for use in industrial automation, renewable energy systems, and electric vehicles due to their high power density, rapid charge-discharge cycles, and endurance. However, their efficiency depends on precise monitoring and maintenance, where AI excels. AI employs advanced ML algorithms to analyze sensor data, such as voltage, current, and temperature, in real time. These diagnostics detect anomalies, such as imbalances in cell performance or overheating, that could compromise the supercapacitor's functionality. AI systems predict the RUL and State Of Health (SOH) by identifying degradation patterns, enabling proactive maintenance, and preventing failures. Additionally, AI-driven diagnostics optimize operational parameters by dynamically adjusting charging and discharging cycles to reduce wear and improve energy efficiency. This real-time adaptability extends the device's lifespan and ensures consistent performance under varying environmental and load conditions. By providing detailed insights into supercapacitor behavior, AI enhances reliability and scalability, ensuring these devices play a critical role in sustainable energy systems and high-demand applications [42, 43].

AI-DRIVEN PROCESS OPTIMIZATION AND CONTROL

AI-driven process optimization and control transform energy systems by enhancing efficiency, reliability, and scalability. Through machine learning and advanced algorithms, AI analyzes real-time data from energy systems, identifying patterns and optimizing operations. In renewable energy, AI adjusts parameters for solar, wind, and bioenergy systems to maximize output under dynamic conditions. For energy storage, AI ensures precise charge-discharge cycles, extending battery life and efficiency. Additionally, AI-driven control systems enable dynamic grid management, balancing energy supply and demand while seamlessly integrating renewables. This ensures cost-effective, sustainable, and adaptive energy processes, accelerating the transition to clean energy technologies. Fig. (**4**) illustrates the integration of AI in optimizing energy conversion processes, including solar-to-electric and wind-to-storage systems. It showcases real-time data analytics and adaptive control mechanisms enabled by AI. These advancements ensure optimal energy flow and reduce inefficiencies, highlighting AI's role in accelerating the adoption of renewable energy technologies [44].

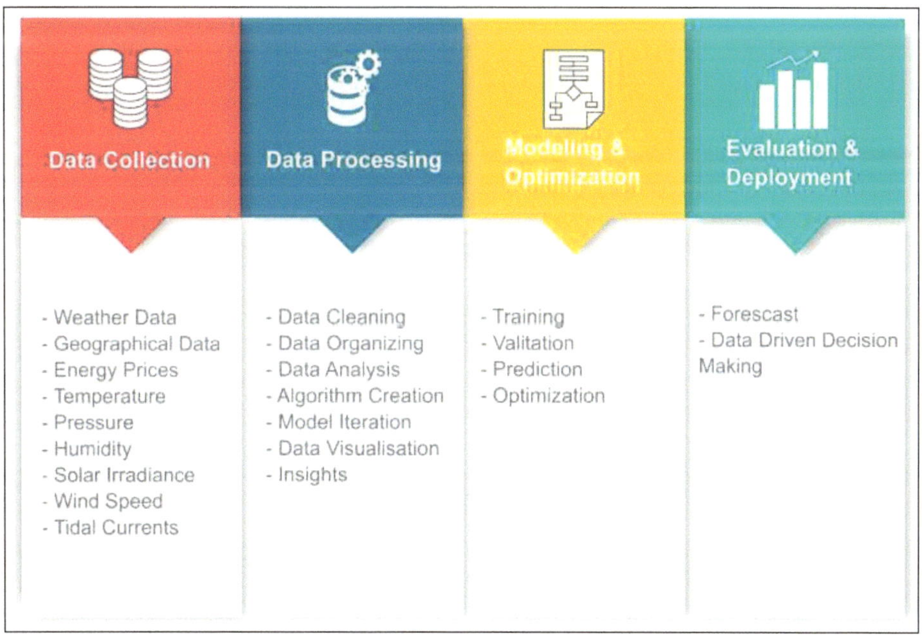

Fig. (4). AI-Driven Process Optimization Across Energy Conversion Systems for Real-Time Efficiency Gains. Reprinted with permission from ref [45]. © 2023 by the authors. Licensee MDPI, Basel, Switzerland.

SMART CHARGING AND DISCHARGING STRATEGIES

Smart charging and discharging strategies, enabled by AI, play a critical role in optimizing energy storage systems, particularly in applications like EVs, renewable energy integration, and grid management. These strategies leverage advanced AI algorithms to dynamically monitor and control charging and discharging cycles, ensuring maximum efficiency, extended lifespan, and reliability of energy storage devices [46].

AI systems analyze real-time data such as battery State Of Charge (SOC), SOH, and external variables like electricity demand, grid conditions, and energy prices. Based on this analysis, they optimize the timing and intensity of charging and discharging processes. AAI balances energy supply and demand in renewable energy systems, for example, by directing excess energy from solar or wind sources to storage during periods of peak output and releasing it during times of high demand.

In EVs, AI-driven strategies minimize battery wear by avoiding overcharging or deep discharging, enhancing longevity. Predictive algorithms also integrate user behavior and travel patterns to ensure efficient charging schedules. For grid-level applications, smart strategies support frequency regulation and peak load management by deploying stored energy at optimal intervals [47].

Furthermore, ML models predict energy usage trends, enabling preemptive adjustments to charging protocols that prevent power losses and reduce operational costs. These intelligent strategies enhance overall system efficiency and facilitate seamless integration of intermittent renewable sources, contributing to a sustainable and resilient energy infrastructure. By enabling adaptive energy management, AI-driven smart charging and discharging strategies are pivotal for advancing next-generation energy storage solutions.

ENERGY FLOW MANAGEMENT IN HYBRID SYSTEMS

It examines how AI can enhance the operation and integration of hybrid energy systems, which effectively meet energy demands by combining multiple energy sources, including solar, wind, and conventional power generation. To maintain system stability, dependability, and peak performance in hybrid systems, controlling the energy flow between various sources and storage components, such as batteries, is essential. In this context, AI is important because it facilitates the monitoring, forecasting, and control of energy flow in real-time.

Artificial intelligence models, specifically machine learning algorithms, facilitate the dynamic management of energy resources. They achieve this by accurately forecasting energy generation from renewable sources, leveraging predictive analysis of meteorological conditions, time-based variables, and historical data. By analyzing these inputs, AI systems can determine the optimal combination of energy sources to meet demand, reducing reliance on non-renewable backup generators and minimizing fuel consumption. To ensure that excess energy produced during periods of high renewable output is effectively stored and utilized when production declines, ML algorithms can also forecast the demand for energy storage [48].

Moreover, AI can optimize the energy flow between generation, storage, and consumption points in hybrid systems by controlling inverters, batteries, and other key components. This results in minimizing energy losses, maximizing storage capacity, and enhancing overall system efficiency. By continuously learning from data, AI can adjust energy flow strategies to respond to changing environmental conditions, load variations, and system performance, thereby improving the adaptability and sustainability of hybrid energy systems. Additionally, AI-driven predictive maintenance helps ensure that all components of the hybrid system operate at peak performance, reducing downtime and extending the system's lifespan. Overall, AI enhances energy flow management in hybrid systems by providing intelligent, data-driven decision-making capabilities that optimize resource use, improve system integration, and support the transition to sustainable energy solutions [49]. Fig. (**5**) illustrates AI's role in managing energy flow across hybrid systems, which combine solar, wind, and storage units. AI algorithms predict energy generation and optimize flow to minimize losses. The visual emphasizes the seamless integration of diverse energy sources, improving overall system adaptability and performance in renewable energy networks.

TESLA'S AUTOBIDDER PLATFORM FOR ENERGY STORAGE OPTIMIZATION

The application of Artificial Intelligence (AI) in energy storage technologies has been revolutionized by Tesla's Autobidder platform, an advanced energy trading and management system. Autobidder utilizes machine learning algorithms to autonomously optimize the economic value and dispatch of distributed energy resources, particularly large-scale battery installations. One of the most prominent implementations of this technology is at the *Hornsdale Power Reserve (HPR)* in South Australia—the world's largest lithium-ion battery storage facility, boasting a capacity of 150 MW/194 MWh. This installation plays a crucial role in stabilizing grid operations, enhancing the integration of renewable energy, and significantly reducing electricity costs.

Fig. (5). AI-Facilitated Energy Flow Management in Hybrid Renewable Energy Systems. This is an AI-generated image taken from freepik.com.

OPERATIONAL MECHANISM OF AUTOBIDDER

Tesla's Autobidder serves as an automated energy trading platform, utilizing real-time data analytics and predictive algorithms to optimize energy flows. It optimally schedules the charging and discharging of energy storage systems based on fluctuating electricity market prices, grid demands, and the availability of renewable energy. Through machine learning models trained on extensive datasets—including historical energy prices, weather patterns, and demand forecasts—Autobidder predicts variations in renewable energy generation and strategically deploys stored energy to maximize profitability. Unlike conventional energy trading methods, Autobidder executes trades autonomously, reacting to market signals within milliseconds and optimizing energy dispatch for maximum economic return.

IMPACT ON THE HORNSDALE POWER RESERVE (HPR)

The deployment of Autobidder at the Hornsdale Power Reserve has significantly bolstered energy reliability and cost efficiency. Since its integration, HPR has contributed to enhanced grid stability and substantial cost savings. The system provides rapid-response frequency control services, mitigating the risks of blackouts and reinforcing energy security during critical grid disturbances.

Remarkably, during major energy events, HPR's operations led to a 90% reduction in grid service costs, generating approximately $40 million in savings within its first year. This achievement not only highlights the economic advantages of AI-driven optimization but also demonstrates its effectiveness in integrating renewable energy sources. By managing surplus energy from solar and wind during peak production, Autobidder enables seamless discharge during high-demand periods, stabilizing grid fluctuations.

TECHNOLOGICAL ADVANTAGES

Several technological innovations underpin the success of Tesla's Autobidder platform. Its real-time data analytics enable precise energy dispatch by continuously monitoring market signals, weather conditions, and grid demands. The platform's dynamic optimization capabilities enable it to adjust energy strategies instantly, thereby maximizing efficiency and revenue generation. Additionally, Autobidder's scalability makes it suitable for both grid-scale projects and decentralized energy networks, demonstrating its versatility. Its autonomous operation minimizes human intervention, reducing the risk of errors and ensuring consistent market participation.

Tesla's Autobidder platform sets a global benchmark for AI-driven energy storage optimization. Its successful deployment at the Hornsdale Power Reserve exemplifies how intelligent automation can enhance grid reliability, cut operational costs, and support the seamless integration of renewable energy. This case study underscores the transformative potential of AI in optimizing energy storage systems, contributing to smarter and more resilient energy infrastructures worldwide.

GOOGLE'S DEEPMIND AI FOR DATA CENTER ENERGY EFFICIENCY

As global energy demands rise, optimizing energy consumption in large-scale industrial settings has become increasingly critical. Data centers, which power everything from cloud computing to online communications, are among the largest energy consumers worldwide. Addressing this challenge, Google has implemented advanced Artificial Intelligence (AI) through its DeepMind division to enhance energy efficiency in its global network of data centers. This AI-driven optimization initiative has not only reduced energy consumption but also set new standards for sustainable operations in the technology sector. DeepMind's application in Google's data centers showcases the transformative potential of AI in optimizing complex energy systems with real-time data analytics and machine learning models.

OPERATIONAL MECHANISM OF DEEPMIND AI

DeepMind's AI optimizes data center energy usage by leveraging machine learning algorithms that predict and adjust cooling requirements in real time. Data centers are typically cooled using intricate networks of fans, pumps, and cooling towers to prevent overheating. Traditionally, these systems operated on fixed schedules or required manual adjustments, often resulting in inefficiencies. DeepMind's solution, however, introduces a layer of intelligent automation that continuously analyzes data from thousands of sensors distributed across the facility. The AI system utilizes deep learning models trained on historical data from Google's data centers, including variables such as server temperatures, energy consumption rates, and weather conditions. By processing this data in real-time, DeepMind dynamically adjusts cooling strategies to maintain optimal temperatures with minimal energy consumption. For instance, if the external temperature drops, the AI can autonomously reduce the workload of cooling towers, thereby saving energy. Similarly, during periods of high computational demand, the system anticipates temperature spikes and optimally configures cooling mechanisms to prevent thermal stress on hardware components. DeepMind's AI also employs reinforcement learning, enabling the system to learn and refine its optimization strategies over time. By continuously experimenting with various cooling configurations and receiving feedback on energy consumption, the AI refines its models to achieve peak efficiency. This adaptive capability ensures that energy savings are not only achieved but also sustained, even as data center demands evolve.

IMPACT ON ENERGY EFFICIENCY AND SUSTAINABILITY

The deployment of DeepMind AI in Google's data centers has led to substantial improvements in energy efficiency. According to Google's official reports, the AI-driven optimization resulted in a 40% reduction in energy used for cooling and a 15% overall reduction in Power Usage Effectiveness (PUE). PUE is a standard metric for assessing data center energy efficiency, defined as the ratio of total energy consumed by the facility to the energy consumed by its IT equipment. Achieving a 15% reduction in PUE represents a significant leap toward sustainable operations, as it reduces both energy costs and carbon emissions. Moreover, the environmental impact of these optimizations is profound. Google estimates that the energy saved by DeepMind's intervention is equivalent to removing tens of thousands of cars from the road annually. This initiative aligns with Google's commitment to operating fully carbon-neutral data centers and advancing sustainability goals across its global infrastructure.

ADVANCED PREDICTIVE CAPABILITIES

One of the standout features of DeepMind's AI is its predictive capability. Through advanced time-series analysis, the system anticipates future cooling requirements based on historical patterns and real-time environmental data. This foresight allows the AI to make proactive adjustments, preventing energy wastage before it occurs. For instance, if DeepMind detects a trend in rising temperatures due to increased server load, it can preemptively increase cooling output, avoiding reactive overcooling and minimizing power consumption. These predictive capabilities extend beyond just cooling. Google is exploring how DeepMind can optimize power distribution across its data centers, enhancing load balancing and reducing peak energy consumption. This proactive energy management not only reduces costs but also enhances the overall resilience of data center operations, particularly during periods of high demand.

INTEGRATION WITH RENEWABLE ENERGY SOURCES

DeepMind's AI-driven energy optimization also complements Google's renewable energy initiatives. By dynamically managing energy consumption, the AI allows Google to better align its power usage with the availability of renewable sources such as solar and wind. For example, during periods of high renewable energy generation, DeepMind can ramp up data center processing tasks, maximizing the use of clean energy. Conversely, during lower renewable availability, the AI reduces non-critical processing loads to minimize reliance on grid-based fossil fuels. This synergy between AI optimization and renewable energy integration exemplifies a holistic approach to sustainable energy management. It not only reduces Google's carbon footprint but also serves as a scalable model for other energy-intensive industries seeking to enhance sustainability through smart technologies.

TECHNOLOGICAL INNOVATIONS AND SCALABILITY

The success of DeepMind's AI optimization in Google's data centers underscores several key technological innovations. First, its **real-time data processing** capabilities allow it to react instantly to changes in environmental conditions and server demands. Second, **machine learning-driven predictive analytics** enhances its ability to foresee energy demands and optimize resource allocation accordingly. Finally, its **reinforcement learning mechanisms** enable continuous improvement over time, making the system more efficient as more data is collected. Importantly, this technology is highly scalable. Google has already begun deploying AI-driven optimizations across its global network of data centers, demonstrating the platform's robustness in varying climatic and operational conditions. This scalability potential indicates that similar AI-driven energy optimizations could be extended to other industrial sectors, such as manufacturing, logistics, and even urban energy grids.

Google's deployment of DeepMind AI in its data centers represents a groundbreaking advancement in energy optimization. By harnessing real-time data analytics, predictive modeling, and machine learning, DeepMind has successfully reduced cooling energy consumption by 40% and achieved a 15% improvement in overall energy efficiency. These optimizations not only enhance Google's sustainability efforts but also serve as a blueprint for AI-driven energy management across high-demand industries. This case study demonstrates how intelligent automation can contribute to achieving sustainable development goals, reducing carbon footprints while ensuring reliable and cost-effective energy usage.

STRATEGIC PARTNERSHIPS BETWEEN ACADEMIA AND INDUSTRY

The successful commercialization of AI-driven energy technologies heavily relies on strategic collaborations between academia and industry. Academic institutions contribute cutting-edge research, theoretical modeling, and experimental breakthroughs that drive technological innovation. For instance, joint projects between universities and industry leaders, such as Siemens, GE Renewable Energy, and Tesla, have accelerated advancements in smart grids, battery optimization, and renewable energy forecasting. These collaborations enable the transfer of theoretical research into practical, deployable solutions. In particular, public-private partnerships have played a crucial role in scaling AI technologies from laboratory research to full-scale deployment. Government programs, such as the U.S. Department of Energy's ARPA-E (Advanced Research Projects Agency-Energy), fund collaborative projects that bridge academic research and industrial applications, reducing market-entry barriers for innovative technologies. These partnerships not only facilitate technology development but also address regulatory hurdles, standardization, and market integration. In the context of energy systems, AI-driven optimization of grid infrastructure, predictive maintenance of energy storage devices, and renewable energy forecasting have benefited significantly from these synergistic efforts.

TECHNOLOGY READINESS LEVELS (TRLs) AND THEIR RELEVANCE

The successful commercialization of AI-driven energy technologies heavily relies on Technology Readiness Levels (TRLs), which serve as a standardized framework to evaluate the maturity of emerging technologies, particularly in high-impact sectors like energy. The TRL scale ranges from basic principles (TRL 1) to fully operational technology (TRL 9). In the field of AI-driven energy solutions, understanding the TRL of each innovation is crucial for identifying its commercial viability and scaling potential. For example, machine learning algorithms for predictive maintenance in lithium-ion batteries are currently at TRL 7–8, with demonstrable field applications in electric vehicles and grid storage. In contrast, AI-driven quantum computing for energy optimization remains at TRL 3–4, primarily in experimental and proof-of-concept stages. By mapping AI technologies onto the TRL scale, stakeholders can prioritize investment and deployment strategies based on maturity and market readiness.

ROLE OF STARTUPS AND SMES IN ADVANCING AI-DRIVEN ENERGY TECHNOLOGIES

Startups and Small and Medium-sized Enterprises (SMEs) play a pivotal role in driving innovation and commercialization of AI technologies in the energy sector. Unlike large corporations, these agile entities often focus on niche technologies and rapid prototyping, enabling faster development cycles and market adaptation. Startups such as Voltaiq, which specializes in predictive analytics for battery health monitoring, and Uptake, which leverages AI for predictive maintenance in industrial energy systems, have significantly contributed to improving efficiency and reliability in energy technologies. SMEs also facilitate the regional adoption of AI solutions, especially in decentralized energy systems and microgrids. Their ability to customize AI-driven solutions for local energy demands and grid configurations accelerates the deployment of sustainable technologies in emerging markets. Government-backed incubators and innovation hubs provide further support to these enterprises by offering financial assistance, infrastructure, and networking opportunities. Additionally, collaboration among startups, industry leaders, and academic research labs helps bridge the gap between innovative concepts and large-scale implementation. Programs like the Energy Accelerator and Greentown Labs offer platforms for these collaborations, fostering innovation while reducing commercialization timelines.

QUANTUM COMPUTATION FOR ENHANCED ENERGY OPTIMIZATION

Quantum computation represents a frontier technology with the potential to revolutionize energy optimization by solving complex problems that are currently intractable for classical computers. In energy systems, tasks such as optimizing grid operations, enhancing energy storage efficiency, and improving renewable energy forecasting involve computationally intensive processes. Quantum algorithms, such as Quantum Approximate Optimization Algorithm (QAOA) and Variational Quantum Eigensolver (VQE), can process vast datasets exponentially faster than traditional methods, enabling real-time energy management and advanced predictive analytics. For instance, quantum computation can optimize the dispatch of Distributed Energy Resources (DERs) across smart grids by rapidly solving multi-variable constraints that are influenced by fluctuating demand, renewable energy variability, and grid stability. Moreover, the application of quantum machine learning in material discovery could accelerate breakthroughs in battery technology, fuel cell efficiency, and supercapacitor performance by accurately modeling atomic interactions. However, current quantum computing technologies are at Technology Readiness Level (TRL) 3–4, primarily in experimental stages, and require significant advancements before they can be implemented on a large scale. Nevertheless, as quantum hardware matures, its integration with AI-driven energy management platforms could redefine optimization strategies in sustainable energy systems.

FEDERATED LEARNING FOR DECENTRALIZED ENERGY MANAGEMENT

Federated learning, a decentralized machine learning approach, allows energy systems to collaboratively train algorithms across distributed data sources while maintaining data privacy. This is particularly relevant for energy systems that span multiple locations, such as regional power grids, decentralized solar installations, and microgrids. In traditional machine learning models, data must be centrally collected and processed, posing risks to privacy and data security. Federated learning mitigates these issues by enabling local energy nodes to train models independently, sharing only model updates rather than raw data. This distributed learning paradigm is highly advantageous for predictive maintenance in energy storage systems and real-time demand forecasting in smart grids. For example, decentralized wind farms can use federated learning to optimize turbine performance by collectively analyzing weather patterns and mechanical stresses without compromising proprietary data. Additionally, federated learning enhances cybersecurity by reducing centralized data vulnerabilities, which is critical for safeguarding energy infrastructure against cyber threats. Future advancements in federated learning are expected to align with global data protection regulations such as the General Data Protection Regulation (GDPR) and the Data Governance Act. This alignment not only facilitates broader adoption in energy markets but also strengthens trust among stakeholders in decentralized energy ecosystems.

DIGITAL TWIN TECHNOLOGIES FOR REAL-TIME OPTIMIZATION

Digital twins—virtual replicas of physical energy systems—are transforming the way energy technologies are monitored, optimized, and maintained. Through real-time synchronization, digital twins offer in-depth insights into system behavior, enabling predictive maintenance and optimization of energy assets, such as solar panels, wind turbines, and grid components. AI-driven digital twins utilize real-time sensor data to simulate operational conditions, predict equipment failures, and optimize energy flows across distributed networks. For example, in large-scale solar farms, digital twins can forecast variations in energy output based on environmental data, panel degradation, and shading effects. These predictions enable dynamic adjustments, thereby enhancing energy yield and extending asset life. Similarly, in wind energy, digital twins analyze turbine performance under varying wind speeds and stress conditions, recommending real-time adjustments to blade pitch and rotation speeds to maximize energy capture. Furthermore, digital twins contribute to grid resilience by simulating load balancing and power distribution strategies during peak demand or unexpected outages. By leveraging digital twins, energy operators can make data-driven decisions that optimize energy production, minimize downtime, and enhance safety across their energy infrastructures.

ANTICIPATED GLOBAL MARKET GROWTH AND POLICY TRENDS

The global market for AI-driven energy solutions is projected to grow substantially over the next decade, driven by rising energy demands and increasing commitments to sustainability. According to recent market analyses, the AI energy market is expected to reach approximately $20 billion by 2030, with a Compound Annual Growth Rate (CAGR) of over 25%. This growth is largely driven by innovations in smart grids, predictive maintenance, and renewable energy optimization, all of which are powered by AI technologies. Policy trends are also shaping the deployment of AI in energy systems. International agreements such as the Paris Climate Accord and the European Green Deal emphasize the integration of AI and digital technologies to enhance energy efficiency and reduce carbon emissions. Additionally, regional policies like the U.S. Infrastructure Investment and Jobs Act provide substantial funding for smart grid modernization and AI-based energy projects. These policy frameworks are designed to incentivize the adoption of AI-driven energy solutions, accelerating the transition toward cleaner and more resilient energy infrastructures.

ALIGNING WITH SUSTAINABLE DEVELOPMENT GOALS (SDGs)

The integration of AI technologies in energy systems directly supports the United Nations Sustainable Development Goals (SDGs), particularly SDG 7 (Affordable and Clean Energy) and SDG 13 (Climate Action). By optimizing renewable energy systems, enhancing grid stability, and reducing energy wastage, AI-driven solutions contribute to sustainable energy accessibility and climate mitigation. Furthermore, technologies like federated learning and digital twins promote resource efficiency and resilience in energy infrastructures, aligning with global sustainability targets. To enhance the chapter's real-world relevance, we will explicitly map these AI advancements to measurable indicators outlined in SDG 7 and SDG 13. This alignment will provide a clearer demonstration of how AI-driven innovations are contributing to global sustainability efforts.

CHALLENGES IN AI-DRIVEN ENERGY SYSTEMS

It addresses the hurdles in applying AI to energy technologies. Since accurate AI model training requires dependable, high-resolution data, data shortages and quality issues represent a major obstacle. Furthermore, because complicated algorithms often operate as "black boxes," making it challenging to comprehend their decision-making process, the interpretability of AI models remains a concern. Generalization across diverse energy systems can also be problematic, as models trained on specific datasets may not perform well in different environments. Additionally, ethical and environmental implications, such as data privacy and the carbon footprint of AI computation, need to be considered in the widespread deployment of AI in energy systems [50].

DATA SCARCITY AND QUALITY ISSUES

A significant limitation in AI applications for energy systems is the scarcity and quality of available data. AI models, particularly ML algorithms, require large volumes of high-quality, representative datasets to function effectively. However, in many energy sectors, such as renewable energy, operational data can be sparse, inconsistent, or incomplete, making it difficult to train robust models. For example, energy systems in remote locations or developing regions may not have sufficient monitoring infrastructure to collect the necessary real-time data for training AI models. Additionally, data gathered from sensors or other devices may contain noise, inaccuracies, or gaps that can degrade model performance. Inaccurate or low-quality data can lead to suboptimal predictions, resulting in inefficiencies in energy production or consumption management. Therefore, data preprocessing, augmentation, and robust data collection strategies are crucial for mitigating these challenges [51, 52].

MODEL INTERPRETABILITY

Another major challenge in AI adoption in energy systems is the interpretability of models, particularly in the case of DL or complex algorithms. Neural network-based AI models, in particular, function as "black boxes," with decision-making processes that are opaque and difficult for humans to comprehend. In sectors such as the energy industry, where trust, accountability, and transparency are essential, this lack of interpretability presents significant issues. For example, when AI-driven systems are used for critical decisions, such as energy distribution or fault detection, stakeholders must be able to understand and justify how and why certain decisions were made. The inability to interpret the model's reasoning can lead to a lack of trust in AI-driven decisions and reluctance to adopt these systems at scale. In response, a growing field of research is focused on improving the transparency of AI algorithms through methods such asxplainable AI (XAI), which aims to make AI models more interpretable and user-friendly, particularly in high-stakes applications like energy systems [53, 54].

GENERALIZATION ACROSS DIVERSE SYSTEMS

AI models trained on specific datasets or environments may struggle to generalize when deployed in different energy systems or regions. For instance, a model trained on data from a solar farm in one geographic location may not perform optimally in another region with different weather patterns, solar irradiance levels, or system configurations. This lack of generalization arises because AI models can become overfitted to the data they are trained on, leading to reduced performance when faced with new or unseen conditions. Furthermore, energy systems are often complex and subject to local regulatory, economic, and technological variations, which can make it difficult to apply a one-size-fits-all AI solution. To address this, models need to be adaptable, and training datasets should ideally include diverse, representative data from multiple sources and environments to improve model robustness and scalability [55, 56].

SCALABILITY OF AI SOLUTIONS

While AI models may work well for small-scale or localized energy systems, scaling these solutions to larger, more complex networks presents another set of challenges. Hybrid energy systems, for instance, which combine solar, wind, and conventional power sources, are inherently complex and require real-time optimization across numerous components. As these systems scale, the volume of data and the computational demands placed on AI algorithms increase significantly. Additionally, managing energy flow in large grids involves a multitude of variables, such as storage systems, demand response, and distribution networks, which can overwhelm current AI solutions. Therefore, developing scalable AI architectures capable of handling vast amounts of real-time data and providing timely, accurate decisions is a key challenge. Distributed AI systems, edge computing, and advanced optimization techniques are potential solutions, but these technologies still require significant research and development before they can be widely implemented [57].

ETHICAL AND ENVIRONMENTAL IMPLICATIONS

As AI becomes increasingly integral to energy systems, ethical and environmental concerns must also be taken into account. Large volumes of data are utilized by AI models, which can raise privacy concerns, particularly when sensitive customer data is employed in predictive maintenance or smart grid applications. To prevent abuse and maintain public confidence, this data must be collected, stored, and processed in accordance with established ethical guidelines and data protection laws. Moreover, AI algorithms often require substantial computational power, which, depending on the energy source, can contribute to increased carbon emissions. Training large-scale models, particularly deep learning networks, requires significant energy consumption, raising concerns about the environmental impact of AI. Thus, developing energy-efficient AI techniques, such as more efficient algorithms or utilizing renewable energy for AI computations, is essential for mitigating the environmental footprint of AI systems [58].

REGULATORY AND POLICY CHALLENGES

A lack of standardized regulations and policies also hampers the integration of AI into energy systems. Many energy sectors operate in highly regulated environments, and the introduction of AI introduces new challenges for policymakers who must ensure that AI applications align with safety, reliability, and fairness standards. For example, AI-driven decisions regarding grid balancing or demand forecasting must comply with existing regulations related to grid security, resource allocation, and pricing. The lack of clear and unified regulatory frameworks may create uncertainties and legal hurdles for companies looking to deploy AI technologies. Policymakers will need to create comprehensive guidelines that address the ethical, technical, and operational aspects of AI in energy systems [59].

HUMAN FACTORS AND WORKFORCE IMPLICATIONS

The integration of AI into energy systems also raises human factors and workforce implications. The deployment of AI-driven systems may lead to job displacement or necessitate the acquisition of new skills by the existing workforce. In particular, skilled workers with expertise in traditional energy systems may need to adapt to new roles, focusing on managing AI systems, interpreting model outputs, and handling unforeseen issues that AI systems may not address. Concerns regarding an excessive dependence on automation and the possible loss of human oversight are also raised by the incorporation of AI into decision-making processes. A balanced and robust energy workforce depends on AI tools that enhance human judgment rather than replace it [60].

While AI holds enormous potential to revolutionize energy systems by optimizing performance, improving efficiency, and facilitating the transition to renewable energy sources, its successful implementation is fraught with challenges. Overcoming data quality issues, ensuring model interpretability, addressing scalability concerns, mitigating ethical and environmental risks, and navigating regulatory complexities are all essential for the future of AI in energy. By continuing to address these challenges, researchers and practitioners can unlock the full potential of AI to create more efficient, sustainable, and resilient energy systems worldwide [61].

FUTURE DIRECTIONS: SCALING AI FOR GLOBAL ENERGY SUSTAINABILITY

The emerging trends and technological advancements hold the potential to transform the application of AI in energy conversion and storage technologies. As the global demand for sustainable energy grows, the convergence of AI with advanced computational tools, materials science, and systems engineering offers promising pathways to address existing challenges and unlock new opportunities.

INTEGRATION OF AI WITH EMERGING TECHNOLOGIES

The integration of AI with cutting-edge technologies such as quantum computing, the Internet of Things (IoT), and 5G networks promises to revolutionize the energy sector.

Quantum Computing

Quantum computing can significantly enhance AI capabilities by solving optimization problems and performing high-dimensional calculations far more efficiently than classical computing. For instance, quantum algorithms can optimize energy grids, accelerate the discovery of materials or batteries, and enable faster simulations of energy storage systems [62].

Internet of Things (IoT)

IoT devices generate vast amounts of data from sensors in energy systems, including smart grids, solar panels, and wind turbines. AI can leverage this real-time data for predictive analytics, fault detection, and adaptive control, improving system reliability and efficiency [63].

5G Networks

High-speed 5G connectivity enhances the transmission of real-time data from IoT devices, enabling faster and more reliable AI-driven decision-making. This is crucial for applications such as dynamic energy management and decentralized energy systems [64].

FEDERATED LEARNING FOR ENERGY APPLICATIONS

Federated learning is a cutting-edge method of AI training in which several dispersed devices work together to develop a model without exchanging local input. This has significant implications for energy systems:

Enhanced Data Privacy

Federated learning enables AI model training without transferring sensitive energy data, addressing privacy concerns in smart grids and distributed energy systems [65, 66].

Collaboration Across Regions

This approach enables energy systems in different geographical areas to work together to improve AI models, thereby enhancing theireneralization and robustness [66].

Reduced Computational Costs

Federated learning reduces the computing load on centralized servers by distributing the training process across multiple devices, thereby enabling AI to be deployed by smaller energy operators [67].

ADVANCED AI ALGORITHMS FOR RENEWABLE ENERGY

Optimizing energy production and consumption will be greatly aided by the creation of more complex AI algorithms specifically designed for renewable energy applications.

Hybrid AI Models

Combining ML, DL, and reinforcement learning can lead to more accurate predictions and control strategies. For example, hybrid models can optimize wind farm performance by simultaneously analyzing weather data, turbine efficiency, and energy demand patterns [68].

Adaptive AI Systems

AI systems capable of self-learning and adaptation can improve their performance over time by incorporating new data and feedback. This is particularly useful in dynamic environments such as solar and wind energy systems [69].

DIGITAL TWIN TECHNOLOGIES

A game-changing tool in energy management is digital twin technology, which creates a virtual version of a physical energy system.

Predictive Analytics

Digital twins can simulate energy systems under various scenarios, enabling predictive analytics for maintenance, fault detection, and performance optimization.

System Optimization

Operators can reduce risks and expenses by testing various configurations and strategies in a virtual setting before implementing them in the real world, leveraging AI and digital twins.

Case Study Applications

Examples include the use of digital twins for optimizing solar panel layouts, enhancing wind turbine designs, and managing energy flow in hybrid systems [70, 71].

Fig. (**6**) presents a digital twin of a renewable energy system created using AI. The virtual model simulates real-time performance under varying conditions, offering predictive insights for maintenance and optimization. Digital twins enhance system reliability and efficiency, making them critical tools for managing dynamic energy systems sustainably.

AI-DRIVEN MATERIALS DISCOVERY

AI is set to revolutionize materials science by accelerating the discovery and optimization of materials for energy applications.

Battery Materials

ML algorithms can analyze vast datasets of material properties to identify candidates for high-performance battery electrodes and electrolytes. As a result, next-generation batteries with greater energy densities and longer lifespans are being developed more quickly [73].

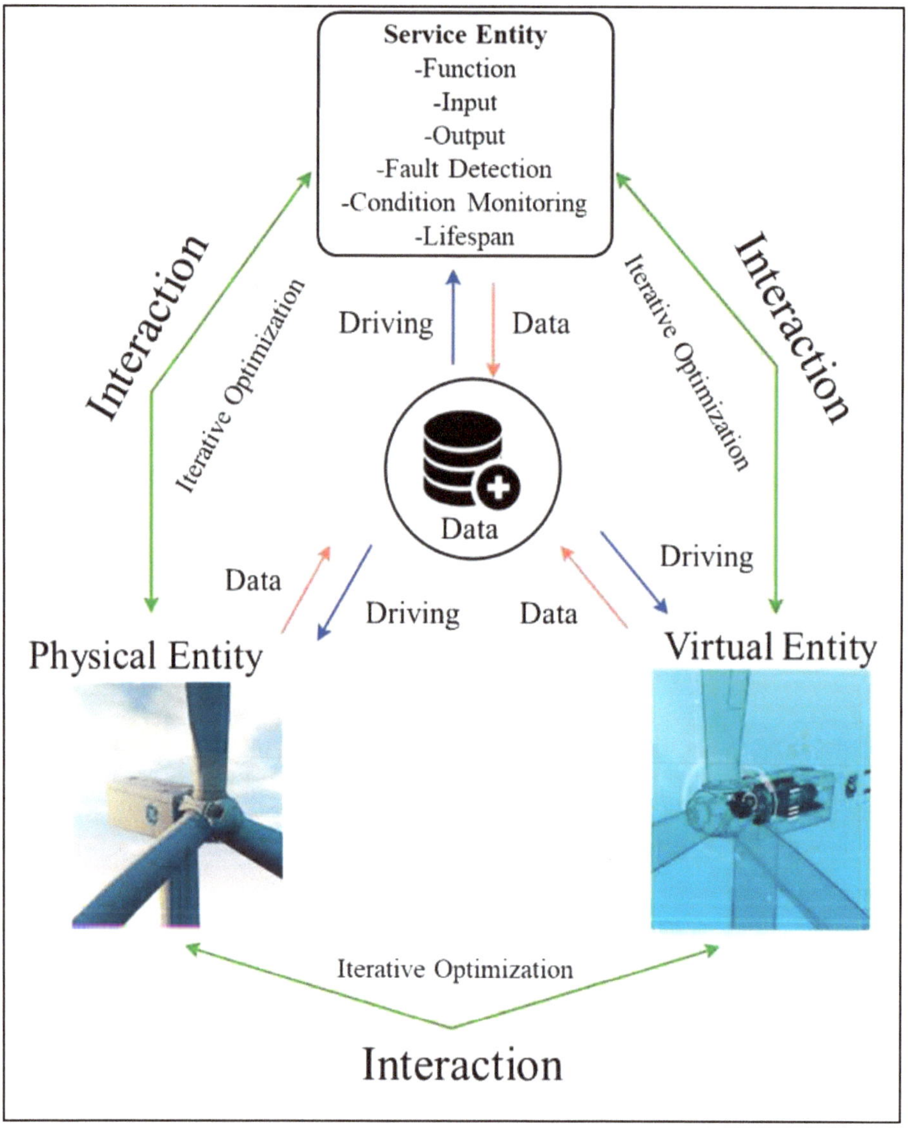

Fig. (6). Digital Twin Technology Enabled by AI for Predictive Energy System Management. Reprinted with permission from ref [72]. © 2023 by the authors. Licensee MDPI, Basel, Switzerland.

Catalyst Design

AI can optimize catalysts for hydrogen production, fuel cells, and other energy storage technologies by predicting their efficiency and stability under different conditions [74].

Thermal Energy Materials

Advanced algorithms can identify materials with superior thermal conductivity and stability for applications in thermal energy storage and conversion [75].

AI-ENHANCED ENERGY STORAGE SYSTEMS

AI will play a critical role in advancing energy storage technologies, which are vital for stabilizing renewable energy systems.

Smart Battery Management Systems

AI can optimize the charging and discharging cycles of batteries, extending their lifespan and improving energy efficiency. Predictive maintenance, utilizing AI algorithms, can detect and address issues before they lead to failure [76].

Hydrogen Storage Optimization

AI can model and simulate hydrogen storage systems, enabling the development of safer and more efficient storage solutions for fuel cell technologies [77].

Dynamic Energy Allocation

By integrating AI with energy storage systems, operators can dynamically allocate energy resources according to demand, thereby enhancing the reliability of renewable energy grids [78].

DECENTRALIZED ENERGY SYSTEMS

The shift toward decentralized energy systems, such as microgrids and peer-t--peer energy trading, is being accelerated by the use of AI.

Microgrid Optimization

AI algorithms can manage the energy flow within microgrids, ensuring optimal use of local renewable energy resources while maintaining grid stability [79].

Peer-to-Peer Energy Trading

Blockchain-powered AI systems enable secure and transparent energy trading between consumers and producers, creating decentralized energy markets [80].

Resilience in Disaster Scenarios

AI-driven decentralized systems can operate autonomously during natural disasters, ensuring continued energy supply to critical facilities [81].

AI FOR GRID MODERNIZATION

Modernizing electrical grids to accommodate increasing renewable energy penetration requires advanced AI-driven solutions.

Load Forecasting

AI models can accurately predict energy demandenabling more efficient grid operations and reducing energy waste [82].

Grid Stability

AI can identify and respond to grid disruptions by analyzing real-time data from sensors and IoT devices, thereby enhancg overall stability [83].

Renewable Integration

Through real-time supply and demand balancing, AI can help intermittent renewable energy sources integrate seamlessly into current systems [84].

ETHICAL AND SUSTAINABLE AI DEVELOPMENT

Future innovations in AI for energy systems must prioritize ethical and sustainable development.

Energy-Efficient AI Models

Developing AI algorithms with lower computational requirements can reduce the environmental impact of AI training and deployment.

Transparency and Accountability

Ensuring that AI systems are transparent and interpretable is critical for building trust and meeting regulatory requirements.

Equitable Access

Efforts should be made to ensure that AI technologies benefit all regions, including developing countries, to promote global energy equity.

COLLABORATION BETWEEN ACADEMIA, INDUSTRY, AND POLICY

Collaboration between academia, industry, and policymakers is vital for advancing the role of AI in energy conversion and storage technologies. Academic institutions are at the forefront of developing innovative AI algorithms and exploring their applications to address complex energy challenges. Industry stakeholders play a crucial role in adopting and scaling these solutions, investing in AI-driven technologies to optimize operations, enhance efficiency, and minimize environmental impacts. Policymakers, on the other hand, play a crucial role in creating a regulatory and economic framework that promotes responsible AI development and deployment. By providing incentives for sustainable practices and establishing guidelines to mitigate potential risks, governments can encourage widespread adoption of AI in energy systems. This tri-sector collaboration ensures that research and innovations are aligned with real-world needs, industry applications are informed by cutting-edge science, and policies promote equitable and ethical advancements in AI for a sustainable energy future.

CONCLUDING REMARKS

AI is revolutionizing the landscape of energy conversion and storage technologies, offering innovative solutions to the complex challenges of modern energy systems. This chapter has highlighted the transformative role of AI in optimizing energy processes, from improving the efficiency of renewable energy systems to extending the lifespan of energy storage devices. By leveraging advanced computational techniques, such as ML, DL, and neural networks, AI enables precise modeling, real-time diagnostics, and predictive analytics, thereby enhancing the overall performance, reliability, and scalability of sustainable energy systems. In energy conversion, AI-driven optimization of solar, wind, and bioenergy systems has demonstrated significant advancements in efficiency and reliability. For instance, AI algorithms accurately predict solar irradiance and wind patterns, enabling dynamic adjustments to system parameters and minimizing energy losses. Similarly, AI optimizes biomass conversion processes by identifying optimal operating conditions and feedstock properties, contributing to cleaner and more efficient energy production. The role of AI in energy storage technologies has been equally impactful. From accelerating the discovery of advanced materials for batteries to implementing predictive maintenance in Li-ion and solid-state batteries, AI has addressed critical issues related to capacity degradation, thermal stability, and system safety. AI-powered real-time diagnostics for fuel cells and supercapacitors further guarantee their scalability and dependability for a range of uses, such as grid-level storage and EVs. AI has also facilitated the integration of hybrid systems and smart grids with renewable energy sources, enabling dynamic energy management. By optimizing charging and discharging strategies, managing energy flows, and supporting decentralized energy systems, AI contributes to the stability and adaptability of energy networks, crucial for accommodating fluctuating renewable energy inputs. Despite these advancements, challenges remain in the widespread implementation of AI in energy systems. Data quality and availability, model generalization, and ethical considerations, such as the energy consumption of AI models, are critical areas that require attention. Continued collaboration between academia, industry, and policymakers will be essential to address these challenges and unlock the full potential of AI in energy applications.

ACKNOWLEDGEMENTS

I would like to sincerely thank my distinguished instructors and PhD Scholars for their invaluable advice, thought-provoking conversations, and unwavering support during the writing of this book chapter. Their guidance has significantly enhanced the quality of my work and refined my understanding of the subject. For creating a lively research environment and giving the tools required to complete this work, I am extremely grateful to Prof. Anand Srivastava, the Honorable Vice Chancellor of Netaji Subhas University of Technology.

REFERENCES

[1] A.N. Abdalla, M.S. Nazir, H. Tao, S. Cao, R. Ji, M. Jiang, and L. Yao, "Integration of energy storage system and renewable energy sources based on artificial intelligence: An overview", *J. Energy Storage,* vol. 40, p. 102811, 2021.
[http://dx.doi.org/10.1016/j.est.2021.102811]

[2] N. Kumar, and Prabhansu, "Artificial intelligence and machine learning applications in energy storage system: technology overview and perspectives", *Emerging Trends in Energy Storage Systems and Industrial Applications,* no. Jan, pp. 1-26, 2023.
[http://dx.doi.org/10.1016/B978-0-323-90521-3.00014-4]

[3] K. Chakrapani, T. Kavitha, M. Iqubal Safa, M. Kempanna, and B. Chakrapani, "Applications of artificial intelligence in intelligent combustion and energy storage technologies", *Applications of Big Data and Artificial Intelligence in Smart Energy Systems,* vol. 2, pp. 27-45, 2023.
[http://dx.doi.org/10.1201/9781003440864-2]

[4] T. Ahmad, H. Zhu, D. Zhang, R. Tariq, A. Bassam, F. Ullah, A.S. AlGhamdi, and S.S. Alshamrani, "Energetics Systems and artificial intelligence: Applications of industry 4.0", *Energy Rep.,* vol. 8, pp. 334-361, 2022.
[http://dx.doi.org/10.1016/j.egyr.2021.11.256]

[5] Maciej Serda, "The role of mechanical energy storage systems based on artificial intelligence techniques in future sustainable energy systems", *Int. J. Electr. Eng. Sustain.,* vol. 7, no. 1, pp. 01-31, 2023.
[http://dx.doi.org/10.2/JQUERY.MIN.JS]

[6] Won Shin, Jeongyun Han, Wonjong Rhee, "AI-assistance for predictive maintenance of renewable energy systems", *Energy.* Volume 221, 2021, 119775, ISSN 0360-5442.
[http://dx.doi.org/10.1016/j.energy.2021.119775]

[7] J.D. Rodríguez-García, J. Moreno-León, M. Román-González, and G. Robles, "Introducing artificial intelligence fundamentals with learning ML: Artificial intelligence made easy", *ACM International Conference Proceeding Series,* vol. vol. 3, 2020pp. 18-20
[http://dx.doi.org/10.1145/3434780.3436705]

[8] X. Wang, Y. Han, V.C.M. Leung, D. Niyato, X. Yan, and X. Chen, *Fundamentals of Artificial Intelligence.* Edge AI, 2020, pp. 33-47.
[http://dx.doi.org/10.1007/978-981-15-6186-3_3]

[9] Z. Waszczyszyn, *Fundamentals of Artificial Neural Networks.*, 1999, pp. 1-51.
[http://dx.doi.org/10.1007/978-3-7091-2484-0_1]

[10] J. Li, M.S. Herdem, J. Nathwani, and J.Z. Wen, "Methods and applications for artificial intelligence, big data, internet of things, and blockchain in smart energy management", *Energy and AI,* vol. 11, p. 100208, 2023. [http://dx.doi.org/10.1016/j.egyai.2022.100208]

[11] A. Energy, "Energy and AI citation for published version", *Energy AI,* vol. 1, p. 100002, 2020. [http://dx.doi.org/10.1016/j.egyai.2020.100002]

[12] N. M. Kumar, "Distributed energy resources and the application of AI, IoT, and blockchain in smart grids", *Energies,* vol. 13, no. 21, p. 5739, 2020. [http://dx.doi.org/10.3390/EN13215739]

[13] V. Melinda, T. Williams, J. Anderson, J.G. Davies, and C. Davis, "Enhancing waste-to-energy conversion efficiency and sustainability through advanced artificial intelligence integration", *International Transactions on Education Technology (ITEE),* vol. 2, no. 2, pp. 183-192, 2024. [ITEE]. [http://dx.doi.org/10.33050/itee.v2i2.597]

[14] M. Ashraf, M. Ayaz, M. Khan, S.F. Adil, W. Farooq, N. Ullah, and M. Nawaz Tahir, "Recent trends in sustainable solar energy conversion technologies: Mechanisms, prospects, and challenges", *Energy Fuels,* vol. 37, no. 9, pp. 6283-6301, 2023. [http://dx.doi.org/10.1021/acs.energyfuels.2c04077]

[15] A. Mohammad, and F. Mahjabeen, "Revolutionizing solar energy: The impact of artificial intelligence on photovoltaic systems", *International Journal of Multidisciplinary Sciences and Arts,* vol. 2, no. 3, 2023. [http://dx.doi.org/10.47709/ijmdsa.v2i1.2599]

[16] Y. Zhou, "Artificial intelligence in renewable systems for transformation towards intelligent buildings", *Energy and AI,* vol. 10, p. 100182, 2022. [http://dx.doi.org/10.1016/j.egyai.2022.100182]

[17] W.M. Shaban, A.E. Kabeel, M. El Hadi Attia, and F.M. Talaat, "Optimizing photovoltaic thermal solar systems efficiency through advanced artificial intelligence driven thermal management techniques", *Appl. Therm. Eng.,* vol. 247, p. 123029, 2024. [http://dx.doi.org/10.1016/j.applthermaleng.2024.123029]

[18] M. L. T. Zulu, R. P. Carpanen, and R. Tiako, "A comprehensive review: study of artificial intelligence optimization technique applications in a hybrid microgrid at times of fault outbreaks", *Energies,* vol. 16, no. 4, p. 1786, 2023. [http://dx.doi.org/10.3390/EN16041786]

[19] M.J. Sammar, M.A. Saeed, S.M. Mohsin, S.M.A. Akber, R. Bukhsh, M. Abazeed, and M. Ali, "Illuminating the future: A comprehensive review of AI-based solar irradiance prediction models", *IEEE Access,* vol. 12, pp. 114394-114415, 2024. [http://dx.doi.org/10.1109/ACCESS.2024.3402096]

[20] A.N. Akpolat, E. Dursun, and A.E. Kuzucuoglu, "AI-aided control of a power converter in wind energy conversion system", *Proceedings - 2020 Innovations in Intelligent Systems and Applications Conference, ASYU 2020,* Oct. 2020, doi: 10.1109/ASYU50717.2020.9259877. [http://dx.doi.org/10.1109/ASYU50717.2020.9259877]

[21] Z. Liu, Y. Sun, C. Xing, J. Liu, Y. He, Y. Zhou, and G. Zhang, "Artificial intelligence powered large-scale renewable integrations in multi-energy systems for carbon neutrality transition: Challenges and future perspectives", *Energy and AI,* vol. 10, p. 100195, 2022. [http://dx.doi.org/10.1016/j.egyai.2022.100195]

[22] M. Hamza Zafar, N. Mujeeb Khan, M. Mansoor, A. Feroz Mirza, S. Kumayl Raza Moosavi, and F. Sanfilippo, "Adaptive ML-based technique for renewable energy system power forecasting in hybrid PV-Wind farms power conversion systems", *Energy Convers. Manage.,* vol. 258, p. 115564, 2022. [http://dx.doi.org/10.1016/j.enconman.2022.115564]

[23] M.S.H. Lipu, M.S. Miah, M.A. Hannan, A. Hussain, M.R. Sarker, A. Ayob, M.H.M. Saad, and M.S. Mahmud, "Artificial intelligence based hybrid forecasting approaches for wind power generation: progress, challenges and prospects", *IEEE Access,* vol. 9, pp. 102460-102489, 2021. [http://dx.doi.org/10.1109/ACCESS.2021.3097102]

[24] A.D.A. Bin Abu Sofian, H.R. Lim, H. Siti Halimatul Munawaroh, Z. Ma, K.W. Chew, and P.L. Show, "Machine learning and the renewable energy revolution: Exploring solar and wind energy solutions for a sustainable future including innovations in energy storage", *Sustain. Dev. (Bradford),* vol. 32, no. 4, pp. 3953-3978, 2024. [http://dx.doi.org/10.1002/sd.2885]

[25] M. Liao, and Y. Yao, "Applications of artificial intelligence-based modeling for bioenergy systems: A review", *Glob. Change Biol. Bioenergy,* vol. 13, no. 5, pp. 774-802, 2021. [http://dx.doi.org/10.1111/gcbb.12816]

[26] L. Saju, D. Selvaraj, and T. Vairaperumal, "Artificial intelligence and machine intelligence: modeling and optimization of bioenergy production", *Computer Vision and Machine Intelligence for Renewable Energy Systems,* no. Jan, pp. 163-176, 2025. [http://dx.doi.org/10.1016/B978-0-443-28947-7.00009-4]

[27] M. Khan, "Applications of machine learning in thermochemical conversion of biomass-a review", *Fuel,* vol. 332, p. 126055, 2023. [http://dx.doi.org/10.1016/J.FUEL.2022.126055]

[28] A. Sakheta, R. Nayak, I. O'Hara, and J. Ramirez, "A review on modelling of thermochemical processing of biomass for biofuels and prospects of artificial intelligence-enhanced approaches", *Bioresour. Technol.,* vol. 386, p. 129490, 2023. [http://dx.doi.org/10.1016/j.biortech.2023.129490] [PMID: 37460019]

[29] N. Mehraj, C. Mateu, and L.F. Cabeza, "Use of artificial intelligence methods in designing thermal energy storage tanks: A bibliometric analysis", *J. Energy Storage,* vol. 97, p. 112794, 2024. [http://dx.doi.org/10.1016/j.est.2024.112794]

[30] A. Sai Ramesh, S. Vigneshwar, S. Vickram, S. Manikandan, R. Subbaiya, N. Karmegam, and W. Kim, "Artificial intelligence driven hydrogen and battery technologies – A review", *Fuel,* vol. 337, p. 126862, 2023. [http://dx.doi.org/10.1016/j.fuel.2022.126862]

[31] K. Liu, Z. Wei, C. Zhang, Y. Shang, R. Teodorescu, and Q. L. Han, "Towards long lifetime battery: AI-based manufacturing and management", *IEEE/CAA J. Autom. Sin.,* vol. 9, no. 7, pp. 1139-1165, 2022. [http://dx.doi.org/10.1109/JAS.2022.105599]

[32] G. Xu, M. Jiang, J. Li, X. Xuan, J. Li, T. Lu, and L. Pan, "Machine learning-accelerated discovery and design of electrode materials and electrolytes for lithium ion batteries", *Energy Storage Mater.,* vol. 72, p. 103710, 2024. [http://dx.doi.org/10.1016/j.ensm.2024.103710]

[33] C. Chen, D.T. Nguyen, S.J. Lee, N.A. Baker, A.S. Karakoti, L. Lauw, C. Owen, K.T. Mueller, B.A. Bilodeau, V. Murugesan, and M. Troyer, "Accelerating computational materials discovery with machine learning and cloud high-performance computing: from large-scale screening to experimental validation", *J. Am. Chem. Soc.,* vol. 146, no. 29, pp. 20009-20018, 2024. [http://dx.doi.org/10.1021/jacs.4c03849] [PMID: 38980280]

[34] M. Pooyandeh, and I. Sohn, "Smart lithium-ion battery monitoring in electric vehicles: an AI-empowered digital twin approach", *Mathematics,* vol. 11, no. 23, p. 4865, 2023. [http://dx.doi.org/10.3390/MATH11234865]

[35] G. Krishna, "Advanced battery management system enhancement using IoT and ML for predicting remaining useful life in Li-ion batteries", *Sci. Rep.,* vol. 14, no. 1, pp. 1-18, 2024. [http://dx.doi.org/10.1038/s41598-024-80719-1]

[36] V. Vakharia, M. Shah, P. Nair, H. Borade, P. Sahlot, and V. Wankhede, "Estimation of lithium-ion battery discharge capacity by integrating optimized explainable-AI and stacked LSTM model", *Batteries,* vol. 9, no. 2, p. 125, 2023. [http://dx.doi.org/10.3390/BATTERIES9020125]

[37] B. Ramasubramanian, R. P. Rao, V. Chellappan, and S. Ramakrishna, "Towards sustainable fuel cells and batteries with an AI perspective", *Sustainability,* vol. 14, no. 23, p. 16001, 2022. [http://dx.doi.org/10.3390/SU142316001]

[38] V. Mounica, and Y. P. Obulesu, "Hybrid power management strategy with fuel cell, battery, and supercapacitor for fuel economy in hybrid electric vehicle application", *Energies,* vol. 15, no. 12, p. 4185, 2022. [http://dx.doi.org/10.3390/EN15124185]

[39] H. Jondhle, A.B. Nandgaonkar, S. Nalbalwar, and S. Jondhle, "An artificial intelligence and improved optimization-based energy management system of battery-fuel cell-ultracapacitor in hybrid electric vehicles", *J. Energy Storage,* vol. 74, p. 109079, 2023. [http://dx.doi.org/10.1016/j.est.2023.109079]

[40] X. Liu, K. Fan, X. Huang, J. Ge, Y. Liu, and H. Kang, "Recent advances in artificial intelligence boosting materials design for electrochemical energy storage", *Chem. Eng. J.,* vol. 490, p. 151625, 2024. [http://dx.doi.org/10.1016/j.cej.2024.151625]

[41] M. Fayyazi, "Artificial intelligence/machine learning in energy management systems, control, and optimization of hydrogen fuel cell vehicles", *Sustainability,* vol. 15, no. 6, p. 5249, 2023. [http://dx.doi.org/10.3390/SU15065249]

[42] S. Naeem, A. Ali, K. Memon, M. Bavluwala, U.P. Shinde, and A.V. Patil, "A review of flexible high-performance supercapacitors for the internet of things (IoT) and artificial intelligence (ai) applications", *Energy and Thermofluids Engineering,* vol. 3, no. 2, pp. 1-9, 2023. [http://dx.doi.org/10.38208/ete.v3.734]

[43] I.A. Khan, M. Khaleghiabbasabadi, D. Silvestri, A.A. Mazari, S. Wacławek, B. Chahkandi, and M. Gheibi, "A scenario-based genetic algorithm for controlling supercapacitor aging and degradation in the industry 4.0 era", *Eng. Appl. Artif. Intell.,* vol. 133, p. 108015, 2024. [http://dx.doi.org/10.1016/j.engappai.2024.108015]

[44] A.K. Jabakumar, "Optimizing energy storage systems with AI-based control strategies", *Research Journal of Computer Systems and Engineering,* vol. 5, no. 1, pp. 95-105, 2024. [http://dx.doi.org/10.52710/rjcse.98]

[45] L. A. Yousef, H. Yousef, and L. Rocha-Meneses, "Artificial intelligence for management of variable renewable energy systems: a review of current status and future directions", *Energies,* vol. 16, no. 24, p. 8057, 2023. [http://dx.doi.org/10.3390/EN16248057]

[46] P. Biswas, A. Rashid, A. Biswas, M.A.A. Nasim, S. Chakraborty, K.D. Gupta, and R. George, "AI-driven approaches for optimizing power consumption: a comprehensive survey", *Discover Artificial Intelligence,* vol. 4, no. 1, p. 116, 2024. [http://dx.doi.org/10.1007/s44163-024-00211-7]

[47] A. R. Singh, R. S. Kumar, K. R. Madhavi, F. Alsaif, M. Bajaj, and I. Zaitsev, "Optimizing demand response and load balancing in smart EV charging networks using AI integrated blockchain framework", *Sci. Rep.,* vol. 14, no. 1, pp. 1-22, 2024. [http://dx.doi.org/10.1038/s41598-024-82257-2]

[48] D. M. T. E. Ali, V. Motuzienė, and R. Džiugaitė-Tumėnienė, "AI-driven innovations in building energy management systems: a review of potential applications and energy savings", *Energies,* vol. 17, no. 17, p. 4277, 2024. [http://dx.doi.org/10.3390/EN17174277]

[49] J.H. Cavalcanti, T. Kovacs, A. Ko, and K. Pocsarovszky, "Production system efficiency optimization through application of a hybrid artificial intelligence solution", *Int. J. Comput. Integrated Manuf.,* vol. 37, no. 6, pp. 790-807, 2024. [http://dx.doi.org/10.1080/0951192X.2023.2257661]

[50] T.M. Olatunde, A.C. Okwandu, D.O. Akande, and Z.Q. Sikhakhane, "Reviewing the role of artificial intelligence in energy efficiency optimization", *Engineering Science & Technology Journal,* vol. 5, no. 4, pp. 1243-1256, 2024. [http://dx.doi.org/10.51594/estj.v5i4.1015]

[51] A. Gangwal, A. Ansari, I. Ahmad, A.K. Azad, and W.M.A. Wan Sulaiman, "Current strategies to address data scarcity in artificial intelligence-based drug discovery: A comprehensive review", *Comput. Biol. Med.,* vol. 179, p. 108734, 2024. [http://dx.doi.org/10.1016/j.compbiomed.2024.108734] [PMID: 38964243]

[52] Z. Allal, H.N. Noura, O. Salman, and K. Chahine, "Machine learning solutions for renewable energy systems: Applications, challenges, limitations, and future directions", *J. Environ. Manage.,* vol. 354, p. 120392, 2024. [http://dx.doi.org/10.1016/j.jenvman.2024.120392] [PMID: 38387355]

[53] L. Baur, K. Ditschuneit, M. Schambach, C. Kaymakci, T. Wollmann, and A. Sauer, "Explainability and interpretability in electric load forecasting using machine learning techniques – a review", *Energy and AI,* vol. 16, p. 100358, 2024. [http://dx.doi.org/10.1016/j.egyai.2024.100358]

[54] K. Ukoba, K.O. Olatunji, E. Adeoye, T.C. Jen, and D.M. Madyira, "Optimizing renewable energy systems through artificial intelligence: Review and future prospects", *Energy Environ.,* vol. 35, no. 7, pp. 3833-3879, 2024. [http://dx.doi.org/10.1177/0958305X241256293]

[55] Y. Li, "Artificial intelligence-based methods for renewable power system operation", *Nat. Rev. Electr. Eng.,* vol. 1, no. 3, pp. 163-179, 2024. [http://dx.doi.org/10.1038/s44287-024-00018-9]

[56] M. Shoaei, Y. Noorollahi, A. Hajinezhad, and S.F. Moosavian, "A review of the applications of artificial intelligence in renewable energy systems: An approach-based study", *Energy Convers. Manage.,* vol. 306, p. 118207, 2024. [http://dx.doi.org/10.1016/j.enconman.2024.118207]

[57] S.S. Binyamin, S.A. Ben Slama, and B. Zafar, "Artificial intelligence-powered energy community management for developing renewable energy systems in smart homes", *Energy Strategy Reviews,* vol. 51, p. 101288, 2024. [http://dx.doi.org/10.1016/j.esr.2023.101288]

[58] V. Jain, and A. Mitra, *Ethical Implications of Artificial Intelligence in Promoting Sustainable Clean Energy Solutions,* pp. 96-118. [http://dx.doi.org/10.4018/979-8-3693-6567-0.CH006]

[59] S.R. Joshua, S. Park, and K. Kwon, "Knowledge-based modeling approach: A schematic design of artificial intelligence of things (AIoT) for hydrogen energy system", *2024 IEEE 14th Annual Computing and Communication Workshop and Conference, CCWC 2024,* pp. 235–241, 2024, doi: 10.1109/CCWC60891.2024.10427681. [http://dx.doi.org/10.1109/CCWC60891.2024.10427681]

[60] A. Khamaj, A.M. Ali, R. Saminathan, and S. M, "Human factors engineering simulated analysis in administrative, operational and maintenance loops of nuclear reactor control unit using artificial intelligence and machine learning techniques", *Heliyon,* vol. 10, no. 10, p. e30866, 2024. [http://dx.doi.org/10.1016/j.heliyon.2024.e30866] [PMID: 38770317]

[61] M. Peruzzini, A. Brunzini, and B. Hasanain, "The role of ergonomic and human factors in sustainable manufacturing: a review", *Machines,* vol. 12, no. 3, p. 159, 2024.

[http://dx.doi.org/10.3390/MACHINES12030159]

[62] P. Whig, R. Remala, K.R. Mudunuru, and S.J. Quraishi, *Integrating AI and Quantum Technologies for Sustainable Supply Chain Management,* pp. 267-283. [http://dx.doi.org/10.4018/979-8-3693-4107-0.CH018]

[63] F.A. Alijoyo, "AI-powered deep learning for sustainable industry 4.0 and internet of things: Enhancing energy management in smart buildings", *Alex. Eng. J.,* vol. 104, pp. 409-422, 2024. [http://dx.doi.org/10.1016/j.aej.2024.07.110]

[64] Z.A. Bhat, I.B. Sofi, and I.S. Masoodi, *Smart Energy-Saving Solutions Based on Artificial Intelligence and Other Emerging Technologies for 5G Wireless and Beyond Networks Communications*, 2024. [http://dx.doi.org/10.1007/978-981-99-8771-9_5]

[65] A. Kumar, Y. Yanamala, S. Suryadevara, V. Dinesh, and R. Kalli, "Balancing innovation and privacy: the intersection of data protection and artificial intelligence", *Int. J. Mach. Learn. Res. Cybersecur. Artif. Intell.,* p. 1, 2024.

[66] T. Jelinek, A. Bhave, N. Buchoud, M.M. Bühler, P. Glauner, O. Inderwildi, M. Kraft, C. Mok, K. Nübel, and A. Voss, "International collaboration: Mainstreaming artificial intelligence and cyberphysical systems for carbon neutrality", *IEEE Transactions on Industrial Cyber-Physical Systems,* vol. 2, pp. 26-34, 2024. [http://dx.doi.org/10.1109/TICPS.2024.3351624]

[67] A. Kristian, T. Sumarsan Goh, A. Ramadan, A. Erica, and S. Visiana Sihotang, "Application of AI in optimizing energy and resource management: Effectiveness of deep learning models", *International Transactions on Artificial Intelligence (ITALIC),* vol. 2, no. 2, pp. 99-105, 2024. [http://dx.doi.org/10.33050/italic.v2i2.530]

[68] B.N. Alhasnawi, S.M.M. Almutoki, F.F.K. Hussain, A. Harrison, B. Bazooyar, M. Zanker, and V. Bureš, "A new methodology for reducing carbon emissions using multi-renewable energy systems and artificial intelligence", *Sustain Cities Soc.,* vol. 114, p. 105721, 2024. [http://dx.doi.org/10.1016/j.scs.2024.105721]

[69] S. Saravanan, R. Khare, K. Umamaheswari, S. Khare, B. S. K. Gowda, and S. Boopathi, *AI and ML adaptive smart-grid energy management systems: exploring advanced innovations.,* pp. 166-196. [http://dx.doi.org/10.4018/978-1-6684-9214-7.CH006]

[70] F.B. Ismail, H. Al-Faiz, H. Hasini, A. Al-Bazi, and H.A. Kazem, "A comprehensive review of the dynamic applications of the digital twin technology across diverse energy sectors", *Energy Strategy Reviews,* vol. 52, p. 101334, 2024. [http://dx.doi.org/10.1016/j.esr.2024.101334]

[71] V.A. Arowoiya, R.C. Moehler, and Y. Fang, "Digital twin technology for thermal comfort and energy efficiency in buildings: A state-of-the-art and future directions", *Energy and Built Environment,* vol. 5, no. 5, pp. 641-656, 2024. [http://dx.doi.org/10.1016/j.enbenv.2023.05.004]

[72] M. Ibrahim, "Digital twin as a virtual sensor for wind turbine applications", *Energies,* vol. 16, no. 17, p. 6246, 2023. [http://dx.doi.org/10.3390/EN16176246]

[73] A. Zanoletti, A. Cornelio, E. Galli, M. Scaglia, A. Bonometti, A. Zacco, L.E. Depero, A. Gianoncelli, and E. Bontempi, "AI-driven identification of a novel malate structure from recycled lithium-ion batteries", *Environ. Res.,* vol. 267, p. 120709, 2025. [http://dx.doi.org/10.1016/j.envres.2024.120709] [PMID: 39733987]

[74] I.T. Bello, R. Taiwo, O.C. Esan, A.H. Adegoke, A.O. Ijaola, Z. Li, S. Zhao, C. Wang, Z. Shao, and M. Ni, "AI-enabled materials discovery for advanced ceramic electrochemical cells", *Energy and AI,* vol. 15, p. 100317, 2024. [http://dx.doi.org/10.1016/j.egyai.2023.100317]

[75] Y. Liu, O.C. Esan, Z. Pan, and L. An, "Machine learning for advanced energy materials", *Energy and AI,* vol. 3, p. 100049, 2021.
[http://dx.doi.org/10.1016/j.egyai.2021.100049]

[76] M. K. Farman, J. Nikhila, A. B. Sreeja, B. S. Roopa, K. Sahithi, and D. Gireesh Kumar, "AI-enhanced battery management systems for electric vehicles: advancing safety, performance, and longevity", *E3S Web Conf.,* vol. 591, p. 04001, 2024.
[http://dx.doi.org/10.1051/E3SCONF/202459104001]

[77] M.H. Elkholy, M. Elymany, S. Ueda, I.T. Halidou, H. Fedayi, and T. Senjyu, "Maximizing microgrid resilience: A two-stage AI-Enhanced system with an integrated backup system using a novel hybrid optimization algorithm", *J. Clean. Prod.,* vol. 446, p. 141281, 2024.
[http://dx.doi.org/10.1016/j.jclepro.2024.141281]

[78] T. Yuvaraj, K.R. Devabalaji, and M.K. Tangirala, "Optimal allocation of battery energy storage systems using artificial intelligence techniques", *Renewable Energy for Plug-In Electric Vehicles,* no. Jan, pp. 129-155, 2024.
[http://dx.doi.org/10.1016/B978-0-443-28955-2.00009-3]

[79] A. Mansour-Saatloo, Y. Pezhmani, M.A. Mirzaei, B. Mohammadi-Ivatloo, K. Zare, M. Marzband, and A. Anvari-Moghaddam, "Robust decentralized optimization of Multi-Microgrids integrated with Power-to-X technologies", *Appl. Energy,* vol. 304, p. 117635, 2021.
[http://dx.doi.org/10.1016/j.apenergy.2021.117635]

[80] T. AlSkaif, J.L. Crespo-Vazquez, M. Sekuloski, G. van Leeuwen, and J.P.S. Catalao, "Blockchain-based fully peer-to-peer energy trading strategies for residential energy systems", *IEEE Trans. Industr. Inform.,* vol. 18, no. 1, pp. 231-241, 2022.
[http://dx.doi.org/10.1109/TII.2021.3077008]

[81] H. Hafeznia, and B. Stojadinović, "Resilience-based decision support system for installing standalone solar energy systems to improve disaster resilience of rural communities", *Energy Strategy Reviews,* vol. 54, p. 101489, 2024.
[http://dx.doi.org/10.1016/j.esr.2024.101489]

[82] M. Ali, M. Khalid, and M.M. Gulzar, "Transforming the grid: AI, ML, renewable, storage, EVs, and prosumers", *Intelligent Learning Approaches for Renewable and Sustainable Energy,* no. Jan, pp. 3-30, 2024.
[http://dx.doi.org/10.1016/B978-0-443-15806-3.00001-2]

[83] N.D. Noviati, S.D. Maulina, and S. Smith, "Smart Grids: Integrating AI for Efficient Renewable Energy Utilization", *International Transactions on Artificial Intelligence (ITALIC),* vol. 3, no. 1, pp. 1-10, 2024.
[http://dx.doi.org/10.33050/italic.v3i1.644]

[84] M. Kiasari, M. Ghaffari, and H. H. Aly, "A comprehensive review of the current status of smart grid technologies for renewable energies integration and future trends: the role of machine learning and energy storage systems", *Energies,* vol. 17, no. 16, p. 4128, 2024.
[http://dx.doi.org/10.3390/EN17164128]

CHAPTER 5

AI-Driven Discovery and Modeling of Electrochemical Materials

Soumya Rai[1,*], Jahanvi Thakur[1], Anshi Pandey[1] and N. L. Singh[2]

[1] *Research Lab for Energy Systems, Department of Physics, Netaji Subhas University of Technology, Dwarka, New Delhi, India*

[2] *Department of Nanotechnology, Delhi Skill Entrepreneurship University, Dwarka, New Delhi, India*

Abstract: This chapter delves into the transformative role of Artificial Intelligence (AI) in accelerating the discovery and modeling of electrochemical materials, with a focus on enhancing their performance, sustainability, and industrial relevance. By leveraging AI techniques such as machine learning, deep learning, and reinforcement learning, researchers are addressing key challenges in material optimization, catalyst selection, and performance prediction. The chapter highlights how AI enables rapid screening, predictive modeling, and real-time adaptability, which are critical for advancing technologies such as hydrogen production, battery systems, and electrochemical sensors. Case studies from industry, including AI-integrated electrolyzers, flow battery management, and AI-guided catalyst platforms, illustrate real-world applications and the progression of technology readiness. Furthermore, the integration of AI innovations with the United Nations Sustainable Development Goals (SDGs) is discussed, including direct links to clean energy, climate action, and responsible production. Commercialization pathways, such as patent trends, startup ecosystems, and AI-as-a-Service (AIaaS) models, are examined to contextualize the industrial deployment of these innovations within the frameworks of Industry 4.0 and the hydrogen economy. Concluding insights underscore AI's growing role in shaping next-generation electrochemical systems through data-driven design, cross-sector collaboration, and sustainable innovation.

Keywords: AI optimization, Artificial intelligence, Battery optimization, Carbon emission, Deep learning, Electrochemical cells, Electrochemical reactors, Electrochemical sensors, Hydrogen production, Machine learning, Sustainable energy.

* **Corresponding author Soumya Rai:** Research Lab for Energy Systems, Department of Physics, Netaji Subhas University of Technology, Dwarka, New Delhi, India; E-mail: soumyarai.sr16@gmail.com

Shreya Sharma, Peeyush Phogat, Ranjana Jha & Sukhvir Singh (Eds.)

INTRODUCTION

Artificial Intelligence (AI) is transforming the design of electrochemical reactors and systems, offering innovative tools to address energy efficiency and sustainability needs. The integration of AI in electrochemical engineering enables optimized design, predictive maintenance, and enhanced control over critical parameters, which are essential for applications in sustainable energy [1]. This chapter examines the fundamental principles of AI-driven electrochemical system design, highlighting the potential for deep learning, machine learning, and data-driven optimization to enhance reactor performance. By reducing energy demands and enabling real-time adjustments, AI contributes to sustainable, efficient electrochemical solutions, with significant implications for industries striving to meet global energy goals.

Overview of AI in Electrochemical Design

The role of artificial intelligence in electrochemical system design is pivotal, bringing unprecedented advancements to both research and practical applications. Traditionally, designing electrochemical reactors, which are crucial in fields such as energy storage, environmental sensing, and chemical synthesis, has been based on iterative testing, empirical relationships, and direct human input. These approaches, however, often fall short in addressing the complex, multivariate relationships within the reactor environment, where factors such as temperature, pressure, and current density intricately affect performance [2]. AI-driven approaches, particularly Machine Learning (ML) and deep learning, enable the processing and analysis of vast datasets, which can reveal patterns and insights beyond the reach of traditional methods [3]. In reactor design, ML models can predict system behavior under varying conditions, allowing engineers to optimize materials, geometries, and operational settings more effectively [4]. Deep learning methods, such as artificial neural networks, can simulate intricate reaction kinetics and energy flows within the reactor, enabling the prediction of outcomes for specific design choices. By generating simulations at high speed, AI reduces the time and resources needed for experimentation [5]. AI's real-time data processing and adaptive learning capabilities also support continuous improvement in reactor operations. With predictive maintenance algorithms, electrochemical systems can detect potential faults before they become critical, extending the reactor's lifecycle and minimizing downtime [6]. AI can also respond to data from sensors in real-time, adjusting operational parameters to sustain optimal performance, which is particularly valuable in renewable energy applications where supply and demand fluctuate. Moreover, the rapid expansion of AI applications in this field is driven by the need for sustainable energy solutions. AI-optimized reactors play a crucial role in hydrogen production, battery systems, and carbon capture technologies, which are essential for reducing greenhouse gas emissions and transitioning to cleaner energy sources [7]. For example, AI-driven models can enhance the efficiency of hydrogen electrolyzers by precisely controlling factors such as temperature and electrolyte concentration, resulting in higher outputs with reduced energy consumption. The widespread application of AI in electrochemical design marks a paradigm shift in how engineers and scientists approach system optimization. As the field advances, AI is expected to continue driving more efficient, adaptable, and sustainable designs, making it an invaluable asset in the global effort to meet ambitious energy and environmental goals.

Sustainable Energy Goals and AI Innovations

In the context of global sustainability targets, artificial intelligence emerges as a powerful catalyst for innovation in electrochemical systems. Sustainable energy goals, as outlined by the United Nations' Sustainable Development Goals (SDGs), emphasize the importance of clean energy production, efficient resource use, and reducing carbon footprints [8]. Electrochemical systems, including batteries, fuel cells, and hydrogen electrolyzers, play a central role in achieving these goals. However, their traditional design and operational processes often entail energy losses and inefficiencies, which present obstacles to large-scale sustainable energy deployment. AI innovations help tackle these challenges by enabling real-time optimization and efficient design processes for electrochemical reactors. For example, AI algorithms can be applied to refine material selection and reactor configuration, two factors that significantly impact the sustainability of energy systems [9]. Materials optimized through AI-based predictive models can improve system durability and efficiency, which in turn minimizes waste and reduces the need for frequent replacements. Additionally, AI tools support researchers in developing new, sustainable materials by predicting their properties and potential reactions under various conditions, shortening development cycles and reducing resource expenditure.

These advancements directly support several UN SDGs, notably: SDG 7 (Affordable and Clean Energy), by enhancing the efficiency and scalability of clean energy systems; SDG 9 (Industry, Innovation, and Infrastructure), through the acceleration of innovation in electrochemical technologies; SDG 12 (Responsible Consumption and Production), by minimizing material waste and optimizing resource use; and SDG 13 (Climate Action), by enabling the development of low-emission technologies. By integrating AI into the design and operation of electrochemical systems, researchers and industries can align their innovations with global sustainability frameworks, contributing to long-term energy resilience and environmental protection.

Another critical aspect of AI's contribution to sustainable energy goals is its ability to enhance energy efficiency across electrochemical processes. In electrochemical energy storage and conversion systems, maintaining a balance between input and output energy is crucial. AI can continuously monitor and adjust operating conditions such as voltage, current density, and electrolyte concentration to maintain the highest possible efficiency under variable loads [10]. This adaptability is particularly beneficial for renewable energy applications, where intermittent energy sources, such as solar and wind, create fluctuating input conditions. AI innovations also facilitate the integration of carbon-reduction strategies in electrochemical systems. For instance, in carbon capture and utilization processes, AI-driven electrochemical systems can help optimize reaction conditions, maximizing carbon conversion while minimizing energy consumption [11]. By enhancing the efficiency of carbon capture technologies, AI facilitates the achievement of net-zero emissions targets, which are becoming increasingly critical in the fight against climate change. As AI technologies evolve, their role in promoting sustainable energy practices within electrochemical systems will expand. Machine learning, big data analytics, and predictive modeling offer promising avenues for reducing environmental impact and maximizing efficiency. Together, these AI-driven approaches not only support immediate sustainability goals but also contribute to a long-term transition toward cleaner, more resilient energy systems. In this regard, AI serves as both a transformative tool and an enabler of sustainable innovations within the electrochemical industry. To summarize the broader implications, Table **1** illustrates how various AI capabilities in electrochemical systems align with specific SDG targets and commercial outcomes, bridging scientific innovation with societal and industrial relevance.

Table 1. Alignment of AI capabilities in electrochemical systems with sustainable development goals (SDGs) and commercial benefits.

AI Capability	Electrochemical Application	Related SDG(s)	Commercial/Industrial Benefit
Predictive Modeling and Simulation	Material discovery (*e.g.*, catalysts, electrodes)	SDG 7: Affordable and Clean Energy SDG 9: Industry, Innovation and Infrastructure.	Faster innovation, reduced R and D costs.
Process Optimization	Electrolyser operation, battery cycling	SDG 12: Responsible Consumption and Production.	Improved efficiency, extended system lifespan
Predictive Maintenance	Flow batteries, fuel cells	SDG 13: Climate Action.	Reduced downtime, increased reliability

(Table 1) cont.....

AI Capability	Electrochemical Application	Related SDG(s)	Commercial/Industrial Benefit
AI-as-a-Service (AIaaS)	Cloud platforms for materials design	SDG 17: Partnerships for the Goals.	Accessible tools for SMEs/startups, scalability
Digital Twins and Real-time Monitoring	Smart grid integration, virtual power plants	SDG 11: Sustainable Cities and Communities.	Grid stability, renewable energy adoption
Patent Mapping and Market Prediction	Technology transfer, commercialization strategies	SDG 8: Decent Work and Economic Growth	Informed investment and licensing decisions

Key Objectives of AI-Driven Reactor Design

The primary objectives of integrating AI into electrochemical reactor design are to improve system efficiency, enhance sustainability, and facilitate adaptive, real-time control over processes. Achieving these objectives involves a combination of predictive modeling, process optimization, and material innovation—all essential to meet the demands of modern energy and environmental challenges [12]. First and foremost, AI enhances efficiency in reactor design by optimizing operational parameters that directly affect energy conversion rates, such as voltage, pressure, and temperature. Through machine learning, researchers can analyze historical data from multiple reactor systems, identifying the optimal set points for each variable to minimize energy losses and increase output. Deep learning algorithms, particularly neural networks, play a crucial role in simulating complex reaction kinetics within the reactor. These simulations enable engineers to anticipate the outcomes of various design choices, thereby reducing trial-and-error experimentation and conserving time and resources. Sustainability is another central objective, with AI playing a critical role in minimizing the environmental footprint of electrochemical reactors. AI models can optimize material selection to increase durability and reduce the need for resource-intensive replacements, thus lowering waste [13]. Furthermore, AI-driven innovations are being increasingly applied to the design of reactors capable of utilizing renewable or recyclable materials, aligning with the principles of circular economy practices. By optimizing the reactor design process, AI helps ensure that resources are used efficiently, reducing the system's overall environmental impact.

Another objective of AI-driven design is to enable real-time, adaptive control within electrochemical systems. Traditional reactors require periodic maintenance and manual adjustments to sustain optimal performance [14]. However, AI algorithms embedded within these systems enable autonomous decision-making, where the reactor can self-adjust based on real-time data from sensors. This adaptability is particularly useful in renewable energy applications, where fluctuations in input energy (such as solar or wind) can affect output consistency. By autonomously adjusting operational parameters to maintain efficiency, AI-driven reactors can effectively handle these variations. Additionally, AI's predictive capabilities facilitate preventive maintenance, extending the lifespan of electrochemical systems and reducing downtime. By analyzing trends in operational data, AI can identify signs of wear or potential issues before they lead to failures, prompting timely interventions. This predictive maintenance not only improves the reactor's longevity but also reduces the resources needed for repairs or replacements, contributing to sustainable operation. In summary, AI-driven reactor design prioritizes efficiency, sustainability, and adaptability, positioning AI as a vital tool in addressing modern energy challenges. By meeting these objectives, AI empowers electrochemical reactors to support cleaner, more resilient energy systems, aligned with today's sustainable energy targets.

FUNDAMENTALS OF ELECTROCHEMICAL REACTORS AND SYSTEMS

Electrochemical reactors are vital components in processes where chemical energy is converted into electrical energy and vice versa, providing sustainable solutions for industries such as energy storage, fuel cells, hydrogen production, and wastewater treatment [15]. Electrochemical reactors typically consist of an electrolyte, electrodes, and an external power source to drive the reaction. In these systems, the chemical reactions occur at the electrode-electrolyte interface, and the efficient management of reactants, products, and heat is essential for maintaining stable operation and maximizing reaction efficiency. Two primary configurations of electrochemical reactors are the batch reactor and the continuous-flow reactor [16]. Batch reactors are commonly used in laboratory settings and applications where flexibility and control over reaction conditions are essential. Continuous-flow reactors, on the other hand, are favored for large-scale industrial processes due to their ability to operate steadily and for prolonged periods [17]. However, both types present unique challenges in terms of energy efficiency, scalability, and the consistent quality of electrochemical products. Traditional design methods for electrochemical reactors are often limited by the complexity of electrochemical reactions and their high sensitivity to operating parameters. Advances in Artificial Intelligence (AI) have recently provided promising solutions to these challenges, optimizing reactor performance and contributing to more sustainable process designs.

Types and Operating Principles of Electrochemical Reactors

Electrochemical reactors come in various designs, each tailored to meet specific operational and functional requirements. The most common types are batch reactors and continuous-flow reactors, which serve as foundational models for laboratory experiments and industrial-scale applications, respectively [18]. Batch reactors operate by processing a fixed quantity of reactant within a confined space, allowing for precise control over reaction conditions such as concentration, temperature, and reaction time. These reactors are well-suited for research and development because they enable detailed observation and manipulation of variables within a closed environment, making them ideal for small-scale production or experimental analysis. Continuous-flow reactors, in contrast, allow for a constant input of reactants and an uninterrupted output of products, enabling uninterrupted reaction processes. Due to their high throughput and efficiency, continuous-flow reactors are widely used in industrial settings where consistent and large-scale production is necessary [19]. In these reactors, the reactants flow through a series of electrodes, where they undergo controlled electrochemical transformations, making them highly efficient for processes such as electrolysis, fuel cell reactions, and large-scale chemical synthesis. The continuous nature of these reactors makes them inherently suitable for scalable, industrial applications, though the requirement for constant monitoring and precise parameter control can make their operation challenging.

In both types, electrodes play a crucial role, serving as sites for oxidation and reduction reactions, while the electrolyte facilitates the movement of ions to sustain these reactions. The choice of electrode material, electrolyte composition, and operational parameters such as temperature and current density directly impact reactor efficiency and the quality of the end products. Recent advancements in AI have enabled enhanced optimization of these factors, helping to overcome limitations in traditional design by automating adjustments based on real-time data, predicting optimal conditions, and minimizing energy wastage in both batch and continuous-flow reactors.

Batch and Continuous-Flow Reactors

The complex nature of continuously operated reactors makes their management more challenging and necessitates sophisticated control systems to handle variations. Batch reactors and continuous-flow reactors are fundamental to electrochemical processing, each serving distinct purposes and offering unique advantages in specific contexts. As industries seek efficient, high-output production methods, continuous-flow reactors are often integrated with AI-driven technologies to enhance performance. AI algorithms can process real-time data from sensors to predict optimal operating conditions, detect anomalies, and make automated adjustments, enabling continuous reactors to operate more efficiently and reliably in high-demand settings [20]. Thus, while batch reactors remain crucial for exploratory work, continuous-flow reactors have become indispensable in industrial applications, especially when enhanced with AI technologies. Here is an overview of the two major types of electrochemical reactors:

a. **Batch Reactors:** Batch reactors operate by introducing a fixed quantity of reactants into a closed container where the reaction proceeds until completion. This setup enables precise control over reaction variables, such as reactant concentration, temperature, and pressure, making batch reactors highly suitable for laboratory experimentation and processes that require fine-tuned reaction conditions [21]. Commonly used in research and small-scale production, batch reactors enable scientists to closely monitor reaction kinetics, facilitating adjustments to maximize yields and study new materials. Additionally, the closed nature of batch reactors minimizes the influence of external factors, leading to high repeatability in experimental settings. However, batch reactors have limitations, particularly in terms of scalability and efficiency. Processing one batch at a time inherently restricts production capacity and introduces periods of downtime during cleaning, refilling, and preparatory steps. Moreover, batch reactors can struggle with heat management, as exothermic reactions can lead to local temperature spikes that require careful regulation to avoid inconsistent product quality or safety risks. Despite these challenges, batch reactors remain invaluable in Research and Development due to their adaptability and control over reaction parameters. Fig. (**1**) depicts a labelled schematic of a batch reactor for specific purposes.
b. **Continuous-flow Reactors:** Continuous-flow reactors differ fundamentally in that reactants are introduced and products removed on an ongoing basis, facilitating a constant reaction process. These reactors are optimized for large-scale production and are a common choice for industrial electrochemical processes, such as fuel cell reactions, hydrogen production, and large-volume chemical synthesis [23]. Continuous-flow reactors allow for steady-state operation, meaning that reactions can be conducted at a consistent rate without interruption, thereby maximizing throughput and minimizing downtime. The design of continuous-flow reactors as illustrated in Fig. (**2**) also enhances thermal and mass transfer, as the constant flow facilitates even distribution of reactants and heat, promoting reaction efficiency [24]. However, continuous-flow reactors require rigorous parameter monitoring and control, as deviations in temperature, flow rate, or reactant concentration can quickly impact overall process stability and product quality.

Operating Limitations and Challenges

The operation of electrochemical reactors, whether batch or continuous-flow, presents several limitations and challenges, especially when aiming for efficient and sustainable production.

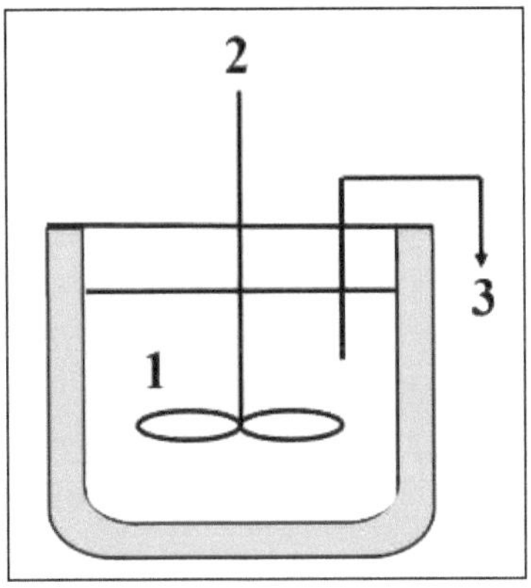

Fig. (1). Schematic of a Batch Reactor for Controlled Laboratory Reactions and Small-Scale Production, having: Stirrer **(1)** Ensures uniform mixing of reactants, Electrode/Probe **(2)** Monitors and controls key parameters such as pH, temperature, or potential within the reactor, Outlet/Flow Path **(3)** Facilitates the removal of products. Reprinted from [22] Copyright © 2021 Wiley Online Library.

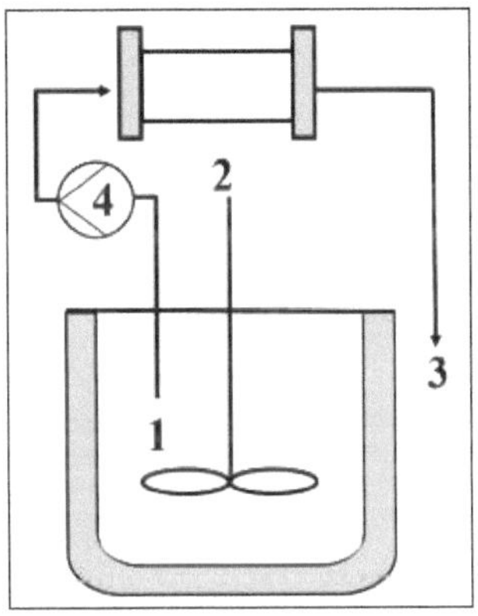

Fig. (2). Electrochemical reactor setup illustrating key components: a stirrer **(1)** for consistent mixing, electrode setup **(2)** for electrochemical processes, flow path **(3)** for guiding reactants, and a pump **(4)** to control fluid flow within the reaction chamber. This configuration supports precise and efficient electrochemical reactions within the reactor. Reprinted from [22] Copyright © 2021 Wiley Online Library.

a. **Scalability and Cost:** One of the primary challenges is scaling electrochemical processes from laboratory settings to industrial production. Batch reactors, for example, are challenging to scale due to their inherent operational constraints, which limit the processing volume and necessitate periodic shutdowns [25]. Continuous-flow reactors, although more scalable, require significant capital investment in equipment, as well as comprehensive monitoring and control systems to ensure operational stability [26].
b. **Thermal Management**: In electrochemical processes, temperature plays a critical role in determining reaction rates and product quality. Batch reactors often experience local temperature spikes, especially in exothermic reactions,

which can lead to inconsistent product quality if not effectively managed [27]. Continuous-flow reactors mitigate some thermal issues due to the constant flow of reactants, which distributes heat more evenly throughout the system. However, managing thermal loads remains complex and necessitates the use of advanced cooling and control systems to prevent overheating or thermal runaway.

c. **Energy Efficiency**: Electrochemical processes are inherently energy-intensive, and optimizing energy consumption is essential for sustainable operation [28]. While continuous-flow reactors can offer better energy efficiency due to steady-state operation, they require sophisticated energy management strategies to minimize waste. Batch reactors, on the other hand, often suffer from efficiency losses associated with the downtime required for cleaning and refilling.
d. **Control of Reaction Conditions**: Achieving consistent reaction conditions is crucial for high-quality electrochemical production. In batch reactors, even small variations in initial reactant concentrations or temperature can have a significant impact on the final product. Continuous-flow reactors offer more control but require precise monitoring of parameters and rapid adjustments to accommodate fluctuations in flow rates or reactant properties. This complexity can lead to operational challenges that impact reactor reliability.
e. **Environmental Impact and Waste Management**: Electrochemical reactors generate byproducts, some of which can be hazardous or require further processing. Batch reactors, due to their limited scale, are generally easier to clean and manage waste for, but they produce waste in smaller, less predictable quantities. Continuous-flow reactors generate larger amounts of waste that must be efficiently managed to comply with environmental regulations, adding complexity to operational oversight [29].

Comparison of Conventional and AI-Enhanced Design

The design of electrochemical reactors has traditionally been based on empirical knowledge and incremental improvements. Conventional approaches rely on established principles of chemistry, materials science, and engineering to optimize parameters such as electrode material, electrolyte composition, and temperature settings. However, these approaches can be limited by the complexity of electrochemical reactions, the numerous variables involved, and the dynamic nature of industrial applications.

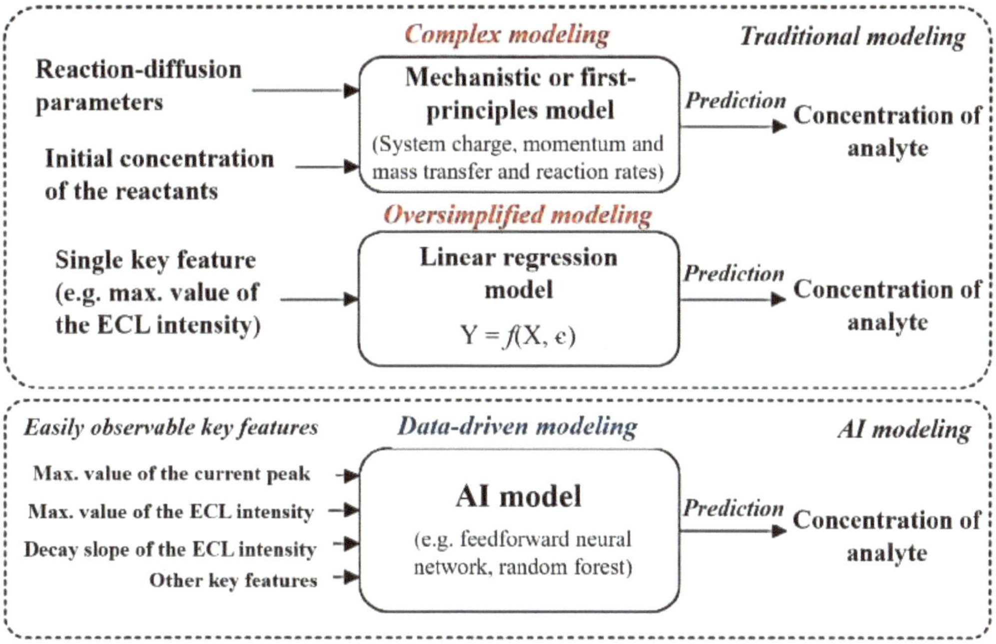

Fig. (3). Flowchart depicting the comparison of traditional and artificial intelligence (AI) modeling in the estimation of the analyte concentration. Reprinted from [30] Copyright © 1996-2024 MDPI (Basel, Switzerland).

In conventional electrochemical reactor design, as depicted in Fig. (**3**), engineers optimize each parameter manually, typically through extensive trial-and-error experimentation or by following well-established models. While effective for certain applications, this method can be time-consuming, resource-intensive, and lacking in flexibility. Moreover, conventional design often struggles to adapt to fluctuations in operating conditions or unexpected changes, which can hinder efficiency and limit scalability. Energy efficiency is often suboptimal in these systems, and maintaining consistency across large production volumes can be challenging. The integration of AI into reactor design represents a paradigm shift, enabling data-driven optimization and adaptive control [31]. AI systems utilize large datasets and sophisticated algorithms to analyze multiple parameters simultaneously and identify patterns that may not be obvious through traditional methods. Machine learning models, for instance, can predict optimal reaction conditions, reducing the need for extensive manual calibration. By continuously analyzing real-time data, AI systems can also detect anomalies early and make automated adjustments, improving both safety and efficiency. Below is a concise tabular comparison of conventional designs *versus* AI-enhanced designs across various parameters given in Table **2**.

Table 2. Comparison of conventional designs *versus* AI-enhanced designs of electrochemical reactors across various parameters.

Parameter	Conventional Design	AI-enhanced Design
Speed of Optimization	Rapid optimization is enabled by machine learning, processing large data sets to find optimal settings in real-time.	A slow, iterative testing process that is inefficient, especially when multiple variables are adjusted.
Flexibility and Adaptability	Highly adaptable, dynamically adjusting to changes in feedstock composition, flow rates, and temperature.	Limited adaptability; struggles to maintain stability with fluctuations in operating conditions.
Energy and Resource Efficiency	Optimizes energy use by adjusting parameters based on real-time data, minimizing wastage.	Operates within a fixed parameter range, often resulting in inefficiencies when conditions vary.
Predictive Maintenance and Safety	Provides predictive maintenance, reducing downtime and enhancing safety by anticipating potential failures.	Relies on scheduled maintenance and may experience unexpected breakdowns due to a lack of predictive capability.
Scalability and Consistency	Relies on scheduled maintenance and may experience unexpected breakdowns due to a lack of predictive capability.	Effective at smaller scales but requires extensive recalibration and testing for larger, high-demand setups.

AI TECHNIQUES FOR REACTOR DESIGN AND SIMULATION

The application of AI in reactor design and simulation is transforming how electrochemical systems are engineered and optimized. Leveraging advanced algorithms, AI enables the design of reactors that meet complex specifications and enhances system efficiency. AI-driven methods, such as Machine Learning (ML), Deep Learning (DL), and Reinforcement Learning (RL), each bring unique capabilities to reactor design [32]. Machine learning algorithms predict critical properties and optimize operational parameters, enhancing predictive capabilities and fine-tuning reactor performance for diverse applications. Deep learning techniques offer high-fidelity simulations for reaction kinetics and structural analysis, enabling more precise modeling of complex electrochemical reactions. Finally, reinforcement learning introduces adaptability into system design by allowing the reactor to learn from continuous feedback, adjusting in real-time for optimal performance [33]. These AI techniques help address limitations in traditional reactor design, such as the trial-and-error approach and limited predictive accuracy. Through AI, electrochemical reactors can achieve enhanced precision, energy efficiency, and operational resilience, aligning with the demands of modern sustainable energy solutions. Furthermore, by combining these AI methodologies, electrochemical systems can be designed and simulated with a degree of accuracy and functionality that traditional models cannot achieve, thereby revolutionizing the development of reactors for sustainable energy applications.

Machine Learning for Predictive Design Optimization

Machine Learning (ML) has emerged as a key tool for optimizing the design and performance of electrochemical reactors, allowing for precise predictions and proactive adjustments to process parameters. In electrochemical systems, the variability of parameters like temperature, pressure, pH, and electrolyte concentration can significantly impact efficiency and output. ML algorithms, such as regression models, classification algorithms, and clustering techniques, excel at analyzing large datasets to detect patterns and relationships among these variables, helping predict optimal conditions for enhanced performance [34]. Predictive design optimization through ML extends to selecting suitable materials for reactor components, such as catalysts, electrodes, and electrolytes. Algorithms can analyze extensive datasets to identify materials with desirable properties, such as high conductivity, durability, or cost-effectiveness, which aids in developing reactors with increased efficiency and reduced operational costs. By processing historical and real-time data, ML can detect correlations between input variables and outcomes, forecasting how alterations in operating conditions may influence system performance. In practice, ML-based predictive models have enhanced efficiency in various electrochemical systems, including fuel cells, batteries, and hydrogen production reactors [35]. For instance, ML models have been used to predict degradation rates in battery electrodes, optimizing operational settings to prolong lifespan. Additionally, ML enables real-time optimization by providing continuous updates on system status, allowing operators to adjust parameters on the fly for consistent performance. Thus, ML fosters a data-driven approach to reactor design and process control, making electrochemical reactors more adaptable, efficient, and aligned with sustainability objectives.

Property Prediction and Process Optimization

Machine learning has become instrumental in property prediction and process optimization for electrochemical reactors. Predicting material properties, such as conductivity, stability, and reaction rates, is fundamental in selecting materials that suit specific electrochemical processes. ML algorithms utilize historical data to analyze material behavior under varied conditions, enabling more accurate predictions about how these properties will influence reactor performance. For example, regression models can predict properties such as ionic conductivity or charge transfer resistance based on input features, providing critical insights into the suitability of a material for a given application. Beyond material properties, ML excels in process optimization, which involves fine-tuning operational parameters to maximize reactor efficiency. Parameters such as temperature, pressure, voltage, and electrolyte concentration have a direct impact on electrochemical reaction rates, energy consumption, and product yield. ML models can analyze correlations between these parameters and reactor performance, optimizing conditions to achieve the desired outcomes. By incorporating extensive datasets, algorithms can predict how minor adjustments to process variables will impact efficiency, enabling dynamic and precise control over reactor operations. Process optimization also benefits from unsupervised ML methods like clustering, which groups data points based on similarities to reveal hidden patterns and insights. Clustering can identify operational states associated with optimal or suboptimal performance, guiding operators toward effective process configurations. For instance, in hydrogen production reactors, clustering may identify distinct operating conditions that maximize hydrogen yield while minimizing energy input. Additionally, ML-based optimization enhances scalability by automating routine adjustments, enabling systems to maintain high efficiency without constant human intervention. This capability is especially valuable in industrial settings where reactors operate continuously, and real-time adjustments are necessary for consistent performance. Reinforcement learning, a subset of ML, is increasingly applied here to create adaptive models that respond dynamically to changes in process conditions, ensuring steady output despite fluctuations. Finally, property prediction and process optimization through ML support sustainability objectives by enabling energy-efficient reactor operation and reducing material waste. Algorithms can identify operating parameters that minimize energy consumption and extend the lifetime of reactor components, lowering the overall environmental footprint of electrochemical processes. In doing so, ML facilitates the development of reactors that are both economically and environmentally sustainable, paving the way for AI-enhanced electrochemical systems that meet today's energy demands [36].

Predictive analysis involves eight steps, as shown in Fig. (**4**). The first step is to clearly define the objectives and understand the specific predictions required, which ensures alignment with business or research goals. Next, gather relevant data from credible sources and thoroughly clean and preprocess it. This data preparation step involves managing missing values, normalizing variables, and splitting the data into training and testing sets to prevent overfitting. Following this, perform Exploratory Data Analysis (EDA) to identify underlying patterns, relationships, and trends, which help in selecting meaningful features. With insights from EDA, engage in feature engineering by creating new variables or transforming existing ones to enhance the predictive power of the model. Once the data is prepared, select an appropriate algorithm based on the problem type, such as linear regression for continuous data or decision trees for classification. Train the model on the training dataset, optimizing its parameters to improve accuracy and performance. After training, evaluate the model's effectiveness using validation metrics such as accuracy, precision, and recall, ensuring that it generalizes well to unseen data. Finally, deploy the model in a real-world setting and monitor its performance, updating it periodically as data patterns evolve to maintain predictive accuracy. This cyclical approach ensures continuous improvement in prediction quality [37].

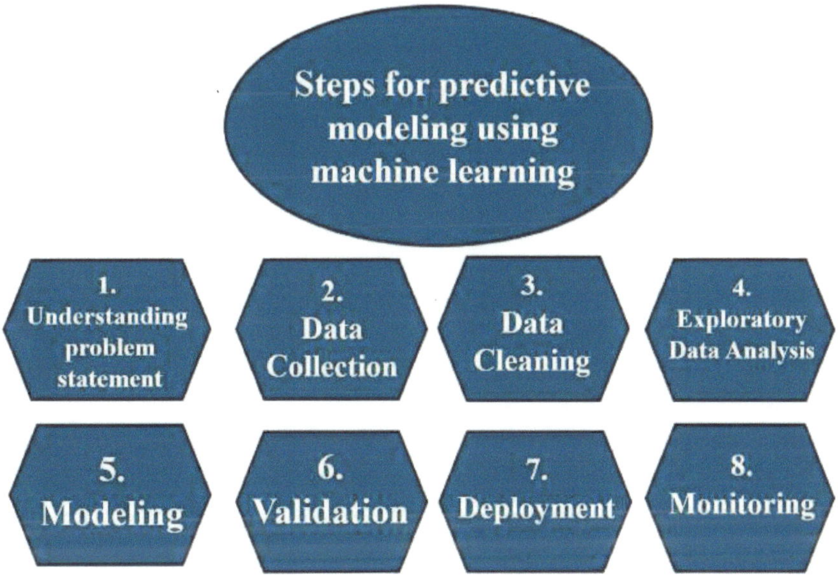

Fig. (4). An overview of the predictive analysis process, illustrating the eight essential steps: defining objectives, collecting data, data cleaning and preprocessing, exploratory data analysis, feature engineering, model selection, training and evaluation, and deployment with continuous monitoring. This structured approach enables accurate forecasting by leveraging historical data, refining model performance, and ensuring adaptability over time.

Operating Limitations and Challenges

While machine learning offers promising advancements in optimizing electrochemical reactors, several operating limitations and challenges must be addressed to harness its potential fully. One of the primary challenges is the quality and availability of data required to train accurate ML models. Electrochemical systems often involve complex reactions influenced by numerous variables, and collecting comprehensive datasets that cover the full range of operating conditions can be challenging. Inadequate data can lead to inaccurate predictions, limiting the reliability of ML-driven optimizations. Another challenge is the interpretability of machine learning models. Many ML algorithms, particularly deep learning models, function as "black boxes," making it difficult to understand how input features are transformed into predictions [38]. This lack of transparency can hinder the adoption of ML in reactor design, as operators may be reluctant to rely on models they cannot fully understand or justify. Developing interpretable models or integrating explainable AI techniques is crucial to gaining user trust in ML-driven optimizations. Model generalizability is another limitation, as ML models trained on specific datasets may not perform accurately when applied to different reactors or conditions. Variability in operating environments, such as fluctuations in temperature or humidity, can affect the applicability of models across settings [39]. Ensuring that ML models are adaptable to various reactor types and conditions is essential for scaling their use in industrial applications. Transfer learning, where models trained on one dataset are fine-tuned for a new, related dataset, is a potential solution, though it requires careful implementation. The integration of ML into reactor control systems also presents technical challenges, including latency in data processing and response. Real-time optimization relies on the rapid analysis of data and the adjustment of reactor parameters; however, delays in data processing can reduce the effectiveness of ML-driven adjustments. Additionally, the computational resources required for real-time ML processing may be prohibitive in some applications, especially those with limited budgets or stringent energy constraints. Finally, the deployment of ML models for reactor optimization raises concerns regarding security and privacy. In industrial settings, sensitive operational data must be protected from unauthorized access, especially if models rely on cloud-based data storage and processing. Robust cybersecurity measures are needed to safeguard data integrity and protect proprietary information. Addressing these limitations will be essential to leverage ML for reactor design and optimization. As data quality improves and techniques for model interpretability, generalizability, and security evolve, ML's role in optimizing electrochemical reactors will continue to expand, unlocking new potential for sustainable energy solutions.

Deep Learning for Reaction Kinetics and Structural Simulation

Deep Learning (DL) represents an advanced branch of machine learning distinguished by its ability to process complex, high-dimensional data through neural networks with multiple layers. In the field of electrochemical reactor design, DL techniques have shown great promise for simulating reaction kinetics and structural properties with a high degree of precision. Fig. (**5**) illustrates a diagram that depicts the relationships among Artificial Intelligence (AI), Machine Learning (ML), Neural Networks (NN), and Deep Learning (DL). Reaction kinetics, which govern the rate at which reactions occur within electrochemical systems, are fundamental to optimizing reactor performance. DL models, particularly Convolutional Neural Networks (CNNs) and Recurrent Neural Networks (RNNs) [40], offer powerful capabilities for modeling these intricate reaction pathways, analyzing data on reactant concentration, temperature, and pressure to forecast reaction rates under various conditions. Structural simulation is another critical area where DL excels, especially when simulating complex electrode and electrolyte structures. CNNs, often used in image processing, can be applied to structural modeling by analyzing data from techniques like X-ray diffraction or scanning electron microscopy [41]. This approach enables DL models to simulate microstructural changes within reactor components, such as electrode degradation over time or electrolyte dissolution, which directly impact reactor efficiency and longevity. By understanding these structural changes, operators can make proactive adjustments to enhance performance and extend the lifespan of reactor components. Another notable DL application is in the optimization of heterogeneous catalytic reactions. Many electrochemical processes involve catalysts that facilitate reactions at the electrode interface. DL models can analyze massive datasets on catalyst morphology, surface area, and particle size to predict optimal catalyst configurations for specific reactions. This insight allows for the design of reactors that maximize reaction rates while minimizing material costs. Deep Reinforcement Learning (DRL), a combination of DL and reinforcement learning, is emerging as a promising tool for simulating and optimizing electrochemical systems. DRL algorithms can be trained to navigate complex decision-making spaces, adjusting variables like current density, temperature, and pH in response to changing conditions [42]. In fuel cells, for instance, DRL has been employed to adjust operating parameters, maintaining high efficiency even as cell conditions vary. The application of DL in electrochemical systems is still in its early stages, but its potential for improving reactor design is immense. By providing detailed insights into reaction kinetics and structural behavior, DL-based simulations help identify optimal operating conditions and anticipate potential issues before they arise. Additionally, DL models are increasingly being integrated with real-time monitoring systems, enabling continuous updates to reactor parameters based on current conditions. This adaptability makes DL an invaluable asset in achieving sustainable and efficient reactor designs.

Neural Networks for Kinetics

Neural Networks (NNs) are increasingly used to model reaction kinetics in electrochemical systems, offering a powerful approach to understanding and predicting the speed of chemical reactions under varying conditions. Reaction kinetics, the study of reaction rates and their dependence on parameters like temperature, pressure, concentration, and catalyst presence, is crucial in optimizing electrochemical processes. Traditional methods often require extensive experimentation or complex analytical modeling, which can be time-consuming and prone to limitations in accuracy. In contrast, neural networks excel in handling large datasets and capturing complex, non-linear relationships, making them ideal for modeling intricate reaction pathways. One of the primary applications of neural networks in kinetics is the ability to analyze time-series data from electrochemical reactions. For instance, Recurrent Neural Networks (RNNs), which are particularly suited for sequential data, can model how reaction rates change over time in response to adjustments in parameters [44]. RNNs capture dependencies between different reaction stages, providing valuable insights into the evolution of reactions as they progress, which is critical for optimizing both reaction rates and product yield. Convolutional Neural Networks (CNNs), typically used for image processing, have also been adapted to model kinetics, particularly by interpreting structural information about catalysts and reactants. CNNs analyze input data such as electrode surface morphology or catalyst shape to identify features that influence reaction rates [45]. This capability is particularly beneficial in systems where surface reactions play a significant role, as it provides a deeper understanding of how surface characteristics influence reaction dynamics, which can be leveraged to optimize electrode and catalyst design. A notable advantage of neural networks is their ability to learn and adapt continuously. Through feedback loops, NNs can be trained with real-time data from ongoing processes, allowing them to adjust predictions and improve accuracy continuously. This adaptability is particularly valuable in dynamic environments, such as industrial reactors, where fluctuating conditions impact reaction kinetics. Real-time data collection and processing make NNs an invaluable tool for enhancing reaction efficiency and stability. By applying neural networks to kinetics, electrochemical reactor designs can be optimized with unprecedented precision. Through data-driven predictions, reactor parameters can be adjusted in real-time, resulting in energy savings, reduced operational costs, and a minimized environmental impact. The insights provided by neural networks enable researchers and engineers to accurately predict reaction outcomes, facilitating the development of sustainable, high-efficiency electrochemical reactors tailored to specific reactions and operational conditions.

Reinforcement Learning for Adaptive System Design

Reinforcement Learning (RL) is transforming adaptive system design in electrochemical reactors by introducing a level of flexibility and real-time responsiveness that conventional design methods cannot achieve, as shown by its architecture in Fig. (**6a**). RL is a subset of machine learning where an agent learns to make sequential decisions by interacting with an environment, receiving feedback, and optimizing its actions based on the rewards it receives. This approach is especially valuable in electrochemical systems, where conditions such as temperature, pressure, and concentration vary continuously and require adaptive responses to maintain optimal reactor performance. In electrochemical reactors, RL can dynamically adjust critical parameters, such as voltage, electrolyte concentration, and reaction time, to optimize reactor efficiency and product yield [46]. Unlike traditional optimization methods, which often rely on predefined models, RL agents learn through trial and error, refining their strategies over time to identify the most effective operating conditions. This iterative learning process enables RL to adapt to unique or unpredictable scenarios, such as sudden fluctuations in reactant quality or power supply variations, making it particularly well-suited for real-world industrial applications. One compelling application of RL in adaptive system design is in fuel cells, where stability and efficiency are critical. In these systems, RL algorithms can monitor and adjust operating parameters in response to fluctuating demand or environmental conditions. For instance, RL can control the distribution of reactants in a fuel cell stack to maintain consistent power output, minimizing waste and ensuring that the system operates within safe limits. By continuously adapting to real-time feedback, RL-based designs can extend the life and efficiency of fuel cells, making them more sustainable and cost-effective. RL also enables multi-objective optimization, balancing competing factors such as energy consumption, production rate, and environmental impact. For example, in electrochemical reactors used for hydrogen production, an RL algorithm may optimize the process to achieve maximum hydrogen yield while minimizing energy input and emissions [47]. Through reward functions that assign higher values to desired outcomes, RL agents learn to make decisions that align with sustainability goals, ultimately resulting in reactors that are not only efficient but also environmentally friendly. A key feature of RL is its capacity to handle complex, high-dimensional data, which is common in electrochemical systems where multiple variables interact. Advanced RL methods, such as Deep Reinforcement Learning (DRL), combine RL with deep learning to manage these data-rich environments, making it possible to control reactors with many interdependent parameters as depicted in Fig. (**6b**). DRL has been particularly effective in scenarios where traditional RL struggles, allowing reactors to adjust to complex interactions within the system and maintain performance in real-time. Despite its advantages, RL in reactor design poses challenges, including the need for substantial computational power and training time. RL agents require numerous iterations to learn optimal strategies, which may involve significant simulation or experimental resources. However, recent advances in transfer learning and model-based RL are helping mitigate these challenges by enabling agents to leverage knowledge from related tasks, thereby reducing training requirements.

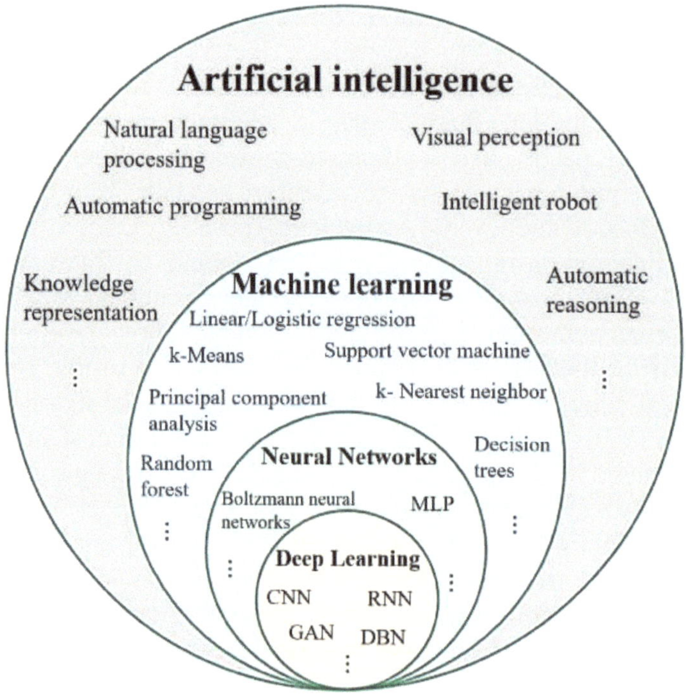

Fig. (5). Diagram depicting the relationship between Artificial Intelligence (AI), Machine Learning (ML), Neural Networks (NN), and Deep Learning (DL), illustrating various network types: MLP (multilayer perceptron), CNN (Convolutional Neural Network), RNN (Recurrent Neural Network), DBN (Deep Belief Network), and GAN (Generative Adversarial Network). This hierarchy shows how deep learning techniques build on neural network architectures within the broader fields of ML and AI. Reprinted from [43] Copyright © 1996-2024 MDPI (Basel, Switzerland) .

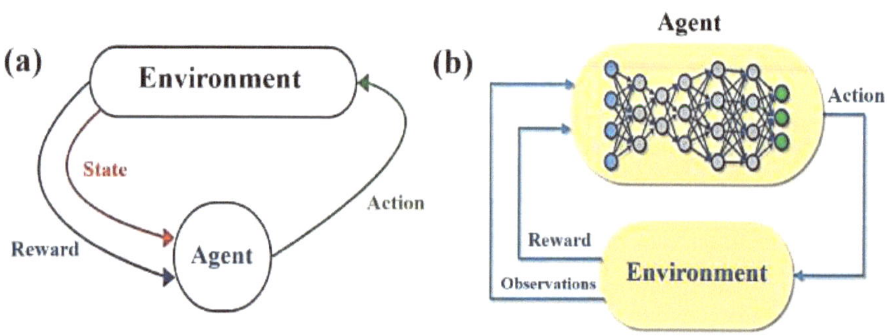

Fig. (6). **(a)** Reinforcement learning architecture. **(b)** Deep reinforcement learning architecture. Reprinted from [48] Copyright © 2024 IEEE .

DATA-DRIVEN PROCESS OPTIMIZATION AND MAINTENANCE

In electrochemical systems, data-driven process optimization and maintenance integrate Artificial Intelligence (AI) and Machine Learning (ML) with continuous data collection to enhance system efficiency, reliability, and longevity [49]. By utilizing real-time data from sensors embedded in electrochemical cells, these systems enable dynamic adjustments to core operational parameters, such as voltage, temperature, and pressure. This data-centric approach enables electrochemical reactors to optimize performance by automatically adjusting conditions in response to operational fluctuations, achieving high levels of precision and efficiency that surpass those of traditional control methods. Predictive maintenance, a key component of this framework, minimizes unexpected downtimes and extends equipment life by forecasting potential malfunctions before they occur. This is accomplished through ML algorithms that identify patterns in data and detect subtle anomalies that may indicate emerging issues. Proactively addressing these issues reduces the need for reactive maintenance, lowers operating costs, and extends the system's lifespan. Data-driven optimization also facilitates resource conservation by identifying inefficiencies and suggesting adjustments to reduce energy usage and waste. As industries increasingly align with sustainable goals, AI-driven systems contribute to eco-friendly practices, making electrochemical technology an adaptable and resource-efficient solution to meet the complex demands of modern energy infrastructure.

Real-Time Data and Predictive Maintenance

Real-time data acquisition, combined with AI-driven predictive maintenance, has transformed maintenance strategies within electrochemical systems, replacing traditional reactive or scheduled maintenance with continuous, adaptive monitoring. This approach relies on advanced AI algorithms and sensor networks to capture, process, and analyze operational data instantaneously, covering critical parameters such as voltage, current, temperature, and pressure. Fig. (7) illustrates an AI-based predictive maintenance framework. By continuously comparing live data against ideal operating benchmarks, predictive maintenance systems detect even slight deviations from normal behavior that signal potential issues, including resistance build-up, overvoltage, or thermal inconsistencies. For instance, in battery systems, real-time monitoring allows AI algorithms to analyze trends in voltage and current fluctuations, which may signal early-stage battery degradation or a decline in cell efficiency [50]. Upon detecting such changes, the AI model generates alerts, enabling timely interventions that prevent larger malfunctions and minimize wear and tear. This continuous monitoring reduces the need for manual inspections, as maintenance personnel are alerted to emerging issues immediately, allowing for precise maintenance scheduling based on the actual health of the system rather than arbitrary timelines. Predictive maintenance relies heavily on machine learning, where algorithms learn from historical performance data to anticipate faults before they fully manifest. Techniques such as pattern recognition, regression, and neural networks enable AI to detect both short-term anomalies and long-term performance degradation, allowing for maintenance tailored to the unique conditions of each system. An additional benefit is the AI system's adaptability; as data accumulates, the algorithms become more accurate at predicting potential issues, creating an evolving model that improves maintenance precision over time. In high-energy systems, such as fuel cells, where sustained operational efficiency is crucial, AI-driven predictive maintenance proves invaluable [51]. By identifying issues such as catalyst degradation or membrane fouling, which can compromise efficiency and safety, real-time predictive systems protect both the equipment and the surrounding environment. Additionally, predictive maintenance aligns with sustainability goals by reducing waste and extending equipment life, lowering the ecological footprint associated with frequent replacements or repairs. Through intelligent monitoring and proactive fault prevention, real-time data and predictive maintenance optimize electrochemical processes, ensuring reliability and reducing both financial and environmental costs associated with system operation.

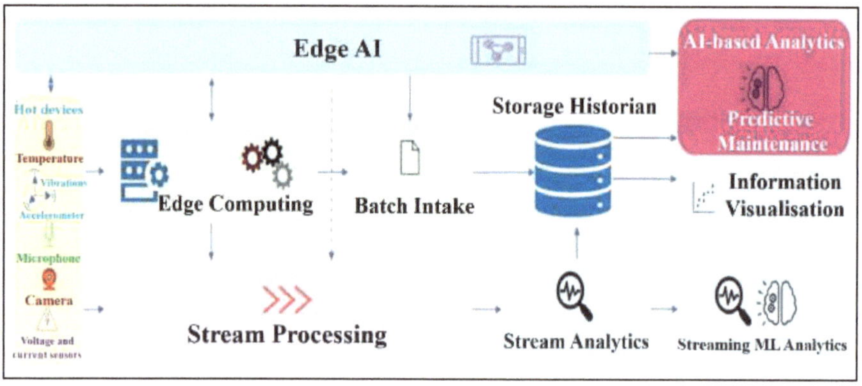

Fig. (7). AI-based predictive maintenance framework. Reprinted from [52] Copyright © 2021 Artificial Intelligence for Digitising Industry: Applications.

Anomaly Detection in Electrochemical Cells

Anomaly detection within electrochemical cells is a crucial component of predictive maintenance, as it allows operators to identify irregularities that could indicate emerging faults or inefficiencies in the system. Electrochemical processes involve intricate interactions between current, voltage, temperature, and pressure, which collectively influence reaction rates and system stability [53]. Anomalies in these variables may indicate faults such as resistance buildup, electrolyte degradation, or current inconsistencies, which, if undetected, could compromise cell performance or lead to equipment failure. AI models, particularly machine learning algorithms such as regression, clustering, and neural networks, play a pivotal role in identifying these anomalies. Clustering algorithms, for example, analyze operational data to detect deviations from normal groupings based on historical performance, enabling the quick identification of abnormalities in parameters such as temperature and voltage. Machine learning models learn from historical data, forming a baseline of normal conditions. Any deviation beyond expected ranges is flagged as an anomaly. A subtle but sustained increase in operating temperature, for instance, could indicate internal resistance or impending thermal runaway, a condition where unchecked heat accumulation leads to uncontrollable temperature increases.

In systems utilizing advanced AI techniques, such as Long Short-Term Memory (LSTM) networks, temporal patterns in time-series data are crucial for recognizing trends and predicting future values [54]. LSTM models analyze sequential data, spotting deviations in trends over time, which signal potential failures before they escalate. When current, voltage, or temperature values deviate significantly from predicted values, the system raises an alert. These alerts allow maintenance teams to conduct proactive interventions, effectively reducing downtime and preventing severe faults. An example of anomaly detection's utility is found in lithium-ion battery systems, where thermal runaway remains a primary safety concern. Traditional monitoring methods may overlook minor fluctuations, whereas AI-driven anomaly detection can flag incremental changes that may signify early-stage failure. This early intervention reduces the chance of fires or explosions, ensuring safety in high-risk settings. Anomaly detection provides numerous benefits for electrochemical system maintenance, including extended system longevity, enhanced safety, and lower operational costs. By catching minor deviations early, maintenance teams can implement minor adjustments, eliminating the need for more costly repairs later. Additionally, detecting anomalies reduces resource wastage and conserves equipment, further aligning with eco-friendly operational goals. Through its accurate, real-time fault detection, AI-driven anomaly detection transforms electrochemical system maintenance, providing a critical mechanism for sustaining performance, reducing expenses, and enhancing system safety.

Case Study: AI-Enabled Predictive Maintenance in Fuel Cells

AI-enabled predictive maintenance has proven particularly valuable in fuel cell systems, where operational stability is crucial for efficient and reliable performance. Fuel cells are widely used due to their high energy density and low emissions; however, they require continuous monitoring and maintenance to prevent issues such as membrane thinning, fuel starvation, or catalyst degradation [55]. Traditional maintenance methods, which rely on periodic inspections, may overlook subtle degradation between inspections, often resulting in costly repairs or unexpected downtimes. A case study on AI-enabled predictive maintenance in hydrogen fuel cells highlights how AI technology can reduce these risks. In this case, a fleet of hydrogen fuel cells was equipped with sensors capturing real-time data on temperature, current density, voltage, and gas flow rates [56]. AI algorithms processed this data and compared it to historical performance, training predictive models that detected early signs of common faults. For instance, gradual decreases in current density were linked to fuel starvation caused by minor clogging in the gas flow channels. The AI system flagged this anomaly, prompting maintenance crews to clean the channels before the issue escalated, preventing an eventual shutdown. Another example from the case study involves monitoring for catalyst degradation, a frequent issue in fuel cells that affects efficiency. AI algorithms trained on historical degradation patterns could recognize early indicators of catalyst wear, such as slight changes in voltage patterns, that are often missed by traditional monitoring methods. By predicting this degradation early, operators were able to replace the catalyst layer at an optimal time, reducing operational downtime and maximizing cell efficiency.

The AI-enabled predictive maintenance strategy yielded substantial benefits. Downtime across the fuel cell fleet was reduced by 30%, with maintenance costs decreasing by nearly 20% due to fewer emergency repairs and optimized resource allocation [57]. Additionally, the fuel cells' lifespan increased by an average of 15%, resulting in long-term savings and a lower environmental impact due to reduced resource consumption and waste. Furthermore, by catching early signs of degradation, predictive maintenance ensured that the fuel cells maintained high efficiency and minimized emissions, aligning with environmental sustainability goals. Overall, this case study demonstrates the advantages of integrating AI-based predictive maintenance into fuel cells and similar electrochemical systems. By detecting faults early, predictive maintenance reduces operational costs, enhances efficiency, and contributes to sustainability objectives. These findings highlight the transformative impact of AI in managing electrochemical systems, ensuring both performance reliability and longevity for fuel cells in the context of clean energy solutions.

Optimization of Key Process Parameters

Optimizing key process parameters such as temperature, pressure, and voltage is essential for achieving maximum efficiency and reliability in electrochemical systems. By utilizing AI and machine learning algorithms, real-time adjustments to these parameters can be made in response to changing operational conditions, significantly improving system performance and reducing energy consumption. AI-driven systems continuously monitor operational data, evaluating and optimizing these variables to maintain ideal reaction conditions, minimize energy wastage, and extend equipment life. Machine learning models, trained on historical and real-time data, enable AI systems to predict the most efficient settings for each parameter under various load conditions. For instance, a slight variation in operating temperature might result in energy losses or trigger unwanted side reactions, potentially affecting the overall efficiency of the system. By analyzing temperature fluctuations and their impact on energy output, AI can adjust the system to maintain an optimal thermal range, thereby reducing energy usage while safeguarding components from thermal stress [58].

Pressure is another critical parameter, especially in processes such as hydrogen generation or fuel cell operation, where maintaining precise pressure levels maximizes reaction rates and minimizes gas waste. AI algorithms track real-time pressure data, making instantaneous adjustments to compensate for fluctuations, ensuring efficient gas flow and maximizing product yield [59]. Similarly, voltage optimization in battery systems ensures that energy is stored and released at safe and efficient levels, avoiding overcharging, which can lead to degradation or even safety hazards. AI-based voltage regulation extends battery life, enhances storage efficiency, and reduces the environmental impact by lowering the frequency of replacements. AI-driven optimization considers the interdependencies between these parameters, adjusting temperature, pressure, and voltage simultaneously to enhance system performance. This holistic approach is especially beneficial for complex processes, such as electrolysis, where slight variations in temperature and voltage can significantly impact hydrogen output and electrode durability. By leveraging AI to monitor these relationships, operators can achieve a finely-tuned balance across all parameters, resulting in optimized performance without the trial-and-error methods traditionally required. The optimization of these parameters is not only a technical advancement but also a contributor to sustainability. By reducing energy and material waste, AI-driven optimization aligns with eco-friendly practices and lowers operating costs, enhancing the economic viability of electrochemical technologies. Thus, through data-driven process optimization, AI provides a robust framework for improving the efficiency, safety, and sustainability of electrochemical systems.

Control of Temperature, Pressure, and Voltage

Temperature, pressure, and voltage control are central to maintaining efficient, safe, and long-lasting operations in electrochemical systems. These parameters influence reaction kinetics, system efficiency, and longevity, and their real-time regulation is critical for high-performance applications. AI systems, with their capacity for instant adjustments, provide advanced control over these parameters, creating stability within electrochemical reactions even under fluctuating operating conditions [60]. Temperature control is crucial, particularly in high-temperature systems such as fuel cells and electrochemical reactors. AI-driven temperature regulation minimizes the risk of thermal stress by detecting and adjusting for fluctuations before they cause damage. For instance, in fuel cells, where catalysts may degrade under excess heat, AI systems continuously monitor temperatures, adjusting inputs or initiating cooling mechanisms as needed. This dynamic control prevents overheating, maintaining optimal reaction rates and extending the lifespan of components. Similarly, in electrolyzers, precise thermal management enhances hydrogen yield and reduces the energy costs associated with cooling or reheating the system, thereby maximizing efficiency and promoting resource conservation. Pressure control is equally essential, particularly in hydrogen production or battery systems, where controlled pressure levels optimize reaction rates and maintain efficiency. Real-time pressure monitoring enables AI algorithms to detect variations, adjusting inputs to maintain stable pressures and prevent efficiency losses. By maintaining pressure at ideal levels, the system minimizes the energy required for compressing gases, thereby reducing operating costs and enhancing the durability of sensitive components, such as membranes and seals. In fuel cell stacks, pressure control also contributes to uniform gas distribution across cells, maximizing the system's overall power output and energy efficiency. Voltage regulation, meanwhile, plays a critical role in managing the electrochemical reaction's pace and intensity. AI-driven voltage control prevents over-voltage conditions that can degrade electrodes or lead to safety issues [61]. In applications such as battery storage, overcharging can lead to thermal runaway—a potentially hazardous phenomenon that AI algorithms can mitigate by adjusting the voltage according to battery conditions. In hydrogen generation, voltage adjustments align reaction rates with ideal conditions, increasing hydrogen output and reducing energy waste.

AI algorithms can simultaneously coordinate temperature, pressure, and voltage adjustments, creating a harmonized control system that further optimizes overall performance. In an electrochemical reactor, for example, a rise in temperature might require a voltage decrease to prevent undesired reactions, a balance that AI systems handle in real-time. By learning from historical data, these systems identify ideal parameter settings under various conditions, reducing the need for manual input and increasing efficiency. Overall, AI-based control of temperature, pressure, and voltage results in improved process stability, safety, and resource efficiency. As these control systems evolve, they will contribute to more sustainable, high-performance electrochemical applications, enhancing both operational performance and environmental responsibility.

SUSTAINABILITY AND EFFICIENCY THROUGH AI INTEGRATION

The transformative role of AI in sustainability within electrochemical systems has become a focal point in modern energy technologies, where efficiency and eco-friendliness are primary goals. Through AI-enhanced design and optimization, electrochemical reactors and systems can achieve new levels of performance while reducing environmental impacts. Central to this integration is AI's ability to process and analyze large data sets, allowing for real-time optimization and the identification of operational inefficiencies. For example, Machine Learning (ML) algorithms can fine-tune parameters such as current density, voltage, and temperature within reactors to reduce energy consumption while maximizing reaction rates and output quality [62]. Another crucial aspect of AI-driven sustainability is reducing the carbon footprint within electrochemical processes. AI models can predict and control carbon emissions by optimizing reactions and materials that reduce CO_2 production. Furthermore, AI can aid in the design of carbon-capture techniques in electrochemical reactors, which contribute directly to climate change mitigation by capturing CO_2 from industrial emissions. By minimizing energy losses and extending the lifespan of equipment through predictive maintenance, AI contributes to sustainable energy practices practically and cost-effectively. Additionally, AI plays a crucial role in optimizing the selection and utilization of sustainable materials, including eco-friendly electrolytes, catalysts, and electrode materials that offer enhanced performance with minimal environmental impact. Advanced algorithms can identify materials with lower ecological footprints while maintaining or improving performance standards, making AI integration a practical solution for reducing resource dependency. Overall, AI-powered sustainability in electrochemical systems not only aligns with global environmental goals but also enhances operational efficiency, making it a key driver in the transition toward greener, more sustainable industrial practices [63].

Reducing Energy Consumption and Carbon Footprint

Reducing energy consumption and carbon footprint in electrochemical systems is imperative for sustainable industry practices, and AI has emerged as a powerful tool to address these challenges. Electrochemical processes, while already efficient compared to traditional energy conversion methods, can experience significant gains in energy efficiency when AI is applied. By utilizing data-driven insights, AI models can identify patterns in energy usage and pinpoint areas of unnecessary energy consumption, allowing for optimization strategies tailored to each system's unique operating conditions. Machine learning algorithms, for instance, can be employed to dynamically adjust operational parameters such as voltage and current density, thereby minimizing the energy required for reactions without compromising output. AI-powered predictive maintenance, another important application, can reduce energy wastage by identifying potential equipment failures before they lead to inefficiencies or downtime. This allows for timely interventions, reducing the need for energy-intensive repairs or replacements and extending the equipment's operational life [64]. As shown in Fig. (**8**), on the carbon reduction front, AI-driven systems can help reduce emissions by optimizing reaction conditions to minimize CO_2 production. Algorithms can model the thermodynamic and kinetic properties of reactions, identifying optimal conditions that reduce carbon emissions. For example, in fuel cells, AI can fine-tune reaction rates to enhance fuel efficiency while reducing Greenhouse Gas (GHG) emissions [65]. Additionally, AI can enable electrochemical systems to operate in cycles that maximize the potential for CO_2 capture and storage. Another significant avenue is the design of electrochemical processes that favor low-carbon inputs and renewable energy sources. AI can predict the effects of substituting traditional inputs with low-emission alternatives, evaluating the impact on performance, efficiency, and carbon footprint. This aligns electrochemical systems with renewable energy sources, such as solar or wind, through intelligent load balancing that reduces reliance on fossil fuels. AI's ability to simulate the environmental impact of electrochemical reactions at a granular level empowers industries to take proactive steps toward carbon neutrality. Overall, AI serves as an essential ally in achieving low-energy, low-emission electrochemical processes, contributing to a sustainable energy landscape and reducing the environmental footprint of industrial processes.

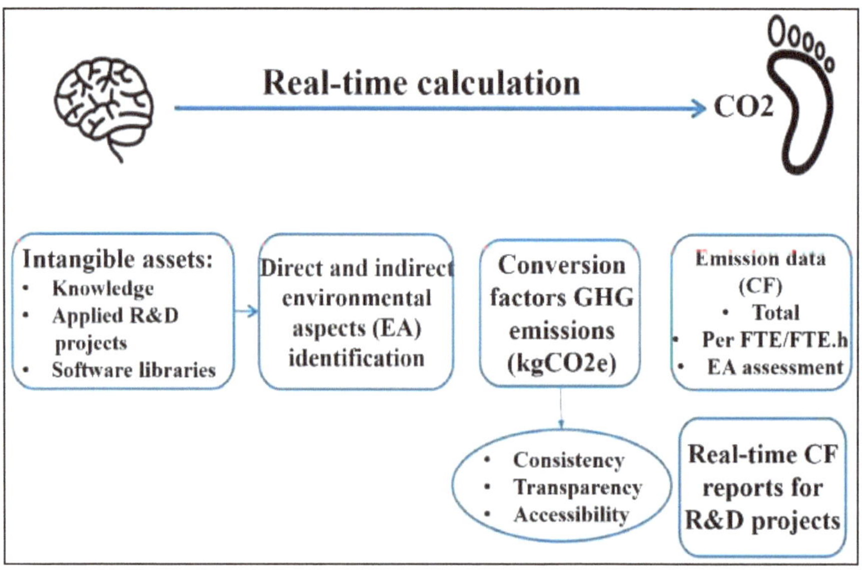

Fig. (8). Illustration of GHG emissions linked to intangible assets, highlighting metrics such as FTE (full-time equivalent), CF (carbon footprint), and EA (environmental aspects). Emissions are measured in $kgCO_2e$ (kilograms of carbon dioxide equivalent), providing insights into greenhouse gas impacts per unit of labor and environmental factors. Reprinted from [66] Copyright © 1996-2024 MDPI (Basel, Switzerland).

AI Strategies for Carbon Reduction

Artificial intelligence is revolutionizing carbon reduction strategies in electrochemical systems by offering new approaches to emissions management and resource efficiency. One of the primary ways AI contributes to carbon reduction is by optimizing operating conditions to lower carbon dioxide (CO_2) emissions in real-time. By analyzing large datasets from reactor conditions, AI models can identify optimal settings that maximize the reaction efficiency while minimizing CO_2 output. For instance, Machine Learning (ML) algorithms can predict the relationship between reaction kinetics and carbon emissions, enabling adjustments in temperature, pressure, or reactant concentrations to achieve the lowest possible emissions without compromising the system's performance. Moreover, AI-driven design can explore new materials and catalysts that reduce carbon emissions during electrochemical reactions. Traditional methods of material discovery are time-intensive and often limited by trial and error. However, AI, especially deep learning, accelerates this process by simulating the properties and interactions of potential materials, identifying those with lower carbon footprints and efficient catalytic behaviors. For example, AI can suggest materials that either facilitate the breakdown of carbon compounds or inhibit CO_2 production altogether, making reactors more environmentally friendly from a materials perspective [67]. AI also plays a role in developing predictive maintenance strategies that contribute to carbon reduction. By identifying potential issues before they lead to significant equipment failures, AI-based maintenance systems can prevent the excessive energy usage and emissions associated with unscheduled shutdowns or repairs. This predictive approach not only extends the lifespan of electrochemical equipment but also reduces the carbon emissions linked to the manufacture, transportation, and installation of replacement parts. AI's ability to integrate renewable energy sources into electrochemical processes further supports efforts to reduce carbon emissions. For instance, AI algorithms can control the timing and intensity of electrochemical reactions to coincide with periods of high renewable energy availability, such as when solar or wind power is most abundant. This synchronization minimizes dependence on fossil fuel energy sources and reduces the indirect carbon footprint associated with the grid [68].

Additionally, intelligent load balancing supported by AI enables electrochemical systems to optimize energy use and avoid peak grid hours, during which fossil fuel energy is often more prevalent. Finally, AI supports the development of carbon capture mechanisms within electrochemical systems. By monitoring the conditions within reactors, AI models can adjust parameters to enhance the capture efficiency of CO_2. This application is particularly valuable for industries seeking to implement carbon-neutral or carbon-negative processes. In effect, AI strategies for carbon reduction provide electrochemical systems with the capability to operate sustainably, meeting energy demands while aligning with environmental policies and goals. Overall, AI is essential in achieving carbon reduction in electrochemical systems. Through parameter optimization, material innovation, predictive maintenance, renewable integration, and enhanced carbon capture, AI-driven solutions contribute to a cleaner, more sustainable future.

Case Study: Carbon Capture in Electrochemical Systems

Carbon capture in electrochemical systems has become an innovative method for reducing CO_2 emissions, with the aid of AI enhancing the efficiency and feasibility of these processes [69]. This case study examines the application of AI-driven carbon capture technology within an industrial electrochemical reactor used for chemical synthesis, showcasing the role of AI in reducing environmental impact. The electrochemical carbon capture process generally involves the reaction of CO_2 with specialized materials in the reactor to convert it into a stable compound, effectively "locking away" the carbon. Traditional approaches to carbon capture often face challenges in energy efficiency and process control. However, with the integration of AI, these limitations can be overcome through data-driven adjustments in real-time. Machine learning algorithms play a crucial role in managing the electrochemical conditions required for optimal CO_2 capture, including voltage, pressure, and reactant concentration. In this case, an AI-based predictive model is utilized to continuously adjust these parameters, ensuring that the system operates in conditions where CO_2 capture is maximized while maintaining low energy consumption [70]. In practice, the AI model analyzes data collected from the reactor's sensors, which monitor the CO_2 concentration, temperature, and pressure within the system. By processing this data, the AI model predicts the rate of CO_2 capture and identifies the precise conditions required to enhance capture efficiency. For instance, when CO_2 levels in the exhaust gas increase, the model dynamically modifies the voltage and reactant concentrations to encourage higher absorption rates. This real-time optimization prevents unnecessary energy use and ensures that the process remains as efficient as possible. Additionally, AI enhances the durability and lifespan of the capture materials. The electrochemical process can degrade capture materials over time, reducing their efficiency and requiring frequent replacement. AI helps to mitigate this by monitoring material performance and adjusting the reactor conditions to reduce stress on these materials. This capability not only lowers maintenance costs but also minimizes the carbon footprint associated with material replacement. A key outcome from this case study is the significant reduction in CO_2 emissions, demonstrating AI's potential to make carbon capture economically viable on a large scale. The AI-driven approach lowered the reactor's energy demand by nearly 20% compared to non-AI-assisted systems, directly reducing operational costs and environmental impact [71]. The success of this case illustrates how AI can drive electrochemical carbon capture forward, paving the way for more sustainable industrial practices.

Optimizing Material Selection for Sustainability

Optimizing material selection for sustainability in electrochemical systems is fundamental to reducing environmental impact and achieving efficient, long-lasting performance. AI facilitates the discovery and selection of materials with high performance and low environmental impact, a crucial step toward developing sustainable electrochemical technologies. One major focus in material optimization is identifying eco-friendly catalysts, electrode materials, and electrolytes that not only maximize efficiency but also align with environmental and sustainability goals, as depicted in Fig. (**9**). AI models, particularly those utilizing deep learning and machine learning, play a vital role in material discovery. Traditional methods of material development, often based on trial and error, are time-consuming and resource-intensive [72]. AI models expedite this process by predicting the properties of various materials and simulating their performance under different conditions. For example, AI-driven computational models can predict properties such as conductivity, stability, and catalytic efficiency, which are critical for electrochemical systems. This predictive capability enables researchers to identify materials with optimal properties while avoiding those with potentially harmful environmental effects. In the realm of catalysts, AI aids in discovering materials that can accelerate electrochemical reactions without compromising sustainability. For instance, catalysts derived from abundant and non-toxic elements, such as iron, cobalt, and nitrogen, can serve as more sustainable alternatives to traditional, scarce, or toxic catalysts. AI models trained on databases of known materials can suggest combinations of these elements that offer high catalytic efficiency with minimal environmental impact. Furthermore, AI-driven design strategies can help develop nanostructured catalysts with larger surface areas, reducing the quantity of material needed and enhancing the sustainability of the process [73]. Another important aspect is the optimization of electrolyte selection. Many electrolytes used in traditional systems contain toxic or corrosive substances, posing environmental hazards. AI allows for the exploration of biodegradable or low-toxicity alternatives by simulating their stability and ionic conductivity in electrochemical reactions [74]. By analyzing the environmental impact of different electrolyte formulations, AI can help in selecting greener options without compromising system performance. In electrochemical storage systems, for example, AI-guided electrolyte selection can enhance energy efficiency while maintaining eco-friendly standards. AI also contributes to optimizing electrode materials by identifying those with long lifespans and minimal ecological footprint. For instance, AI algorithms can simulate the degradation mechanisms in various electrode materials under operating conditions, enabling the prediction of their durability and efficiency over time. Sustainable options such as carbon-based materials, which are abundant and have a low environmental impact, are often recommended by AI models due to their favorable lifecycle assessments. By reducing the frequency of material replacement, the environmental burden associated with electrode manufacturing and disposal is significantly lowered.

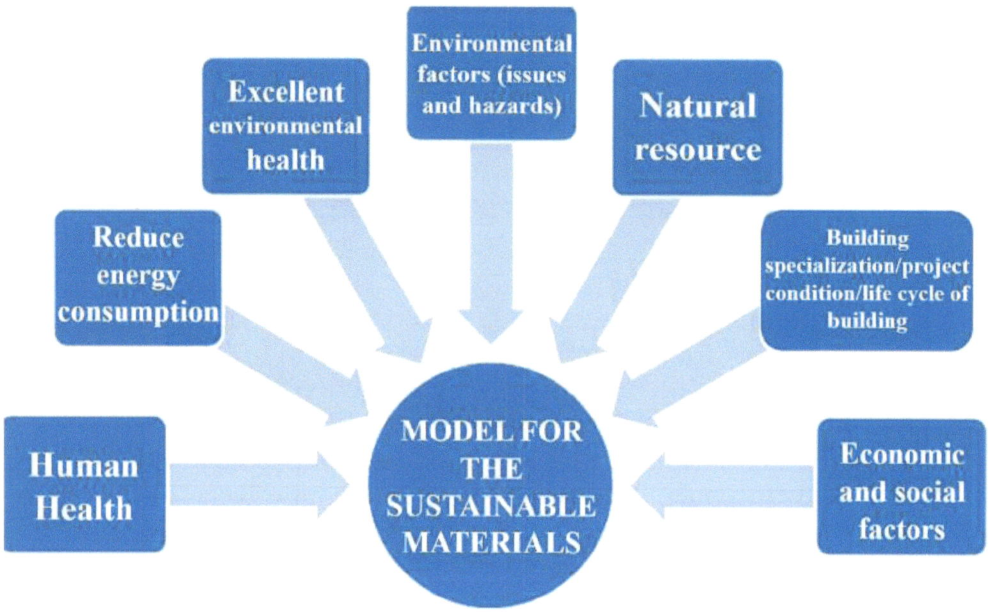

Fig. (9). Model illustrating the sustainable material selection. Reprinted from [75] Copyright © 1996-2024 MDPI (Basel, Switzerland).

Lastly, the concept of recyclability is integral to AI-driven sustainable material selection. By identifying materials that can be easily separated and reused, AI enhances the sustainability of electrochemical systems throughout their lifecycle. This includes recommending materials that maintain performance through recycling processes or that can be decomposed with minimal energy. In summary, AI enables the efficient selection of sustainable materials across catalysts, electrolytes, and electrodes, optimizing electrochemical systems for environmental compatibility, performance, and durability. Through AI, electrochemical systems can meet both operational demands and sustainability goals, advancing the field toward a greener future. Machine learning algorithms process large volumes of data collected from various sensors, identifying patterns and correlations that human analysts might overlook, thereby generating actionable insights promptly. One significant application of AI-enhanced electrochemical sensors is in predictive maintenance for industrial systems. These sensors can monitor equipment health and performance metrics in real-time, detecting anomalies that signal potential failures. For instance, an electrochemical sensor used in a manufacturing plant may monitor chemical concentrations, temperature, and pressure. If the sensor data deviates from normal patterns, the AI system alerts maintenance teams to investigate before a failure occurs. This predictive capability reduces downtime and maintenance costs, promoting operational efficiency. In environmental monitoring, AI-enabled electrochemical sensors provide real-time data on pollutants, heavy metals, and other contaminants in water and air. Traditional monitoring methods often involve complex sample processing and result in delayed responses, limiting timely action to environmental hazards. AI sensors, however, analyze data instantly, offering real-time insights into contamination levels. For example, an electrochemical sensor integrated with AI algorithms can monitor heavy metal concentrations in wastewater treatment facilities [76]. The AI system continuously processes sensor data, automatically adjusting treatment processes to ensure regulatory compliance and protect public health.

Another area of significant impact is in energy systems, where AI-enhanced sensors monitor battery performance and health. In lithium-ion batteries, electrochemical sensors measure parameters such as voltage, current, and temperature. By employing AI algorithms, the data collected can predict battery life and optimize charging cycles, improving both performance and safety. Advanced machine learning models analyze historical data to predict potential failure points, enabling proactive maintenance and extending battery longevity. Additionally, AI integration allows for the development of smart sensor networks, where multiple sensors communicate and share data. In agricultural applications, for instance, a network of electrochemical sensors can monitor soil moisture, nutrient levels, and pH, providing farmers with comprehensive insights to optimize irrigation and fertilization [77]. The AI system analyses this data to recommend specific actions, enhancing crop yield while minimizing resource waste. Moreover, AI techniques, such as deep learning, are applied to improve sensor calibration and accuracy. Calibration is often a tedious and error-prone process in traditional sensors. By leveraging large datasets and employing AI algorithms, researchers can develop self-calibrating sensors that maintain high accuracy over time, significantly reducing the need for manual calibration. As these technologies continue to evolve, their impact on industry practices and environmental management is set to increase, making AI-enhanced electrochemical sensors a critical component of modern process monitoring solutions.

CASE STUDIES ON AI-ENHANCED ELECTROCHEMICAL SYSTEMS

Case studies on AI-enhanced electrochemical systems highlight the practical applications and benefits AI brings to electrochemical technologies in sustainable energy [78]. These examples demonstrate how AI-driven approaches enhance the efficiency, scalability, and cost-effectiveness of systems such as hydrogen production, battery development, and sensor technology, with the goal of meeting global energy demands while minimizing environmental impact. The role of AI in hydrogen production and electrolyzers demonstrates significant potential for reducing the energy intensity required to produce hydrogen [79]. Traditional electrolyzers rely on precise control of current density, electrode activity, and electrolyte composition, all of which AI can help regulate by predicting optimal parameters and dynamically adjusting them in real time. This approach improves production rates and stability, paving the way for hydrogen as a viable renewable energy carrier. AI's involvement in battery design, particularly in lithium-ion and flow batteries, facilitates more effective energy storage solutions, which are critical for the grid integration of renewable sources. Through machine learning algorithms, AI helps refine parameters such as electrolyte concentration, electrode composition, and temperature management, ultimately increasing battery capacity, cycle life, and safety. Advanced AI models analyze patterns from extensive datasets, guiding the design process to develop batteries with enhanced storage and discharge capabilities. In addition to hydrogen and batteries, electrochemical sensors benefit significantly from AI-driven data processing for real-time monitoring. Sensors integrated with AI algorithms enable predictive maintenance by detecting and diagnosing issues before they impact performance. These sensors are increasingly deployed in various industries, from automotive to environmental monitoring, ensuring that systems operate within optimal parameters. Through these case studies, it is evident that AI-driven electrochemical systems provide the dual benefits of enhancing performance and supporting sustainability.

AI in Hydrogen Production and Battery Design

Artificial Intelligence (AI) plays a crucial role in advancing hydrogen production and battery design, two key components of sustainable energy systems. In hydrogen production, AI-driven optimization of electrolyzers has proven essential in reducing the energy demands associated with hydrogen generation [80]. Hydrogen, a clean fuel with extensive applications in transportation, industry, and energy storage, has traditionally faced barriers related to high production costs and energy inefficiencies. By employing AI techniques, these barriers are being progressively addressed. AI algorithms streamline hydrogen production processes by enabling precise control over critical parameters such as electrode materials, electrolyte composition, and current density. Machine learning (ML) models can learn from vast data sets collected during electrolysis, identifying optimal operating conditions that maximize hydrogen output while minimizing energy consumption. Reinforcement learning, a subset of AI, enables electrolyzers to autonomously adjust their operating parameters in real-time, responding to fluctuations in electricity availability from renewable sources. This adaptability is particularly valuable for grid balancing, where hydrogen production can increase during periods of excess renewable energy generation. Similarly, in battery design, AI significantly improves the performance, safety, and lifespan of modern batteries, particularly lithium-ion and emerging solid-state batteries. AI algorithms analyze large volumes of data from battery testing, including charge-discharge cycles, electrolyte interactions, and thermal responses, to enhance battery capacity and safety features. For instance, predictive analytics in Battery Management Systems (BMS) can detect signs of degradation early on, preventing issues like thermal runaway and extending battery life.

Moreover, generative AI models aid in designing new battery chemistries by predicting material properties and their interactions, accelerating the development of higher-energy-density batteries. Through these AI-driven insights, researchers can develop battery systems that strike a balance between energy density and stability, which is essential for Electric Vehicles (EVs) and grid storage [81]. The integration of AI in hydrogen and battery technologies has the potential to transform global energy systems. By reducing production costs, increasing efficiency, and enhancing safety, AI-driven advancements in hydrogen and battery design are paving the way for a more sustainable and resilient energy future. These innovations bring us closer to realizing hydrogen-powered economies and expanding the deployment of clean energy storage solutions.

Case Study: AI-Based Optimization in Hydrogen Electrolyzers

Hydrogen production through electrolysis, although environmentally beneficial, has traditionally been costly and energy-intensive, limiting its widespread adoption. AI-based optimization in electrolyzer technology addresses these challenges by streamlining the production process, reducing energy consumption, and enhancing system efficiency. A case study focusing on an AI-enhanced Proton Exchange Membrane (PEM) electrolyzer demonstrates how machine learning and reinforcement learning algorithms have transformed this technology. In a PEM electrolyzer, the electrolyte material, typically a polymer, facilitates ion exchange between electrodes, producing hydrogen gas. Optimal operation requires precise control of variables such as current density, voltage, temperature, and electrolyte composition. Machine Learning (ML) algorithms can analyze historical data from past electrolysis cycles, identifying trends and conditions that maximize hydrogen yield while minimizing energy use [82]. In this case study, supervised learning models were developed using data on current density, electrode condition, and voltage requirements, creating predictive models that enable real-time control of production parameters. By implementing reinforcement learning, the system autonomously adjusts operating conditions in response to fluctuating renewable electricity availability, a common scenario in solar or wind-powered electrolysis plants. For instance, when excess solar power is available, the AI system dynamically increases production to store surplus energy in hydrogen form, providing a buffer for grid stability. Conversely, during periods of lower renewable output, the AI reduces operations to prevent energy drain, thereby achieving a balance between energy production and storage. This optimization aligns with sustainable energy goals, as the electrolyzer efficiently operates based on real-time data.

One challenge in PEM electrolysis is the degradation of electrodes, especially the anode. AI-based maintenance prediction models help mitigate this by monitoring performance indicators, such as voltage increases or output reductions, which signal potential electrode wear [83]. By predicting maintenance needs, these AI models significantly reduce downtime and extend the lifespan of electrolyzer components, thereby directly impacting cost efficiency. The case study also highlights the environmental benefits achieved through AI optimization. Reduced energy demands lower the carbon footprint of hydrogen production, while optimized electrolyzer operation decreases waste and improves overall sustainability. These improvements are crucial for large-scale hydrogen production facilities seeking to serve as suppliers of hydrogen fuel for transportation and industrial applications. In summary, this AI-based optimization case study underscores how advanced algorithms can unlock new levels of efficiency, reliability, and sustainability in hydrogen production. The integration of machine learning and reinforcement learning in PEM electrolyzers showcases AI's potential to drive sustainable hydrogen production, supporting the transition to cleaner energy sources. With such advancements, hydrogen production is becoming an increasingly viable component of the renewable energy landscape.

Case Study: Hystar's HyPilot Project-Advancing Green Hydrogen Production

Hystar, a Norwegian cleantech company, has launched the HyPilot project to advance the commercialization of its next-generation Proton Exchange Membrane (PEM) electrolyser technology. Located at the Kårstø Gas Processing Plant in Rogaland, Norway, the project involves deploying a 1.5 MW containerized PEM electrolyser system designed to produce green hydrogen with significantly improved efficiency compared to conventional systems. This initiative is a collaborative effort with major industrial partners, including Equinor, Yara Clean

Ammonia, Gassco, and ABB. It is supported by Enova, a Norwegian government-owned enterprise that promotes sustainable energy solutions. The HyPilot project strategically aims to validate Hystar's patented electrolyser under real-world operating conditions, particularly under intermittent power scenarios commonly associated with renewable energy sources. Over a 10,000-hour operational period, the project will generate extensive performance data related to system durability, efficiency, and adaptability. This long-term field testing not only supports technology validation but also positions Hystar's solution for broader commercial deployment. By demonstrating high technology readiness in collaboration with established industrial players, the HyPilot project represents a significant step toward scaling green hydrogen production and integrating AI-compatible electrolysis systems into future energy infrastructures.

Battery System Improvements with AI

AI-driven improvements in battery systems are revolutionizing energy storage, a cornerstone of sustainable energy solutions. With the rising demand for reliable energy storage solutions for renewable sources, the optimization of battery systems using AI offers substantial benefits, including enhanced efficiency, improved safety, and extended longevity. This case study focuses on lithium-ion batteries, widely used in Electric Vehicles (EVs) and grid storage, and explores how AI is transforming battery management and design [84]. Lithium-ion batteries, although efficient, have inherent challenges, including a limited lifespan, overheating risks, and degradation over time. AI algorithms tackle these issues by enabling Battery Management Systems (BMS) to monitor and predict battery behavior under various conditions. Through machine learning, predictive analytics, and deep learning models, AI enables the early detection of performance degradation and overheating, thereby preventing issues such as thermal runaway. This predictive capability is vital in EVs, where battery reliability and safety are paramount. One application of AI is in optimizing charging cycles to prolong battery life. Supervised learning algorithms analyze historical data from charge-discharge cycles, identifying optimal charging patterns that minimize wear on the electrodes. Reinforcement learning models then adapt these charging patterns in real time, based on usage and environmental factors, ensuring the battery operates under conditions that maximize its lifespan. For example, in high-temperature scenarios, the BMS may lower the charging speed to avoid overheating, extending both battery safety and longevity. Generative AI also plays a significant role in enhancing battery design. Through simulations and data-driven predictions, AI identifies optimal materials and chemistries, including novel electrolyte compositions or electrode structures that improve energy density and durability. Researchers can simulate thousands of material interactions to pinpoint the most promising combinations, a process that traditionally required time-consuming experimentation. The discovery of lithium iron phosphate ($LiFePO_4$) as an alternative to lithium cobalt oxide is one example where AI-driven simulations guided material selection. In practical terms, AI-driven battery improvements contribute to cost savings for manufacturers, reduced environmental impact, and greater adoption of EVs and renewable energy storage. For instance, Tesla's use of AI in optimizing battery management has been instrumental in achieving longer-range EVs and reducing battery degradation, contributing to their leadership in the EV market [85]. This case study illustrates the transformative potential of AI in battery technology, where enhanced safety, efficiency, and sustainability enable broader applications across various industries. AI-enhanced batteries are crucial for addressing today's energy challenges, driving advancements in transportation, energy storage, and the integration of renewables in energy grids.

Case Study: AI-Enhanced Predictive Maintenance in Flow Battery Systems

Artificial Intelligence (AI) is becoming increasingly crucial in enhancing the performance of flow battery systems, particularly for large-scale grid energy storage applications. Known for their scalability and long lifespan, flow batteries are complex systems that require meticulous monitoring of various parameters, including temperature, pressure, electrolyte concentration, and voltage. Traditionally, maintaining these systems involved scheduled inspections or reactive measures in response to system failures. However, this method often results in unexpected downtimes and decreased system efficiency. To address these challenges, companies such as NenPower are incorporating AI-driven predictive maintenance platforms into flow battery infrastructure. These platforms continuously analyze real-time data from sensors embedded throughout the battery system. Advanced machine learning algorithms process this data to identify subtle anomalies or trends that might signal carly signs of component wear, electrolyte imbalance, membrane fouling, or pump failures. By detecting these potential issues before they worsen, AI enables proactive maintenance scheduling, focusing on specific components at optimal times rather than adhering to fixed intervals. This approach leads to fewer operational disruptions, lower maintenance costs, and a longer equipment lifespan. Additionally, AI models can dynamically adjust charging and discharging cycles based on usage patterns and environmental conditions, thereby improving overall energy efficiency. In the realm of grid-scale applications, such intelligent monitoring and control mechanisms enhance the competitiveness and reliability of flow batteries. As energy demands increase and the shift to renewable energy accelerates, AI-enabled flow batteries provide a robust solution for long-duration energy storage with minimal human intervention, contributing to greater system resilience and sustainability.

Case Study: Capalo AI's Virtual Power Plants for Energy Storage Optimization

Capalo AI, a Finland-based startup, is revolutionizing the operation of battery energy storage systems through the use of artificial intelligence. Their platform functions as a Virtual Power Plant (VPP), utilizing AI algorithms to forecast renewable energy generation, predict consumer demand, and optimize the scheduling of battery charging and discharging accordingly. By evaluating real-time information such as weather patterns, electricity market rates, and grid limitations, the platform makes dynamic, data-driven choices to optimize energy efficiency and financial returns for battery owners. This AI-based strategy enables storage systems to adapt flexibly to changes in both supply and demand, effectively stabilizing the grid. The platform also offers operators insights on reducing energy waste and enhancing battery health. By doing so, Capalo AI facilitates the efficient integration of renewable energy sources, such as solar and wind, into the power grid, while also enhancing the profitability of energy storage systems. These solutions demonstrate how AI is advancing the Technology Readiness Level (TRL) of smart energy systems, providing scalable, commercially viable tools that tackle real-world energy management challenges in decentralized power networks.

AI in Electrochemical Sensors for Process Monitoring

The integration of Artificial Intelligence (AI) in electrochemical sensors has significantly transformed the landscape of process monitoring across various industries. Electrochemical sensors are pivotal for detecting and quantifying chemical substances, providing critical information about the conditions of processes in real time. When paired with AI algorithms, these sensors not only enhance measurement accuracy but also facilitate predictive analytics, enabling proactive decision-making and process optimization [86]. Electrochemical sensors operate by converting chemical signals into electrical signals, enabling the monitoring of parameters such as pH, ion concentration, and the presence of specific molecules. Fig. (**10**) shows the schematic diagram of the electrochemical sensor. The working principle is as follows: firstly, a certain external voltage is applied to the electrode; then, a material with a specific electrochemical activity reacts in a redox reaction around the electrode, generating charge transfer and further forming current. The current will be transmitted through the conduction system of the electrodes to the signal analysis system for amplification. Traditional sensors, while effective, often generate vast amounts of data that can overwhelm human analysts. This is where AI comes into play. Machine learning and deep learning algorithms can process and analyze these data streams efficiently, identifying patterns and trends that may not be apparent through manual analysis. This capability is particularly important in environments where conditions fluctuate rapidly and accurate data is crucial for maintaining operational efficiency. One of the primary applications of AI-enhanced electrochemical sensors is in predictive maintenance for industrial operations. Predictive maintenance utilizes real-time data collected from sensors to anticipate equipment failures before they occur. For instance, an electrochemical sensor installed in a manufacturing process can monitor various parameters, such as chemical concentrations, temperature, and pressure. AI algorithms can continuously analyze this data, learning from historical patterns to predict potential anomalies. If sensor readings deviate from established norms, the AI system can trigger alerts, prompting maintenance teams to investigate potential issues before they become significant. This proactive approach not only minimizes equipment downtime but also reduces maintenance costs and enhances overall operational efficiency.

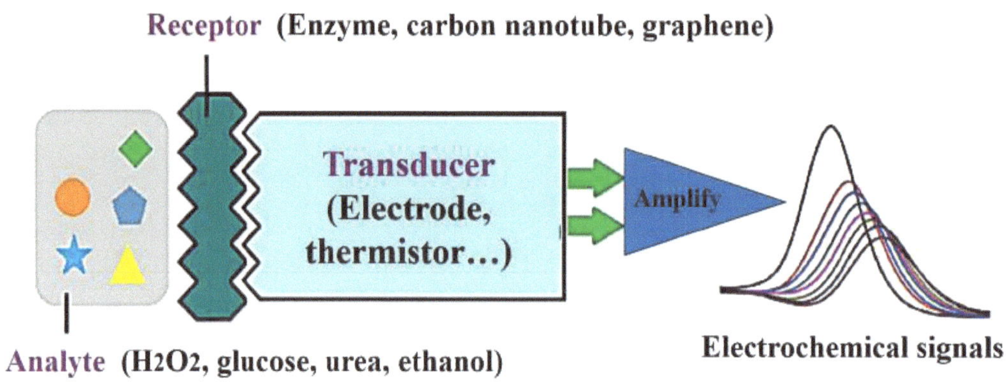

Fig. (10). Diagram of an electrochemical sensor illustrating key components: analyte, receptor, transducer, and amplifier. The analyte binds to the receptor, triggering the transducer to convert the interaction into a measurable electrical signal, which is then amplified for accurate detection and analysis. Reprinted from [87] Copyright © 1996-2024 MDPI (Basel, Switzerland).

Environmental monitoring is another critical area benefiting from AI-integrated electrochemical sensors. Traditional methods of monitoring environmental pollutants often involve complex procedures that can delay results, thereby hindering timely responses to potential hazards. AI-enhanced electrochemical sensors provide real-time data analysis capabilities, enabling instant insights into the levels of contaminants, such as heavy metals and volatile organic compounds, in water and air. For example, an electrochemical sensor designed to monitor heavy metal concentrations in wastewater treatment facilities can utilize AI algorithms to assess incoming data continuously. The AI system can automatically adjust treatment processes based on real-time readings, ensuring compliance with regulatory standards and protecting public health. In the realm of energy systems, AI-enhanced electrochemical sensors play a pivotal role in monitoring battery performance. Lithium-ion batteries, widely used in various applications ranging from electric vehicles to renewable energy storage, require precise monitoring of parameters such as voltage, current, and temperature. By incorporating AI algorithms, these sensors can analyze data to predict battery life and optimize charging cycles. Machine learning models can utilize historical performance data to forecast potential failure points, enabling timely interventions that enhance safety and extend the lifespan of the batteries [88]. This capability is becoming increasingly important as the demand for efficient and reliable energy storage solutions continues to grow. Moreover, the advent of smart sensor networks represents a significant advancement in process monitoring. In agriculture, for example, a network of electrochemical sensors can monitor various soil parameters, including moisture levels, nutrient concentrations, and pH values. By integrating AI, the data from these sensors can be analyzed to provide farmers with actionable insights. The AI system can recommend optimal irrigation schedules or fertilization strategies based on real-time data, thereby enhancing crop yields while minimizing resource wastage. This targeted approach not only increases agricultural productivity but also supports sustainable farming practices.

AI techniques are also being employed to improve the calibration and accuracy of electrochemical sensors. Calibration is a crucial aspect of sensor performance, often requiring manual adjustments that can introduce errors and inconsistencies. AI algorithms can analyze large datasets to develop self-calibrating sensors that maintain accuracy over time. This advancement significantly reduces the need for routine manual calibrations, streamlining operations and ensuring consistent performance. Furthermore, the use of AI in data fusion enhances the capabilities of electrochemical sensors by integrating data from multiple sources. This fusion of data allows for a more comprehensive understanding of the process environment. For example, in industrial settings, data from electrochemical sensors can be combined with information from temperature sensors, pressure gauges, and other monitoring devices. AI algorithms can then analyze this multifaceted dataset to provide a holistic view of process conditions, enabling more informed decision-making and improved operational control [89].

Case Study*: *XtalPi's AI-Guided Catalyst Discovery

XtalPi, a technology company at the intersection of AI, quantum science, and material discovery, is leveraging computational power to accelerate the identification of new electrochemical catalysts. Initially focused on pharmaceuticals, the company has broadened its AI-driven platform to materials science, where it assists in designing catalysts for fuel cells, batteries, and hydrogen production. By employing advanced machine learning models and quantum mechanical simulations, XtalPi can predict the properties of numerous materials at a fraction of the time and cost of traditional experimental methods. This AI-guided discovery process enables the rapid screening of catalyst candidates, facilitating researchers and commercial developers in identifying materials with optimal activity, stability, and selectivity. The approach minimizes trial-and-error in the lab, shortens development cycles, and enables more targeted experimentation. By collaborating with industrial partners, XtalPi brings these computationally identified materials closer to commercialization, advancing their Technology Readiness Level. Their platform exemplifies how AI is transforming material innovation, enabling the faster and more cost-effective discovery of next-generation electrochemical materials, and aligning them with real-world energy applications.

CHALLENGES AND FUTURE DIRECTIONS

As AI integration in electrochemical systems advances, various challenges emerge that must be addressed to facilitate large-scale adoption. The most significant hurdles include scalability, industrial integration, data security, and the adaptation of advanced AI frameworks, such as self-learning systems and predictive analytics. Firstly, scaling AI applications in electrochemical reactors requires extensive data sets for model training and validation. AI-driven electrochemical designs often rely on advanced machine learning and deep learning models that require vast amounts of process data [90]. However, data availability is often limited due to proprietary restrictions or insufficient process monitoring. Moreover, scaling AI to work effectively in industrial settings requires systems to operate in real-time; however, electrochemical processes are typically complex, dynamic, and nonlinear, making real-time data processing particularly challenging. Additionally, integrating AI models for electrochemical applications involves aligning multiple systems and databases across an organization, which presents logistical and interoperability challenges, especially in industries with existing legacy systems. Another significant challenge lies in the security, privacy, and management of data in AI-based electrochemical applications. AI solutions often require access to highly sensitive operational data, raising concerns over privacy and intellectual property. The growing reliance on data sharing and remote access for AI systems exposes them to cyber threats, potentially compromising data integrity and system safety. Moreover, regulatory frameworks surrounding data use in AI are still evolving, and industries may face challenges in adhering to diverse regulations across different regions.

Lastly, the future of AI-enhanced electrochemical systems is evolving rapidly, with trends such as self-learning systems and predictive analytics set to play a crucial role in their development. Self-learning systems enable AI to adapt and optimize autonomously, potentially transforming electrochemical processes by making them more adaptable and efficient. Predictive analytics, which anticipates system behavior based on historical and real-time data, could improve fault detection and maintenance, minimizing downtime. However, implementing such advanced AI models requires high processing power and computational resources, which may not be readily available in all industrial environments. These trends also require advanced training and upskilling of the workforce, adding to the financial and time investments necessary for successful adoption. Overcoming these challenges will be crucial for the future direction of AI-driven electrochemical technology, requiring collaboration between industry stakeholders, technology providers, and regulatory bodies. By addressing scalability, data management, security, and technological advancements, the field can progress towards creating more efficient, adaptive, and secure electrochemical systems. Fig. (**11**) illustrates a flowchart that outlines the various challenges encountered in electrochemical systems.

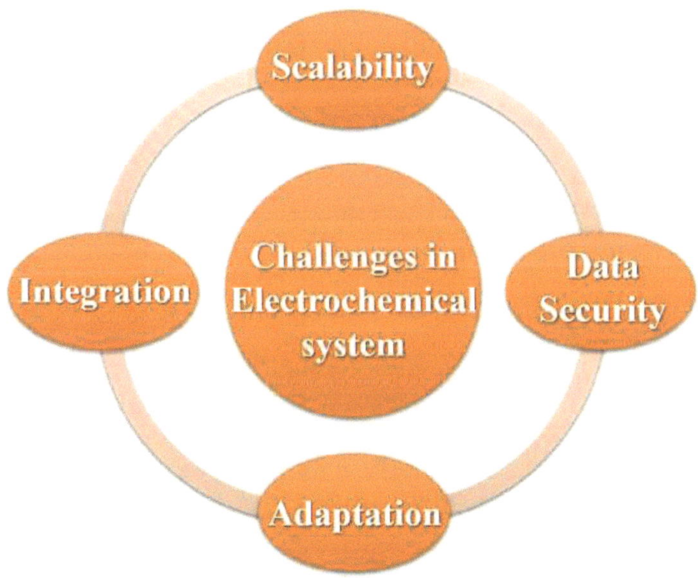

Fig. (11). Flowchart illustrating the various challenges encountered in electrochemical systems.

Scalability and Industrial Integration of AI Solutions

Scalability in AI-driven electrochemical solutions is crucial for industries seeking to deploy AI-enhanced designs across multiple operational units or facilities. Scaling up AI systems from lab-scale prototypes to full industrial implementations requires extensive effort and is often limited by several factors.

One primary constraint is the quality and volume of data available. Electrochemical processes involve complex interactions among materials, electric fields, and chemical reactions, requiring AI models to be trained on comprehensive datasets to ensure accurate predictions and control [91]. However, data collected in laboratories often differ from industrial-scale data, where noise, equipment variability, and environmental factors play a much larger role. Therefore, creating reliable AI models requires high-quality data that accurately represents these conditions, which may not always be readily available. Industrial integration also requires AI systems to communicate effectively with existing equipment, databases, and control systems. Many industries still rely on legacy systems, which often lack the necessary interoperability for AI systems to access and utilize their data. Developing AI solutions that are compatible with existing equipment or establishing protocols for data standardization across systems can be both costly and time-consuming. Furthermore, any industrial implementation must consider process reliability, which means that AI-based systems must be capable of performing consistently across various operational scenarios without risking productivity or safety.

In addition to these technical challenges, the industrial integration of AI into electrochemical systems faces economic and human resource barriers. AI solutions often require a significant initial investment in infrastructure, including upgrades to equipment, software integration, and personnel training [92]. Return On Investment (ROI) for AI in electrochemical systems may take time to realize, which can deter companies from fully committing to these innovations. Moreover, organizations must invest in skilled personnel who can maintain and troubleshoot these AI systems. Integrating AI into daily operations also demands upskilling or hiring data scientists and engineers proficient in electrochemical processes and AI, which can further raise costs. Another significant aspect of scalability is the computational demand of AI models, particularly for electrochemical systems that operate in real time. Real-time AI applications, such as predictive maintenance or process optimization, require substantial computational power and storage. Cloud computing and edge computing offer potential solutions by allowing data to be processed off-site or closer to the data source, respectively. However, these solutions introduce complexity to data management and raise concerns about latency, which is crucial for applications that require rapid response times. The path forward for scalable AI integration in the electrochemical industry involves a combination of technological advancements and organizational changes. Collaborative efforts between AI developers, industrial stakeholders, and regulatory authorities can help establish data-sharing frameworks that streamline integration while respecting proprietary information and intellectual property rights [93]. Additionally, industry-focused training programs can bridge skill gaps, equipping workers with the knowledge required to manage AI-based systems effectively. Successfully scaling AI-driven electrochemical systems also requires the development of adaptable AI models that can self-tune to handle variations in the industrial environment. By incorporating adaptability, industries can deploy systems that dynamically adjust to various operating conditions, making AI a viable and scalable solution in electrochemical industries.

Security, Privacy, and Data Challenges

As AI solutions become integrated into electrochemical systems, data security, privacy, and management challenges become critical areas of concern. Electrochemical processes often involve highly sensitive operational and material data that, if exposed, could reveal proprietary technologies or compromise intellectual property. For instance, details about reactor design, material compositions, or process efficiencies are often considered trade secrets, making data security a top priority. The increasing reliance on AI-based systems, particularly those that require internet connectivity for data sharing and remote monitoring, has amplified the risk of cyber threats. Electrochemical industries are vulnerable to cyberattacks that could disrupt operations or result in data theft. For example, hackers could potentially manipulate process parameters, leading to system malfunctions, compromised product quality, or even hazardous conditions. Therefore, implementing robust cybersecurity protocols to protect AI-enabled electrochemical systems is crucial. Privacy concerns also arise when AI systems collect and analyze data at high levels of granularity. Regulatory frameworks governing data privacy and security vary by region, making compliance a complex process. For instance, data protection regulations like the General Data Protection Regulation (GDPR) in the European Union impose strict data handling requirements, even for industrial data. This regulatory landscape requires electrochemical companies deploying AI to establish protocols for data collection, storage, and sharing that adhere to legal and ethical standards. Balancing the need for extensive data to train AI models with privacy requirements adds a layer of complexity to the deployment of AI. Data quality and integrity pose additional challenges in AI applications for electrochemical processes. Data-driven AI models depend on the quality and accuracy of data for training and prediction; however, electrochemical data can be inconsistent due to variations in equipment, environmental conditions, or data collection methodologies [94]. Establishing data standardization practices can improve data quality; however, discrepancies may still arise across different operating units or facilities.

Additionally, incomplete data sets can lead to biased AI models, which reduces their effectiveness and potentially results in suboptimal decisions. To address these challenges, electrochemical industries must adopt robust data management and security frameworks. Data encryption, access controls, and regular audits can enhance security and limit the potential for data breaches. Moreover, implementing secure data-sharing protocols, such as federated learning, can enable organizations to train AI models without transferring sensitive data outside company networks, thereby mitigating privacy risks. Further, organizations can adopt ethical AI practices by embedding transparency into their AI systems, such as explainable AI (XAI) models that allow users to understand the reasoning behind AI decisions [95]. Transparent AI systems foster trust among stakeholders and ensure that AI implementations align with ethical standards and regulatory requirements. Looking ahead, addressing these security, privacy, and data challenges will be crucial for scaling AI in electrochemical industries. By adopting a proactive approach to data security and privacy, and by fostering compliance with regulatory frameworks, organizations can better safeguard their AI systems and the valuable data they handle, ensuring that AI serves as a secure and reliable tool in the future of sustainable electrochemical systems.

FUTURE TRENDS

Self-Learning Systems and Predictive Analytics

Self-learning systems and predictive analytics represent the next wave of innovation in AI-enhanced electrochemical systems, promising to elevate process optimization, fault detection, and maintenance to new levels of efficiency and autonomy. Self-learning AI systems, also known as adaptive or dynamic AI, are designed to evolve independently based on new data, identifying patterns, and refining their models without human intervention. These systems could play a transformative role in electrochemical processes by continuously adapting to changing operating conditions, raw material variability, and external environmental factors. In electrochemical reactors, self-learning systems could significantly improve process control and operational stability. By autonomously tuning parameters such as voltage, temperature, and chemical concentrations, these systems can enhance the consistency and efficiency of electrochemical reactions. Additionally, self-learning systems enable continuous improvement of predictive maintenance. By analyzing vast amounts of historical and real-time data, these AI systems can detect potential malfunctions or performance declines before they impact operations, minimizing downtime and reducing costs associated with unplanned maintenance. For example, self-learning systems could be programmed to monitor voltage fluctuations in electrochemical cells, using this data to predict issues like electrode degradation or electrolyte depletion [96].

Predictive analytics further expands the capabilities of AI in electrochemical industries by leveraging statistical and machine learning techniques to forecast future operational outcomes based on historical data. For instance, predictive models can anticipate changes in reaction efficiency based on fluctuations in temperature or pH levels, enabling proactive adjustments that maintain optimal performance. Predictive analytics can also facilitate energy savings by forecasting periods of high energy consumption and adjusting system settings accordingly. This capability aligns with sustainability goals, enabling industries to minimize resource consumption and reduce their environmental impact. Despite the promising potential of self-learning systems and predictive analytics, implementing these advanced AI solutions presents challenges. High computational requirements mean that organizations must invest in robust IT infrastructure capable of supporting real-time data processing. Moreover, self-learning systems require careful monitoring to ensure they adapt correctly without introducing errors or biases. Additionally, interpreting predictive analytics results requires skilled personnel who understand both AI and electrochemical processes, highlighting the need for continued investment in workforce training. The integration of these AI technologies into electrochemical systems may also prompt the development of new industry standards and regulatory frameworks. Self-learning AI systems, for instance, operate autonomously, potentially introducing ethical concerns around accountability and control [97]. Organizations adopting self-learning AI may need to establish guidelines for oversight, ensuring that these systems make safe and ethical decisions. In the coming years, self-learning systems and predictive analytics are likely to become integral components of electrochemical industries, shaping a future where processes are more efficient, adaptive, and sustainable. With continued advancements in AI technology, these trends have the potential to redefine traditional electrochemical systems, making them smarter, more resilient, and better aligned with industry and environmental goals. The path forward will involve overcoming technical, ethical, and regulatory challenges to fully harness the potential of these innovations for the benefit of industries and society.

Commercialization Pathways and Industry Relevance

The integration of artificial intelligence into electrochemical systems is no longer limited to research laboratories; it is steadily moving toward scalable, commercial solutions. This shift toward commercialization is supported by several key pathways, including a growing patent landscape, an expanding startup ecosystem, and the emergence of AI-as-a-Service (AIaaS) models tailored to materials science and energy technologies. Recent years have seen a significant increase in patent filings related to the AI-driven discovery and optimization of electrochemical materials, including catalysts for hydrogen production, battery electrodes, and solid-state electrolytes. These patents indicate not only technological innovation but also a clear intention to secure intellectual property for future industrial deployment. For example, companies such as Siemens, IBM, and Mitsubishi are actively filing patents in AI-powered battery diagnostics and electrolysis systems, reflecting the commercial potential of these innovations. Simultaneously, a vibrant startup ecosystem is developing around AI in electrochemistry. Startups such as XtalPi, Emvolon, and Capalo AI are using machine learning and computational chemistry to create platforms for rapid material screening, virtual power plant optimization, and autonomous process control. These ventures bridge the gap between laboratory-scale innovation and market-ready products by offering scalable and modular AI tools that can be readily integrated into industrial workflows.

Furthermore, the rise of AI-as-a-Service (AIaaS) platforms is broadening access to these technologies. Businesses are no longer required to create their own AI infrastructures; instead, they can opt for cloud-based platforms that provide pre-trained models and customizable analytics specifically designed for electrochemical applications. This transition democratizes access to high-performance computing, accelerating adoption across various industries, including energy storage, green hydrogen, and fuel cell technologies. These advancements align closely with the objectives of Industry 4.0, which focuses on digital transformation, smart automation, and data-driven manufacturing. In the context of the burgeoning hydrogen economy, AI plays a crucial role in enhancing the design and operation of electrolyser systems, facilitating real-time diagnostics, and optimizing the integration of renewable energy sources. The merging of AI, electrochemistry, and industrial automation thus marks a significant advancement toward more sustainable, intelligent, and commercially viable energy technologies.

CONCLUSION

This chapter explored the transformative role of artificial intelligence in the discovery, modeling, and deployment of advanced electrochemical materials, framing AI as a catalyst for innovation in sustainable energy technologies. By addressing the limitations of traditional trial-and-error approaches, AI empowers rapid material screening, performance prediction, and process optimization. AI methodologies—particularly machine learning, deep learning, and reinforcement learning—have been demonstrated to revolutionize the understanding of structure-property relationships, reaction kinetics, and real-time operational behaviors in electrochemical systems. The integration of AI into hydrogen production, battery engineering, and sensor design demonstrates its far-reaching impact across multiple energy platforms. Case studies have highlighted how AI-driven models optimize key performance metrics such as overpotential, charge/discharge rates, and material stability—directly improving the viability and scalability of these technologies. Industrial implementations showcased applications like intelligent electrolyzers and AI-enhanced flow battery systems, illustrating the convergence of research innovation and market readiness.

Importantly, the chapter emphasized AI's alignment with global sustainability efforts, particularly the United Nations Sustainable Development Goals (SDGs). AI-augmented electrochemical systems contribute to the development of clean energy, reduced emissions, and more resource-efficient processes. Predictive maintenance and anomaly detection help reduce waste and operational downtimes, while AI-assisted material selection supports environmentally conscious design choices, such as eco-friendly catalysts or low-carbon materials. The discussion also acknowledged challenges related to data privacy, model transparency, and deployment scalability. Overcoming these barriers will require standardized protocols, secure data infrastructures, and interdisciplinary collaboration between researchers, industry, and policymakers. Emerging commercialization strategies—such as AI-as-a-Service (AIaaS), intellectual property trends, and startup activity—signal a growing ecosystem supporting AI-driven electrochemical innovation.

Looking ahead, autonomous self-optimizing systems and AI-led materials discovery platforms will shape the next generation of electrochemical technologies. These advancements promise not only improved performance and reliability but also stronger alignment with environmental and industrial goals. As AI continues to drive data-informed design and sustainable innovation, it stands poised to redefine the landscape of electrochemical materials and reinforce its central role in building a cleaner energy future.

ACKNOWLEDGEMENTS

Authors Soumya Rai and Chhaya Ravi Kant would like to acknowledge the support of Prof. Ranjana Jha, Vice-Chancellor of Indira Gandhi Delhi Technical University for Women, Delhi, for providing the essential resources required for this work. Soumya Rai gratefully acknowledges the financial support provided by Indira Gandhi Delhi Technical University for Women, Delhi. Authors Jahanvi Thakur, Anshi Pandey, and Nand Lal Singh extend their heartfelt gratitude to Prof. Anand Srivastava, Vice-Chancellor of Netaji Subhas University of Technology, for his encouragement in advancing research excellence. Moreover, we wish to acknowledge the valuable insights of the researchers in this field, which have significantly enriched this study.

REFERENCES

[1] A. Al-Othman, M. Tawalbeh, R. Martis, S. Dhou, M. Orhan, M. Qasim, and A. Ghani Olabi, "Artificial intelligence and numerical models in hybrid renewable energy systems with fuel cells: Advances and prospects", *Energy Convers. Manage.*, vol. 253, p. 115154, 2022.

[http://dx.doi.org/10.1016/j.enconman.2021.115154]

[2] Available from: https://www.proquest.com/openview/9609de62b48f4747b3d05215646f1561/1?pq-origsite=gscholar&cbl=18750&diss=y

[3] N.L. Rane, M. Paramesha, S.P. Choudhary, & J. Rane. "Artificial Intelligence, Machine Learning, and Deep Learning for Advanced Business Strategies". *A Review. Partners Universal International Innovation Journal (PUIIJ)*, vol. 02, no. 03, pp. 147–171, 2024. [http://dx.doi.org/10.5281/zenodo.12208298]

[4] M. Bracconi, "Intensification of catalytic reactors: A synergic effort of Multiscale Modeling, Machine Learning and Additive Manufacturing", *Chem. Eng. Process.,* vol. 181, p. 109148, 2022. [http://dx.doi.org/10.1016/j.cep.2022.109148]

[5] L.T. Zhu, X-Z. Chen, B. Ouyang, W-C. Yan, H. Lei, Z. Chen, and Z-H. Luo, "Review of machine learning for hydrodynamics, transport, and reactions in multiphase flows and reactors", *Ind. Eng. Chem. Res.,* vol. 61, no. 28, pp. 9901-9949, 2022. [http://dx.doi.org/10.1021/acs.iecr.2c01036]

[6] I. Ahmad, "Advances in Machine Learning for Monitoring, Control, and Optimization of Temperature of Reactors", 2023. [http://dx.doi.org/10.20944/preprints202309.1318.v1]

[7] T. Ahmad, D. Zhang, C. Huang, H. Zhang, N. Dai, Y. Song, and H. Chen, "Artificial intelligence in sustainable energy industry: Status Quo, challenges and opportunities", *J. Clean. Prod.,* vol. 289, p. 125834, 2021. [http://dx.doi.org/10.1016/j.jclepro.2021.125834]

[8] B. Ramasubramanian, R. P. Rao, V. Chellappan, and S. Ramakrishna, *Towards Sustainable Fuel Cells and Batteries with an AI Perspective,* 2022. [http://dx.doi.org/10.3390/su142316001]

[9] B. Ramasubramanian, R. P. Rao, V. Chellappan, and S. Ramakrishna, "Towards sustainable fuel cells and batteries with an ai perspective", *Sustainability,* vol. 14, no. 23, p. 16001, Nov. 2022. [http://dx.doi.org/10.3390/SU142316001]

[10] K. Liu, Z. Wei, C. Zhang, Y. Shang, R. Teodorescu, and Q. L. Han, "Towards long lifetime battery: ai-based manufacturing and management", *IEEE/CAA J Autom Sinica,* vol. 9, no. 7, pp. 1139-1165, 2022. [http://dx.doi.org/10.1109/JAS.2022.105599]

[11] Available from: https://books.google.co.in/books?hl=en&lr=&id=FysfEQAAQBAJ&oi=fnd&pg=PA159&dq=in+carbon+capture+and+utilization+processes,+AI-driven+electrochemical+systems+can+help+optimize+reaction+conditions,+maximizing+carbon+conversion+while+minimizing+energy+consumption.+&ots=SYE5TW5Rtw&sig=3n8JKQYhGAHhcAho79MupzD26J4&redir_esc=y#v=onepage&q&f=false

[12] M. G. Shirkoohi, R. D. Tyagi, P. A. Vanrolleghem, and P. Drogui, "Artificial intelligence techniques in electrochemical processes for water and wastewater treatment: a review", *J Environ Health Sci Eng,* vol. 20, no. 2, pp. 1089-1109, 2022. [http://dx.doi.org/10.1007/S40201-022-00835-W]

[13] R. Chaturvedi, "Maximizing towards the sustainability: integrating materials, energy, and resource efficiency in revolutionizing manufacturing industry", *E3S Web Conf,* vol. 453, p. 01036, 2023. [http://dx.doi.org/10.1051/E3SCONF/202345301036]

[14] B. Senthil Rathi, P. Senthil Kumar, S. Sanjay, M. Prem Kumar, and G. Rangasamy, "Artificial intelligence integration in conventional wastewater treatment techniques: techno-economic evaluation, recent progress and its future direction", *Int. J. Environ. Sci. Technol.,* vol. 2024, pp. 1-26, 2024. [http://dx.doi.org/10.1007/s13762-024-05725-2]

[15] S.P.S. Badwal, S.S. Giddey, C. Munnings, A.I. Bhatt, and A.F. Hollenkamp, "Emerging

electrochemical energy conversion and storage technologies", *Front Chem.,* vol. 2, no. SEP, p. 79, 2014.
[http://dx.doi.org/10.3389/fchem.2014.00079] [PMID: 25309898]

[16] T. Noël, Y. Cao, and G. Laudadio, "The fundamentals behind the use of flow reactors in electrochemistry", *Acc. Chem. Res.,* vol. 52, no. 10, pp. 2858-2869, 2019.
[http://dx.doi.org/10.1021/acs.accounts.9b00412] [PMID: 31573791]

[17] G. R, V. Thangarasu, A. Vinayakaselvi M, and A. Ramanathan, "A critical review of recent advancements in continuous flow reactors and prominent integrated microreactors for biodiesel production", *Renew. Sustain. Energy Rev.,* vol. 154, p. 111869, 2022.
[http://dx.doi.org/10.1016/j.rser.2021.111869]

[18] O. Garcia-Rodriguez, E. Mousset, H. Olvera-Vargas, and O. Lefebvre, "Electrochemical treatment of highly concentrated wastewater: A review of experimental and modeling approaches from lab- to full-scale", *Crit. Rev. Environ. Sci. Technol.,* vol. 52, no. 2, pp. 240-309, 2022.
[http://dx.doi.org/10.1080/10643389.2020.1820428]

[19] L. Buglioni, F. Raymenants, A. Slattery, S.D.A. Zondag, and T. Noël, "Technological innovations in photochemistry for organic synthesis: flow chemistry, high-throughput experimentation, scale-up, and photoelectrochemistry", *Chem. Rev.,* vol. 122, no. 2, pp. 2752-2906, 2022.
[http://dx.doi.org/10.1021/acs.chemrev.1c00332] [PMID: 34375082]

[20] Q. Huang, S. Peng, J. Deng, H. Zeng, Z. Zhang, Y. Liu, and P. Yuan, "A review of the application of artificial intelligence to nuclear reactors: Where we are and what's next", *Heliyon,* vol. 9, no. 3, p. e13883, 2023.
[http://dx.doi.org/10.1016/j.heliyon.2023.e13883] [PMID: 36895398]

[21] Available from: https://books.google.co.in/books?hl=en&lr=&id=2nLl6SJ8RfMC&oi=fnd&pg=PR4&dq=Batch+reactors+operate+by+introducing+a+fixed+quantity+of+reactants+into+a+closed+container+where+the+reaction+proceeds+until+completion.+This+setup+allows+for+precise+control+over+reaction+variables+such+as+reactant+concentration,+temperature,+and+pressures&ots=PrfmMwuvdx&sig=ExjjPzEdbePoFKOWezM0Wvuc_rs&redir_esc=y#v=onepage&q&f=false

[22] I. Pottratz, C. Schmidt, I. Müller, and C. Hamel, "Immobilization of β-galactosidase on monolithic discs for the production of prebiotics galacto-oligosaccharides", In: *Chem Ing Tech* vol. 93. , 2021, no. 5, pp. 838-843.
[http://dx.doi.org/10.1002/cite.202000231]

[23] N.C. Neyt, and D.L. Riley, "Application of reactor engineering concepts in continuous flow chemistry: a review", *React. Chem. Eng.,* vol. 6, no. 8, pp. 1295-1326, 2021.
[http://dx.doi.org/10.1039/D1RE00004G]

[24] A. Tanimu, S. Jaenicke, and K. Alhooshani, "Heterogeneous catalysis in continuous flow microreactors: A review of methods and applications", *Chem. Eng. J.,* vol. 327, pp. 792-821, 2017.
[http://dx.doi.org/10.1016/j.cej.2017.06.161]

[25] G. Caygill, M. Zanfir, and A. Gavriilidis, "Scalable reactor design for pharmaceuticals and fine chemicals production. 1: Potential scale-up obstacles", *Org. Process Res. Dev.,* vol. 10, no. 3, pp. 539-552, 2006.
[http://dx.doi.org/10.1021/op050133a]

[26] T. Noël, Y. Su, and V. Hessel, "Beyond organometallic flow chemistry: The principles behind the use of continuous-flow reactors for synthesis", *Top. Organomet. Chem.,* vol. 57, pp. 1-41, 2015.
[http://dx.doi.org/10.1007/3418_2015_152]

[27] D. Levin, "Managing hazards for scale up of chemical manufacturing processes", *ACS Symposium Series* vol. 1181, 2014, pp. 3-71.
[http://dx.doi.org/10.1021/bk-2014-1181.ch001]

[28] J. Tang, C. Zhang, X. Shi, J. Sun, and J.A. Cunningham, "Municipal wastewater treatment plants

coupled with electrochemical, biological and bio-electrochemical technologies: Opportunities and challenge toward energy self-sufficiency", *J. Environ. Manage.*, vol. 234, pp. 396-403, 2019. [http://dx.doi.org/10.1016/j.jenvman.2018.12.097] [PMID: 30639863]

[29] T. Muddemann, D. Haupt, M. Sievers, and U. Kunz, "Electrochemical reactors for wastewater treatment", *ChemBioEng Rev.*, vol. 6, no. 5, pp. 142-156, 2019. [http://dx.doi.org/10.1002/cben.201900021]

[30] E. C. Rivera, "Data-driven modeling of smartphone-based electrochemiluminescence sensor data using artificial intelligence", *Sensors,* vol. 20, no. 3, p. 625, 2020. [http://dx.doi.org/10.3390/S20030625]

[31] A. Cardenas, G.T. Cuadrado, K.M. Martinez, M. Ali, M. Khayyat, and G. Szekely, "Data-driven optimization of chemical processes", *Sustainable Process Engineering,* no. Jul, pp. 294-326, 2024. [http://dx.doi.org/10.1515/9783111028163-014/HTML]

[32] J. Benavides-Hernández, and F. Dumeignil, "From characterization to discovery: Artificial intelligence, machine learning and high-throughput experiments for heterogeneous catalyst design", *ACS Catal.,* vol. 14, no. 15, pp. 11749-11779, 2024. [http://dx.doi.org/10.1021/acscatal.3c06293]

[33] B.K.M. Powell, D. Machalek, and T. Quah, "Real-time optimization using reinforcement learning", *Comput. Chem. Eng.,* vol. 143, p. 107077, 2020. [http://dx.doi.org/10.1016/j.compchemeng.2020.107077]

[34] P. Dhawas, M.A. Ramteke, A. Thakur, P.V. Polshetwar, R.V. Salunkhe, and D. Bhagat, *Big Data Analysis Techniques: Data Preprocessing Techniques, Data Mining Techniques, Machine Learning Algorithm, Visualization.* Available from: https://services.igi-global.com/resolvedoi/resolve.aspx?doi=10.4018/979-8-3693-0413-6.ch007 [http://dx.doi.org/10.4018/979-8-3693-0413-6.ch007]

[35] B. Ramasubramanian, R. P. Rao, V. Chellappan, and S. Ramakrishna, "Towards sustainable fuel cells and batteries with an ai perspective", *Sustainability,* vol. 14, no. 23, p. 16001, 2022. [http://dx.doi.org/10.3390/SU142316001]

[36] Available from: https://www.proquest.com/openview/9609de62b48f4747b3d05215646f1561/1?pq-origsite=gscholar&cbl=18750&diss=y

[37] Available from: https://books.google.co.in/books?hl=en&lr=&id=AtrPEAAAQBAJ&oi=fnd&pg=PA1975&dq=An+overview+of+the+predictive+analysis+process+using+ML,+defining+objectives,+collecting+data,+data+cleaning+and+preprocessing,+exploratory+data+analysis,+feature+engineering,+model+selection,+training+and+evaluation,+and+deployment+with+continuous+monitoring.+&ots=DiZh2zC7rW&sig=WKnG7HA_p3r1JTvx1Vg3scuPLu4&redir_esc=y#v=onepage&q&f=false

[38] V. Hassija, V. Chamola, A. Mahapatra, A. Singal, D. Goel, K. Huang, S. Scardapane, I. Spinelli, M. Mahmud, and A. Hussain, "Interpreting black-box models: A review on explainable artificial intelligence", *Cognit. Comput.,* vol. 16, no. 1, pp. 45-74, 2024. [http://dx.doi.org/10.1007/s12559-023-10179-8]

[39] A.F. Al-Nouti, M. Fu, and N.D. Bokde, "Reservoir operation based machine learning models: Comprehensive review for limitations, research gap, and possible future research direction", *Knowledge-Based Engineering and Sciences,* vol. 5, no. 2, pp. 75-139, 2024. [http://dx.doi.org/10.51526/kbes.2024.5.2.75-139]

[40] A. Bagheri, *Applications of deep learning and time-series analysis in dynamic process optimization and decision making,* 2024. Available from: https://hdl.handle.net/2097/44421

[41] C. Li, D. Wang, and L. Kong, "Application of machine learning techniques in mineral classification for scanning electron microscopy - energy dispersive X-ray spectroscopy (SEM-EDS) images", *J. Petrol. Sci. Eng.,* vol. 200, p. 108178, 2021. [http://dx.doi.org/10.1016/j.petrol.2020.108178]

[42] X. Chen, G. Qu, Y. Tang, S. Low, and N. Li, "Reinforcement learning for selective key applications in power systems: Recent advances and future challenges", *IEEE Trans. Smart Grid,* vol. 13, no. 4, pp. 2935-2958, 2022. [http://dx.doi.org/10.1109/TSG.2022.3154718]

[43] S. Li, Y. Q. Deng, Z. L. Zhu, H. L. Hua, and Z. Z. Tao, "A comprehensive review on radiomics and deep learning for nasopharyngeal carcinoma imaging", *Diagnostics,* vol. 11, no. 9, p. 1523, 2021. [http://dx.doi.org/10.3390/DIAGNOSTICS11091523]

[44] K.G. Sharma, N.S. Kaisare, and H. Goyal, "A recurrent neural network model for biomass gasification chemistry", *React. Chem. Eng.,* vol. 7, no. 3, pp. 570-579, 2022. [http://dx.doi.org/10.1039/D1RE00409C]

[45] S.H. Yang, E-B. Park, S.Y. Cho, Y.S. Kang, H-A. Ju, Y. Jeon, D. Yang, S-D. Yim, S. Lee, and Y-M. Kim, "Deep learning morphological distribution analysis of metal alloy catalysts in proton exchange membrane fuel cells", *Mater. Today Energy,* vol. 36, p. 101348, 2023. [http://dx.doi.org/10.1016/j.mtener.2023.101348]

[46] K. Scott, "The continuous stirred tank electrochemical reactor. An overview of dynamic and steady state analysis for design and modelling", *J. Appl. Electrochem.,* vol. 21, no. 11, pp. 945-960, 1991. [http://dx.doi.org/10.1007/BF01077579]

[47] Hassan, Qusay, Hafedh, Saadoon Abdul, Mohammed, Hussein Burhan, Abdulrahman, Imad Saeed, Salman, Hayder M. and Jaszczur, Marek., "A review of hydrogen production from bio-energy, technologies and assessments", *Energy Harvesting and Systems,* vol. 372, no. 1, p. 20220117, 2024. [http://dx.doi.org/10.1515/ehs-2022-0117]

[48] W. Wang, H. Liu, W. Lin, and Y. Chen, "Investigation on works and military applications of artificial intelligence", *IEEE Access,* 2020. Available from: https://ieeexplore.ieee.org/abstract/document/9143084/

[49] T. Ahmad, R. Madonski, D. Zhang, C. Huang, and A. Mujeeb, "Data-driven probabilistic machine learning in sustainable smart energy/smart energy systems: Key developments, challenges, and future research opportunities in the context of smart grid paradigm", *Renew. Sustain. Energy Rev.,* vol. 160, p. 112128, 2022. [http://dx.doi.org/10.1016/j.rser.2022.112128]

[50] J. Zhao, X. Feng, M.K. Tran, M. Fowler, M. Ouyang, and A.F. Burke, "Battery safety: Fault diagnosis from laboratory to real world", *J. Power Sources,* vol. 598, p. 234111, 2024. [http://dx.doi.org/10.1016/j.jpowsour.2024.234111]

[51] O. Vermesan, *et al.,* "AI and IIoT-based predictive maintenance system for soybean processing," Artificial Intelligence for Digitising Industry: Applications, pp. 327–352, Sep. 2021. [http://dx.doi.org/10.1201/9781003337232-27]

[52] O. Vermesan, "AI and IIoT-based predictive maintenance system for soybean processing", *Artificial Intelligence for Digitising Industry: Applications,* no. Sep, pp. 327-352, 2021. [http://dx.doi.org/10.1201/9781003337232-27]

[53] K. Bhaskar, A. Kumar, J. Bunce, J. Pressman, N. Burkell, and C. D. Rahn, "Data-driven thermal anomaly detection in large battery packs", *Batteries,* vol. 9, no. 2, p. 70, 2023. [http://dx.doi.org/10.3390/BATTERIES9020070]

[54] M. Abotaleb, and P.K. Dutta, "Optimizing long short-term memory networks for univariate time series forecasting: a comprehensive guide", *Hybrid Information Systems: Non-Linear Optimization Strategies with Artificial Intelligence,* no. Jul, pp. 427-442, 2024. [http://dx.doi.org/10.1515/9783111331133-020]

[55] J. Zhao, and X. Li, "A review of polymer electrolyte membrane fuel cell durability for vehicular applications: Degradation modes and experimental techniques", *Energy Convers. Manage.,* vol. 199, p. 112022, 2019.

[http://dx.doi.org/10.1016/j.enconman.2019.112022]

[56] J.J. Hwang, "Review on development and demonstration of hydrogen fuel cell scooters", *Renew. Sustain. Energy Rev.,* vol. 16, no. 6, pp. 3803-3815, 2012. [http://dx.doi.org/10.1016/j.rser.2012.03.036]

[57] H. Alqahtani, and G. Kumar, "Machine learning for enhancing transportation security: A comprehensive analysis of electric and flying vehicle systems", *Eng. Appl. Artif. Intell.,* vol. 129, p. 107667, 2024. [http://dx.doi.org/10.1016/j.engappai.2023.107667]

[58] S.N.A.B.M. Nashruddin, F.H.M. Salleh, R.M. Yunus, and H.B. Zaman, "Artificial intelligence–powered electrochemical sensor: Recent advances, challenges, and prospects", *Heliyon,* vol. 10, no. 18, p. e37964, 2024. [http://dx.doi.org/10.1016/j.heliyon.2024.e37964] [PMID: 39328566]

[59] Y. Qiu, T. Zeng, C. Zhang, G. Wang, Y. Wang, Z. Hu, Meng Yan, and Z. Wei, "Progress and challenges in multi-stack fuel cell system for high power applications: Architecture and energy management", *Green Energy and Intelligent Transportation,* vol. 2, no. 2, p. 100068, 2023. [http://dx.doi.org/10.1016/j.geits.2023.100068]

[60] S. Rashidi, N. Karimi, B. Sunden, K.C. Kim, A.G. Olabi, and O. Mahian, "Progress and challenges on the thermal management of electrochemical energy conversion and storage technologies: Fuel cells, electrolysers, and supercapacitors", *Pror. Energy Combust. Sci.,* vol. 88, p. 100966, 2022. [http://dx.doi.org/]

[61] Antonopoulos "Artificial intelligence and machine learning approaches to energy demand-side response: A systematic review," Renewable and Sustainable Energy Reviews, vol. 130, p. 109899, Sep. 2020. [http://dx.doi.org/10.1016/j.pecs.2021.100966]

[62] I. Antonopoulos, V. Robu, B. Couraud, D. Kirli, S. Norbu, A. Kiprakis, D. Flynn, S. Elizondo-Gonzalez, and S. Wattam, "Artificial intelligence and machine learning approaches to energy demand-side response: A systematic review", *Renew. Sustain. Energy Rev.,* vol. 130, p. 109899, 2020. [http://dx.doi.org/10.1016/j.rser.2020.109899]

[63] T. Ahmad, H. Zhu, D. Zhang, R. Tariq, A. Bassam, F. Ullah, A.S. AlGhamdi, and S.S. Alshamrani, "Energetics Systems and artificial intelligence: Applications of industry 4.0", *Energy Rep.,* vol. 8, pp. 334-361, 2022. [http://dx.doi.org/10.1016/j.egyr.2021.11.256]

[64] T. Matijašević, T. Antić, and T. Capuder, "A systematic review of machine learning applications in the operation of smart distribution systems", *Energy Rep.,* vol. 8, pp. 12379-12407, 2022. [http://dx.doi.org/10.1016/j.egyr.2022.09.068]

[65] F. Mütter, C. Berger, B. Königshofer, M. Höber, C. Hochenauer, and V. Subotić, "Artificial intelligence for solid oxide fuel cells: Combining automated high accuracy artificial neural network model generation and genetic algorithm for time-efficient performance prediction and optimization", *Energy Convers. Manage.,* vol. 291, p. 117263, 2023. [http://dx.doi.org/10.1016/j.enconman.2023.117263]

[66] E. Loyarte-López, M. Barral, and J. C. Morla, "Methodology for carbon footprint calculation towards sustainable innovation in intangible assets", *Sustainability,* vol. 12, no. 4, p. 1629, 2020. [http://dx.doi.org/10.3390/SU12041629]

[67] H. Chen, Y. Zheng, J. Li, L. Li, and X. Wang, "AI for nanomaterials development in clean energy and carbon capture, utilization and storage (CCUS)", *ACS Nano,* vol. 17, no. 11, pp. 9763-9792, 2023. [http://dx.doi.org/10.1021/acsnano.3c01062] [PMID: 37267448]

[68] K. Ukoba, K.O. Olatunji, E. Adeoye, T.C. Jen, and D.M. Madyira, "Optimizing renewable energy systems through artificial intelligence: Review and future prospects", *Energy Environ.,* vol. 35, no. 7, pp. 3833-3879, 2024.

[http://dx.doi.org/10.1177/0958305X241256293]

[69] M. Rahimi, A. Khurram, T.A. Hatton, and B. Gallant, "Electrochemical carbon capture processes for mitigation of CO 2 emissions", *Chem. Soc. Rev.*, vol. 51, no. 20, pp. 8676-8695, 2022. [http://dx.doi.org/10.1039/D2CS00443G] [PMID: 36177895]

[70] E.G. Al-Sakkari, A. Ragab, H. Dagdougui, D.C. Boffito, and M. Amazouz, "Carbon capture, utilization and sequestration systems design and operation optimization: Assessment and perspectives of artificial intelligence opportunities", *Sci. Total Environ.*, vol. 917, p. 170085, 2024. [http://dx.doi.org/10.1016/j.scitotenv.2024.170085] [PMID: 38224888]

[71] Z. Liu, Y. Sun, C. Xing, J. Liu, Y. He, Y. Zhou, and G. Zhang, "Artificial intelligence powered large-scale renewable integrations in multi-energy systems for carbon neutrality transition: Challenges and future perspectives", *Energy and AI,* vol. 10, p. 100195, 2022. [http://dx.doi.org/10.1016/j.egyai.2022.100195]

[72] J. Li, K. Lim, H. Yang, Z. Ren, S. Raghavan, P-Y. Chen, T. Buonassisi, and X. Wang, "AI applications through the whole life cycle of material discovery", *Matter,* vol. 3, no. 2, pp. 393-432, 2020. [http://dx.doi.org/10.1016/j.matt.2020.06.011]

[73] L. Han, and Z. Xiang, "Intelligent design and synthesis of energy catalytic materials", *Fundamental Research,* vol. 5, no. 2, pp. 624-639, 2025. [http://dx.doi.org/10.1016/j.fmre.2023.10.012] [PMID: 40242526]

[74] N. Yadav, “Artificial intelligence in heavy metals detection: Methodological and ethical challenges,” *Hygiene and Environmental Health Advances*, vol. 7, p. 100071, Sep. 2023. [http://dx.doi.org/10.1016/J.HEHA.2023.100071]

[75] S. M. Hatefi, H. Asadi, G. Shams, J. Tamošaitienė, and Z. Turskis, "Model for the sustainable material selection by applying integrated dempster-shafer evidence theory and additive ratio assessment (aras) method", *Sustainability,* vol. 13, no. 18, p. 10438, 2021. [http://dx.doi.org/10.3390/SU131810438]

[76] A. E. Alprol, A. T. Mansour, M. E. E. D. Ibrahim, and M. Ashour, "Artificial intelligence technologies revolutionizing wastewater treatment: current trends and future prospective", *Water,* vol. 16, no. 2, p. 314, 2024. [http://dx.doi.org/10.3390/W16020314]

[77] N. Yadav, B.M. Maurya, D. Chettri, Pooja, C. Pulwani, M. Jajula, S.S. kanda, H.W.S. babu, A. Elangovan, P. Velusamy, M. Iyer, and B. Vellingiri, "Artificial intelligence in heavy metals detection: Methodological and ethical challenges", *Hygiene and Environmental Health Advances,* vol. 7, p. 100071, 2023. [http://dx.doi.org/10.1016/j.heha.2023.100071]

[78] S. Li, H.O. Gao, and F. You, "AI for science in electrochemical energy storage: A multiscale systems perspective on transportation electrification", *Nexus,* vol. 1, no. 3, p. 100026, 2024. [http://dx.doi.org/10.1016/j.ynexs.2024.100026]

[79] Chinedu Ibegbulam, and C. Ibegbulam, "Machine learning for green hydrogen production", *Computer Science & IT Research Journal,* vol. 4, no. 3, pp. 368-385, 2023. [http://dx.doi.org/10.51594/csitrj.v4i3.1253]

[80] S. Su, X. Yan, K. Agbossou, R. Chahine, and Y. Zong, "Artificial intelligence for hydrogen-based hybrid renewable energy systems: A review with case study", *J. Phys. Conf. Ser.,* vol. 2208, no. 1, p. 012013, 2022. [http://dx.doi.org/10.1088/1742-6596/2208/1/012013]

[81] M. Ahmed, Y. Zheng, A. Amine, H. Fathiannasab, and Z. Chen, "The role of artificial intelligence in the mass adoption of electric vehicles", *Joule,* vol. 5, no. 9, pp. 2296-2322, 2021. [http://dx.doi.org/10.1016/j.joule.2021.07.012]

[82] S. Iqbal, K. Aftab, F. tul Jannat, M. Ali Baig, and U. Kalsoom, A bibliographic analysis of optimization of hydrogen production *via* electrochemical method using machine learning., *Fuel,* vol. 372, p. 132126, 2024. [http://dx.doi.org/10.1016/j.fuel.2024.132126]

[83] M. Batool, O. Sanumi, and J. Jankovic, "Application of artificial intelligence in the materials science, with a special focus on fuel cells and electrolyzers", *Energy and AI,* vol. 18, p. 100424, 2024. [http://dx.doi.org/10.1016/j.egyai.2024.100424]

[84] M. S. H. Lipu, "Artificial intelligence approaches for advanced battery management system in electric vehicle applications: a statistical analysis towards future research opportunities", *Vehicles,* vol. 6, no. 1, pp. 22-70, 2024. [http://dx.doi.org/10.3390/VEHICLES6010002]

[85] B. Olorunfemi, "The innovations driving tesla's success: Disruptions, competition, business model, customer transformation, and entrepreneurial strategies", *Qeios,* no. Apr, 2024. [http://dx.doi.org/10.32388/HA56OH.2]

[86] A. Cernat, A. Groza, M. Tertis, B. Feier, O. Hosu-Stancioiu, and C. Cristea, "Where artificial intelligence stands in the development of electrochemical sensors for healthcare applications-A review", *Trends Analyt. Chem.,* vol. 181, p. 117999, 2024. [http://dx.doi.org/10.1016/j.trac.2024.117999]

[87] K. Chen, W. Chou, L. Liu, Y. Cui, P. Xue, and M. Jia, "Electrochemical sensors fabricated by electrospinning technology: an overview", *Sensors,* vol. 19, no. 17, p. 3676, 2019. [http://dx.doi.org/10.3390/S19173676]

[88] J. Zhao, X. Feng, Q. Pang, M. Fowler, Y. Lian, M. Ouyang, and A.F. Burke, "Battery safety: Machine learning-based prognostics", *Pror. Energy Combust. Sci.,* vol. 102, p. 101142, 2024. [http://dx.doi.org/10.1016/j.pecs.2023.101142]

[89] M.A. Bappy, M. Ahmed, and M.A. Rauf, "Exploring the Integration of Informed Machine Learning in Engineering Applications: A Comprehensive Review", *SSRN Electronic Journal,* 2024. [http://dx.doi.org/10.2139/SSRN.4785058]

[90] S.P. Stier, C. Kreisbeck, H. Ihssen, M.A. Popp, J. Hauch, K. Malek, M. Reynaud, T.P.M. Goumans, J. Carlsson, I. Todorov, L. Gold, A. Räder, W. Wenzel, S.T. Bandesha, P. Jacques, F. Garcia-Moreno, O. Arcelus, P. Friederich, S. Clark, M. Maglione, A. Laukkanen, I.E. Castelli, J. Carrasco, M.C. Cabanas, H.S. Stein, O. Ozcan, D. Elbert, K. Reuter, C. Scheurer, M. Demura, S.S. Han, T. Vegge, S. Nakamae, M. Fabrizio, and M. Kozdras, "Materials acceleration platforms (MAPs): Accelerating materials research and development to meet urgent societal challenges", *Adv. Mater.,* vol. 36, no. 45, p. 2407791, 2024. [http://dx.doi.org/10.1002/adma.202407791] [PMID: 39239995]

[91] X. Liu, K. Fan, X. Huang, J. Ge, Y. Liu, and H. Kang, "Recent advances in artificial intelligence boosting materials design for electrochemical energy storage", *Chem. Eng. J.,* vol. 490, p. 151625, 2024. [http://dx.doi.org/10.1016/j.cej.2024.151625]

[92] M. Elahi, S. O. Afolaranmi, J. L. Martinez Lastra, and J. A. Perez Garcia, "A comprehensive literature review of the applications of ai techniques through the lifecycle of industrial equipment", *Discov Artif Intell,* vol. 3, no. 1, pp. 1-78, 2023. [http://dx.doi.org/10.1007/S44163-023-00089-X]

[93] Etinosa Igbinenikaro, and A.O. Adewusi, "Policy recommendations for integrating artificial intelligence into global trade agreements", *International Journal of Engineering Research Updates,* vol. 6, no. 1, 2024. [http://dx.doi.org/10.53430/ijeru.2024.6.1.0022]

[94] J. Zhao, X. Qu, Y. Wu, M. Fowler, and A.F. Burke, "Artificial intelligence-driven real-world battery diagnostics", *Energy and AI,* vol. 18, p. 100419, 2024.

[http://dx.doi.org/10.1016/j.egyai.2024.100419]

[95] R. Dwivedi, D. Dave, H. Naik, S. Singhal, R. Omer, P. Patel, B. Qian, Z. Wen, T. Shah, G. Morgan, and R. Ranjan, "Explainable AI (XAI): Core ideas, techniques, and solutions", *ACM Comput. Surv.,* vol. 55, no. 9, pp. 1-33, 2023. [http://dx.doi.org/10.1145/3561048]

[96] K. Stecuła, R. Wolniak, and W. W. Grebski, "Ai-driven urban energy solutions—from individuals to society: a review", *Energies,* vol. 16, no. 24, p. 7988, 2023. [http://dx.doi.org/10.3390/EN16247988]

[97] A. Jedličková, "Ethical approaches in designing autonomous and intelligent systems: a comprehensive survey towards responsible development", *AI Soc.,* no. Aug, pp. 1-14, 2024. [http://dx.doi.org/10.1007/S00146-024-02040-9/METRICS]

CHAPTER 6

Ethical Considerations and Challenges in AI Adoption for Sustainable Energy

Tarun Kumar[1,*] and **Dushyant Kumar**[1]

[1] *Department of Physics, Indian Institute of Technology Jodhpur, Rajasthan-342030, India*

Abstract: Artificial Intelligence (AI) holds immense potential to revolutionize various sectors, including sustainable energy, finance, grid management, transportation, and healthcare. By optimizing resource use, predicting maintenance needs, and enabling smarter energy distribution, AI can significantly contribute to achieving sustainable energy goals. However, integrating AI in sustainable energy systems also raises numerous ethical considerations and challenges that must be addressed to ensure equitable and responsible use. The rapidly growing carbon footprint of AI, driven by the substantial energy required to train increasingly complex Machine Learning (ML) models, has raised significant concerns. These concerns raise questions about the true potential of AI in achieving sustainability goals. This chapter explores the ethical implications of AI adoption in the sustainable energy sector. It critically examines the ethical risks and responsibilities surrounding the integration of AI into sustainable energy infrastructure, addressing issues such as data privacy, algorithmic bias, transparency, and socioeconomic impact. As AI algorithms become integral to energy systems, stakeholders must have access to information about model architectures, data sources, and decision criteria. Bias and fairness represent another crucial dimension. AI models can inadvertently perpetuate biases present in training data, potentially exacerbating existing inequalities. Researchers emphasize the need for robust approaches to mitigate bias and ensure equitable access to energy resources. Privacy and data security are ongoing challenges in the AI-driven energy landscape. These systems rely on vast amounts of data, and protecting user privacy while securing sensitive information is paramount. Differential privacy and federated learning have been proposed to address these concerns. Striking a balance between energy efficiency and computational demands is also critical. While AI can optimize energy consumption, it requires substantial computational resources. Researchers have explored the environmental impact of AI deployment, emphasizing the need for sustainable practices. In conclusion, the responsible adoption of AI in sustainable energy requires interdisciplinary collaboration, robust regulations, and continuous ethical scrutiny. Policymakers, researchers, and practitioners must draw insights from relevant studies and frameworks to effectively navigate these challenges. The adoption of Green AI is a better alternative to conventional AI for producing accurate results with lower computational costs.

[*] **Corresponding author Dushyant Kumar:** Department of Physics, Indian Institute of Technology Jodhpur, Rajasthan-342030, India; E-mail: dushyant@nsut.ac.in

Shreya Sharma, Peeyush Phogat, Ranjana Jha & Sukhvir Singh (Eds.)

Keywords: AI adoption, Artificial intelligence, Carbon footprint, Climate mitigation, Data integrity, Data privacy, Economic implications, Energy justice, Energy storage optimization, Grid optimization, Sustainable energy, Tectonic data collection.

INTRODUCTION

AI and energy are the new power couple in the global arena. The Digital Revolution, also known as the 4th Industrial Revolution, has already begun; Artificial Intelligence (AI) and Machine Learning (ML) models hold the largest share in it. The Recent advances in AI have benefited humankind in numerous ways. AI holds the potential to process vast amounts of data, analyze complex patterns, and predict the most favourable outcome. Artificial intelligence (AI) has a strong global adoption rate, with its footprint visible in every sector, including transportation, agriculture, and policy. Among these, the energy sector has garnered significant attention [1 - 5]. As the world is transitioning from conventional energy resources to more sustainable alternatives, AI plays a significant role in this sector. One of the major contributions of AI is its ability to forecast energy supply and demand more accurately. This capability helps in planning energy distribution, optimizing resources, and increasing the efficiency of the grid system. Additionally, AI enhances financial gains by managing resources like wind power stations, solar plants, and hydroelectric plants more efficiently and sustainably [6]. With the optimization of algorithms, data security, and integrity, AI holds the potential for eco-centric sustainable development, which is the core of the 21st-century development process. Most governments, which are likely transitioning towards clean energy, are considering the adoption of AI in governance, planning, and execution, as well as designing sustainable development models. With the ever-increasing demand for power and the changing geopolitical landscape, it's high time for nations to secure their energy infrastructure and supply chain continuity. Here, sustainable sources of energy can play a pivotal role in reducing energy consumption. AI can help nations achieve their net emissions targets and better manage climate change, through effective emission tracking and waste management [6, 7]. Since AI impacts numerous aspects of our lives, it has become essential for governments worldwide to develop policies and frameworks that guide the various stakeholders, including academic institutions, public and private bodies, and civil society, to ensure the ethical use of AI. Major focus areas regarding the ethical use of AI include proportionality and safeguarding human rights, adaptive governance and collaboration, responsibility and accountability, transparency and explainability, auditability and traceability, sustainability, and non-discrimination. Some of the acts or laws passed on AI regulation across the globe include: The European Union AI Act, 2024, which categorizes AI based on risk as unacceptable risk, high-risk, and limited-risk AI systems. This act prohibits systems that include social scoring, manipulative AI, real-time remote biometric identification in public spaces, and AI that exploits vulnerabilities of sensitive attributes, such as political beliefs and race. High-risk AI systems are subject to strict regulations, for instance, in critical infrastructure, education, and employment. The provider must ensure risk management, human oversight. Limited-risk AI systems are subject to transparency rules that include notification to users by the system regarding their interaction with AI.

In contrast to the EU, the US is moving forward with a decentralized framework in AI regulation. States like California are leading the way in AI regulation with proposed laws aimed at enhancing accountability, eliminating discrimination, and regulating business data usage.

In the Asia-Pacific region, countries such as Singapore, Japan, and Australia are leading the way with laws for AI regulation in place. Singapore was the first nation in the world to launch a Model AI governance framework and has also introduced its first edition of the National AI Strategy.

However, certain challenges, such as the increasing complexity of algorithms in improving performance, biases, governance, data availability, and privacy, further add to the perplexities and resource requirements [8, 9]. The vast number of data centres holding immense training data requires refrigerating with large volumes of water, thus increasing AI's overall carbon footprint.

AI, ETHICS, AND SHARED RESPONSIBILITY IN GOVERNANCE

AI governance should incorporate stakeholder responsibilities and their ethical compliance. A multilevel government framework should involve coordination between governments, citizens, and corporations, focusing on building trust to enhance integrity and competence [10]. On the other hand, a cohesive framework proposes a review of AI governance models to enhance coherence among stakeholders, yet in an adaptable manner, addressing public distrust and privacy concerns [11].

Another aspect is the stakeholders' responsibilities, which involve several dimensions, including the government's role in ensuring accountability and transparency, corporate responsibility aimed at developing with ethical standards and respecting the fundamental rights of humans, and citizen engagement, encompassing the encouragement of public participation in the AI governance model to build trust and credibility.

Moreover, ethical compliance is another major factor to consider when incorporating ethical regulations into AI engagement. This entails legal binding norms established by government agencies, as well as AI literacy and capacity building, among other initiatives.

Several Sustainable Development Goals (SDGs) framed by the United Nations are associated with certain ethical themes in AI integration with energy solutions, like:

SDG 1: End Poverty in All Forms: ML algorithms can effectively predict the supply and demand of energy, helping to make the process more inclusive and promote social justice.

SDG 7: Ensure access to affordable, reliable, sustainable, and modern energy for all. AI integration with the energy grid, conducted in an ethical manner, will help ensure that energy is accessible to all sections of society affordably and reliably.

SDG 8: Promotion of sustained, inclusive, and sustainable economic growth: The consideration of AI in conjunction with sustainable energy resources is directly proportional to more sustained economic growth, as AI helps eliminate human error and enhance grid reliability, management, and proper energy channeling through optimized evaluation mechanisms.

SDG 9: Promote sustainable and inclusive industrial innovation and infrastructure: AI integration with sustainable energy infrastructure helps the world build a resilient ecosystem to meet energy needs and adapt to a more inclusive distribution of energy and industrialization, promoting growth for all sections of society equally.

SDG 10: Reduce inequalities within and among countries: The Majority of the people around the world are facing acute energy shortages. A significant portion of energy infrastructure is dedicated to the wealthier sections of society and cities. This inequality can be addressed by integrating AI in energy infrastructure, which supports a sustainable approach using bias-free ML models to identify demand and supply, promoting inclusive energy distribution.

SDG 11: Promote the building of sustainable cities and communities: The transition towards sustainable development depends on the development of sustainable infrastructure in our cities, including sustainable transportation, inclusive urbanization, and disaster-resilient energy infrastructure.

SDG 12: Responsible Production and Consumption: The goal involves the responsible use of resources, reducing waste, and enhancing resource efficiency.

AI-powered energy infrastructure is the core for enhancing efficiency and optimizing the sustainable use and distribution of energy.

SDG 13: Combat climate change and its impacts: Climate is the most hampered aspect of human development in an unsustainable manner. The impacts of rising sea levels and Earth's temperature have already begun to appear, including floods, changing weather patterns, and the unpredictable nature of natural disasters worldwide. This has made the sustainable approach to development the urgency of the hour, where the energy infrastructure must be overhauled to meet energy needs without disturbing nature and overconsuming the resources of future generations. It is our ethical responsibility to adopt and promote sustainable consumption practices that respect the Earth's resources.

ETHICAL FRAMEWORKS FOR AI IN SUSTAINABILITY

AI has transformed our view of sustainable development models drastically. Ethical frameworks for AI aim to ensure that such technologies contribute positively to environmental, social, and economic goals while minimizing the negative impacts. With the rising challenges due to climate change and increasing pressure on the energy infrastructure worldwide, we must fast-track the research and development of sustainable energy solutions. Effects of climate change have started being visible as rising sea levels with global temperature increased by 1.5°C [9]. Extreme weather events, continuously rising carbon emissions, and declining carbon sinks have led governments and organizations worldwide to recognize the urgency of taking effective steps to mitigate climate change and enhance adaptability.

As defined, "Sustainable AI is a movement to foster change in the entire lifecycle of AI products (*i.e.*, idea generation, training, re-tuning, implementation, governance) towards greater ecological integrity and social justice." AI holds pivotal importance in our efforts to achieve net-zero emissions [12] (Table **1**).

Table 1. List of sectors benefiting from the AI revolution.

Sr. No.	Sector	Sustainable Impact
1.	Manufacturing processes	30-50% decline in carbon emissions [13].
2.	Intelligent Transportation Systems	60% decrease in CO_2 emissions [14].
3.	Natural gas industry	>70% of the industry in this sector leverages AI for forecasting the weather and thus optimizing the resources and planning [13].
4.	Solar energy sector	AI helps to improve the solar energy yield by 25%.

(Table 1) cont.....

Sr. No.	Sector	Sustainable Impact
5.	Wind energy sector	AI enhances the safety of wind turbine operations and mitigates exposure to risks due to faulty equipment [15].
6.	Automotive AI industry	AI improves the safety and reliability of e-vehicles and has the potential to capture a $7 billion market by 2027.

A critical aspect of these frameworks is creating models that account for transparency and accountability to avoid unintended consequences. These aspects include clear communication about the purpose of algorithms, limitations, and environmental impact during their lifecycle [16]. Other ethical dimensions include fairness and inclusivity. AI models should strive to avoid inequities, particularly for vulnerable social communities. Therefore, frameworks should have mechanisms to assess and mitigate any form of bias, ensuring equitable resource distribution and benefits among all sections of society.

Privacy and data protection are another pillar of ethical frameworks for AI [17]. Many AI-driven sustainability solutions heavily rely on data collection and analysis, such as in climate modelling or energy distribution optimization. AI should be modelled to adhere to the rights of an individual to have privacy and protection for data collected. Proper guidelines and policies need to be established for the corporate world to strike a balance between the need for data-driven development and the personal privacy of every individual [18].

Lastly, these AI models should address the sustainability of AI development and deployment. Although carbon emissions from AI-based technologies are relatively lower than those from humans, the substantial electricity consumption by AI data centres and energy-intensive ML models results in a significantly high carbon footprint for AI [19, 20]. This undermines the environmental benefits of AI. To address this, ethical policies highly recommend strategies such as enhancing computational efficiency and utilizing renewable energy sources to power the data centers that support AI technologies [21].

Data Integrity and Equality

Ensuring data integrity and equality in AI is crucial for fostering trust, fairness, and accuracy in data-driven AI models. Data integrity refers to the accuracy, consistency, and reliability of data throughout its lifecycle. Maintaining high data integrity is essential to prevent biases and errors in AI systems. This includes robust data verification, transparency in data handling, mitigation of risks associated with data manipulation and corruption, and accountability in the event of error or fraud [22]. Policies must be established to prioritize data governance, enabling the monitoring and maintenance of data quality and informed decision-making [23]. Equality is another dimension in addressing data bias and algorithms to ensure fair treatment and outcomes for all groups and individuals. Addressing data equality requires identifying and mitigating system biases that might exist in the system training datasets or decision-making processes. For instance, AI-driven systems sourcing from historical datasets might have societal inequalities and biases, and their use will amplify or perpetuate these biases if not addressed timely. Data integrity and data equality are interconnected concepts. Poor data integrity, such as inaccurate datasets, can exacerbate AI results. Conversely, ensuring data equality that represents all sections of the population without undue favour will automatically uphold the data integrity process. This necessitates careful examination or preprocessing, stakeholder involvement in data curation, processing, and analysis, and adherence to principles like FAIR (Findability, Accessibility, Interoperability, and Reusability) [24].

Economic Implications of AI-adoption

There is no doubt that the economic implications of AI integration in the energy sector will have tremendous implications for the global economy, ranging from cost reductions and efficiency improvements to distribution optimization and resource management [25]. AI-driven solutions can reduce the costs of energy generation by up to 20% in renewable energy systems [26]. AI technologies, such as predictive analytics and optimization models, will enable energy infrastructure to operate more effectively and efficiently. These advancements surely reduce operational costs and human errors, strengthening economic growth in the renewable energy sector [4, 27]. Several AI techniques, including artificial neural networks, Fuzzy Logic Control (FLC), particle swarm optimization, and ant colony optimization, are utilized to optimize renewable energy systems [27]. AI can be implemented using either of these three methods:

Artificial Neural Networks (ANN)

Artificial Neural Networks in the Optimization of Renewable Energy. Artificial neural networks are computer models that mimic the neural networks found in the human brain [28]. In renewable energy optimization, ANNs are applied to predict and manage the energy output from resources such as solar and wind [29]. They can predict complex data patterns to generate precise predictions about energy output, which can be useful for optimizing the efficiency and reliability of renewable energy systems. For instance, ANNs can predict the generation of solar power depending on weather data. In this way, better management of the grid can be achieved, and less energy waste.

Fuzzy Logic Control (FLC) in Renewable Energy Systems

FLC is a type of AI that deals with approximate reasoning rather than fixed and exact [30]. FLC manages and controls hybrid systems in renewable energy systems, combining different kinds of renewable energy sources like solar and wind [31]. FLC considers the variability or uncertainty of renewable energies and can make decisions based on imprecise inputs to ensure the smooth running of energy production. For instance, an FLC can control the flow of power between a solar panel, wind turbine, and energy storage system to ensure a stable energy supply [32].

Particle Swarm Optimization (PSO) for Renewable Energy Layout

Particle Swarm Optimization (PSO) is a computational method that iteratively optimizes a problem by trying to improve a candidate solution. PSO plays a detrimental role in the optimal placement of energy-production units, such as wind turbines or solar panels, thereby helping to optimize the energy output process and minimize costs [33]. Using the simulation behaviour of a swarm of particles, *i.e.*, potential solutions, one can find the best possible configuration for installing renewable energy infrastructure.

Ant Colony Optimization (ACO) in Smart Grids

ACO is a probability-based technique useful for solving computational problems that can be reduced to finding good paths through graphs. It is useful in optimizing the route and distribution of electricity, ensuring efficient and reliable energy delivery. It mimics the behavior of ants searching for food, thus finding the best paths for electricity flow, which helps reduce energy losses and improves grid stability [34].

Economic Opportunities and Workforce Transformation

AI also has the potential to create new economic opportunities, such as jobs in AI development, renewable energy, and efficiency services. However, this may simultaneously disrupt traditional energy jobs, particularly in the fossil fuel industries, and automation in the renewable energy sector. As per the International Renewable Energy Agency (IRENA) estimation, renewable energy jobs could increase to 42 million globally by 2050, with major roles being AI-related, like data analytics, ML, and system integration [34]. However, workforce displacement remains a concern. Policymakers must address these challenges by promoting reskilling initiatives and training for the present workforce, and by incorporating advanced skills and AI techniques into the educational curriculum of institutions for the upcoming workforce [35].

Moreover, integrating AI into the existing infrastructure requires significant improvements and investments, including the installation of advanced sensors, computational infrastructure, and AI software. While it may seem challenging, the investment cost can be recovered quickly with the potential benefits of AI integration. A study by PwC estimates that AI adoption in the energy sector will contribute $3.5 trillion to global GDP by 2030 [36].

Cost Reductions and Efficiency Gains

The integration of AI systems in energy infrastructure will help optimize energy resources and consumption through smart grids. For example, predictive maintenance using AI reduces downtime in energy supply plants, saving around 15% of operational costs annually [37]. A report by Siemens predicts that AI-enabled energy systems can achieve efficiency gains of 15-25%, thereby saving billions of dollars globally every year.

In addition, the adoption of AI algorithms for energy storage and management helps improve battery performance and longevity. Such optimization is beneficial in regions that are heavily reliant on solar and wind energy, where energy storage systems powered by AI can help reduce storage costs.

Equity and Access Challenges

Uneven distribution of resources has long been an issue in the upliftment of marginalized sections of society. Using AI, even distribution and fast connectivity can be provided to these vulnerable sections of the population. Due to a vast disparity in resource distribution, the majority of marginalized communities, particularly in the Global South, lack proper access to the energy needed for their daily usage. These sections generally belong to poor farmers, labourers, and a certain group of the poor section of society who do not have access to basic amenities critical for living. A proper framework for energy redistribution and energy justice should be established to include these vulnerable sections. Still, wealthier nations and corporations often have dominant access to AI infrastructure, leaving developing regions behind. Approximately 70% of global AI investment is allocated to North America, Europe, and China, while only 5% is directed toward Africand South Asia [36]. This global disparity in resource allocation directly hampers global energy transition and the fight against climate change. Thus, more targeted funding, democratic allocation of investments, and collaboration between the Global North and South in AI technologies are the need of the hour.

Environmental and Economic Co-benefits

Fighting global climate change is a central driving force behind the incorporation of AI in the energy sector. According to the World Wind Energy Association, the optimization of energy infrastructure requires AI, which will help reduce global CO_2 emissions by 1.5-2.5 gigatons annually. This impact addresses climate change and reduces healthcare costs associated with air pollution, potentially saving $200-300 billion annually in healthcare expenditures. AI-integrated sensors in e-vehicles help optimize energy usage while maximizing the vehicle's cost-effectiveness and maintaining battery lifetime. Renewable energy sources offer a fluctuating power supply, mandating grid optimization, where AI-based solutions offer the best possible management. For instance, a neural network developed by DeepMind (a subsidiary of Google) can predict wind power output 36 hours in advance. This technological revolution helps in increasing the commercial value of wind energy by 20%. This marvelous technological feat also helps in scheduling and managing high-powered tasks according to peak power output time frames. Another example is Enel, an energy company that manages a platform named EnelX, which helps optimize energy distribution and consumption. ML algorithm-based models assist in analyzing large amounts of data from various sources, such as weather prediction, energy production, peak consumption, and energy market data.

Several sensors and cameras can help inspect transmission lines 24/7, reducing inspection costs by approximately 25% and predicting any maintenance issues for a timely response. This combined effort of humans and AI can increase energy uptime by 20%. There are numerous other examples of private players entering the AI-based energy solution space, such as Tesla, NextEra, and Duke Energy, among others. These efforts will have a substantial impact on climate mitigation, thereby gifting a livable world to future generations.

AI IN VARIOUS SUSTAINABLE ENERGY SECTORS

AI holds untapped potential that can revolutionize our transition to clean energy solutions. With global efforts underway to develop methods for decarbonization, carbon capture, and climate mitigation, AI has the potential to significantly enhance these initiatives, as shown in Fig. (**1**).

AI in the Solar Energy Sector

AI-powered solar farms are soon going to be a reality. Managing, optimizing, and maintaining such large-scale farms will be easy using AI and ML-based algorithms. The sector will be transformed from solar energy generation to grid optimization, load management, and energy distribution by integrating AI-based technology sensors, thereby helping to accelerate the transition to renewable energy sources. Solar panel tracking systems, when integrated with AI, can orient and position the panels to always face the direction of maximum solar input, based on weather data and patterns [38, 39]. AI can help with the regular inspection of panels and the grid system to prevent potential failures and predict maintenance needs, thereby lowering operating costs and reducing downtime, while increasing the lifespan of the solar plant.

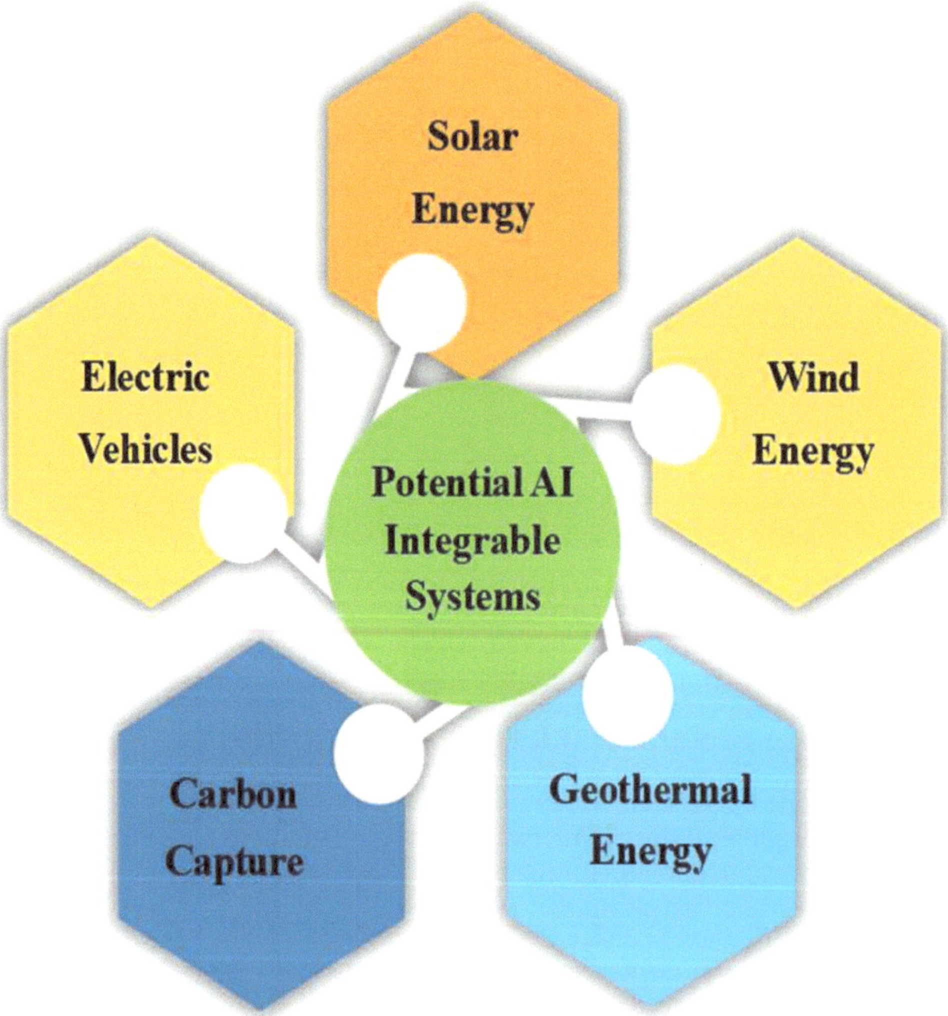

Fig. (1). AI-integrated systems in sustainable energy solutions.

AI in the Wind Energy Sector

According to the World Wind Energy Association (WWEA), the global capacity of wind energy systems is expected to exceed 1000 GW by 2024, representing a total of 54% increase in wind energy generated compared to 2019 [39]. But this jump in wind energy production demands both logistical and financial improvements. AI perspectives in this sector are significant, as seen in aerodynamic optimization [39, 40], wind turbine position optimization [40], blade shape optimization [41, 42], and wind speed prediction, among others. Artificial Neural Networks (ANNs) can be widely employed for data acquisition and processing related to wind energy parameters, thereby optimizing wind farm output.

AI in the Geothermal Sector

Geothermal energy uses the earth's natural heat with common fluids found in geothermal reservoirs, including water and steam [43]. Since these sites are located closer to tectonic faults and fractures and experience high temperatures, their exploitation is highly challenging. Still, Geothermal energy is one of the most sustainable sources of energy. To effectively utilize such resources, AI can aid in optimizing reservoir storage, collecting tectonic data, and evaluating maintenance.

AI in Carbon Capture and Decarbonization

Sustainability does not just lie in exploring new sustainable energy sources, but also in minimizing greenhouse gas emissions from existing sources. This incorporates the option of carbon capture and decarbonization in the transition to clean energy sources. Carbon capture involves capturing carbon dioxide (CO_2) emissions from sources like power plants and industrial facilities before they enter the atmosphere. This captured carbon is then transported and stored in underground facilities and formations. This entire process has a vast scope for AI integration in optimizing transportation and storage facilities. By assisting in the development of new, greener, and cost-effective fuels, grid management, demand-side flexibility, and renewable energy asset management, AI plays a significant role in carbon capture and the decarbonization of the world's economies [44]. Several private players and government organizations are now taking steps to develop technological solutions to address carbon emissions and help mitigate the ongoing deterioration of carbon sinks worldwide.

Several policies can be formulated for the targeted, sustainable integration of AI in energy infrastructure, as shown in Table **2**.

Table 2. Policy roadmap for ethical AI in the energy sector.

Focus Area	Relevance
AI in Smart grids	Crucial for secure and reliable energy distribution and grid management. Customization should also be incorporated to make such AI-enabled systems cyberattack-proof.
AI in climate-based policy making	Essential for climate mitigation and enhancing the integration and efficiency of sustainable energy sources. Optimization of AI frameworks with sustainable energy sources must also be prioritized, along with the operationalization of such plants.
AI in risk analysis and management	Critical evaluation and identification to mitigate any risk. Integration of the risk assessment mechanisms and AI deployment for management.
ASHES Framework	Focuses on assessing, strategizing, harmonizing, executing, and sustaining AI applications in the energy sector.
Lifecycle approach	Structured methodology to include ethical principles in AI development phases and operation to build trust and reliability in energy systems [45].
Multidisciplinary collaboration	Emphasizes multidisciplinary and multi-level cooperation among different stakeholders, from energy generation and management to distribution to the end user.

CHALLENGES WITH AI

Undoubtedly, AI will lead to a greener energy transition in global efforts. However, AI needs to consume less energy than it saves to be a viable solution in the energy sector. This interplay between energy consumption and saving creates several challenges in the field of AI integration and interoperability that must be targeted for sustainable energy transition, as shown in Fig. (**2**). Following are the roadblocks and challenges ahead in merging AI with sustainable energy systems successfully:

Data Privacy and Security

AI gathers large amounts of data, including sensitive information about consumers and infrastructure. This data needs to be protected at all costs, as it could be a potential cyber-target and expose the vulnerabilities of a nation's grid system. Ensuring the privacy and security of this data is crucial. Regulatory frameworks and secure connections must be established to avoid any unauthorized access and cyberattacks [46].

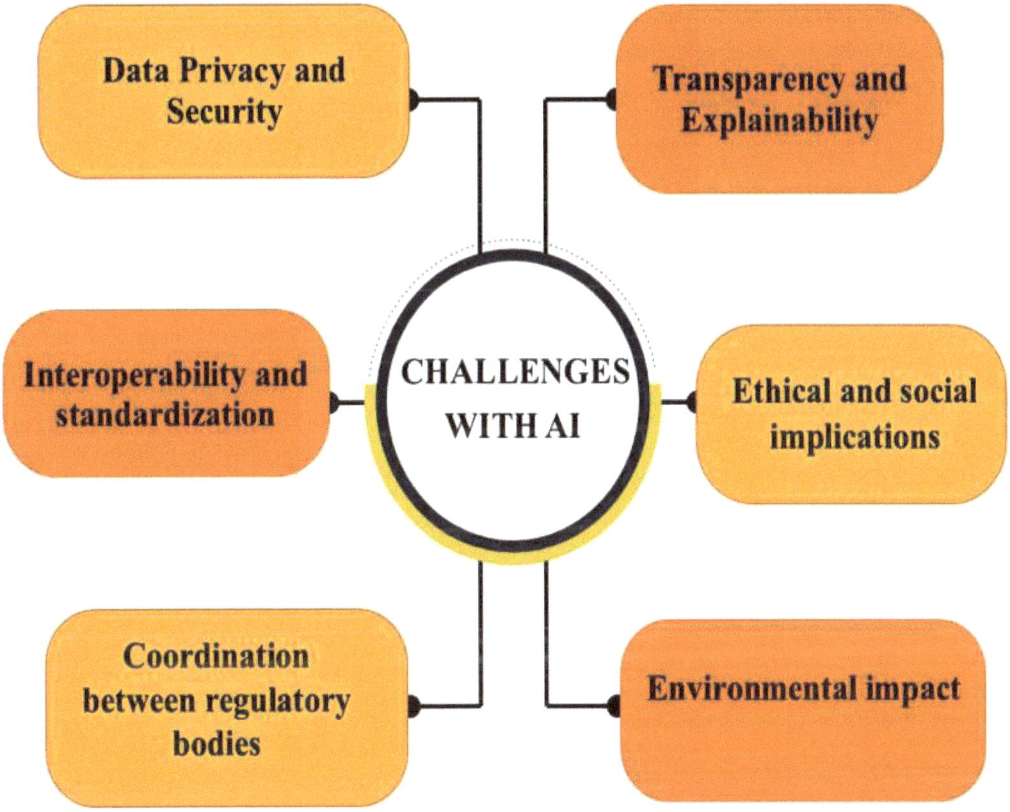

Fig. (2). Several challenges faced in AI-integrated systems for sustainable energy.

Transparency and Explainability

AI models are typically complex and opaque in terms of their actions and reliability. This lack of transparency acts as a barrier to the adoption of AI among stakeholders. Thus, sincere efforts must be made to ensure the transparency and accountability of such technology, which will have control of our most crucial infrastructures [47].

Interoperability and Standardization

For seamless integration with a wide range of sensors and models, AI systems must be interoperable with existing infrastructure and flexible enough to be compatible with future systems. This requires certain parameters and standards to be established for proper integration facilitation. Guidelines and policies should be established to check the interoperability and standardization of the system with the energy infrastructure [46].

Ethical and Social Implications

AI deployment in the energy sector will have huge ethical and social implications, like job displacement and biased algorithmic decisions. This all needs to be regulated and mitigated through the implementation of proper policies and frameworks. Developers must prioritize designing AI systems that are morally fair, protect values that align with societal norms, and prevent discriminatory outcomes. Results and decisions taken by the AI models must be understandable and communicable to the stakeholders. Algorithms lacking transparency in the system can lead to mistrust and suspicion among stakeholders, making the adoption and integration of AI more challenging.

Coordination Between Regulatory Bodies

AI adoption and integration require a lot of cooperation between several regulatory bodies, both at the state and federal levels [48]. This seems challenging but highly essential for the seamless transition and integration of AI with the energy infrastructure globally.

Incentives and Funding

The adoption of AI in the energy sector requires significant funding and incentives. This necessitates continuous funding mechanisms and the research and development of new methods and materials to make integration smoother and more consumer-friendly.

Environmental Impact

Although AI appears to have a significant impact on the energy sector, AI itself presents challenges in terms of energy consumption. A large amount of data collection, processing, and analysis also requires large data centres with huge data storage capabilities. These large-sized data centres require continuous cooling systems, thus enlarging the carbon footprint of AI in itself. These large training models required for AI need to be run continuously, thus increasing their energy consumption manifold. For instance, training a model such as the Generative Pre-trained Transformer 3 (GPT-3) is estimated to use just under 1,300 megawatt-hours (MWh) of electricity. This is roughly equivalent to the annual power consumption of 130 homes in the US. Therefore, serious efforts are required to undertake research and development of efficient cooling mechanisms and systems.

AI holds immense scope in terms of climate justice, targeting the equitable distribution of resources and thus reducing disparities, avoiding a disproportionate share of the climate crisis for future generations and vulnerable sections of society, and enhancing transparency in resource allocation [49]. AI-based systems, particularly those focused on optimizing renewable energy sources, also help reduce our carbon footprint, enhance climate modeling, and improve energy efficiency. Thus, the ethical deployment of AI must be approached through environmental protection policies, increased transparency, inclusivity, and social justice.

CONCLUDING REMARKS

We humans have come a long way technologically, and AI has revolutionized the way we use technology in our daily lives. Soon, AI integration in the energy infrastructure will become a reality, significantly impacting our transition to a sustainable future. To make this transformation smooth and successful, certain measures need to be followed like developing clear instructions and policies for such systems integration, data privacy and protection, cybersecurity challenges, incorporating interdisciplinary collaborations in ML modelling, investment in research and development of such integrated mechanisms and reduction in energy consumption of AI-based energy solutions, and equitable access of energy to all facets of society based on AI integrated systems must be ensured.

REFERENCES

[1] S. Tiwari, "Artificial Intelligence (AI) in the Sustainable Energy Sector", *Engineering Proceedings,* vol. 37, no. 1, p. 11, 2023. [http://dx.doi.org/10.3390/ECP2023-14609]

[2] L. Bolte, and A. van Wynsberghe, "Sustainable AI and the third wave of AI ethics: a structural turn", *AI and Ethics,* no. Jul, 2024. [http://dx.doi.org/10.1007/s43681-024-00522-6]

[3] Y. Hou, and Q. Wang, *Big data and artificial intelligence application in energy field: a bibliometric analysis,* 2023. [http://dx.doi.org/10.1007/s11356-022-24880-y]

[4] Z. Liu, Artificial intelligence powered large-scale renewable integrations in multi-energy systems for carbon neutrality transition: Challenges and future perspectives *Elsevier B.V.* Nov. 01, 2022. [http://dx.doi.org/10.1016/j.egyai.2022.100195]

[5] T. Saheb, and M. Dehghani, *Artificial intelligence for Sustainability in Energy Industry: A Contextual Topic Modeling and Content Analys,* 2022.

[6] D.B. Olawade, O.Z. Wada, A.C. David-Olawade, O. Fapohunda, A.O. Ige, and J. Ling, "Artificial intelligence potential for net zero sustainability: Current evidence and prospects", *Next Sustainability,* vol. 4, p. 100041, 2024. [http://dx.doi.org/10.1016/j.nxsust.2024.100041]

[7] E. Latif, X. Zhai, and L. Liu, "AI Gender Bias, Disparities, and Fairness: Does Training Data Matter?", 2023. http://arxiv.org/abs/2312.10833

[8] N. Truong, K. Sun, S. Wang, F. Guitton, and Y. Guo, "Privacy preservation in federated learning: An insightful survey from the GDPR perspective", *Comput. Secur.,* vol. 110, p. 102402, 2021. [http://dx.doi.org/10.1016/j.cose.2021.102402]

[9] C. Ding, J. Ke, M. Levine, J. Granderson, and N. Zhou, "Potential of artificial intelligence in reducing energy and carbon emissions of commercial buildings at scale", *Nat. Commun.*, vol. 15, no. 1, p. 5916, 2024.
[http://dx.doi.org/10.1038/s41467-024-50088-4] [PMID: 39004671]

[10] H. Choung, P. David, and J. S. Seberger, "A Multilevel Framework for AI Governance 1 A Multilevel Framework for AI Governance", 2023.

[11] P. Robles, and D. J. Mallinson, "Catching up with AI: Pushing toward a cohesive governance framework", Jun. 01, 2023, John Wiley and Sons Inc.
[http://dx.doi.org/10.1111/polp.12529]

[12] A. van Wynsberghe, "Sustainable AI: AI for sustainability and the sustainability of AI", *AI and Ethics,* vol. 1, no. 3, pp. 213-218, 2021.
[http://dx.doi.org/10.1007/s43681-021-00043-6]

[13] L. Chen, Artificial intelligence-based solutions for climate change: a review', Oct. 01, 2023, Springer Science and Business Media Deutschland GmbH, 2023.
[http://dx.doi.org/10.1007/s10311-023-01617-y]

[14] M. Elassy, M. Al-Hattab, M. Takruri, and S. Badawi, "Intelligent transportation systems for sustainable smart cities", Jun. 01, 2024, Elsevier Ltd.
[http://dx.doi.org/10.1016/j.treng.2024.100252]

[15] S. Dörterler, S. Arslan, and D. Özdemir, Unlocking the potential: A review of artificial intelligence applications in wind energy', Dec. 01, 2024, John Wiley and Sons Inc.
[http://dx.doi.org/10.1111/exsy.13716]

[16] L. Floridi, and J. Cowls, "A unified framework of five principles for AI in society", *SSRN Electronic Journal,* no. Jun, 2019.
[http://dx.doi.org/10.2139/ssrn.3831321]

[17] Data privacy, ethics and protection guidance note on big data for achievement of the 2030 agenda.

[18] I.D. Raji, and J. Buolamwini, *Actionable Auditing: Investigating the Impact of Publicly Naming Biased Performance Results of Commercial AI Products*.www.aaai.org
[http://dx.doi.org/10.1145/3306618.3314244]

[19] B. Tomlinson, R.W. Black, D.J. Patterson, and A.W. Torrance, "The carbon emissions of writing and illustrating are lower for AI than for humans", *Sci. Rep.,* vol. 14, no. 1, p. 3732, 2024.
[http://dx.doi.org/10.1038/s41598-024-54271-x] [PMID: 38355820]

[20] E. Strubell, A. Ganesh, and A. McCallum, "Energy and policy considerations for deep learning in NLP", 2019. http://arxiv.org/abs/1906.02243
[http://dx.doi.org/10.18653/v1/P19-1355]

[21] P. Henderson, J. Hu, J. Romoff, E. Brunskill, D. Jurafsky, and J. Pineau, "Towards the systematic reporting of the energy and carbon footprints of machine learning", 2020. http://arxiv.org/abs/2002.05651

[22] P. Bourhis, D. Deutch and Y. Moskovitch, "Analyzing data-centric applications: Why, what-if, and how-to," 2016 IEEE 32nd International Conference on Data Engineering (ICDE), Helsinki, Finland, 2016, pp. 779-790.
[http://dx.doi.org/10.1109/ICDE.2016.7498289]

[23] V. Khatri, and C.V. Brown, "Designing data governance", *Commun. ACM,* vol. 53, no. 1, pp. 148-152, 2010.
[http://dx.doi.org/10.1145/1629175.1629210]

[24] M.D. Wilkinson, M. Dumontier, I.J.J. Aalbersberg, G. Appleton, M. Axton, A. Baak, N. Blomberg, J.W. Boiten, L.B. da Silva Santos, P.E. Bourne, J. Bouwman, A.J. Brookes, T. Clark, M. Crosas, I. Dillo, O. Dumon, S. Edmunds, C.T. Evelo, R. Finkers, A. Gonzalez-Beltran, A.J.G. Gray, P. Groth, C.

Goble, J.S. Grethe, J. Heringa, P.A.C. 't Hoen, R. Hooft, T. Kuhn, R. Kok, J. Kok, S.J. Lusher, M.E. Martone, A. Mons, A.L. Packer, B. Persson, P. Rocca-Serra, M. Roos, R. van Schaik, S.A. Sansone, E. Schultes, T. Sengstag, T. Slater, G. Strawn, M.A. Swertz, M. Thompson, J. van der Lei, E. van Mulligen, J. Velterop, A. Waagmeester, P. Wittenburg, K. Wolstencroft, J. Zhao, and B. Mons, "The FAIR Guiding Principles for scientific data management and stewardship", *Sci. Data,* vol. 3, no. 1, p. 160018, 2016.
[http://dx.doi.org/10.1038/sdata.2016.18] [PMID: 26978244]

[25] F. Alhusaini, S. Yaakob, and F. Zaman Rokhani, *Integrating Artificial Intelligence in Power Plant Management: A Review of Recent Applications and Future Directions,* 2024.

[26] I. - International Energy Agency, *Renewables 2022,* 2022.www.iea.org

[27] I. Renewable Energy Agency, *Renewable energy and jobs: Annual review 2023.,* 2023.www.irena.org

[28] G. D'Angelo, F. Palmieri, and A. Robustelli, "Artificial neural networks for resources optimization in energetic environment", *Soft Comput.,* vol. 26, no. 4, pp. 1779-1792, 2022.
[http://dx.doi.org/10.1007/s00500-022-06757-x]

[29] J. Jamii, M. Mansouri, M. Trabelsi, M.F. Mimouni, and W. Shatanawi, "Effective artificial neural network-based wind power generation and load demand forecasting for optimum energy management", *Front. Energy Res.,* vol. 10, p. 898413, 2022.
[http://dx.doi.org/10.3389/fenrg.2022.898413]

[30] G. Sharma, V.V. Raju, H. Dhall, P. Sudan, B. Reddy, and I. Alpackaya, Fuzzy logic-based energy management in smart grids for renewable integration.*E3S Web of Conferences.* EDP Sciences, 2024.
[http://dx.doi.org/10.1051/e3sconf/202451101013]

[31] Sm. Joys Mary, Sr. Babu, and D. Winston, 'Fuzzy logic based control of a grid connected hybrid renewable energy sources', *Int J Sci Eng Res*, vol. 5, no. 4, 2014, [Online]. Available: http://www.ijser.org

[32] T. Hinokuma, H. Farzaneh, A. Shaqour, and M. Sorrentino, "Techno-economic analysis of a fuzzy logic control based hybrid renewable energy system to power a university campus in Japan", 2021.
[http://dx.doi.org/10.3390/en14071960]

[33] K. Veeramachaneni, M. Wagner, U.-M. O'reilly, and F. Neumann, Optimizing energy output and layout costs for large wind farms using particle swarm optimization. 2012.
[http://dx.doi.org/10.1109/CEC.2012.6253002]

[34] Mosqueira-Rey, E., Hernández-Pereira, E., Alonso-Ríos, D. "Human-in-the-loop machine learning: a state of the art". *Artif Intell Rev* 56, p. 3005–3054. 2023.
[http://dx.doi.org/10.1007/s10462-022-10246-w]

[35] S.F. Bello, I.U. Wada, and B. Olukayode, Sakiru Folarin Bello; Ifeoluwa Uchechukwu Wada; Olukayode B Ige; Ernest C Chianumba; Samod Adetunji Adebayo, "AI-driven predictive maintenance and optimization of renewable energy systems for enhanced operational efficiency and longevity", *International Journal of Science and Research Archive,* vol. 13, no. 1, pp. 2823-2837, 2024.
[http://dx.doi.org/10.30574/ijsra.2024.13.1.1992]

[36] unctad, 'value creation and capture: implications for developing countries', 2019.

[37] W. Tao, S. Weng, X. Chen, F.B. ALHussan, and M. Song, "Artificial intelligence-driven transformations in low-carbon energy structure: Evidence from China", *Energy Econ.,* vol. 136, p. 107719, 2024.
[http://dx.doi.org/10.1016/j.eneco.2024.107719]

[38] A. Mohammad, and F. Mahjabeen, "Revolutionizing solar energy: The impact of artificial intelligence on photovoltaic systems", *International Journal of Multidisciplinary Sciences and Arts,* vol. 2, no. 3, 2023.
[http://dx.doi.org/10.47709/ijmdsa.v2i1.2599]

[39] M. Yin, Z. Yang, Y. Xu, J. Liu, L. Zhou, and Y. Zou, "Aerodynamic optimization for variable-speed

wind turbines based on wind energy capture efficiency", *Appl. Energy,* vol. 221, pp. 508-521, 2018. [http://dx.doi.org/10.1016/j.apenergy.2018.03.078]

[40] X. Gao, H. Yang, and L. Lu, "Optimization of wind turbine layout position in a wind farm using a newly-developed two-dimensional wake model", *Appl. Energy,* vol. 174, pp. 192-200, 2016. [http://dx.doi.org/10.1016/j.apenergy.2016.04.098]

[41] C.M. Chan, H.L. Bai, and D.Q. He, "Blade shape optimization of the Savonius wind turbine using a genetic algorithm", *Appl. Energy,* vol. 213, pp. 148-157, 2018. [http://dx.doi.org/10.1016/j.apenergy.2018.01.029]

[42] S. Sahibzada, F. S. Malik, S. Nasir, and S. K. Lodhi, "Generative ai driven aerodynamic shape optimization: a neural network-based framework for enhancing performance and efficiency,", *International Journal of Innovative Research in Computer Science and Technology,*. vol. 13, no. 1, pp. 98–105, Jan. 2025. [http://dx.doi.org/10.1016/j.geothermics.2022.102348]

[43] T. Muther, F.I. Syed, A.T. Lancaster, F.D. Salsabila, A.K. Dahaghi, and S. Negahban, "Geothermal 4.0: AI-enabled geothermal reservoir development- current status, potentials, limitations, and ways forward", *Geothermics,* vol. 100, p. 102348, 2022. [http://dx.doi.org/10.1016/j.geothermics.2022.102348]

[44] E.G. Al-Sakkari, A. Ragab, H. Dagdougui, D.C. Boffito, and M. Amazouz, "Carbon capture, utilization and sequestration systems design and operation optimization: Assessment and perspectives of artificial intelligence opportunities", *Sci. Total Environ.,* vol. 917, p. 170085, 2024. [http://dx.doi.org/10.1016/j.scitotenv.2024.170085] [PMID: 38224888]

[45] N. El-Haber, D. Burnett, A. Halford, K. Stamp, D. De Silva, M. Manic, and A. Jennings, "A lifecycle approach for artificial intelligence ethics in energy systems", *Energies,* vol. 17, no. 14, p. 3572, 2024. [http://dx.doi.org/10.3390/en17143572]

[46] D.D. Slate, *Adoption of artificial intelligence by electric utilities,* 2024. http://jmc.stanford.edu/artificial-intelli- [http://dx.doi.org/10.2139/ssrn.4847872]

[47] N. Balasubramaniam, M. Kauppinen, A. Rannisto, K. Hiekkanen, and S. Kujala, "Transparency and explainability of AI systems: From ethical guidelines to requirements,", *Inf Softw Technol.* vol. 159, Jul. 2023. [http://dx.doi.org/10.1016/j.infsof.2023.107197]

[48] B.C. Cheong, "Transparency and accountability in AI systems: safeguarding wellbeing in the age of algorithmic decision-making", *Frontiers in Human Dynamics,* vol. 6, p. 1421273, 2024. [http://dx.doi.org/10.3389/fhumd.2024.1421273]

[49] M. Coeckelbergh, "AI for climate: freedom, justice, and other ethical and political challenges", *AI and Ethics,* vol. 1, no. 1, pp. 67-72, 2021. [http://dx.doi.org/10.1007/s43681-020-00007-2]

CHAPTER 7

Future Directions: AI's Role in Shaping the Future of Electrochemical Technologies

Prashanth S. Adarakatti[1,*]

[1] *Department of Chemistry, SVM Arts, Science and Commerce College, Ilkal, India*

Abstract: Artificial Intelligence (AI) is revolutionizing electrochemical technologies by spurring advancements in material discovery, process optimization, and predictive modeling. By enabling the rapid screening and creation of innovative electrode materials, electrolytes, and catalysts, advanced machine learning algorithms and neural networks significantly reduce the time and expense associated with conventional research. By analyzing data in real-time and making well-informed decisions, AI-powered solutions enhance the sustainability and effectiveness of electrochemical processes, including chemical synthesis, water treatment, and energy storage. Artificial Intelligence (AI) models excel at understanding the intricacies of electrochemical systems, providing valuable insights into device performance and refining reaction conditions to achieve optimal results. Advances in battery, fuel cell, and electrolyzer technology are made possible by predictive modeling, which facilitates the development of high-performance materials and systems. Additionally, by optimizing processes and reducing human involvement, AI-driven automation in industrial and laboratory environments speeds up scaling and commercialization. AI and electrochemical technologies are being integrated for specific uses where accuracy and speed of analysis are essential, such as biosensing and diagnostics. Customized solutions are being developed to tackle issues in environmental monitoring and healthcare by utilizing AI's capabilities. This investigation demonstrates how AI has the potential to transform electrochemical technologies and provide long-term solutions to the world's energy and environmental challenges. AI has the potential to significantly influence the direction of electrochemical research and its real-world applications by stimulating innovation and improving operational effectiveness.

Keywords: Biosensing, Catalysts, Electrode materials, Energy storage, Environmental monitoring, Machine learning algorithms, Neural networks, Predictive modeling, Real-time data analysis, Sustainability, Water treatment.

* **Corresponding author Prashanth S. Adarakatti:** Department of Chemistry, SVM Arts, Science and Commerce College, Ilkal, India; E-mail: prashanthsa143@gmail.com

Shreya Sharma, Peeyush Phogat, Ranjana Jha & Sukhvir Singh (Eds.)

INTRODUCTION

Modern society relies heavily on electrochemical technologies, particularly for chemical synthesis, energy conversion, and storage [1]. These technologies utilize the motion of ions and electrons, transforming chemical energy into electrical energy or vice versa. The development of next-generation electronic gadgets, the advancement of clean energy solutions, and the reduction of carbon footprints all depend on key applications such as batteries, fuel cells, electrolyzers, and sensors [2]. Rechargeable batteries, such as lithium-ion (Li-ion) and solid-state batteries, are among the most well-known electrochemical systems. The power is anything from electric cars to mobile devices. As clean substitutes for fossil fuel-based power generation, fuel cells—which produce electricity *via* the electrochemical reaction of hydrogen and oxygen—are being investigated more and more. In contrast, electrolyzers facilitate the production of hydrogen from water, a crucial step in achieving sustainable energy transitions. Despite their potential, these technologies face several obstacles that necessitate creative solutions, including affordability, scalability, durability, and efficiency [3, 4].

Due in large part to the complexity of the materials involved and the subtleties of their behavior under actual working conditions, electrochemical systems continue to face performance and reliability limits after decades of research and advancement. The need for a more comprehensive, data-driven strategy that utilizes sophisticated algorithms, simulation tools, and computational techniques to forecast, evaluate, and enhance electrochemical processes is becoming increasingly apparent in order to overcome these challenges [5]. Numerous scientific and engineering fields have undergone significant changes in recent decades due to the rapid development of Artificial Intelligence (AI). Artificial Intelligence (AI), particularly Machine Learning (ML) and Deep Learning (DL), has demonstrated its ability to solve complex optimization problems, provide predictive analytics in various domains, including materials science and healthcare, and uncover significant patterns from vast datasets [6]. AI is a game-changing tool in both industry and research because of its capacity to handle vast amounts of data and identify minute correlations within it [7].

Artificial Intelligence (AI) has gained popularity in the field of electrochemical technologies as a valuable tool for enhancing the understanding and performance of electrochemical systems [8]. The design of new materials or reaction conditions may be optimized, future behaviors can be predicted, and experimental data from electrochemical cells can be processed using AI algorithms. AI is particularly adept at evaluating data from simulations and high-throughput tests, which enables scientists to identify potential materials and reaction pathways that would otherwise require years of trial and error [9]. Neural networks, support vector machines, and decision trees are examples of machine learning approaches commonly used to predict important factors such as efficiency, longevity, and thermal stability, as well as to evaluate the behavior of electrochemical systems [10]. These techniques simplify both the discovery process and the optimization of current technologies. They can be applied in various electrochemical domains, ranging from battery development to fuel cell optimization [11]. There is considerable promise in combining AI with electrochemical technology to address the persistent challenges that conventional electrochemical systems have encountered. The potential of AI to speed up electrochemical material discovery and innovation is among its most alluring benefits. In a fraction of the time required by traditional experimental approaches, researchers can use machine learning to predict the behavior of novel compounds, assess complex material properties and interactions, and determine the optimal configurations for energy storage or conversion devices [12].

AI also enables the real-time monitoring and management of electrochemical processes, which helps prevent errors before they occur and provides valuable insights into system performance [13]. AI, for instance, can monitor fuel cell efficiency, optimize battery charge/discharge cycles, or identify early degradation indicators, all of which increase system longevity and lower maintenance costs. AI-driven optimization is also used in the creation of novel electrodes and materials. It can be quite time-consuming and resource-intensive to screen thousands of potential candidates when creating novel materials for electrochemical applications [14]. This is accelerated by AI, which eliminates the need for time-consuming trial-and-error techniques by evaluating data from computer models and experimental tests to anticipate the most promising materials. Development cycles are significantly shortened by this data-driven approach, which facilitates the advancement of energy storage and conversion technologies [15].

Last but not least, AI can help electrochemical technologies scale for large-scale uses. AI can help optimize design, manufacturing, and operational strategies to ensure that these technologies are not only efficient but also commercially feasible, whether they are being developed for grid-scale energy storage or hydrogen production through water electrolysis [16]. In conclusion, unlocking the next generation of energy systems hinges on the integration of AI and electrochemical technology. AI has the potential to spur innovation in materials science, process optimization, and predictive maintenance by improving the speed, precision, and efficiency of research and development. AI will become more and more important as electrochemistry develops in order to solve the world's energy problems, hasten the switch to sustainable energy sources, and usher in a new era of electrochemical technology [17] (Fig. **1**).

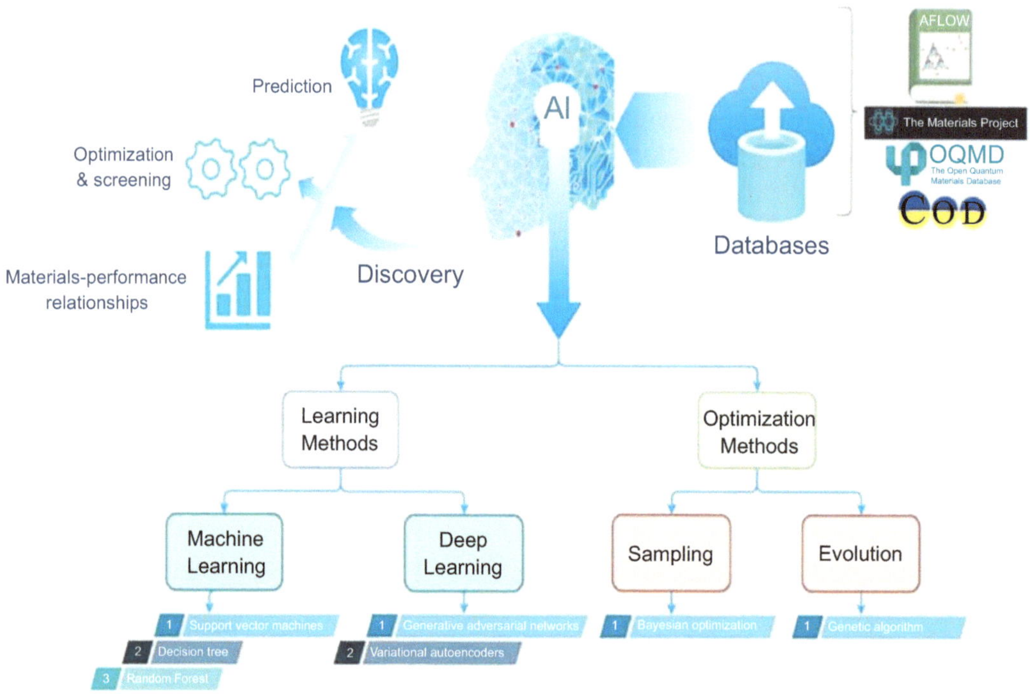

Fig. (1). Schematic representation of AI-driven materials discovery through databases, learning methods, and optimization techniques for performance enhancement, reproduced with permission from Elsevier 2024 [18].

Understanding Electrochemical Processes

Electrons are transferred between species in chemical processes, which are at the heart of basic electrochemical reactions, the foundation of electrochemical technologies. The laws of oxidation and reduction (redox reactions) regulate these processes, which usually take place at the interface between an electrode and an electrolyte [19]. One species loses electrons through oxidation and another gains electrons through reduction in a redox process. For instance, in a basic galvanic cell, a type of battery, a metal (such as zinc) loses electrons at the anode during the oxidation reaction, and ions (like copper ions) gain electrons at the cathode during the reduction reaction, forming solid copper. An electric current is produced when electrons move from the anode to the cathode *via* an external circuit. The circuit inside the cell is completed when ions in the electrolyte migrate to equalize charge imbalances [20]. These fundamental ideas form the basis for a wide range of electrochemical devices, including chemical production processes such as electrolysis and energy storage devices like batteries. The effectiveness of these redox processes, the characteristics of the electrodes and electrolyte materials, and the conditions under which the reactions occur (such as temperature, pressure, and concentration) all have a significant impact on the system's performance and efficiency.

Important Applications of Electrochemical Technology: Electrolyzers, Fuel Cells, and Batteries

Batteries, fuel cells, and electrolyzers are the primary applications of electrochemical technologies. Energy storage, conversion, and chemical synthesis are at the heart of each of these systems, which use electrochemical reactions for particular purposes [21].

Batteries: The most well-known use of electrochemical processes is probably in rechargeable batteries. Electrical energy can be stored in these devices as chemical energy and *vice versa*, thanks to electrochemical reactions [22]. Lithium-ion (Li-ion), sodium-ion, and new solid-state batteries are the most popular varieties. Ions in these batteries generate and store energy as they travel between the cathode and anode through the electrolyte during cycles of charge and discharge [23]. The longevity, effectiveness, and safety of these systems are important topics for continued study and development.

Fuel Cells: Fuel cells use an electrochemical reaction with an oxidizing agent (usually oxygen) to directly transform the chemical energy of a fuel (usually hydrogen) into electrical energy [24]. Proton Exchange Membrane (PEM) fuel cells, the most well-known type, power everything from cars to portable devices. Fuel cells are a clean alternative to conventional energy sources, as they generate power without releasing greenhouse gases, unlike burning. Long-term durability, system cost, and fuel storage remain issues, though [25].

Electrolyzers: These devices convert water into compounds, most notably hydrogen, through electrochemical processes [26]. Water is split into hydrogen and oxygen by applying electrical energy in a process known as water electrolysis. Green hydrogen, which can be used as a sustainable energy carrier for various industrial purposes, is produced using this method. To scale up hydrogen production and integrate it into renewable energy sources, advancements in electrolyzer technology are essential [27].

Electrochemical Engineering Difficulties

Despite the enormous potential of electrochemical technologies, several obstacles hinder their widespread adoption and effectiveness. These difficulties stem from both the technological constraints of existing devices and the complex nature of the materials and reactions involved [3].

Material Limitations: The materials used for electrodes and electrolytes have a significant impact on the performance of electrochemical systems [28]. The anode and cathode materials of batteries, for example, need to be able to store and release ions effectively without deteriorating over time. Electrodes in fuel cells must also be able to tolerate the corrosive nature of the operating environment while facilitating effective ion and electron transfer. It remains quite challenging to discover and develop new materials that are more economical, durable, and efficient. Although the process is still in its infancy, Artificial Intelligence (AI) and machine learning are beginning to play a significant role in accelerating the discovery of such materials.

Energy Efficiency and Storage Capacity: The effectiveness of energy storage and retrieval is a crucial concern, especially with batteries. The energy density of many modern technologies, including lithium-ion batteries, is limited, which has an immediate impact on the duration between charges [29]. Furthermore, the lifespan of batteries is shortened over time by frequent cycles of charging and discharging. Reducing fuel consumption and attaining high efficiency at low temperatures are persistent issues in fuel cells.

Cost and Scalability: There are several challenges associated with scaling up electrochemical technology for large-scale applications, such as grid storage or hydrogen production. Production procedures are frequently costly and energy-intensive, especially when it comes to high-performance materials. For example, the cost of producing platinum catalysts for fuel cells is prohibitive, and obtaining and processing raw materials such as nickel, cobalt, and lithium is a problem for large-scale battery manufacturing. Furthermore, a key component of future improvements is ensuring that these materials are produced sustainably, especially in light of concerns about supply chain stability and mining methods [30].

Durability and Lifespan: Many electrochemical devices have issues with limited lifespans and deterioration. This may manifest as internal short circuits or capacity fading in batteries, while electrode deterioration over time can reduce fuel cell performance. Concerns about durability are especially important in applications such as grid storage and electric vehicles, where long-term dependability is crucial [31]. Innovative materials, cutting-edge coatings, and a deeper understanding of the underlying degradation mechanisms are needed to address these challenges.

System Integration and Performance Monitoring: Lastly, the smooth coordination of hardware, software, and control systems is necessary for integrating electrochemical systems into practical applications, such as energy grids or transportation networks. By utilizing real-time data collection, predictive analytics, and system modeling to monitor and maintain optimal performance, problems can be avoided, and overall efficiency can be enhanced. More intelligent control and defect detection are made possible by the development of AI and machine learning [32].

AI in Electrochemical Research and Development

Models for Machine Learning (ML) have become essential resources for forecasting how electrochemical systems will behave [17]. The primary benefit of machine learning is its ability to analyze large datasets and identify intricate patterns that are challenging to detect using conventional techniques. In electrochemical research, this aptitude has significant implications for both fundamental understanding and practical application.

A wide range of interrelated factors, such as electrode materials, electrolyte compositions, temperature, and voltage, are involved in electrochemical systems, such as batteries, fuel cells, and electrolyzers [33]. Conventional experimental techniques can be resource- and time-intensive, often requiring hundreds or thousands of trials to identify the optimal materials or conditions. Conversely, machine learning models can quickly analyze simulations and experimental data to forecast system behavior under various circumstances. For instance, ML models have been applied in battery research to forecast thermal behavior, charge/discharge patterns, and battery cycle life, depending on input characteristics such as electrolyte composition and electrode material quality [34]. While unsupervised learning techniques, such as clustering or dimensionality reduction, can identify underlying patterns or anomalies that may indicate degradation or inefficiencies, supervised learning algorithms, like neural networks or Support Vector Machines (SVMs), can translate input data into performance metrics. Similar to this, fuel cell research utilizes machine learning models to predict the electrochemical performance under various operating conditions. Machine learning models can help optimize operational parameters (such as fuel mix, temperature, and pressure) for optimal durability and efficiency by being trained on data from high-throughput tests [35]. To make better design decisions and more accurate lifespan projections, these models can also help identify failure mechanisms (Fig. **2**).

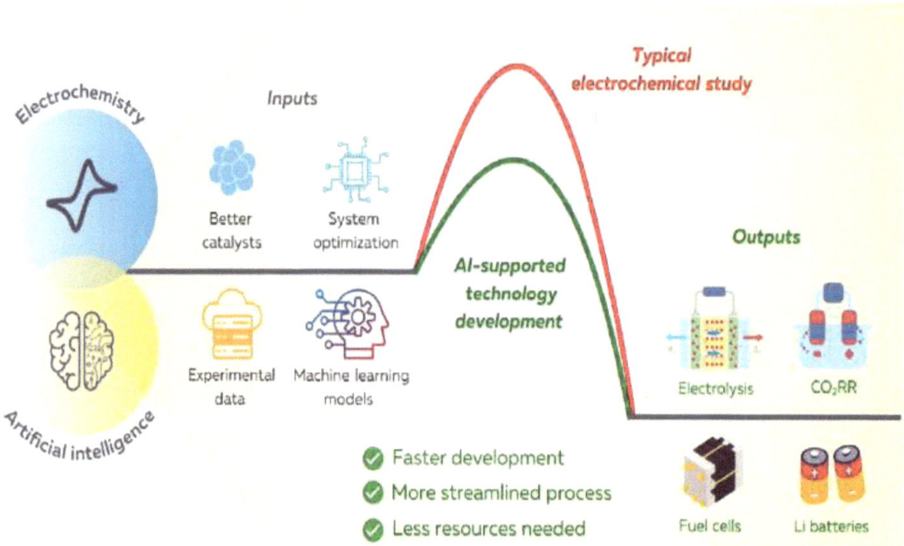

Fig. (2). Schematic image of how artificial intelligence (AI) can approach electrochemical experimental studies, reproduced with permission from Cell Press, 2024 [36].

Data-Informed Methods for Catalyst Design

The effectiveness of many electrochemical processes, particularly those involving energy conversion and storage, depends heavily on the use of catalysts. For example, the electrode catalysts (such as platinum or new materials) in fuel cells and electrolyzers must effectively promote the electrochemical reactions, usually by reducing activation energy and enhancing reaction kinetics [37]. Conventional catalyst design often employs empirical or trial-and-error techniques, which can be both expensive and time-consuming. Catalyst optimization and discovery can be accelerated with the help of AI and machine learning. Large datasets from computational simulations and experimental results are utilized in data-driven techniques to predict the performance of novel catalysts and identify trends. Data on distinct candidate materials under varied reaction conditions are produced by high-throughput screening techniques and incorporated into machine learning algorithms [38]. By learning from the data, these models forecast the stability, selectivity, and catalytic activity of untested materials, providing valuable insights into the most promising candidates for further research. AI models, for instance, can predict the catalytic activity of novel materials in fuel cell Hydrogen Evolution Reactions (HER) or Oxygen Reduction Reactions (ORR) based on electronic structural characteristics, surface shape, and composition [39]. Machine learning algorithms can rapidly assess a material's potential performance in an electrochemical reaction by integrating data from multiple sources, including experimental data, Density Functional Theory (DFT) calculations, and material databases. This greatly speeds up the design cycle. Additionally, by determining the ideal mix of metals, ligands, or other performance-enhancing additions, machine learning can be used to optimize catalyst structure. The field of catalyst design is evolving as a result of this data-driven approach, which enables the discovery of more economical and effective materials. For example, non-precious metal catalysts can be used in fuel cells as an alternative to expensive platinum [16].

AI for Identifying and Improving Reaction Mechanisms

To maximize the efficiency of energy systems, it is crucial to understand the reaction mechanisms underlying electrochemical processes. In the past, determining these mechanisms required a multi-step process that could take years to develop, involving electrochemical modeling, theoretical calculations, and experimental observations. The development of AI and machine learning has enabled academics to employ data-driven methods to identify underlying mechanisms more rapidly and precisely, thereby accelerating this process [40]. The adsorption, desorption, and transfer of ions or electrons at the electrode surface are just a few examples of the numerous intermediary steps that are part of the complex reaction mechanisms observed in many electrochemical processes. Artificial Intelligence (AI) methods, especially deep learning and reinforcement learning, can be used to model these intricate reactions and pinpoint the routes that result in the most effective energy conversion or storage procedures. AI models, for instance, can be used to forecast the formation and consumption rates of chemical intermediates in fuel cell or battery reactions. These forecasts are frequently derived from experimental data, which feeds the model with information about how well electrochemical cells function in various scenarios. The model can then pinpoint crucial phases in the reaction mechanism, such as catalyst poisoning or the accumulation of resistive layers on electrodes, that restrict performance or cause degradation over time. Researchers can utilize this knowledge to inform system modifications that enhance stability and efficiency.

AI-Driven Materials Discovery and Design

A revolutionary era in the study and creation of new materials has begun with the incorporation of Artificial Intelligence (AI) into materials science. By utilizing computational techniques, AI accelerates the discovery, development, and application of materials, particularly those with advanced electrochemical properties [41]. This chapter examines the pivotal role Artificial Intelligence (AI) plays in materials science, with a specific focus on its application in discovering new electrode materials and enabling high-throughput screening for electrochemical systems (Fig. **3**).

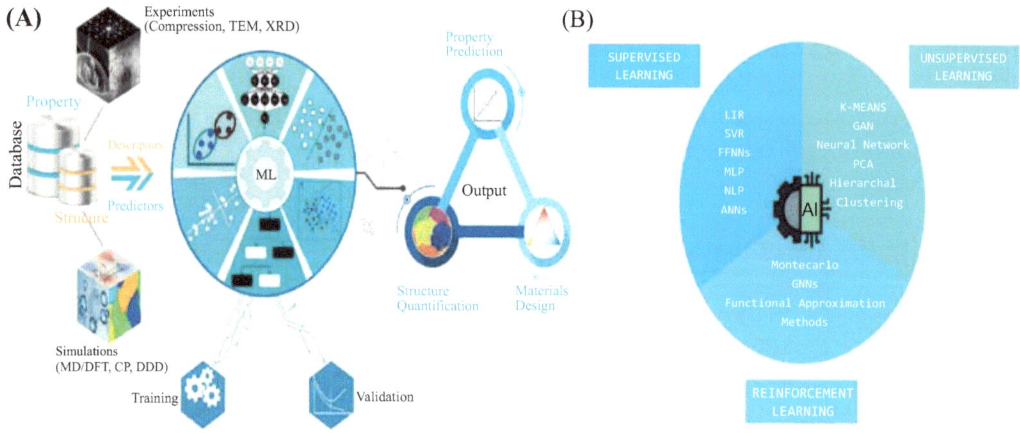

Fig. (3). (A) An outline of the AI-powered materials design process that includes three key components: a material dataset, machine learning models that can use the dataset to learn and interpret representations for particular tasks, and output that produces improved and optimized material properties for the development of advanced materials, reproduced with permission from MDPI, 2021 [42] **(B)** A summary of machine learning approaches emphasizing the three main types - reinforcement learning, supervised learning, and unsupervised learning.

Computational Materials Science: The Role of AI

In materials research, AI-driven computational techniques are transforming simulation, predictive modeling, and material property optimization. Physical, chemical, and electrical properties can be predicted quickly and accurately thanks to Machine Learning (ML) algorithms that have been trained on large datasets [43]. AI models, for instance, can utilize atomic or molecular structures to estimate properties such as mechanical strength, thermal conductivity, and bandgap characteristics. These features significantly reduce the need for labor-intensive experimental processes and computationally expensive simulations. Furthermore, by creating completely original material compositions, generative models such as generative adversarial networks, or GANs, are opening up new possibilities. These tools facilitate the investigation of novel material systems with customized characteristics, thereby expediting the research process and promoting groundbreaking findings [44].

AI in Identifying Novel Electrode Materials

The identification of new electrode materials with ideal electrochemical characteristics is crucial in the pursuit of cutting-edge energy conversion and storage technologies. To anticipate and suggest possible outcomes, Artificial Intelligence (AI) correlates complex datasets, such as chemical compositions, crystal structures, and performance measurements [45]. For instance, by examining millions of compounds in a fraction of the time needed for conventional methods, AI-driven research has effectively identified high-performance cathode and anode materials for lithium-ion batteries. To ensure both theoretical promise and actual feasibility, Reinforcement Learning (RL), a subset of artificial intelligence, has also been used to optimize synthesis routes and processing conditions for these materials.

AI for High-Throughput Screening of Electrochemical Materials

A key component of contemporary materials discovery is High-Throughput Screening (HTS), which enables scientists to assess a large number of material candidates. By automating data processing, feature extraction, and pattern detection from simulation and experimental datasets, AI improves HTS [38]. To identify promising materials for applications such as fuel cells, supercapacitors, and electrocatalysts, advanced AI models can analyze spectral data, electrochemical performance metrics, and structural information. Additionally, feedback loops that repeatedly improve predictions through experimental validation are integrated into AI-powered HTS systems, resulting in a synergistic cycle of optimization and discovery [46]. Particularly in electrochemical systems, the combination of artificial intelligence and materials science presents enormous potential for ground-breaking discoveries. By leveraging AI's predictive capabilities, scientists can address critical issues in healthcare, energy, and the environment, paving the way for a technologically sophisticated and sustainable future (Fig. **4**).

AI for Real-Time Monitoring and Control

A paradigm shift in materials science and engineering has been brought about by the incorporation of Artificial Intelligence (AI) into the real-time monitoring and control of electrochemical systems [51]. Researchers and engineers can operate electrochemical processes with previously unheard-of precision, efficiency, and dependability by utilizing sophisticated machine learning algorithms and autonomous systems [52]. This section examines the significant developments in this field, including autonomous process control, predictive maintenance for system optimization, and machine learning for *in-situ* analysis.

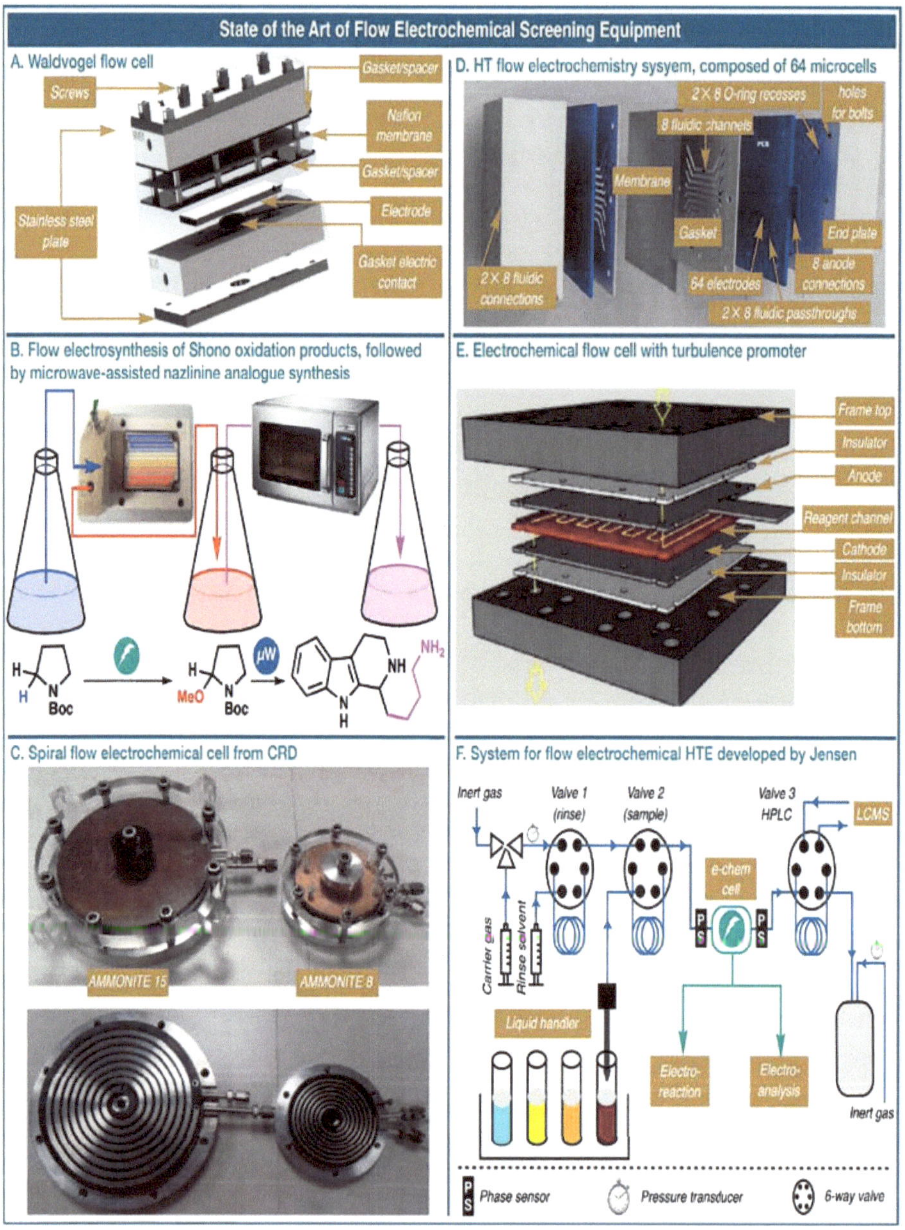

Fig. (4). State of the art of flow electrochemical screening equipment. **(A)** Reproduced with permission from American Chemical Society, 2017 [47]. **(C)** Reproduced with permission from American Chemical Society, 2017 [48]. **(D)** Reproduced with permission from MDPI, 2020 [49]. **(E)** Reproduced with permission from American Chemical Society, 2020 [50].

Machine Learning Algorithms for *In-Situ* Analysis

In-situ analysis has been revolutionized by Machine Learning (ML), enabling the rapid and accurate understanding of real-time data. During studies, electrochemical parameters, including voltage, current, impedance, and reaction kinetics, are analyzed using methods such as supervised learning and reinforcement learning. These algorithms can recognize transient states, forecast response paths, and find minor anomalies that older approaches frequently overlook. For instance, Electrochemical Impedance Spectroscopy (EIS) data can be processed by Convolutional Neural Networks (CNNs) to identify phase shifts or material deterioration in real time [53]. Additionally, real-time feedback is provided by combining ML with spectroscopic tools, allowing researchers to make well-informed adjustments while conducting tests (Fig. **5**).

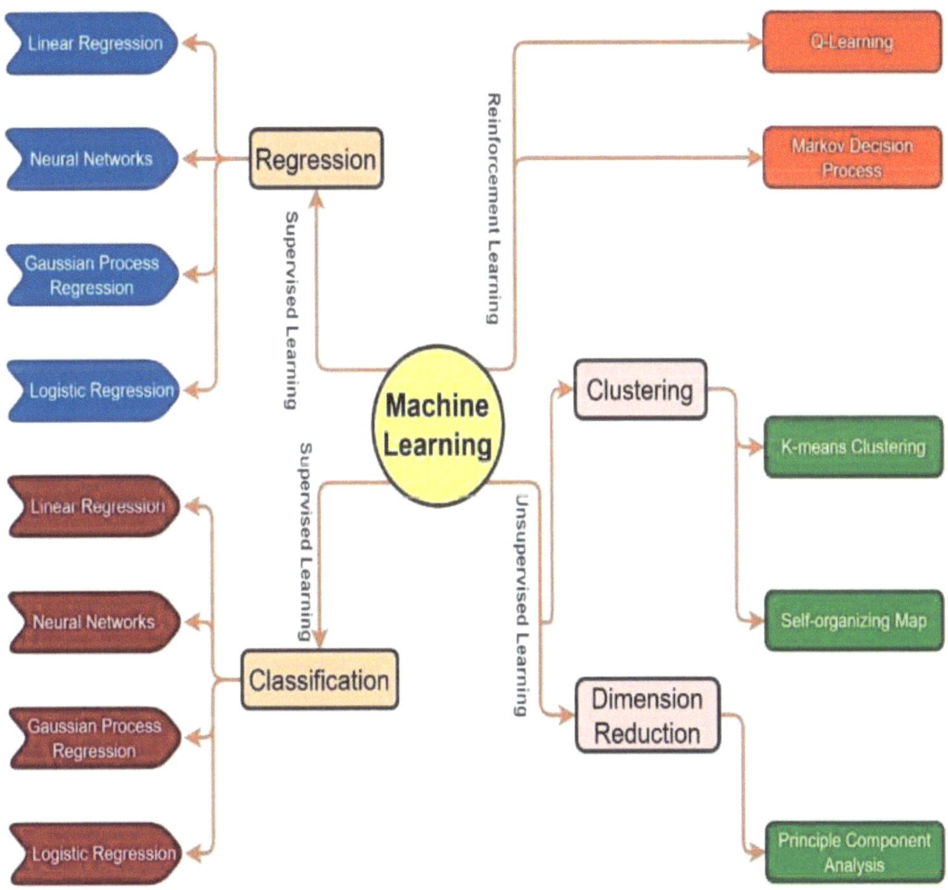

Fig. (5). Schematic illustrating various ML algorithms, reproduced with permission from Elsevier, 2021 [54].

Autonomous Systems for Electrochemical Process Control

AI-powered autonomous systems are revolutionizing electrochemical process control by reducing the need for human involvement. These systems dynamically modify process variables, including temperature, pressure, and reactant flow rates, using AI-powered decision-making frameworks [51]. These systems can enhance product production, mitigate overloading or malfunction hazards, and optimize energy efficiency through real-time data analysis. AI-controlled potentiostats and galvanostats, which adaptively adjust applied voltage or current based on the changing state of the electrochemical system, are a notable example. In industrial applications, where maintaining constant process conditions is crucial for large-scale manufacturing, this type of autonomy is highly beneficial.

Predictive Maintenance and Performance Monitoring in Electrochemical Systems

AI algorithms are used in predictive maintenance to anticipate potential electrochemical system faults before they occur. AI algorithms can identify trends that indicate wear, corrosion, or other forms of degradation by analyzing historical and current operating data. This proactive strategy prolongs the life of vital components, such as electrodes and membranes, reduces maintenance expenses, and minimizes downtime. AI-powered performance monitoring systems also continuously assess the effectiveness and health of the system, giving operators useful information. AI-powered digital twins, for example, can replicate the operation of electrochemical reactors, enabling real-time comparisons between expected and actual behavior to ensure optimal performance [55]. The application of AI to real-time electrochemical system monitoring and control has revolutionary potential in both the scientific and industrial spheres. Predictive maintenance, autonomous process control, and machine learning algorithms are used in these advances to create electrochemical technologies that are more intelligent, effective, and sustainable. In addition to improving existing capabilities, this intersection of electrochemistry and artificial intelligence paves the way for future developments in process optimization and materials discovery.

Optimizing Energy Storage and Conversion Technologies

Technologies for energy conversion and storage have undergone a significant transformation with the rapid development of Artificial Intelligence (AI), which has opened up previously unexplored possibilities for enhancing sustainability, performance, and reliability. AI enables accurate forecasts and optimizations in various fields, including fuel cell systems, battery technologies, and energy management frameworks, by utilizing machine learning algorithms, data-driven models, and computational tools [56]. This chapter examines how AI is revolutionizing specific domains, highlighting significant developments and promising future directions.

Enhancing Battery Technologies Using AI: Li-ion, Solid-State, and Beyond

AI has had a big impact on battery technology research and optimization, especially for lithium-ion (Li-ion) and new solid-state batteries. Machine learning models are used to identify degradation mechanisms, optimize charging procedures, and forecast battery life [57]. AI-powered simulations, for example, aid in the discovery of new materials with enhanced stability and energy density. AI's capacity to simulate ion conductivity and select the most suitable solid electrolytes is advantageous for solid-state batteries, which are hailed as the next big thing in energy storage. By examining electrochemical characteristics and lifespan data, AI facilitates the investigation of other chemistries beyond Li-ion, such as sodium-ion and lithium-sulfur. These developments offer energy storage systems that are safer, more effective, and more durable for uses ranging from electric cars to consumer electronics.

AI in Fuel Cell Performance Prediction and Optimization

By integrating AI, fuel cells—crucial for converting renewable energy—have advanced significantly. Fuel cell performance under various operating conditions, including temperature, pressure, and humidity, can be precisely predicted thanks to AI algorithms [58]. Data-driven models enhance durability and efficiency by optimizing fuel flow rates, selecting membrane materials, and determining optimal catalyst loading. In order to ensure extended operation, AI also helps identify failure modes and mitigate degradation processes. AI helps lower production costs and boost the commercial viability of fuel cells in industrial, residential, and transportation applications by accelerating the design of improved materials and control systems (Fig. **6**).

Smart Grid Integration and Energy Management

Stability, demand forecasting, and energy distribution have become more difficult as a result of the grid's incorporation of renewable energy sources [60]. AI aids in addressing these issues by enabling dynamic energy management and optimizing smart grids. The smooth integration of renewable energy sources like solar and wind is ensured by the high accuracy with which advanced neural networks and reinforcement learning models forecast changes in energy supply and demand. In addition to improving overall grid resilience, AI-powered algorithms enable real-time energy pricing, storage dispatch, and load balancing. AI also optimizes energy storage systems to support grid functions, guaranteeing effective use of stored energy during times of high demand [61]. A sustainable, low-carbon energy future depends on these breakthroughs. To sum up, artificial intelligence has become a key component in the development of energy conversion and storage technologies. AI advances the development of a more resilient and sustainable energy environment by accelerating material discovery, enhancing operational efficiency, and enabling intelligent energy management. Future advancements will probably further combine AI with cutting-edge technologies, leading to innovations in clean energy solutions for a world that is changing quickly.

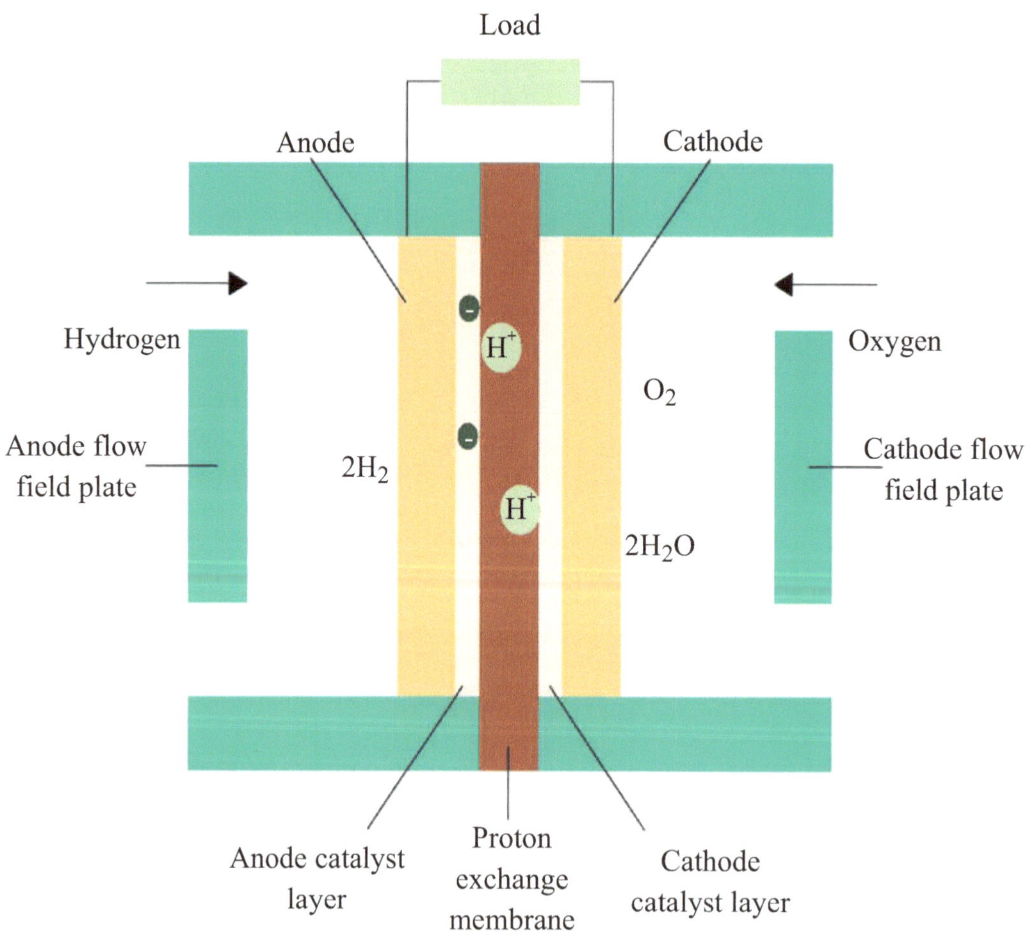

Fig. (6). Schematic diagram of the working principle of PEMFC, reproduced with permission from MDPI, 2024 [59].

AI and Sustainability: Green Electrochemical Technologies

The incorporation of Artificial Intelligence (AI) into green electrochemical technology has created new opportunities to address the world's sustainability issues. AI plays a crucial role in advancing environmentally friendly solutions, as it enhances productivity, reduces resource consumption, and optimizes system performance. The revolutionary effects of AI on carbon capture, water splitting, hydrogen production, and recycling in electrochemical systems are highlighted in this section.

AI's Role in Carbon Capture, Storage, and Conversion

The use of AI models to improve Carbon Capture, Utilization, and Storage (CCUS) operations is growing. The best adsorbents or absorbents for CO_2 sequestration, such as amines or Metal-Organic Frameworks (MOFs), can be predicted by machine learning algorithms that can evaluate large datasets. Furthermore, to enable carbon-neutral industrial processes, AI-driven simulations help determine the ideal conditions for electrochemical CO_2 reduction to value-added products, such as methanol or formic acid [36]. For a comprehensive approach to sustainability, predictive models are also useful in designing systems that combine carbon capture with renewable energy sources.

Electrochemical Water Splitting and Hydrogen Production *via* AI Models

A key component of green energy is the use of water splitting to produce hydrogen. AI utilizes deep learning and high-throughput screening to expedite the search for and optimization of electrocatalysts, such as transition metal oxides or phosphides [62]. By forecasting catalytic activity, stability, and reaction kinetics under various conditions, these models significantly reduce the time and expense of experiments. AI also aids in real-time electrolyzer performance monitoring, ensuring the highest possible hydrogen yield with the least amount of energy. This encourages the use of economical and effective hydrogen generation technologies, which are crucial for developing a hydrogen-based economy (Fig. 7).

AI for Circular Economy and Recycling in Electrochemical Systems

By streamlining recycling procedures in electrochemical systems, such as batteries and fuel cells, Artificial Intelligence (AI) helps accelerate the shift to a circular economy [64]. For example, sophisticated AI systems can efficiently recover vital elements, such as nickel, cobalt, and lithium, by analyzing waste streams. Predictive maintenance and device end-of-life management are also made possible by AI-powered systems, which minimize waste and conserve resources. Additionally, sustainable recycling methods that maximize financial returns while minimizing environmental damage are designed using reinforcement learning approaches. Sustainability objectives can be more effectively met by combining AI with electrochemical technology [65]. These developments point to a time when environmentally friendly inventions will be both commercially and technically practicable, opening the door to a more sustainable world.

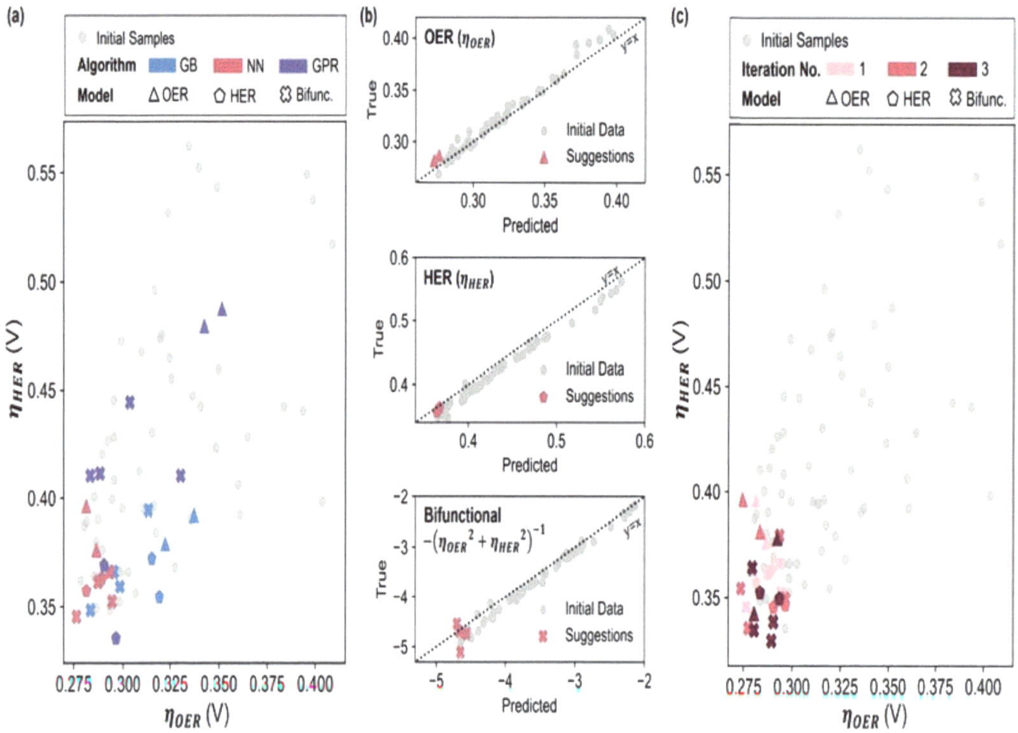

Fig. (7). **(a)** Comparison of experimental η_{HER} and η_{OER} between the initial data set modelled and the performance of the model-suggested compositions of the three ML algorithms. **(b)** True *versus* the NN-predicted values of the initial dataset, alongside the values for the NN-suggested compositions. **(c)** Experimental ZHER and ZOER values for the three NN iterations, reproduced with permission from The Royal Society of Chemistry, 2023 [63].

Evidence-Based Advancements: AI-Driven Improvements in Electrochemical Technologies

AI in Catalyst Design and Optimization

Finding and improving electrocatalysts quickly is one of AI's most important accomplishments. In Hydrogen Evolution Reactions (HER), research has demonstrated that Artificial Intelligence (AI)-powered neural networks can identify materials with up to 50% greater catalytic performance, while reducing catalyst discovery time by up to 70%. One study, for example, utilized AI to screen over 1,000 potential catalyst materials, narrowing the selection to a small number of highly effective ones that were subsequently confirmed through testing [66].

Enhanced Electrochemical Process Efficiency

AI has played a crucial role in enhancing the energy efficiency of electrochemical processes, such as the production of hydrogen through water splitting. Energy efficiency increased by 15% due to advanced AI models optimizing real-time parameters, such as voltage, temperature, and pressure. Commercial generation of green hydrogen is now more viable due to these innovations, which have significantly reduced energy losses and operating expenses [16].

Diagnostics and Predictive Maintenance of Electrochemical Systems

AI has transformed system diagnostics, especially in the energy storage industry. The ability of machine learning systems to anticipate lithium-ion battery failure scenarios has reached 95% accuracy. Thanks to this development, battery life cycles can now be extended by up to 20% with predictive maintenance. Improved dependability and reduced downtime are guaranteed by the ability to forecast performance abnormalities and monitor systems in real-time [67].

Design of Advanced Membranes and Electrodes

Experimental testing has confirmed that polymer electrolyte membranes created using generative AI models have a 30% increase in ionic conductivity. Fuel cells now function significantly better thanks to these advancements, making them more effective tools for producing sustainable energy. Similarly, supercapacitors and other electrochemical devices have become more efficient due to AI-optimized electrode materials [67].

Reduction of Computational Costs in Material Simulations

AI-based surrogate models have achieved a 90% reduction in processing times, significantly reducing computational time for Density Functional Theory (DFT) simulations. Due to computational limitations, screening hundreds of electrode and catalyst materials in a high-throughput manner was previously considered unfeasible [68].

Challenges and Limitations of AI in Electrochemical Research

The application of Artificial Intelligence (AI) in electrochemical research has yielded groundbreaking discoveries, but it is not without its challenges. Significant challenges include issues with data quality and availability, model interpretability, and the integration of these techniques with traditional engineering approaches. These problems must be addressed if AI is to fully realize its potential to enhance electrochemical research and technology [51, 69 - 71].

Data Quality and Availability Issues

For AI-driven models to be trained and validated, high-quality, comprehensive, and trustworthy datasets are necessary. Unfortunately, the subject of electrochemistry sometimes lacks adequate datasets. There are multiple reasons for this restriction:

1. Inconsistent Experimental Protocols

Issue: Highly variable and unstructured data are produced by non-standardized experimental setups, measurement techniques, and reporting standards. Compiling datasets for AI training can be challenging, as research on battery electrode performance often reports characteristics such as cycle life or capacity using diverse methods (*e.g.*, variable current densities or electrolyte compositions).

Impact: AI models trained on such diverse datasets frequently have lower predictive accuracy and poor generalization. An AI model trained on electrode data from a specific experimental setup, for example, might not be able to forecast performance in a slightly different configuration accurately.

Solution: It's crucial to set up uniform procedures for gathering and reporting data. For instance, the electrochemical community should adopt standards similar to the FAIR principles (Findable, Accessible, Interoperable, and Reusable) [72].

2. Lack of Open-Access Databases:

Issue: Data from electrochemical research is frequently scattered and proprietary across academic and industrial silos. For instance, due to concerns about intellectual property, private firms may choose to withhold datasets related to catalyst performance for Hydrogen Evolution Reactions (HER).

Impact: The training of reliable AI models is slowed down, and collaborative development is impeded by the lack of centralized, publicly accessible repositories.

Solution: Electrochemical datasets should be added to collaborative platforms, such as the Materials Project. Initiatives led by the community can establish repositories for particular uses, such as sensors, batteries, and fuel cells.

3. Inadequate Labeling:

Issue: Oftentimes, raw, unlabeled electrochemical experimental data lack metadata like reaction conditions, material qualities, or experimental parameters.

Impact: The accuracy and application of AI models are limited by the inability of supervised learning models to be trained efficiently in the absence of labeled data. For example, if important reaction conditions are not labeled, a model that predicts electrolyte stability may not work.

Solution: Annotating datasets can be aided by the use of automated data-labeling techniques, such as Natural Language Processing (NLP) tools for information extraction from research publications. During data publication, researchers should also concentrate on producing structured datasets with thorough annotations.

To overcome these challenges, community-driven, open-access databases must be established. Initiatives such as the Materials Project and other collaborative platforms should incorporate standardized electrochemical datasets. Standardizing data collection and reporting practices across the scientific community can help improve data consistency. Finally, data augmentation strategies and automated labeling techniques can be used to mitigate the shortage of labeled data, thereby improving model reliability [73].

Model Interpretability and Explainability

The "black-box" nature of many AI algorithms, particularly deep learning models, is a significant barrier in electrochemical research. It can be challenging for scientists to interpret the predictions of these models and relate them to underlying physical or chemical occurrences [74]. This problem can appear in a number of ways:

1. Decision-Making Difficulties:

Issue: Because they don't fully understand how predictions are made, researchers frequently hesitate to use AI models for important judgments. For instance, a deep learning model may accurately forecast the high stability of a novel battery material but be unable to identify the specific chemical characteristics that contribute to this stability.

Impact: The lack of transparency hampers adoption in high-stakes applications, such as catalyst development or energy storage system safety evaluations.

Solution: Explainable AI (XAI) frameworks that can pinpoint important characteristics impacting predictions include SHAP (Shapley Additive Explanations) and LIME (Local Interpretable Model-Agnostic Explanations). SHAP values, for instance, may show how catalytic activity is impacted by particle size or composition [75].

2. Barriers to Trust and Adoption:

Issue: AI models frequently yield outcomes that defy accepted electrochemical theories. For instance, the scientific community may become skeptical if corrosion rate forecasts don't match up well with mechanistic theories.

Impact: The adoption of AI-driven technologies into standard research workflows is slowed down by this skepticism.

Solution: Interpretability can be improved by integrating domain knowledge into AI models [76]. By incorporating first-principles equations into its architecture, Physics-Informed Neural Networks (PINNs) can produce predictions that are consistent with established scientific principles.

3. Challenge in Experimental Validation:

Issue: In order to plan validation studies, experimentalists frequently need to know which variables affect the predictions made by AI models. Black-box models, however, don't offer much direction [77].

Impact: Experimental validation and real-world implementation are delayed by the absence of unambiguous guidance from AI predictions.

Solution: Important parameters can be highlighted by interpretable machine learning models, such as decision trees or linear regression with sparsity constraints. By making it easier to identify important factors, these models allow for more focused studies [78].

Integration of AI with Traditional Electrochemical Engineering Practices

The intricate interaction of ambient factors, reaction kinetics, and material qualities defines electrochemical systems. Although AI excels at identifying patterns and optimizing processes, it remains challenging to integrate its predictions into traditional engineering workflows.

1. Alignment with Mechanistic Knowledge

Issue: Without taking causality into account, AI models frequently rely on correlations, which can lead to predictions that deviate from mechanistic theories. For example, without considering surface electronic states, an AI model can recommend a particular nanostructured catalyst as the best for the Oxygen Reduction Reaction (ORR).

Impact: This discrepancy restricts the adoption of AI suggestions in academic and professional contexts.

Solution: Predictions are guaranteed to follow accepted theories thanks to hybrid models, like PINNs, which incorporate mechanistic knowledge into AI frameworks. For example, integrating AI with Density Functional Theory (DFT) computations can provide insights into catalyst activity.

2. Interdisciplinary Gaps

Issue: Effective cooperation between domain experts and AI experts is crucial for the successful integration of AI into electrochemical research. However, the inability of these organizations to communicate with one another frequently leads to poorly constructed models.

Impact: Since misaligned models fail to consider domain-specific factors, their applicability in the real world is limited.

Solution: The knowledge gap can be closed by promoting interdisciplinary connections through workshops, group projects, and specialist training courses. For instance, collaborative efforts between data scientists and materials scientists can encourage the co-development of AI models specifically designed for electrochemical systems.

3. Real-World Constraints

Issue: Artificial intelligence models developed in regulated laboratory settings may not translate well to industrial settings, where factors such as temperature, pressure, and material impurities vary.

Impact: The real-world implementation of AI predictions is constrained by this discrepancy.

Solution: Model resilience can be increased by incorporating real-world variability into training datasets. In industrial settings, feedback loops that incorporate experimental findings into model retraining cycles can further improve accuracy.

Hybrid models, which combine AI with traditional mechanistic simulations, offer a promising approach. To ensure that predictions remain consistent with recognized theories, Physics-Informed Neural Networks (PINNs), for example, integrate domain-specific knowledge into AI models. Promoting interdisciplinary collaboration through workshops, projects, and training programs can help bridge the knowledge gap between electrochemistry and artificial intelligence. Lastly, incorporating feedback loops and conducting exhaustive experimental testing to verify AI predictions may enhance their dependability and usefulness [79].

Future Trends and Opportunities in AI-Driven Electrochemistry

The discipline is expected to undergo a revolution as a result of the convergence of electrochemistry and Artificial Intelligence (AI), which will enable advances in energy solutions, process optimization, and material discovery. The limits of electrochemical innovation are about to be redefined by cutting-edge technologies like quantum computing, AI-driven cost reduction techniques, and cooperative AI-human synergies.

Quantum Computing and Its Role in Electrochemical Modeling

The computational difficulties in electrochemistry are revolutionized by quantum computing, especially when it comes to simulating intricate processes and electronic structures. Quantum systems, unlike classical computers, can replicate quantum mechanical phenomena on a previously unattainable scale, providing profound insights into catalyst behaviors and reaction mechanisms [80, 81]. For instance, by accurately forecasting energy landscapes and reaction routes, quantum algorithms could optimize the design of electrocatalysts for hydrogen evolution or carbon dioxide reduction. To create hybrid approaches that combine quantum accuracy with AI's capacity to manage massive datasets and identify patterns, this computational capability can be leveraged in conjunction with AI models. With the further development of quantum computing and its integration with AI, a new era of highly effective, data-driven electrochemical research is likely to emerge.

AI for Enhancing Electrochemical Efficiency and Reducing Costs

AI has enormous potential to enhance the efficacy and economy of electrochemical processes. Researchers can minimize energy consumption and material waste by optimizing factors, including electrode materials, electrolyte composition, and reaction conditions, through the use of machine learning models [82]. AI has been used, for example, to find high-performance, reasonably priced substitutes for noble metal catalysts. Furthermore, in large-scale electrochemical systems, such as water electrolyzers or battery production lines, AI-enabled predictive maintenance can reduce downtime and operating expenses. The ongoing development of such applications can accelerate the adoption of sustainable electrochemical technology across industrial sectors.

Collaborative AI-Human Synergies in Electrochemical Innovation

The future of electrochemical research depends on the collaboration of human and AI knowledge in a synergistic manner. While AI excels at data analysis, optimization, and prediction, human researchers tackle complex issues by applying their subject knowledge, creativity, and intuition. Collaborative platforms can enhance experimental design, interpret unusual data, and generate novel hypotheses by combining human creativity with AI's computational power. AI techniques, for instance, can examine vast datasets and recommend promising experimental avenues, which scientists can subsequently confirm and refine [83]. By uniting specialists in AI, materials science, and electrochemistry to tackle global issues in energy, the environment, and healthcare, these partnerships can also promote interdisciplinary innovation.

Case Studies and Industry Applications

Real-world applications are the most effective way to demonstrate the transformative potential of Artificial Intelligence (AI) in electrochemistry. Three specific case studies are highlighted in this section: the application of AI to the development of lithium-ion batteries, improvements to fuel cells, and advancements in electrochemical sensor development.

AI in Lithium-Ion Battery Development

Although lithium-ion (Li-ion) batteries are essential to contemporary energy storage technologies, issues such as capacity deterioration and safety concerns continue to be significant obstacles. By improving performance optimization and accelerating materials discovery, AI has proven crucial in addressing these challenges. An Argonne National Laboratory study, for instance, demonstrated how Machine Learning (ML) was utilized to evaluate over 40,000 potential electrode materials and select those with the highest energy density and cycling stability. Manufacturers are now able to predict degradation patterns thanks to predictive algorithms built on large datasets of battery performance, which has increased battery longevity [84]. An example of a useful industry use is Tesla's use of AI in battery manufacturing. The company utilizes predictive analytics driven by AI to enhance electrode coating process efficiency, thereby reducing production costs and faults. In a similar vein, Panasonic utilizes AI-powered diagnostics to track battery status in real-time, ensuring quality assurance and extending product life. Together, these initiatives demonstrate how AI is driving innovation, reducing development schedules, and enabling the production of high-performance batteries to meet the world's growing energy needs [85].

AI in Fuel Cell Design and Optimization

Fuel cells are essential for renewable energy solutions; however, they have drawbacks, including high costs and limited efficiency. AI is now a vital tool for addressing these obstacles, especially in operational optimization and catalyst design. One noteworthy instance is a partnership between IBM and the National Renewable Energy Laboratory (NREL), where AI algorithms were used to identify novel catalyst formulations that reduce the need for expensive noble metals like platinum. These initiatives lowered material costs without sacrificing functionality [86]. Ballard Power Systems has incorporated Artificial Intelligence (AI) into industrial applications to optimize fuel cell efficiency and monitor it in real time. AI-driven systems anticipate operating inefficiencies and recommend adjustments to maintain thermal stability and optimize power production. Furthermore, Toyota Research Institute simulates fuel cell stack designs using machine learning algorithms, which improves power density and lowers hydrogen usage. These illustrations highlight how AI is increasing the affordability of fuel cells while simultaneously accelerating their adoption as a competitive, sustainable energy source [87, 88].

AI Applications in Electrochemical Sensors

Electrochemical sensors are essential for a wide range of applications, from medical diagnosis to environmental monitoring. By facilitating accurate calibration, sophisticated signal processing, and real-time data interpretation, artificial intelligence has completely changed sensor design. To illustrate the useful applications in air quality monitoring, MIT researchers have created an AI-driven sensor that can identify volatile organic chemicals with improved sensitivity and selectivity [89]. Abbott Laboratories utilizes Artificial Intelligence (AI) algorithms in glucose sensors, such as the FreeStyle Libre, to enhance continuous glucose monitoring in the healthcare industry with increased accuracy and dependability. Similar to this, companies like DeepMind Sensors have utilized neural networks to develop intelligent environmental sensors that can detect contaminants and heavy metals in water sources. These developments demonstrate how AI can be used to advance sensor technology in various fields, thereby increasing accuracy and expanding the application range [90].

CONCLUDING REMARKS

In electrochemical technologies, Artificial Intelligence (AI) has emerged as a disruptive force, solving long-standing problems and creating new opportunities for innovation and creativity. AI has demonstrated the ability to transform various areas in several ways, including accelerating the discovery of new materials, enhancing energy storage systems, improving electrochemical processes, and enabling the creation of sophisticated sensors. Researchers have lowered prices, increased efficiency, and sparked innovations in various applications, including batteries, fuel cells, and electrolyzers, by utilizing Machine Learning (ML), Deep Learning (DL), and other AI-driven approaches. AI's significance as a catalyst for technical developments in this field has been further solidified by its ability to evaluate complex information, predict material behaviors, and provide real-time system monitoring and control. One important takeaway from this chapter is that, to realize AI's promise, it must be seamlessly integrated with human expertise. The interpretability and usefulness of AI's predictions largely depend on the domain-specific expertise of electrochemical engineers, even as the technology excels at analyzing massive datasets and identifying patterns at unprecedented scales and speeds. This collaboration ensures that AI-powered insights are grounded in practical application and thoroughly tested. Collaborative AI-human workflows have the potential to stimulate focused innovation and address urgent issues in environmental sustainability, healthcare, and energy. In summary, the incorporation of AI with electrochemical technologies marks a significant turning point, making a new era of innovation and sustainable growth possible. The results presented in this chapter highlight how AI has the potential to revolutionize system intelligence, process optimization, and material discovery. The electrochemical community is well-positioned to contribute to a more intelligent, environmentally friendly, and resilient future by fostering interdisciplinary cooperation, incorporating ethical considerations, and sustaining consistent investment in AI-driven research.

ACKNOWLEDGEMENTS

Prashanth S. A. acknowledges the SVM Arts, Science and Commerce College, ILKAL for their support and encouragement.

REFERENCES

[1] S.G. Manjushree, S. Ashoka, and P.S. Adarakatti, "A brief review on basic principles of electrochemistry and electrochemical sensing devices".*Real-Time Applications of Advanced Electrochemical Sensing Devices.,* I.O.P. Publishing, Ed., , 2024, pp. 1-1-1-20. [http://dx.doi.org/10.1088/978-0-7503-5377-9ch1]

[2] L. Shreenivasa, S. A. Prashanth, H. Eranjaneya, R. Viswanatha, K. Yogesh, and G. Nagaraju, "Engineering of highly conductive and mesoporous ZrV2O7: a cathode material for lithium secondary

batteries," Journal of Solid State Electrochemistry, vol. 23, pp. 1201-1209, 2019/04/01 2019. [http://dx.doi.org/10.1007/s10008-019-04212-w]

[3] S.P.S. Badwal, S.S. Giddey, C. Munnings, A.I. Bhatt, and A.F. Hollenkamp, "Emerging electrochemical energy conversion and storage technologies", *Front Chem.,* vol. 2, p. 79, 2014. [http://dx.doi.org/10.3389/fchem.2014.00079] [PMID: 25309898]

[4] F.T. Wagner, B. Lakshmanan, and M.F. Mathias, "Electrochemistry and the future of the automobile", *J. Phys. Chem. Lett.,* vol. 1, no. 14, pp. 2204-2219, 2010. [http://dx.doi.org/10.1021/jz100553m]

[5] S.K. Bishnu, S.Y. Alnouri, and D.M. Al-Mohannadi, "Computational applications using data driven modeling in process Systems: A review", *Digital Chemical Engineering,* vol. 8, p. 100111, 2023. [http://dx.doi.org/10.1016/j.dche.2023.100111]

[6] A. Khatoon, A. Ullah, and K.N. Qureshi, "AI models and data analytics: transforming research methods" in *Next Generation AI Language Models in Research,* ed: CRC Press, 2025, pp. 45-85.

[7] U.A.K. Betz, L. Arora, R.A. Assal, H. Azevedo, J. Baldwin, M.S. Becker, S. Bostock, V. Cheng, T. Egle, N. Ferrari, E.K. Schneider-Futschik, S. Gerhardy, A. Hammes, A. Harzheim, T. Herget, C. Jauset, S. Kretschmer, C. Lammie, N. Kloss, S.M. Fernandes, C-G. Mitrofan, I. Myrgorodska, D. Nedbalek, S.G. Neumann, S. Paffenholz, L.P. Ponce, B. Rogell, D. Savic, G. Velikova, C. Schumacher, N. Weisshaar, M. Yahya, J.Y.C. Yang, and G. Zhao, "Game changers in science and technology - now and beyond", *Technol. Forecast. Soc. Change,* vol. 193, p. 122588, 2023. [http://dx.doi.org/10.1016/j.techfore.2023.122588]

[8] J. Benavides-Hernández, and F. Dumeignil, "From characterization to discovery: Artificial intelligence, machine learning and high-throughput experiments for heterogeneous catalyst design", *ACS Catal.,* vol. 14, no. 15, pp. 11749-11779, 2024. [http://dx.doi.org/10.1021/acscatal.3c06293]

[9] A. Lavin, D. Krakauer, H. Zenil, J. Gottschlich, T. Mattson, and J. Brehmer, "Simulation intelligence: Towards a new generation of scientific methods", 2112.03235, 2021.

[10] A. Li, J. Weng, A.C.Y. Yuen, W. Wang, H. Liu, E.W.M. Lee, J. Wang, S. Kook, and G.H. Yeoh, "Machine learning assisted advanced battery thermal management system: A state-of-the-art review", *J. Energy Storage,* vol. 60, p. 106688, 2023. [http://dx.doi.org/10.1016/j.est.2023.106688]

[11] H. Adamu, S.I. Abba, P.B. Anyin, Y. Sani, and M. Qamar, "Artificial intelligence-navigated development of high-performance electrochemical energy storage systems through feature engineering of multiple descriptor families of materials", *Energy Advances,* vol. 2, no. 5, pp. 615-645, 2023. [http://dx.doi.org/10.1039/D3YA00104K]

[12] Z. Yao, Y. Lum, A. Johnston, L.M. Mejia-Mendoza, X. Zhou, Y. Wen, A. Aspuru-Guzik, E.H. Sargent, and Z.W. Seh, "Machine learning for a sustainable energy future", *Nat. Rev. Mater.,* vol. 8, no. 3, pp. 202-215, 2022. [http://dx.doi.org/10.1038/s41578-022-00490-5] [PMID: 36277083]

[13] S.A. Kalogirou, "Artificial intelligence for the modeling and control of combustion processes: a review", *Pror. Energy Combust. Sci.,* vol. 29, no. 6, pp. 515-566, 2003. [http://dx.doi.org/10.1016/S0360-1285(03)00058-3]

[14] R.K. Mishra, D. Mishra, and R. Agarwal, *An artificial intelligence-powered approach to material design.* vol. Vol. I. Cutting-Edge Research in Chemical and Material Science, 2024.

[15] L. Xu, F. Wu, R. Chen, and L. Li, "Data-driven-aided strategies in battery lifecycle management: Prediction, monitoring, and optimization", *Energy Storage Mater.,* vol. 59, p. 102785, 2023. [http://dx.doi.org/10.1016/j.ensm.2023.102785]

[16] X. Liu, K. Fan, X. Huang, J. Ge, Y. Liu, and H. Kang, "Recent advances in artificial intelligence boosting materials design for electrochemical energy storage", *Chem. Eng. J.,* vol. 490, p. 151625,

2024.
[http://dx.doi.org/10.1016/j.cej.2024.151625]

[17] A. Mistry, A.A. Franco, S.J. Cooper, S.A. Roberts, and V. Viswanathan, "How machine learning will revolutionize electrochemical sciences", *ACS Energy Lett.,* vol. 6, no. 4, pp. 1422-1431, 2021. [http://dx.doi.org/10.1021/acsenergylett.1c00194] [PMID: 33869772]

[18] I. T. Bello, R. Taiwo, O. C. Esan, A. H. Adegoke, A. O. Ijaola, and Z. Li, *AI-enabled materials discovery for advanced ceramic electrochemical cells. Energy and AI,* vol. 15, p. 100317, 2024/01/01/ 2024.
[http://dx.doi.org/10.1016/j.egyai.2023.100317]

[19] V.S. Bagotsky, *Fundamentals of electrochemistry.* John Wiley & Sons, 2005. [http://dx.doi.org/10.1002/047174199X]

[20] A.J. Bard, L.R. Faulkner, and H.S. White, *Electrochemical methods: fundamentals and applications.* John Wiley & Sons, 2022.

[21] S. Rashidi, N. Karimi, B. Sunden, K.C. Kim, A.G. Olabi, and O. Mahian, "Progress and challenges on the thermal management of electrochemical energy conversion and storage technologies: Fuel cells, electrolysers, and supercapacitors", *Pror. Energy Combust. Sci.,* vol. 88, p. 100966, 2022. [http://dx.doi.org/10.1016/j.pecs.2021.100966]

[22] B.E. Conway, "Transition from “supercapacitor” to “battery” behavior in electrochemical energy storage", *J. Electrochem. Soc.,* vol. 138, no. 6, pp. 1539-1548, 1991. [http://dx.doi.org/10.1149/1.2085829]

[23] V. Thangadurai, and B. Chen, "Solid Li-and Na-ion electrolytes for next generation rechargeable batteries", *Chem. Mater.,* vol. 34, no. 15, pp. 6637-6658, 2022. [http://dx.doi.org/10.1021/acs.chemmater.2c01475]

[24] L. Carrette, K.A. Friedrich, and U. Stimming, "Fuel cells: principles, types, fuels, and applications", *ChemPhysChem,* vol. 1, no. 4, pp. 162-193, 2000. [http://dx.doi.org/10.1002/1439-7641(20001215)1:4<162::AID-CPHC162>3.0.CO;2-Z] [PMID: 23696319]

[25] A.L. Dicks, and D.A. Rand, *Fuel cell systems explained.* John Wiley & Sons, 2018. [http://dx.doi.org/10.1002/9781118706992]

[26] K. Scott, *Introduction to electrolysis, electrolysers and hydrogen production.* 2019.

[27] S.F. Ahmed, M. Mofijur, S. Nuzhat, N. Rafa, A. Musharrat, S.S. Lam, and A. Boretti, "Sustainable hydrogen production: Technological advancements and economic analysis", *Int. J. Hydrogen Energy,* vol. 47, no. 88, pp. 37227-37255, 2022.
[http://dx.doi.org/10.1016/j.ijhydene.2021.12.029]

[28] C. Zhong, Y. Deng, W. Hu, J. Qiao, L. Zhang, and J. Zhang, "A review of electrolyte materials and compositions for electrochemical supercapacitors", *Chem. Soc. Rev.,* vol. 44, no. 21, pp. 7484-7539, 2015.
[http://dx.doi.org/10.1039/C5CS00303B] [PMID: 26050756]

[29] A.R. Dehghani-Sanij, E. Tharumalingam, M.B. Dusseault, and R. Fraser, "Study of energy storage systems and environmental challenges of batteries", *Renew. Sustain. Energy Rev.,* vol. 104, pp. 192-208, 2019.
[http://dx.doi.org/10.1016/j.rser.2019.01.023]

[30] T.M. Gür, "Review of electrical energy storage technologies, materials and systems: challenges and prospects for large-scale grid storage", *Energy Environ. Sci.,* vol. 11, no. 10, pp. 2696-2767, 2018. [http://dx.doi.org/10.1039/C8EE01419A]

[31] M.A. Hannan, M.M. Hoque, A. Mohamed, and A. Ayob, "Review of energy storage systems for electric vehicle applications: Issues and challenges", *Renew. Sustain. Energy Rev.,* vol. 69, pp. 771-789, 2017.

[http://dx.doi.org/10.1016/j.rser.2016.11.171]

[32] H. Taheri, M. Gonzalez Bocanegra, and M. Taheri, "Artificial intelligence, machine learning and smart technologies for nondestructive evaluation", *Sensors (Basel),* vol. 22, no. 11, p. 4055, 2022. [http://dx.doi.org/10.3390/s22114055] [PMID: 35684675]

[33] S.D. Ebbesen, S.H. Jensen, A. Hauch, and M.B. Mogensen, "High temperature electrolysis in alkaline cells, solid proton conducting cells, and solid oxide cells", *Chem. Rev.,* vol. 114, no. 21, pp. 10697-10734, 2014. [http://dx.doi.org/10.1021/cr5000865] [PMID: 25283178]

[34] Z. Nozarijouybari, and H.K. Fathy, "Machine learning for battery systems applications: Progress, challenges, and opportunities", *J. Power Sources,* vol. 601, p. 234272, 2024. [http://dx.doi.org/10.1016/j.jpowsour.2024.234272]

[35] R. Ding, S. Zhang, Y. Chen, Z. Rui, K. Hua, Y. Wu, X. Li, X. Duan, X. Wang, J. Li, and J. Liu, "Application of machine learning in optimizing proton exchange membrane fuel cells: a review", *Energy and AI,* vol. 9, p. 100170, 2022. [http://dx.doi.org/10.1016/j.egyai.2022.100170]

[36] J. Park, and J. Lee, "Electrochemical energy conversion and storage processes with machine learning", *Trends Chem.,* vol. 6, no. 6, pp. 302-313, 2024. [http://dx.doi.org/10.1016/j.trechm.2024.04.007]

[37] M. Suvarna, and J. Pérez-Ramírez, "Embracing data science in catalysis research", *Nat. Catal.,* pp. 1-12, 2024.

[38] R. Potyrailo, K. Rajan, K. Stoewe, I. Takeuchi, B. Chisholm, and H. Lam, "Combinatorial and high-throughput screening of materials libraries: review of state of the art", *ACS Comb. Sci.,* vol. 13, no. 6, pp. 579-633, 2011. [http://dx.doi.org/10.1021/co200007w] [PMID: 21644562]

[39] M. Karthikeyan, D.M. Mahapatra, A.S.A. Razak, A.A.M. Abahussain, B. Ethiraj, and L. Singh, "Machine learning aided synthesis and screening of HER catalyst: Present developments and prospects", *Catal. Rev., Sci. Eng.,* vol. 66, no. 4, pp. 997-1027, 2024. [http://dx.doi.org/10.1080/01614940.2022.2103980]

[40] P. Pasrija, P. Jha, P. Upadhyaya, M.S. Khan, and M. Chopra, "Machine learning and artificial intelligence: a paradigm shift in big data-driven drug design and discovery", *Curr. Top. Med. Chem.,* vol. 22, no. 20, pp. 1692-1727, 2022. [http://dx.doi.org/10.2174/1568026622666220701091339] [PMID: 35786336]

[41] J.M. Gregoire, L. Zhou, and J.A. Haber, "Combinatorial synthesis for AI-driven materials discovery", *Nature Synthesis,* vol. 2, no. 6, pp. 493-504, 2023. [http://dx.doi.org/10.1038/s44160-023-00251-4]

[42] K. Frydrych, K. Karimi, M. Pecelerowicz, R. Alvarez, F.J. Dominguez-Gutiérrez, F. Rovaris, and S. Papanikolaou, "Materials informatics for mechanical deformation: A review of applications and challenges", *Materials (Basel),* vol. 14, no. 19, p. 5764, 2021. [http://dx.doi.org/10.3390/ma14195764] [PMID: 34640157]

[43] Y. Hong, B. Hou, H. Jiang, and J. Zhang, "Machine learning and artificial neural network accelerated computational discoveries in materials science", *Wiley Interdiscip. Rev. Comput. Mol. Sci.,* vol. 10, no. 3, p. e1450, 2020. [http://dx.doi.org/10.1002/wcms.1450]

[44] W. Yi Wang, J. Li, W. Liu, and Z.K. Liu, "Integrated computational materials engineering for advanced materials: A brief review", *Comput. Mater. Sci.,* vol. 158, pp. 42-48, 2019. [http://dx.doi.org/10.1016/j.commatsci.2018.11.001]

[45] C. Xiouras, F. Cameli, G.L. Quilló, M.E. Kavousanakis, D.G. Vlachos, and G.D. Stefanidis, "Applications of artificial intelligence and machine learning algorithms to crystallization", *Chem. Rev.,*

vol. 122, no. 15, pp. 13006-13042, 2022.
[http://dx.doi.org/10.1021/acs.chemrev.2c00141] [PMID: 35759465]

[46] K. Shahzad, A.I. Mardare, and A.W. Hassel, "Accelerating materials discovery: combinatorial synthesis, high-throughput characterization, and computational advances", *Science and Technology of Advanced Materials: Methods,* vol. 4, p. 2292486, 2024.

[47] C. Gütz, A. Stenglein, and S.R. Waldvogel, *Highly Modular Flow Cell for Electroorganic Synthesis*, 2017.
[http://dx.doi.org/10.1021/acs.oprd.7b00123]

[48] R.A. Green, K.E. Jolley, A.A.M. Al-Hadedi, D. Pletcher, D.C. Harrowven, O. De Frutos, C. Mateos, D.J. Klauber, J.A. Rincón, and R.C.D. Brown, "Electrochemical deprotection of para-methoxybenzyl ethers in a flow electrolysis cell", *Org. Lett.,* vol. 19, no. 8, pp. 2050-2053, 2017.
[http://dx.doi.org/10.1021/acs.orglett.7b00641] [PMID: 28375019]

[49] R. Becker, K. Weber, T.V. Pfeiffer, J. Kranendonk, and K.J. Schouten, "A scalable high-throughput deposition and screening setup relevant to industrial electrocatalysis", *Catalysts,* vol. 10, no. 10, p. 1165, 2020.
[http://dx.doi.org/10.3390/catal10101165]

[50] M. Lehmann, C.C. Scarborough, E. Godineau, and C. Battilocchio, "An electrochemical flow-through cell for rapid reactions", *Ind. Eng. Chem. Res.,* vol. 59, no. 16, pp. 7321-7326, 2020.
[http://dx.doi.org/10.1021/acs.iecr.0c00431]

[51] S.N.A.B.M. Nashruddin, F.H.M. Salleh, R.M. Yunus, and H.B. Zaman, "Artificial intelligence–powered electrochemical sensor: Recent advances, challenges, and prospects", *Heliyon,* vol. 10, no. 18, p. e37964, 2024.
[http://dx.doi.org/10.1016/j.heliyon.2024.e37964] [PMID: 39328566]

[52] M.H. Mobarak, M.A. Mimona, M.A. Islam, N. Hossain, F.T. Zohura, I. Imtiaz, and M.I.H. Rimon, "Scope of machine learning in materials research—A review", *Applied Surface Science Advances,* vol. 18, p. 100523, 2023.
[http://dx.doi.org/10.1016/j.apsadv.2023.100523]

[53] Y. Liu, L. Wang, D. Li, and K. Wang, "State-of-health estimation of lithium-ion batteries based on electrochemical impedance spectroscopy: a review", *Protection and Control of Modern Power Systems,* vol. 8, no. 1, p. 41, 2023.
[http://dx.doi.org/10.1186/s41601-023-00314-w]

[54] Y. Liu, O.C. Esan, Z. Pan, and L. An, "Machine learning for advanced energy materials", *Energy and AI,* vol. 3, p. 100049, 2021.
[http://dx.doi.org/10.1016/j.egyai.2021.100049]

[55] Z. Feng, I. Eiubovi, Y. Shao, Z. Fan, and R. Tan, "Review of digital twin technology applications in hydrogen energy", *CHAIN,* vol. 1, no. 1, pp. 54-74, 2024.
[http://dx.doi.org/10.23919/CHAIN.2024.000001]

[56] X. Chen, H. Gao, Z. Tang, W. Dong, A. Li, and G. Wang, "Optimization strategies of composite phase change materials for thermal energy storage, transfer, conversion and utilization", *Energy Environ. Sci.,* vol. 13, no. 12, pp. 4498-4535, 2020.
[http://dx.doi.org/10.1039/D0EE01355B]

[57] A. Kilic, B. Oral, D. Eroglu, and R. Yildirim, "Machine learning for beyond Li-ion batteries: Powering the research", *J. Energy Storage,* vol. 73, p. 109057, 2023.
[http://dx.doi.org/10.1016/j.est.2023.109057]

[58] V. Subotić, M. Eibl, and C. Hochenauer, "Artificial intelligence for time-efficient prediction and optimization of solid oxide fuel cell performances", *Energy Convers. Manage.,* vol. 230, p. 113764, 2021.
[http://dx.doi.org/10.1016/j.enconman.2020.113764]

[59] Z. Huang, D. Zhang, X. Wang, X. Huang, C. Wang, L. Liao, Y. Dong, X. Hou, Y. Cao, and X. Zhou, "Machine learning prediction of fuel cell remaining life enhanced by variational mode decomposition and improved whale optimization algorithm", *Mathematics,* vol. 12, no. 19, p. 2959, 2024. [http://dx.doi.org/10.3390/math12192959]

[60] M.A. Mohamed, A.M. Eltamaly, H.M. Farh, and A.I. Alolah, *"Energy management and renewable energy integration in smart grid system," in 2015 IEEE international conference on smart energy grid engineering.* SEGE, 2015, pp. 1-6.

[61] A. Ayub Khan, A. Ali Laghari, M. Rashid, H. Li, A. Rehman Javed, and T. Reddy Gadekallu, "Artificial intelligence and blockchain technology for secure smart grid and power distribution Automation: A State-of-the-Art Review", *Sustain. Energy Technol. Assess.,* vol. 57, p. 103282, 2023. [http://dx.doi.org/10.1016/j.seta.2023.103282]

[62] A. Grimm, A. Sainte-Marie, G.J. Kramer, and M. Gazzani, *Modeling photovoltaic-electrochemical water splitting devices for the production of hydrogen under real working conditions*, 2022. [http://dx.doi.org/10.1016/j.ijhydene.2022.01.223]

[63] C.Y.J. Lim, R. I Made, Z.H.J. Khoo, C.K. Ng, Y. Bai, J. Wang, G. Yang, A.D. Handoko, and Y.F. Lim, "Machine learning-assisted optimization of multi-metal hydroxide electrocatalysts for overall water splitting", *Mater. Horiz.,* vol. 10, no. 11, pp. 5022-5031, 2023. [http://dx.doi.org/10.1039/D3MH00788J] [PMID: 37644912]

[64] Z. Ai, A.Y.C. Nee, and S.K. Ong, "Artificial intelligence in electric vehicle battery disassembly: A systematic review", *Automation,* vol. 5, no. 4, pp. 484-507, 2024. [http://dx.doi.org/10.3390/automation5040028]

[65] A. Al-Othman, M. Tawalbeh, R. Martis, S. Dhou, M. Orhan, M. Qasim, and A. Ghani Olabi, "Artificial intelligence and numerical models in hybrid renewable energy systems with fuel cells: Advances and prospects", *Energy Convers. Manage.,* vol. 253, p. 115154, 2022. [http://dx.doi.org/10.1016/j.enconman.2021.115154]

[66] S.N. Steinmann, Q. Wang, and Z.W. Seh, "How machine learning can accelerate electrocatalysis discovery and optimization", *Mater. Horiz.,* vol. 10, no. 2, pp. 393-406, 2023. [http://dx.doi.org/10.1039/D2MH01279K] [PMID: 36541226]

[67] R. Kushwaha, M.K. Singh, S. Krishnan, and D.K. Rai, "Machine learning enabled property prediction of carbon-based electrodes for supercapacitors", *J. Mater. Sci.,* vol. 58, no. 39, pp. 15448-15458, 2023. [http://dx.doi.org/10.1007/s10853-023-08981-8]

[68] A.L. Dias, and T. Rodrigues, "Large language models direct automated chemistry laboratory," ed: Nature Publishing Group UK London, 2023. [http://dx.doi.org/10.1038/d41586-023-03790-0]

[69] J.F. Arinez, Q. Chang, R.X. Gao, C. Xu, and J. Zhang, "Artificial intelligence in advanced manufacturing: Current status and future outlook", *J. Manuf. Sci. Eng.,* vol. 142, no. 11, p. 110804, 2020. [http://dx.doi.org/10.1115/1.4047855]

[70] T. Lombardo, M. Duquesnoy, H. El-Bouysidy, F. Årén, A. Gallo-Bueno, P.B. Jørgensen, A. Bhowmik, A. Demortière, E. Ayerbe, F. Alcaide, M. Reynaud, J. Carrasco, A. Grimaud, C. Zhang, T. Vegge, P. Johansson, and A.A. Franco, "Artificial intelligence applied to battery research: hype or reality?", *Chem. Rev.,* vol. 122, no. 12, pp. 10899-10969, 2022. [http://dx.doi.org/10.1021/acs.chemrev.1c00108] [PMID: 34529918]

[71] C. Li, D. Guo, Y. Dang, D. Sun, and P. Li, "Application of artificial intelligence-based methods in bioelectrochemical systems: Recent progress and future perspectives", *J. Environ. Manage.,* vol. 344, p. 118502, 2023. [http://dx.doi.org/10.1016/j.jenvman.2023.118502] [PMID: 37390578]

[72] E.L. Clark, J. Resasco, A. Landers, J. Lin, L.T. Chung, A. Walton, C. Hahn, T.F. Jaramillo, and A.T.

Bell, "Standards and protocols for data acquisition and reporting for studies of the electrochemical reduction of carbon dioxide", *ACS Catal.*, vol. 8, no. 7, pp. 6560-6570, 2018. [http://dx.doi.org/10.1021/acscatal.8b01340]

[73] F. Esmaeili, E. Cassie, H.P.T. Nguyen, N.O.V. Plank, C.P. Unsworth, and A. Wang, "Utilizing deep learning algorithms for signal processing in electrochemical biosensors: From data augmentation to detection and quantification of chemicals of interest", *Bioengineering (Basel),* vol. 10, no. 12, p. 1348, 2023. [http://dx.doi.org/10.3390/bioengineering10121348] [PMID: 38135939]

[74] G.Z. Yang, J. Bellingham, P.E. Dupont, P. Fischer, L. Floridi, R. Full, N. Jacobstein, V. Kumar, M. McNutt, R. Merrifield, B.J. Nelson, B. Scassellati, M. Taddeo, R. Taylor, M. Veloso, Z.L. Wang, and R. Wood, "The grand challenges of Science Robotics", *Sci. Robot.,* vol. 3, no. 14, p. eaar7650, 2018. [http://dx.doi.org/10.1126/scirobotics.aar7650] [PMID: 33141701]

[75] U. Kamath, and J. Liu, "Introduction to interpretability and explainability," in *Explainable artificial intelligence: An introduction to interpretable machine learning,* ed: Springer, 2021, pp. 1-26. [http://dx.doi.org/10.1007/978-3-030-83356-5_1]

[76] R. Wu, Y. Fujita, and K. Soga, "Integrating domain knowledge with deep learning models: An interpretable AI system for automatic work progress identification of NATM tunnels", *Tunn. Undergr. Space Technol.,* vol. 105, p. 103558, 2020. [http://dx.doi.org/10.1016/j.tust.2020.103558]

[77] D. Castelvecchi, "Can we open the black box of AI?", *Nature,* vol. 538, no. 7623, pp. 20-23, 2016. [http://dx.doi.org/10.1038/538020a] [PMID: 27708329]

[78] J.A. Keith, V. Vassilev-Galindo, B. Cheng, S. Chmiela, M. Gastegger, K.R. Müller, and A. Tkatchenko, "Combining machine learning and computational chemistry for predictive insights into chemical systems", *Chem. Rev.,* vol. 121, no. 16, pp. 9816-9872, 2021. [http://dx.doi.org/10.1021/acs.chemrev.1c00107] [PMID: 34232033]

[79] C. Daniel, J. C. Gehin, K. Laurin-Kovitz, B. Morreale, R. Stevens, and W. Tumas, *Advanced research directions on AI for energy*. 2024. [http://dx.doi.org/10.2172/2340139]

[80] R.R. Nazmutdinov, M.D. Bronshtein, T.T. Zinkicheva, and D.V. Glukhov, "Modeling of electron transfer across electrochemical interfaces: State-of-the art and challenges for quantum and computational chemistry", *Int. J. Quantum Chem.,* vol. 116, no. 3, pp. 189-201, 2016. [http://dx.doi.org/10.1002/qua.25035]

[81] B. Bauer, S. Bravyi, M. Motta, and G.K-L. Chan, "Quantum algorithms for quantum chemistry and quantum materials science", *Chem. Rev.,* vol. 120, no. 22, pp. 12685-12717, 2020. [http://dx.doi.org/10.1021/acs.chemrev.9b00829] [PMID: 33090772]

[82] C. Chen, Y. Zuo, W. Ye, X. Li, Z. Deng, and S.P. Ong, "A critical review of machine learning of energy materials", *Adv. Energy Mater.,* vol. 10, no. 8, p. 1903242, 2020. [http://dx.doi.org/10.1002/aenm.201903242]

[83] S. Bianchini, M. Müller, and P. Pelletier, "Artificial intelligence in science: An emerging general method of invention", *Res. Policy,* vol. 51, no. 10, p. 104604, 2022. [http://dx.doi.org/10.1016/j.respol.2022.104604]

[84] C. Lv, X. Zhou, L. Zhong, C. Yan, M. Srinivasan, Z.W. Seh, C. Liu, H. Pan, S. Li, Y. Wen, and Q. Yan, "Machine learning: an advanced platform for materials development and state prediction in lithium-ion batteries", *Adv. Mater.,* vol. 34, no. 25, p. 2101474, 2022. [http://dx.doi.org/10.1002/adma.202101474] [PMID: 34490683]

[85] D. Sun, D. Guo, Y. Lu, J. Chen, Y. Lu, X. Han, X. Feng, L. Lu, H. Wang, and M. Ouyang, "AI enabled fast charging of lithium-ion batteries of electric vehicles during their life cycle: review, challenges and perspectives", *Energy Environ. Sci.,* vol. 17, no. 20, pp. 7512-7542, 2024. [http://dx.doi.org/10.1039/D4EE03063J]

[86] M.A. Abdelkareem, K. Elsaid, T. Wilberforce, M. Kamil, E.T. Sayed, and A. Olabi, "Environmental aspects of fuel cells: A review", *Sci. Total Environ.,* vol. 752, p. 141803, 2021. [http://dx.doi.org/10.1016/j.scitotenv.2020.141803] [PMID: 32889267]

[87] P. Soni, V. Dave, and N.B. Repalle, "AI based performance boost in solar PV fuel cell hybrids", *International Conference on Renewable Energy, Green Computing, and Sustainable Development* 2023, pp. 3-16.

[88] J.H. Wee, "Applications of proton exchange membrane fuel cell systems", *Renew. Sustain. Energy Rev.,* vol. 11, no. 8, pp. 1720-1738, 2007. [http://dx.doi.org/10.1016/j.rser.2006.01.005]

[89] N. Pouyanfar, S.Z. Harofte, M. Soltani, S. Siavashy, E. Asadian, F. Ghorbani-Bidkorbeh, R. Keçili, and C.M. Hussain, "Artificial intelligence-based microfluidic platforms for the sensitive detection of environmental pollutants: Recent advances and prospects", *Trends in Environmental Analytical Chemistry,* vol. 34, p. e00160, 2022. [http://dx.doi.org/10.1016/j.teac.2022.e00160]

[90] B. Turyasingura, N. Ayiga, F. Kayusi, M. Tumuhimbise, M. Tumuhimbise, and T. Tumushabe, "Application of artificial intelligence (AI) in environment and societal trends: Challenges and opportunities", *Babylonian Journal of Machine Learning,* vol. 2024, pp. 177-182, 2024. [http://dx.doi.org/10.58496/BJML/2024/018]

CHAPTER 8

Integrating AI for Sustainable Energy Solutions

Shilpi Sehrawat[1], **Deepa Sharma**[1,*] and **Purnima Jain**[1,*]

[1] *Department of Chemistry, Netaji Subhas University of Technology, Dwarka, New Delhi-110078, India*

Abstract: AI has revolutionized the energy industry by enhancing scalability, efficiency, and dependability in terms of sustainable energy solutions enabled by AI. This chapter provides an in-depth discussion of AI's critical role in enhancing sustainable energy technologies, including energy storage, grid management, renewable energy generation, and energy consumption optimization. AI techniques such as ML, neural networks, and optimization algorithms are being explored for their potential to forecast the production of renewable energy, maximize the operations of solar panels and wind turbines, and forecast maintenance requirements to reduce expenses and downtime. In the realm of energy storage, AI-driven models in the energy storage space offer precise forecasts of battery health and performance, enabling the development of advanced BMS that optimize the longevity and effectiveness. This chapter covers the essentiality of AI for the integration of various energy sources into smart grids, as this allows for the efficient distribution of energy, facilitating real-time balancing of supply and demand and improved grid stability, and AI applications in demand-side management, where AI algorithms optimize the behaviors related to energy use in the commercial, industrial, and residential domains, resulting in significant energy savings and reduced carbon footprints. This chapter highlights how AI is contributing to the discovery and optimization of materials with improved qualities for energy conversion and storage, thereby accelerating the development of materials with enhanced properties for energy conversion and storage applications. Through a comprehensive analysis of current research and developments, this chapter highlights the revolutionary potential of AI in accomplishing sustainable energy goals. The study offers insights into potential future research areas and the vital importance of interdisciplinary collaboration in harnessing AI to create a more resilient and sustainable energy future.

Keywords: AI algorithms, AI-driven models, Artificial intelligence (AI), Battery management systems (BMS), Energy solutions, Energy transformations, Innovations, Renewable energy, Sustainability.

* **Corresponding authors Deepa Sharma and Purnima Jain:** Department of Chemistry, Netaji Subhas University of Technology, Dwarka, New Delhi-110078, India; E-mails: deepa0910sharma@gmail.com; prnm_j@yahoo.co.in

Shreya Sharma, Peeyush Phogat, Ranjana Jha & Sukhvir Singh (Eds.)

INTRODUCTION

In the 1950s, the emergence of computer-based intelligence programs and neural networks led to the discovery of the Artificial Intelligence (AI) concept, and during this period only the term AI first came into existence. Theoretically, this laid the foundation for AI as a new popular discipline. However, integrating AI and Machine Learning (ML) into sustainable energy applications gained momentum in the late 20th and early 21st century, driven by advances in computational power, data availability, and environmental urgency [1]. The application of AI and ML in sustainable energy solutions has evolved significantly, aligning well with the global push toward clean, efficient, and intelligent energy systems. These technological advancements led to the evolution of smart computers and software programs that possess the ability to mimic human learning and decision-making abilities. Due to this, AI and data mining have grown in importance across numerous academic fields, especially in the energy sector, which is one of the major sectors where AI and ML are found to be extremely helpful. Furthermore, the requirement of high accuracy and faster processes with complex inputs and datasets has made AI an integral part of the rapidly growing energy sectors [2]. Thus, the integration of AI for the enhancement of clean energy has emerged as a robust necessity for the future.

The development of advanced AI-based technologies for the production, distribution, and consumption of energy provides enormous potential, addressing some of the many Sustainable Development Goals (SDGs) either directly or indirectly. A large share of the population still lacks access to affordable and clean energy due to increasing demand and limited availability of petroleum-based resources. On the other hand, changing climatic conditions resulting from large-scale human activities further create a need to develop smart, innovative methods for sustainable energy solutions. Thus, AI is a robust technology for industrial and climate sustainability, facilitating accurate and enhanced estimates of renewable energy, such as wind speed topology and solar energy irradiance predictions, which are vital for achieving optimal energy production and guaranteeing grid resilience and reliability [3, 4].

AI-driven smart grid technologies enhance the reliability and efficiency of energy distribution by dynamically adjusting to fluctuations in demand and supply [5]. It optimizes energy consumption in buildings through predictive analytics and automation, reducing carbon footprints and enhancing sustainability [6]. Furthermore, it also benefits from improved energy efficiency,s AI models enable precise control and optimization of energy consumption patterns, leading to significant reductions in energy use while maintaining operational efficiency [5]. Additionally, AI facilitates the integration of renewable energy sources (such as solar and wind) into existing energy infrastructures, addressing challenges of intermittence and variability [4].

AI techniques are being applied to manage multi-energy systems, demonstrating their potential in large-scale renewable energy integration [7]. In building automation, successful AI implementations have led to significant energy savings and carbon reduction [6]. AI-driven solutions contribute to the decarbonization of energy systems and the integration of clean energy sources, thereby supporting climate action goals [6]. While AI offers promising solutions for sustainable energy, it is essential to consider the broader implications of its integration. There are several challenges associated with ethical considerations, such as data privacy, algorithm biases, which demand robust ethical frameworks and policies [8, 9]. The integration of AI into existing energy infrastructures also presents challenges in terms of scalability, data integration, and the robustness of AI algorithms [5]. Additionally, the potential for job displacement requires strategies that promote human-AI collaboration [8].

FUNDAMENTALS OF SUSTAINABLE ENERGY SYSTEMS

Sustainable Energy Systems (SES) are crucial for meeting the increasing demand for energy while minimizing environmental impacts. These systems prioritize renewable energy sources and energy efficiency to create resilient and low-carbon energy systems for the future. Therefore, they are also known as Renewable Energy Systems (RES) that decentralise energy infrastructure through advanced technologies. The integration of AI into SES is a transformative approach that enhances the efficiency, reliability, and sustainability of EM. Combining AI technologies with the Internet of Things (IoT) and other advanced computing methods offers innovative solutions to the challenges faced by RES, such as variability and intermittency [10]. AI-driven Decision Support Systems (DSS) are crucial for sustainable EM, particularly in smart cities. These systems utilize Machine Learning (ML) and predictive analytics to optimize resource usage and enhance decision-making processes in urban energy systems [11]. These technologies enable real-time monitoring, predictive analytics, and optimization of energy resources, thereby facilitating a more sustainable energy future.

Renewable Energy Sources

Renewable energy is considered the heart of sustainable energy systems. Solar, wind, hydropower, and biomass provide clean, inexhaustible energy that reduces dependence on fossil fuels. However, the variability of renewable sources, such as intermittent sunlight and wind, presents operational challenges. AI-driven predictive models address these issues by analysing environmental data to optimize energy production. For example, solar energy systems utilize AI algorithms to forecast solar irradiance, allowing forrecise scheduling of energy dispatch [12]. In regions with prolonged rainy seasons and limited sunlight, AI combines historical weather data, satellite imagery, and meteorological forecasts to predict solar irradiance. Advanced ML models like deep neural networks are trained on these datasets to identify patterns and correlations even under adverse weather conditions [13]. For instance, AI can utilize cloud cover predictions, atmospheric humidity, and seasonal weather trends to estimate the availability of solar energy. Additionally, hybrid models combining solar data with auxiliary renewable sources, such as wind or hydro energy, optimize energy planning and dispatch, ensuring continuous reliability despite limited solar input [14]. Similarly, wind farms utilize AI to predict wind patterns and optimize turbine efficiency, thereby ensuring maximum energy output [15]. Hydropower plants benefit from AI's ability to manage water resources by predicting inflows and optimizing reservoir operations [16]. Biomass energy systems also rely on AI for feedstock management and process optimization, enhancing the sustainability of bioenergy production [17].

Energy efficiency and Demand-Side Management (DSM)

Energy efficiency focuses on reducing energy consumption through improved technologies and practices, while DSM involves strategies to optimize energy use patterns, particularly during peak demand periods. Both these components together enhance the sustainability and reliability of energy systems. Energy efficiency is achieved by integrating advanced technologies and practices that reduce energy consumption without compromising service quality. Heat pumps are a key technology in enhancing energy efficiency, providing sustainable heating and cooling solutions while offering demand-side flexibility [18]. Smart grid technologies facilitate energy efficiency by enabling real-time monitoring and control of energy use, thus optimizing consumption patterns [19].

DSM systems empower consumers to manage their energy usage, leading to cost savings and improved efficiency by reducing consumption during peak hours [20]. DSM strategies include load scheduling, price-based mechanisms, and incentive programs, which help manage peak demand and integrate renewable energy sources. Automated demand response systems enable dynamic adjustments to energy consumption in response to price signals and grid conditions, promoting flexible and efficient energy use [21]. Hybrid energy systems, which combine renewable energy sources and technologies such as heat pumps, can be optimized for improved performance and efficiency through advanced algorithms and predictive modeling [18]. The integration of renewable energy, distributed generation, and energy storage with DSM systems enhances grid stability and reduces greenhouse gas emissions [22]. Dynamic pricing models and AI-enabled smart meters empower consumers to make energy-efficient decisions, fostering a culture of sustainability.

Smart Grids and Energy Storage

SES is highly reliant on smart grids and energy storage to integrate renewable energy sources. Smart grids enhance the efficiency and reliability of energy distribution, while Energy Storage Systems (ESS) address the intermittency of RES like solar and wind. They both form the backbone of a sustainable energy infrastructure. Smart grids facilitate the integration of RES, reducing greenhouse gas emissions and reliance on fossil fuels. Technologies such as Advanced Metering Infrastructure (AMI) and Distributed Control Systems (DCS) enhance grid reliability and efficiency [23]. Smart grids require substantial technological upgrades to accommodate decentralized energy sources [24]. ML techniques are employed to optimize EM within smart grids, improving their efficiency and resilience [23].

ESS are crucial for managing the intermittency of RES, providing energy time-shifting, capacity backup, and power quality improvements [25]. ESS faces challenges such as charge/discharge cycle issues, safety concerns, and cost factors. Innovations in battery-based and mechanical storage methods are essential for enhancing performance. Strategies for charging and discharging ESS are developed to maximize efficiency and reshape energy consumption patterns, contributing to a more sustainable energy system [26]. Urban smart grids and distributed energy storage are vital for future infrastructure, offering opportunities for sustainable energy generation and reliable systems [27, 28]. While smart grids and ESS are pivotal for sustainable energy systems, they face significant challenges, including regulatory and financial barriers. A holistic approach involving technological innovation, regulatory reform, and financial mechanisms is necessary to overcome these obstacles and fully realize the potential of smart grids and ESS.

Supercapacitor devices have a significant role in energy systems due to their enormous power density, competing favorably with conventional energy storage solutions [29]. To address environmental issues related to the use and storage of renewable resources, supercapacitors with advanced intelligent features were employed to predict and optimize performance-related aspects, including high power densities, higher capacitance, cyclic stability, and specific capacity [30]. AI models, including HGA-LSTM (hybrid genetic algorithm-long short-term memory) and a Recurrent Neural Network (RNN) model, predict capacitance, power density, usable lifecycles, and state of charge for supercapacitors [31].

Decentralized Energy Systems (DES) and Microgrids

DES and microgrids are pivotal in advancing sustainable energy solutions by offering localized, resilient, and efficient alternatives to traditional centralized power systems. DES incorporates solar photovoltaics, wind turbines, and battery storage to create localized power solutions. These systems are supported by innovative technologies, such as AI and blockchain, which enhance their efficiency and resilience. By reducing reliance on centralized power grids, decentralized systems can lower carbon emissions and promote economic growth through local energy production and job creation. The successful deployment of decentralized systems requires supportive policy frameworks and the overcoming of technical and social challenges, such as grid integration and public acceptance [32].

Microgrids effectively incorporate renewable energy sources, facilitating electrification and e-mobility while enhancing disaster preparedness and resilience. They can operate independently or in conjunction with the main grid, providing reliable power during outages and emergencies [33]. Microgrids utilize advanced control algorithms, real-time data analytics, and load management techniques to optimize energy generation and distribution [34]. Blockchain technology, such as the GridCoin algorithm, enhances energy trading within microgrids by providing secure, transparent, and efficient transaction mechanisms [35]. Current research focuses on enhancing optimization techniques, integrating renewable energy sources, and addressing scalability and security challenges in blockchain-enabled microgrids. While DES and microgrids offer numerous benefits, they also face challenges such as maintaining grid stability, addressing cybersecurity concerns, and requiring comprehensive policy support. Addressing these issues is crucial for realizing the full potential of these systems in achieving global sustainability goals [36].

OVERVIEW OF AI

AI plays a pivotal role in advancing SES by enhancing the efficiency, reliability, and integration of renewable energy sources. AI technologies, including ML and deep learning, are employed to optimize energy production, improve predictive maintenance, and streamline EM processes. AI-driven predictive maintenance models, utilizing ML algorithms, can predict equipment failures with high accuracy, reducing unplanned downtime by 35% and improving energy output by 8.5% across RES [37]. These advancements contribute significantly to achieving sustainable development goals and reducing the carbon footprint of energy systems. AI technologies analyze data from installations like solar panels and wind turbines to prevent equipment failures, ensuring continuous energy generation and reducing maintenance costs [38]. AI enhances energy forecasting accuracy, which is crucial for balancing supply and demand, thereby reducing reliance on non-renewable energy sources and enhancing grid stability [39]. AI-driven models improve wind speed forecasts and solar irradiance predictions, which are essential for optimizing renewable energy production and management [40].

While AI offers transformative potential in RES, challenges such as ethical AI adoption, regulatory compliance, and stakeholder engagement must be addressed to ensure responsible AI deployment. Explainable AI (XAI) principles, such as model interpretability and accountability, are crucial for building trust and understanding in AI-driven energy systems [41]. There are several emergent global policies and acts framed by different countries that facilitate the integration of AI in sustainable energy. The Artificial Intelligence Act (AIA) of the European Commission was enacted with regard to the illicit uses of technology, *i.e.*, the overuse or misuse of AI. The act primarily addresses a human-centric approach, ensuring that AI technologies are developed and used in ways that prioritize human rights and safety. However, the AIA does not adequately address the environmental concerns, suggesting that it should adopt an ontocentric perspective to better align with the EU's Green Deal objective. Thus, it highlights the need for this act to incorporate environmental concerns, suggesting that the current focus is too narrow and lacks an ontocentric perspective [42]. A similar act was proposed by New Mexico Governor Michelle Lujan-Grisham on March 22, 2019, by signing a State Bill, the "Energy Transition Act" (ETA), to achieve an enacted goal of Carbon neutrality by 2045. This act aims to significantly reduce greenhouse gas emissions and transition the state towards renewable energy sources. The act anticipates challenges posed by climate change, particularly on renewable energy resources. Studies indicate that wind power may decrease by approximately 13% and solar power by about 4% due to changing climate conditions in New Mexico. It is pivotal in addressing climate change impacts while ensuring energy reliability and economic stability [43, 44]. The integration of AI in the energy sector presents both promising opportunities and significant ethical and social challenges. AI can enhance energy efficiency, reliability, and sustainability, but it also raises concerns about data privacy, algorithmic bias, accountability, and environmental impact. By implementing comprehensive ethical frameworks and fostering collaboration among stakeholders, the energy sector can harness the benefits of AI while mitigating its risks. This balanced approach is essential for a sustainable and equitable energy future.

AI FOR GRID RESILIENCE AND STABILITY

AI plays a crucial role in enhancing grid resilience and stability, addressing the complexities introduced by the integration of renewable energy and the dynamic nature of modern power systems. AI techniques, including ML and Deep Learning (DL), are increasingly employed to improve the reliability and efficiency of power systems by enabling real-time monitoring, predictive maintenance, and adaptive control strategies. These advancements are crucial for maintaining grid stability amid growing energy demands and environmental challenges.

Fault Detection and Preventive Maintenance

The incorporation of hybrid AI models, including Convolutional Neural Networks (CNNs), with traditional power grid systems has resulted in an upgraded and integrated solution. AI-driven predictions and forecasting methodologies were used to optimise power reduction, distribution, and transmission for industrial and residential consumers. Within the framework of the Fourth Industrial Revolution, AI has proven effective in addressing challenges in modern power generation grids. By utilizing real-time data and analyzing internal and external grid faults over three years, hybrid ML models were deployed at end-user locations for fault prediction and detection [45]. Additionally, AI applications in smart grids have been instrumental in predictive maintenance, integrating renewable resources, and strategically enhancing their overall efficiency and reliability [46].

Integration of Distributed Energy Resources (DES)

K. Dasari *et al.* proposed an AI-driven framework for managing DES, using ML and a multi-agent architecture to ensure optimal load balancing and grid stability [47]. By integrating sensor and smart meter data, the system dynamically improves DER management, enhancing load distribution, peak shaving, and voltage regulation. AI self-learning capabilities further optimize control strategies, increasing system resilience. Soft computing methods like neural networks, fuzzy logic, and Genetic Algorithms (GAs) enable complex problem-solving and, when combined with DERs, improve power system efficiency and reliability [48]. A hybrid algorithm by T. Lv *et al.*, combining Rough Set Theory, Hierarchical GA, and NSGA-II, demonstrated effective EM for microgrids in Active Distribution Systems (ADS) [49]. It relates the ADS to different microgrids and validates it using a real system, suggesting that the EM approach is capable of precisely measuring and directing the energy interaction between microgrids, as well as between microgrids and the ADN. Additionally, P. S. Georgilakis revealed the state of the art in advanced computational intelligence, featuring several models and methods for optimizing local energy markets, and offering insights into current and future research directions [50].

Real-time Monitoring and Adaptive Control

AI techniques, such as Artificial Neural Networks (ANN), are employed for real-time monitoring of grid-connected converters, allowing for precise identification of grid impedance and parameter perturbations [51]. Intelligent frameworks, such as Intelligent FaultEdge, utilize predictive analytics and anomaly detection to continuously monitor grid conditions, thereby enhancing fault tolerance and minimizing downtime [52]. AI facilitates adaptive control by dynamically tuning control parameters based on real-time data, improving the stability margin of grid-connected systems. Agent-based distributed AI frameworks predict power needs in mini-grids, enabling adaptive EM that aligns with fluctuating renewable energy outputs [53]. AI-driven frameworks proactively manage potential faults through predictive analytics, enhancing the reliability and safety of smart grid operations [52]. AI supports scenario generation and risk assessment, enabling accurate predictions of system behaviors under varied conditions, which is crucial for optimizing control strategies [54]. While AI offers substantial benefits for grid resilience and stability, challenges remain, such as the need for robust and scalable intelligent systems to handle the increasing complexity of power systems. Future research should focus on overcoming these limitations to fully realize the potential of AI in power system stability and control.

AI Algorithms for Grid Balancing

AI algorithms are essential for managing modern grids that integrate renewable energy and digital technologies. They enable efficient Load Frequency Control (LFC), real-time stability predictions, and the prevention of cascading failures. Optimization techniques like GA and Particle Swarm Optimization (PSO)-based PID controllers outperform traditional methods by reducing overshoot and achieving faster settling times, while ANN-based controllers offer adaptability with quicker response times but higher overshoot [55]. AI enhances dynamic security assessments through scenario generation, incident prediction, and risk analysis, thereby aiding the integration of renewable energy. Decision trees and data-driven methods optimize control strategies and grid reliability [56]. A hybrid algorithm combining Affinity Propagation Graph (APG) and Self-Propagating Graph (SPG) identifies critical nodes, while Unified Power Flow Controllers (UPFCs) regulate power flow to mitigate cascading failure risks and improve grid resilience [57]. Optimized Long Short-Term Memory (LSTM) models, supported by the Guide-Waterwheel Plant Algorithm (Guide-WWPA), enhance prediction accuracy by capturing temporal and nonlinear dependencies. These models are used in Decentralized Smart Grid Control (DSGC) systems to achieve high grid stability prediction accuracy, ensuring efficient EM and fault resistance [58, 59].

AI TRANSFORMED SES

AI-driven transformations in SES are reshaping the scenario of EM and utilization by offering innovative solutions to enhance efficiency, reliability, and sustainability. Despite various challenges, the integration of AI in energy systems possesses immense potential to contribute to sustainable development goals.

Hydrogen Production and Storage

An AI framework has been developed to identify optimal locations for hydrogen storage in salt caverns, utilizing multi-criteria decision-making and geographical data analysis. The method utilized eight ML algorithms, with CatBoost demonstrating the best performance (R^2 of 0.88, MSE of 0.0816) for creating suitability maps for hydrogen storage in rock salt deposits [60]. AI has also enhanced solid-state hydrogen storage materials by improving material screening and design, offering tools for the development of next-generation storage materials [61]. M. Nachtane *et al.* reviewed the role of AI in evaluating composite Hydrogen Storage Vessels (HSVs), contributing to more sustainable designs [62]. For isolated locations, islanded microgrids utilizing Green Hydrogen Energy Storage Systems (GHESS) and AI-based control techniques provide enhanced stability. Experimental results showed that an SNPID controller reduced frequency fluctuations by 87% compared to conventional PID controllers, highlighting the AI potential in microgrid management. Additionally, an AI-driven genetic optimization framework optimized reservoir production and hydrogen recovery by fine-tuning oxygen injection and production parameters [63].

AI techniques like ANN and support vector machines have been applied to Metal-Organic Frameworks (MOFs) for hydrogen adsorption and storage, achieving high prediction accuracy (R^2 of 0.9946) and aiding the development of more efficient storage materials [64]. Another study used AI and high-throughput computational workflows to optimize MOFs for hydrogen storage, identifying top-performing candidates with work capacities greater than 1.00 wt% % at 298.5 K [65]. Lastly, AI-based optimization of hydrogen production power grids aims to enhance grid efficiency and reliability, with simulation platforms used to study safety and stability strategies for new hydrogen projects [66]. A case study to explore "the role of AI in enhancing the development of sustainable clean hydrogen industries" was done by Scatec ASA in Egypt. Besides the transformative potentials of AI, they have acknowledged the challenges. Their research study highlighted the need for strong and strategic partnerships, supportive policies, and investments to enhance the global transition towards green hydrogen through AI-driven innovations and investment modeling, with significantly increased scalability and economic feasibility, supporting Scatec's leadership in sustainable energy [67].

Carbon Capture and Storage (CCS) Technologies

Optimizing natural gas production and CO_2 sequestration while minimizing CO_2 emissions is a major challenge in hydrogen production. K. Katterbauer and colleagues employed AI-based optimization techniques to improve injection patterns and quantify uncertainty using the New Zealand McKee reservoir model, which involved multiple producing wells and a separate CO_2 sequestration reservoir [68]. To achieve net-zero CO_2 emissions by the 2050s, Q. Qerimi and colleagues emphasized the need for updated regulations to support the development and implementation of AI-integrated CCS technologies [69]. AI has revolutionized CCS, optimized complex processes, and aided in greenhouse gas reduction. K. Aliyon *et al.* used AI to forecast utility consumption in absorption-based carbon capture processes, achieving energy-efficient designs with minimal error (0.4% to 3.6%) in various scenarios [70]. X. Chen and colleagues integrated AI with CCS, utilizing a deep belief neural network for power plant carbon capture and particle swarm optimization to optimize operations, reducing costs and emissions while enhancing renewable power utilization [71]. A. M. Nassef employed an Adaptive Neuro-Fuzzy Inference System (ANFIS) combined with advanced optimization techniques to enhance CO_2 solubility in CCS operations [72]. N. Sharma and colleagues modeled CO_2 capture in Indian coal-fired power plants using AI techniques such as ANFIS and multi-gene genetic programming [73], while E.V. Kotov *et al.* applied ML and neural networks for optimized CCS [74]. P.K. Patro and colleagues integrated AI, blockchain, and the IoT to enhance CCUS transparency. AI analyzed sensor data to optimize carbon capturing and offer accurate, tamper-proof information about the CCUS supply chain [75]. J. Sabeena's study on post-combustion CO_2 capture using monoethanolamine (MEA) highlighted the superiority of Bayesian networks and CNN in modeling complex interactions in carbon capture processes [76]. Finally, B. Chennakrishnan and colleagues emphasized the importance of precisely characterizing reservoir parameters for optimizing CCS operations [77].

Climate-Resilient Energy Systems

Extreme weather events can trigger cascading failures in systems, leading to prolonged blackouts. A comprehensive literature review identified challenges in integrating urban morphology into energy system models and proposed a new framework to enhance the resilience of interconnected systems [78]. AI is also revolutionizing crop development by providing powerful processing tools for breeding and improving the accuracy of high-throughput crop genotyping, phenotyping, and envirotyping data. M.H.U. Khan *et al.* discussed the potential of AIn overcoming challenges in multiomics data integration for future breeding [79]. Smart grids, AI, and ML are advancing energy system resilience against climate-related disruptions. J. Nyangon highlighted the effectiveness of proactive smart grid technologies over non-adaptive approaches, emphasizing their role in reducing climate-related expenses and protecting infrastructure from climate change [80]. In agriculture, AI technologies such as crop monitoring, weather forecasting, and precision farming hold promise for building climate resilience and enhancing sustainability [81]. S. Singh and colleagues presented a framework integrating climate risk assessment into corporate operations, combining DL and AI to improve resilience and reduce risks in business ecosystems facing climate threats [82].

Adaptive Energy Management Systems (AEMS)

AEMS are deployed at Electric Vehicle (EV) charging stations, utilizing AI to improve grid efficiency and stability in real time. The EM systems facilitate smooth integration with renewable energy sources, guarantee efficient energy consumption, and reduce the risk of grid overload. Additionally, by providing scalability and resilience for extensive EV deployments, the adaptive strategy opens the door for future smart grid applications [83]. AI model-based algorithms were employed in various ways to design the adaptive controller. The implementation demonstrates the successful integration of solely AI and integrated approaches to an adaptive power system stabilizer to improve the damping and stability of electric generating units [84]. A case study conducted by M.S.K. Asnaz examines the integration of AI into energy management processes in industrial facilities. This study revealed how AI offers a wide range of solutions, from analyzing energy consumption patterns to detecting anomalies to developing energy-saving strategies. In industrial facilities equipped with sensors and IoT devices, big data analytics and machine learning algorithms enable real-time monitoring and management of energy data. The study also discusses how AI utilizes advanced forecasting models and optimization algorithms to balance fluctuations in energy production and ensure energy supply-demand equilibrium, allowing industrial facilities to maintain a continuous energy supply while reducing costs and promoting environmental sustainability in the industrial sector [85].

Smart Home Energy Management Systems (HEMS)

As IoT advances, the need for HEMS is increasing to manage household energy use. K. Kwon *et al.* proposed an AI-based HEMS (AI-HEMS) that improves both energy efficiency and resident satisfaction. The assessment involved selecting a control group of 2281 households and a treatment group of 100 households to measure the treatment group's energy savings relative to the control group, aiming to enhance reliability by eliminating natural energy fluctuation factors. After a 48-day evaluation, the AI-HEMS resulted in a 14% energy-saving rate and a 91% satisfaction rate compared to a control group [86]. Improvements in smart HEMS have been driven by the need to balance user comfort with energy efficiency. The integration of a DL model with a constraint coordination game method achieved a 12% reduction in energy costs for homeowners [87]. AI-based solutions also resulted in a 51.4% cost reduction when comparing smart homes with and without distributed generation and battery banks [88]. Additionally, AI techniques such as ANN and fuzzy logic are used to optimize the scheduling of electrical devices in smart homes, further improving energy consumption efficiency and integrating demand response tools [89].

AI INTEGRATED BLOCKCHAIN FOR DECENTRALIZED ENERGY MARKETS

AI and blockchain are being utilized to enhance smart grid control, decision-making, and the decarbonization of power systems by facilitating the association of prosumers. AI techniques support various services, including energy load prediction and load management, while blockchain ensures secure EM through data immutability and trust mechanisms [90, 91]. A decentralized peer-to-peer (P2P) energy trading platform using blockchain and AI was developed for efficient energy trading, reducing transmission costs by 20% and solar yield prediction errors to 0.11 [92, 93]. A blockchain-based energy trading simulation for Qatar's Education City Community Housing (ECCH), integrated with GIS, demonstrated effective decision-making and transaction modifications in local energy markets, enhancing market dynamics [94]. Hybrid models incorporating blockchain, AI, IoT, and big data are being deployed globally for smart EM, improving resource reliability and performance [95]. Additionally, the combination of these technologies is enhancing market liquidity and interoperability in smart electrical grids, with autonomous supplier-client interactions through smart contracts [96]. Blockchain and AI are also being utilized in decentralized carbon markets to reduce emissions, with blockchain ensuring safe, transparent transactions and AI optimizing carbon credit pricing [97].

AI-DRIVEN CIRCULAR ENERGY SYSTEM

Energy Recycling and Recovery

Lithium-Ion Batteries (LIBs) are excessively exploited at an unprecedented rate to satisfy the demands of contemporary transportation electrification. To support the predesign strategy for the battery management system and battery chemistry, AI was incorporated. In an Economically and Ecologically Sustainable (EES) manner, purposefully predesigned LIBs with the 3R (Reuse–Refurbish–Recover) approach were collaboratively developed methodically and cooperatively [98]. By creating pertinent comparative experiments and questionnaires, S. Ma *et al.* suggest the use of AI to clean energy heating, energy conservation, and recycling transformation. According to the study's findings, AI has a greater impact on clean energy heating and energy conservation. The energy recycling rate is four times higher than the industry standard, and the clean energy recovery rate is essentially regulated between 85% and 95% [99]. M. Fernandez *et al.* optimized renewable energy for the recycling process by using ML techniques. According to research, the use of ML can boost recycling production, reduce greenhouse gas emissions, and decrease energy use by up to 30% [100]. M. Johnson *et al.* addressed the electronic waste (E-waste) problem with a non-destructive RoboCRM system (Fig. **1**). By simply recognizing and classifying e-waste, the automated battery detection system enables recyclers to complete the cycle of battery recovery and resource efficiency [101].

Life Cycle of Renewable Components

To deliver more precise, effective, and thorough assessments, AI and ML approaches are utilized to enhance Lifecycle Assessments (LCA) of wind, solar, and green hydrogen energy systems. The extensive datasets from several phases of the RES lifecycle, including raw material extraction, installation, operation, production, maintenance, and commissioning, are used by AI-driven Lifecycle Assessment (LCA) models [102]. AI can be used in solar power to optimize the placement of solar panels, ensuring they receive the maximum amount of sunshine throughout the day. Similarly, AI systems can instantly adjust the blade angles of wind turbines to maximize energy harvest and reduce system stress. For renewable energy sources to overcome their intermittent nature, energy storage is essential. By predicting patterns of energy production and consumption, AI algorithms optimize ESS. This maximizes the longevity and efficiency of batteries by enabling intelligent charging and discharge [103].

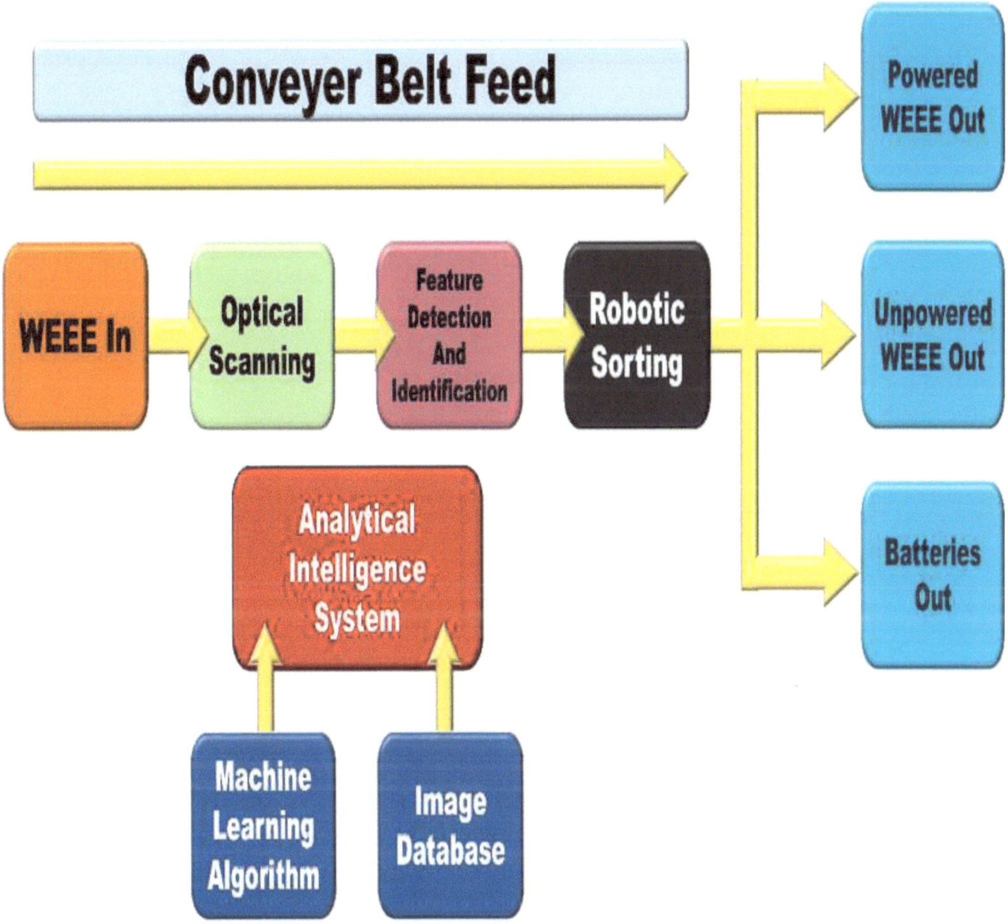

Fig. (1). The proposed battery detection/sorting system design (RoboCRM).

Waste to Energy Conversion

The ML-Driven Predictive Analytical Framework (MLDPAF) has been offered as a way to get ready for waste and EM. To start preparing for energy and waste management, J. Huang and his colleague's research suggested effective methods based on MLDPAF. They employed an improved artificial neural network model to estimate the amount of waste. Then, using ML algorithms based on unstable sustainable energy markets, further improvements are made to garbage collection on energy prices. Fig. (**2**) shows the suggested waste management model [104]. An additional team of researchers is exploring the complex ways in which AI can improve the efficacy and efficiency of waste-to-energy operations. AI enhances data management, analysis, and processing accuracy, enabling more effective waste-to-energy conversion, mitigating negative environmental impacts, and promoting sustainable energy practices [105]. To ensure a constant feed, D.S. Lee *et al.* evaluated the homogeneity of waste inputs. They also used an LSTM neural network architecture to forecast heat values from waste combustion, which significantly improved combustion stability. AI-predicted heat levels and real-time operational parameter adjustments mark a substantial change toward waste management systems that are more responsive and dynamic. Additionally, two significant problems impacting incinerators were addressed by AI-based auxiliary control systems: the increase in the heat value of waste and the unpredictability of heat values in mixed domestic and industrial waste [106]. A procedure for designing and expediting the optimization of the waste-to-energy method utilizing AI technologies was provided by J. Zhou *et al.* The conversion of medical waste to methanol and the application of data-driven process improvement served as examples of the procedures [107]. A novel process for generating Volatile Fatty Acid (VFA) energy precursors from Date Palm Waste (DPW) was optimized using an ANN model. The ANN model receives data from the input layer, then processes it in the hidden layers, and afterward sends the results to the output layer. ANNs were used to optimize a new method for producing VFA energy precursors from DPW. The input layer provides data to the ANN model, which processes it in the hidden layers before sending the results to the output layer [108].

FUTURE DIRECTIONS AND PROSPECTS

The ability of AI to produce pioneering algorithms for SES is being excessively exploited to optimize, design, and enhance the efficacy of the energy systems as sustainable energy solutions. These algorithms promote and enhance the stability and resilience of energy networks. It improves the performance of conventional RES while aiding in forecasting energy supply and demand. Besides, a real-time adaptive decision-making process can become easier and more feasible with smart AI-driven models. These evolutions enable energy systems to dynamically respond to variables such as consumer demands and irregular renewable energy output. This ensures competence and dependability throughout the sustainable energy networks. Table **1** shows the list of AI-based renewable energy systems for sustainable energy solutions.

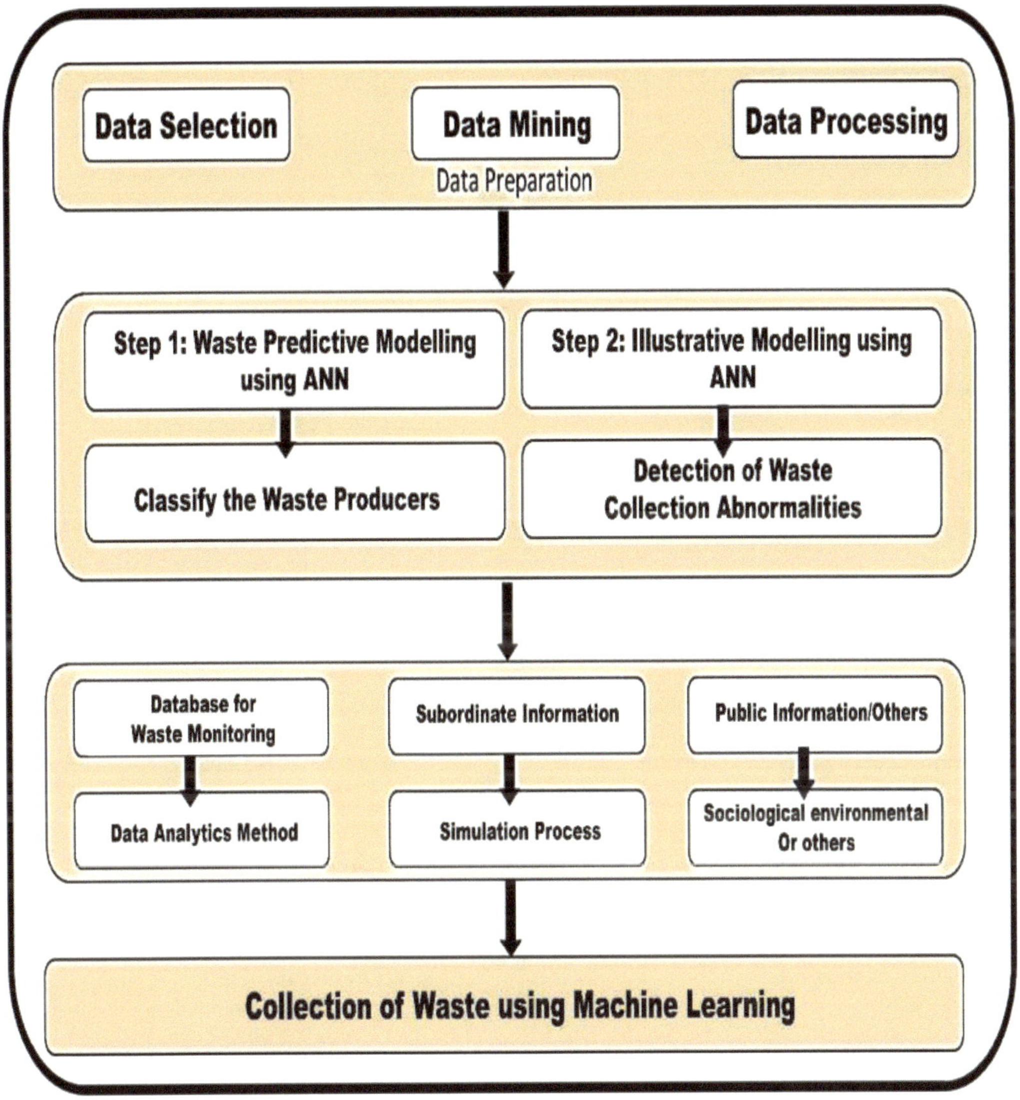

Fig. (2). Proposed model for waste management using MLDPAF.

Table 1. List of AI-based renewable energy systems for sustainable energy solutions.

Title	Impact Metrics and Key Contributions	AI Model Used	References
AI-based grid-connected inverters for power quality improvement in smart grid applications.	Total Harmonic Distortion (THD) is reduced below 5%, control and manage reactive power through integration is managed and controlled, improving the dynamic performance of current tracking.	Adaptive Fuzzy-Neura--Network (AFNN) model, Non-Singular Terminal Sliding Mode Controller (NTSMC)	[109]
Integrating AI Internet of Things and 5G for Next-Generation Smartgrid: A Survey of Trends, Challenges, and Prospects.	Enhanced Security, Autonomous Decision-Making based on real-time data, allowing for self-learning and adaptive responses to environmental changes, Improved Monitoring and Fault Detection for quick response, Integration with IoT and 5G.	Deep Belief Network (DBN) model, CNN algorithm, ANN model, including Whale Optimization-Trained ANN model, Stacked Denoising Autoencoder (SDAE) algorithm, Stacked Autoencoders (SAE) model, Game Theory and Reinforcement Learning (RL) model	[110]
AI-Based Threat Intelligence for Proactive Mitigation of Cyberattacks in Smart Grids	Optimizes energy generation, distribution, and consumption, reducing waste, enhancing the reliability and scalability of renewable energy, Carbon Reduction, Cost Reduction, and resilience, Predictive Analytics, Optimization Algorithms, Real-Time Monitoring, and Autonomous Control.	Random Forest (RF) model, RNN, DL Models, Long Short-Term Memory (LSTM)	[111]
Leveraging AI for Enhanced Sustainable EM	Efficiency of energy, monitoring, and reducing carbon emission, Predictive analytics, and automated decision-making minimize operational costs, improve energy supply reliability.	ML algorithm, Artificial neural network, XAI, Federated Learning (FL) model, Generative Adversarial Networks (GANs)	[112]
DL and AI in Sustainability: A Review of SDG, Renewable Energy, and Environmental Health	Optimizes energy consumption through advanced forecasting and real-time management, easily scalable for large datasets and dynamic systems using IoT and big data analytics, High accuracy in predictions using DL models, optimal resource allocation and usage, Minimizes carbon emissions	CNN, RNN, Generative Adversarial Networks (GANs), Deep Reinforcement Learning (DRL), Generative Adversarial Networks (GANs)	[113]

(Table 1) cont.....

Title	Impact Metrics and Key Contributions	AI Model Used	References
AI-assistance for predictive maintenance of RES	improving the technical inspector's specificity and time efficiency, greater improvements in specificity and time efficiency (24.6% and 25.3%, respectively) when compared with the specialist group (4.7% and 6.4%, respectively).	high-performance DL model based on CNN,	[114]
A new methodology for reducing carbon emissions using multi-RES and AI	By comparing the proposed method with the conventional method, the whale optimization algorithm saved 31.396% per day, and the proposed artificial rabbit's optimization algorithm saved 80.3437% per day.	Improved Artificial Rabbits Optimization Algorithm (IAROA), Honey Badger Algorithm (HBA), and Whale Optimization Algorithm (WOA).	[115]
A new hybrid AI optimal management method for renewable energy communities	The total income is increased by 18.72% compared to utilizing the same management system without exploiting predictions from a forecasting method.	Time Delay Neural Network, stochastic Model Predictive Control.	[116]
Intelligent Combustion Control in Waste-t--Energy Facilities: Enhancing Efficiency and Reducing Emissions Using AI and IoT	AI proposed optimal operation methods, a decrease of 0.66% in incinerator flue gas temperature, 2.41% improved steam flow rate, 60.72% decreased CO emissions, 3.09% increased power generation, and 7.33% decreased NOx emissions.	Intelligent Combustion Control (ICC) system	[117]
Forecasting municipal solid waste generation using Artificial Intelligence models—a case study in India	Lowest Root Mean Square Error (RMSE), highest index of agreement (IA) value, and highest coefficient of determination (R2) value for GA and ANN are more accurate.	Artificial neural network (ANN), (ANFIS), discrete wavelet theory–artificial neural network (DWT-ANN), DWT-ANFIS, genetic algorithm–artificial neural network (GA-ANN), and GA-ANFIS system	[118]

Instantaneously, AI-driven policy and DSS leverage the ability of AI to evaluate extensive datasets, encompassing complex parameters that involve patterns of energy consumption, environmental impact analysis, and economic forecasts. The use of predictive analytics and scenario modeling fosters scientifically robust and data-driven insights, which assist in developing an adaptive energy strategy focusing on low-carbon emissions and equitable resource distribution. AI also helps to achieve renewable energy integration targets through the effective scaling of renewable energy sources, such as solar photovoltaics and wind turbines. AI holds immense potential to revolutionize the design, fabrication, and optimization of sustainable devices, including supercapacitors, by enhancing their stability, lifespan, and capacity with advanced models and algorithms. AI ensures that energy policies are not only theoretically implemented but also practically executed through the assimilation of real-time data with long-term projections in dynamic environments. Likewise, the integration of AI with quantum computation is expected to address the most complex challenges in RES. This proposes unprecedented computational power that enables AI dels and software optimization for highly complex energy networks [119]. AI will revolutionize the energy system to a higher level, enabling adaptive, resilient, and sustainable methods with advanced algorithms and quantum-derived programs to shape better progress towards sustainable energy solutions.

CONCLUSION

The chapter provides insight into the key challenges, efficiency, and critical role of AI in EM, including improving grid stability, integrating renewable energy, enabling predictive maintenance, and facilitating a circular energy system. In conclusion, the integration of AI into SES represents a transformative approach that addresses global energy challenges. Integrating AI into SES enhances the efficiency, reliability, and adaptability of renewable energy, smart grids, and Energy Storage Systems (ESS) through advanced analytics, optimization, and predictive capabilities. AI facilitates real-time decision-making, demand forecasting, and resource management, enabling seamless transitions to DES and microgrids while accelerating the adoption of clean technologies and improving grid stability. The ability of AI to process a large number of datasets, predict outcomes, and make real-time decisions has made it an indispensable tool for accelerating the global energy transition and achieving net-zero emission goals. Emerging technologies, including AI-integrated blockchain and IoT, further enhance transparency and efficiency, creating interconnected and adaptive energy ecosystems. By enabling innovations such as next-generation battery designs, global grid optimization, and carbon capture systems, AI is poised to become the cornerstone of sustainable energy solutions, fostering productivity, resilience, and climate action while promoting socially and environmentally sustainable development.

LIST OF ABBREVIATIONS

ADS	Active Distribution Systems
AI	Artificial intelligence
AMI	Advanced Metering Infrastructure

ANFIS	Adaptive Neuro-Fuzzy Inference System
ANN	Artificial Neural Networks
APG	Affinity Propagation Graph
CCS	Carbon Capture and Storage
CNN	Convolutional Neural Networks
DCS	Distributed Control Systems
DER	Distributed Energy Resources
DES	Decentralized energy systems
DL	Deep Learning
DPW	Date palm waste
DSGC	Decentralized Smart Grid Control
DSM	Demand-side Management
DSS	Decision Support Systems
ECCH	Education City Community Housing
EES	Economically and ecologically sustainable
EM	Energy Management
ESS	Energy Storage Systems
GA	Genetic Algorithm
GHESS	Green Hydrogen Energy Storage Systems
HEMS	Home Energy Management Systems
HSVs	Hydrogen Storage Vessels
IoT	Internet of Things
LCA	Lifecycle assessments
LFC	Load Frequency Control
LIBs	Lithium-ion batteries
LSTM	Long Short-Term Memory
MEA	Monoethanolamine
ML	Machine Learning
MLDPAF	ML-driven predictive analytical framework
MOFs	Metal-Organic Frameworks
P2P	peer-to-peer
RES	Renewable Energy Systems
RNN	Recurrent Neural Network
SDG	Sustainable Development Goals
SES	Sustainable Energy Systems

SPG	Self-Propagating Graph
VFA	Volatile fatty acid
XAI	Explainable AI

ACKNOWLEDGEMENTS

The authors are wholeheartedly thankful to the Netaji Subhas University of Technology for providing the lab facilities and financial aid.

REFERENCES

[1] M. Shoaei, Y. Noorollahi, A. Hajinezhad, and S.F. Moosavian, "A review of the applications of artificial intelligence in renewable energy systems: An approach-based study", *Energy Convers. Manage.,* vol. 306, p. 118207, 2024. [http://dx.doi.org/10.1016/j.enconman.2024.118207]

[2] A. Entezari, A. Aslani, R. Zahedi, and Y. Noorollahi, "Artificial intelligence and machine learning in energy systems: A bibliographic perspective", *Energy Strategy Reviews,* vol. 45, p. 101017, 2023. [http://dx.doi.org/10.1016/j.esr.2022.101017]

[3] R.S. Krishnan, C. Ashokkumar, E. E. Nithila, N. Soundiraraj, P. S. R. Malar and P. A. Rani, "AI-powered demand response mechanisms for sustainable smart grids", 2024 5th International Conference on Electronics and Sustainable Communication Systems (ICESC), Coimbatore, India, 2024, pp. 87-92. [http://dx.doi.org/10.1109/ICESC60852.2024.10690089]

[4] B. Salma, J. Tarik, and L. Roa, "Enhancing renewable energy systems with advanced artificial intelligence solutions", *SCT Proceedings in Interdisciplinary Insights and Innovations,* vol. 2, p. 319, May 2024. [http://dx.doi.org/10.56294/piii2024319]

[5] P. K. Goel, *AI for Energy Efficiency and Conservation,* 2024. [http://dx.doi.org/10.4018/979-8-3693-6567-0.ch003]

[6] Feyisayo Ajayi, Osho Moses Ademola, Kafilat Funmilola Amuda, and Bolape Alade, *AI-driven decarbonization of buildings: Leveraging predictive analytics and automation for sustainable energy management,* 2024.

[7] A.S. Katkar, P.V. Shelar, R.U. Mene, and T. Salve, *Large-Scale Renewable Integration Powered by AI,* no. Oct, pp. 285-306, 2024.

[8] V. Jain, and A. Mitra, *Ethical Implications of Artificial Intelligence in Promoting Sustainable Clean Energy Solutions,* no. July, pp. 96-118, 2024.

[9] V. Jain, and A. Mitra, *Int. Innov.,* no. Aug, pp. 365-382, 2024.

[10] R.S. Krishnan, J.R.F. Raj, P. Saveetha, P.E. Darney, R. Rajkumar, and G.R. Sankar, "Data-Driven decision support system for sustainable energy management: An AI-IoT fusion approach", *2024 Second International Conference on Inventive Computing and Informatics (ICICI),* IEEE, pp. 569-576, 2024. [http://dx.doi.org/10.1109/ICICI62254.2024.00099]

[11] N. MA, "Artificial intelligence-driven decision support systems for sustainable energy management in smart cities", *Int. J. Adv. Comput. Sci. Appl.,* vol. 15, no. 9, 2024.

[12] E. Raafat Maamoun Shouman, Solar power prediction with artificial intelligence In: *Advances in Solar Photovoltaic Energy Systems,* IntechOpen, Feb. 2024. [http://dx.doi.org/10.5772/intechopen.1002726]

[13] K.U. Jaseena, and B.C. Kovoor, *Deterministic weather forecasting models based on intelligent predictors: A survey,* 2022. [http://dx.doi.org/10.1016/j.jksuci.2020.09.009]

[14] O. Mane, A. Zagade, S. Sonpatki, S. Chavan, and K. Nimbalkar, "Forecasting renewable engery production using AI-based weather prediction models", *International Journal for Multidisciplinary Research,* vol. 6, no. 3, 2024.

[15] S. Dörterler, S. Arslan, and D. Özdemir, "Unlocking the potential: A review of artificial intelligence applications in wind energy", *Expert Syst.,* vol. 41, no. 12, p. e13716, 2024. [http://dx.doi.org/10.1111/exsy.13716]

[16] K. Kumar, and R. Saini, "Application of artificial intelligence for the optimization of hydropower energy generation", *EAI Endorsed Transactions on Industrial Networks and Intelligent Systems,* vol. 8, no. 28, p. 170560, 2021. [http://dx.doi.org/10.4108/eai.6-8-2021.170560]

[17] Z. Shi, G. Ferrari, P. Ai, F. Marinello, and A. Pezzuolo, "Artificial intelligence for biomass detection, production and energy usage in rural areas: A review of technologies and applications", *Sustain. Energy Technol. Assess.,* vol. 60, p. 103548, 2023. [http://dx.doi.org/10.1016/j.seta.2023.103548]

[18] M. Jelić, and M. Batić, *Demand-Side Optimization of Hybrid Energy Systems with Heat Pumps,* no. Feb, pp. 392-400, 2024.

[19] M.V. Kumar, R.S.S. Nuvvula, P.P. Kumar, N.H. Haroon, I.W. Suryasa, and U. Priya, "A review on demand side management system and its computer control methods", In: *2023 12th International Conference on Renewable Energy Research and Applications (ICRERA),* IEEE, Aug. 2023, pp. 480–486. [http://dx.doi.org/10.1109/ICRERA59003.2023.10269347]

[20] A.H. Nebey, "Recent advancement in demand side energy management system for optimal energy utilization", *Energy Rep.,* vol. 11, pp. 5422-5435, 2024. [http://dx.doi.org/10.1016/j.egyr.2024.05.028]

[21] D.M. Gado, I. Hamdan, S. Kamel, A.Y. Abdelaziz, and F. Jurado, "Optimizing energy consumption in smart homes: A comprehensive review of demand side management strategies", *2023 IEEE CHILEAN Conference on Electrical, Electronics Engineering, Information and Communication Technologies (CHILECON),* IEEE, pp. 1-10, 2023. [http://dx.doi.org/10.1109/CHILECON60335.2023.10418744]

[22] S. Motahari, and M.R. Rahimpour, "Energy demand management".*Encyclopedia of Renewable Energy, Sustainability and the Environment.* Elsevier, 2024, pp. 33-44. [http://dx.doi.org/10.1016/B978-0-323-93940-9.00248-6]

[23] M. Kiasari, M. Ghaffari, and H. Aly, "A comprehensive review of the current status of smart grid technologies for renewable energies integration and future trends: The role of machine learning and energy storage systems", *Energies,* vol. 17, no. 16, p. 4128, 2024. [http://dx.doi.org/10.3390/en17164128]

[24] Q. Hassan, C-Y. Hsu, K. Mounich, S. Algburi, M. Jaszczur, A.A. Telba, P. Viktor, E. Mahrous Awwad, M. Ahsan, B. Mahmood Ali, A. Khudhair Al-Jiboory, S.N. Henedy, A. Zuhair Sameen, and M. Barakat, "RETRACTED: Enhancing smart grid integrated renewable distributed generation capacities: Implications for sustainable energy transformation", *Sustain. Energy Technol. Assess.,* vol. 66, p. 103793, 2024. [http://dx.doi.org/10.1016/j.seta.2024.103793]

[25] A. Hafezimagham, A. Baghernezhad, N. Tayebi, P. Ghanbari-Mobarakeh, G.B. Gharehpetian, and M. Abedi, "Comprehensive review of energy storage systems for smart grids: Technologies and applications", In: *2024 9th International Conference on Technology and Energy Management (ICTEM),* IEEE, Feb. 2024, pp. 1-8.

[http://dx.doi.org/10.1109/ICTEM60690.2024.10631913]

[26] A. Dudko, and T. Endrjukaite, *Adaptive Charging and Discharging Strategies for Smart Grid Energy Storage Systems,* no. Jan, pp. 77-93, 2024.

[27] A. Chehri, R. Saadane, I. Fofana, and G. Jeon, "Smart grid for sustainable cities", *Strategies and Pathways for Energy Efficiency Solutions,* no. Jan, pp. 317-327, 2022.

[28] A.D. Sanieva, "Smart grids and their role in the sustainable development of energy systems, Ekonomika I upravlenie", *PROBLEMY, RESHENIYA,* vol. 9, no. 9, no. 150, pp. 33-39, 2024.

[29] J. Zhang, M. Gu, and X. Chen, *Supercapacitors for renewable energy applications: A Review,* 2023. [http://dx.doi.org/10.1016/j.mne.2023.100229]

[30] H. Sharma, "A holistic treatise on artificial intelligence (AI) and machine learning (ML) tools for green supercapacitors". In: *Low-carbon Supercapacoitors, RSC Sustainable Energy,* pp. 376-399, Dec. 2023. [http://dx.doi.org/10.1039/BK9781837672479-00376]

[31] Q.A. Sial, U. Safder, S. Iqbal, and R.B. Ali, "Advancement in supercapacitors for IoT applications by using machine learning: Current trends and future technology", *Sustainability (Basel),* vol. 16, no. 4, p. 1516, 2024. [http://dx.doi.org/10.3390/su16041516]

[32] N. N. Omar and M. A. Saleh, "Power to the people: Advancing resilient and sustainable decentralized energy distribution systems", *Proceedings of London International Conferences,* no. 11, pp. 125-139, Sep. 2024.

[33] G.S. Negi, M.K. Gupta, N.K. Saxena, K. Joshi, N. Yamsani, and S. Pant, "Empowering sustainability and resilience: The prominence of microgrids in a decentralized energy future", In: *2024 2nd International Conference on Sustainable Computing and Smart Systems (ICSCSS),* IEEE, pp. 25-31, Jul. 2024. [http://dx.doi.org/10.1109/ICSCSS60660.2024.10625205]

[34] Farhan Mukhtiar, "Comparing microgrid planning and management methods for energy resilience and sustainability", *Power System Technology,* vol. 48, no. 2, pp. 1811-1831, 2024. [http://dx.doi.org/10.52783/pst.758]

[35] M.L.S. Kokila, S. R, P. Kalyanakumar, J. R. Francis Raj, R. S. Krishnan, and S. Gopikumar, "Blockchain-Enabled Energy Trading in Microgrids for Sustainable Computing Infrastructure," In: *2024 5th International Conference on Electronics and Sustainable Communication Systems (ICESC),* IEEE, Aug. 2024, pp. 809-816.

[36] D. L.V. and D. V.A., "Aspects of integration into the electric network of decentralized generation based on renewable energy comments: an overview of issues and tasks for the sustainable development of the energy system.," *Journal of Electrical and power engineering,* vol. 30, no. 1, pp. 22–29, Jun. 2024.

[37] S.F. Bello, I.U. Wada, and B. Olukayode, "AI-driven predictive maintenance and optimization of renewable energy systems for enhanced operational efficiency and longevity", *International Journal of Science and Research Archive,* vol. 13, no. 1, pp. 2823-2837, 2024. [http://dx.doi.org/10.30574/ijsra.2024.13.1.1992]

[38] N.N.M. Helena, H.M. Kehinde, C.P. Agupugo, and C.N.M. Adélia, "The impact of AI on boosting renewable energy utilization and visual power plant efficiency in contemporary construction", *World Journal of Advanced Research and Reviews,* vol. 23, no. 2, pp. 1333-1348, 2024. [http://dx.doi.org/10.30574/wjarr.2024.23.2.2450]

[39] C.A. Nnajiofor, "Leveraging Artificial Intelligence for optimizing renewable energy systems: A pathway to environmental sustainability", *WJARR,* vol. 23, no. 3, pp. 2659-2665, 2024.

[40] R. Raman, S. Gunasekar, D. Kaliyaperumal, and P. Nedungadi, "Navigating the nexus of artificial intelligence and renewable energy for the advancement of sustainable development goals",

Sustainability (Basel), vol. 16, no. 21, p. 9144, 2024. [http://dx.doi.org/10.3390/su16219144]

[41] T. Shahzad, S. Nawaz, and M. Tabassum, *Renewable Energy Deployment and Guidelines for Responsible AI Adoption,* no. Oct, pp. 363-392, 2024.

[42] U. Pagallo, J. Ciani Sciolla, and M. Durante, "The environmental challenges of AI in EU law: lessons learned from the Artificial Intelligence Act (AIA) with its drawbacks", *Transforming Gov.,* vol. 16, no. 3, pp. 359-376, 2022. [http://dx.doi.org/10.1108/TG-07-2021-0121]

[43] A.R.N. R, T. Laishram, and S. Bal, "Energy transition: paving the way for a greener future", *Nanomaterials and Energy,* vol. 12, no. 3, pp. 100-109, 2023. [http://dx.doi.org/10.1680/jnaen.23.00057]

[44] C.K. Ho, E.L. Roesler, T.A. Nguyen, and J. Ellison, *Probabilistic Modeling of Climate Change Impacts on Renewable Energy and Storage Requirements for NM's Energy Transition Act (SAND report).*https://www.osti.gov/biblio/1855051https://www.osti.gov/biblio/1855051 [http://dx.doi.org/10.2172/1855051]

[45] F. M. Almasoudi, *Enhancing Power Grid Resilience through Real-Time Fault Detection and Remediation Using Advanced Hybrid Machine Learning Models,* 2023. [http://dx.doi.org/10.3390/su15108348]

[46] C. Alex Ezeigweneme, "Smart Grids in industrial paradigms: a review of progress, benefits, and maintenance implications: analyzing the role of smart grids in predictive maintenance and the integration of renewable energy sources, along with their overall impact on the industrial landscape", Engineering Science & Technology Journal, vol. 5, no. 1, Jan. 2024. [http://dx.doi.org/10.51594/estj.v5i1.719]

[47] K. Dasari, V.H. Raj, G. Nijhawan, R. Kalra, S. Pahwa, and D.S. Abdul-Zahra, "Integration of AI in distributed energy resource management for enhanced load balancing and grid stability".*E3S Web of Conferences.* EDP Sciences, 2024. [http://dx.doi.org/10.1051/e3sconf/202450503008]

[48] S.S. Patil, S.H. Patil, A.M. Pawar, M. Bewoor, and N.S. Patil, "Soft computing techniques for the integration of distributed energy resources (DERs)", *IJDCT,* vol. 8, no. 2, pp. 2455-7307, 2023.

[49] T. Lv, and Q. Ai, "Interactive energy management of networked microgrids-based active distribution system considering large-scale integration of renewable energy resources", *Appl. Energy,* vol. 163, pp. 408-422, 2016. [http://dx.doi.org/10.1016/j.apenergy.2015.10.179]

[50] P. S. Georgilakis, "Review of computational intelligence methods for local energy markets at the power distribution level to facilitate the integration of distributed energy resources: State-of-the-art and future research", J MDPI AG, Jan. 2020. [http://dx.doi.org/10.3390/en13010186]

[51] Y. Qiu, Y. Wang, Y. Tian, and Z. Chen, "Intelligent stability monitoring and improvement of grid-connected converter under weighted average control", *IET Smart Grid,* vol. 7, no. 6, pp. 776-788, 2024. [http://dx.doi.org/10.1049/stg2.12176]

[52] T. Singh, "Intelligent faultEdge: AI-driven fault-tolerant edge framework for smart grid monitoring in IoT", In: *2024 IEEE 12th International Conference on Intelligent Systems (IS),* IEEE, Aug. 2024, pp. 1–6. [http://dx.doi.org/10.1109/IS61756.2024.10705247]

[53] I.I. Ioannou, S. Javaid, V. Vassiliou, A. Pitsillides, and Y. Tan, "Applying an agent-based distributed AI framework to forecast power for the mini-grid stability", In: *2024 International Conference on Consumer Electronics - Taiwan (ICCE-Taiwan),* IEEE, Jul. 2024, pp. 255–256. [http://dx.doi.org/10.1109/ICCE-Taiwan62264.2024.10674231]

[54] K. Dasari, V. H. Raj, G. Nijhawan, R. Kalra, S. Pahwa, and D. S. Abdul-Zahra, "Integration of AI in distributed energy resource management for enhanced load balancing and grid stability", *E3S Web of Conferences,* vol. 505, p. 03008, Mar. 2024.
[http://dx.doi.org/10.1051/e3sconf/202450503008]

[55] F. Bano, M. Ayaz, D.Z. Baig, and S.M.H. Rizvi, "Intelligent Control Algorithms for Enhanced Frequency Stability in Single and Interconnected Power Systems", *Electronics (Basel),* vol. 13, no. 21, p. 4219, 2024.
[http://dx.doi.org/10.3390/electronics13214219]

[56] I. Alhamrouni, N.H. Abdul Kahar, M. Salem, M. Swadi, Y. Zahroui, D.J. Kadhim, F.A. Mohamed, and M. Alhuyi Nazari, "A comprehensive review on the role of artificial intelligence in power system stability, control, and protection: insights and future directions", *Appl. Sci. (Basel),* vol. 14, no. 14, p. 6214, 2024.
[http://dx.doi.org/10.3390/app14146214]

[57] F. Hayat, M. Adnan, S. Iqbal, and S.E. Gasim Mohamed, "Aperiodic small signal stability method for detection and mitigation of cascading failures in smart grids", *Results in Engineering,* vol. 23, p. 102661, 2024.
[http://dx.doi.org/10.1016/j.rineng.2024.102661]

[58] F.K. Karim, D.S. Khafaga, E-S.M. El-kenawy, M.M. Eid, A. Ibrahim, L. Abualigah, N. Khodadadi, and A.A. Abdelhamid, "Optimized LSTM for accurate smart grid stability prediction using a novel optimization algorithm", *Front. Energy Res.,* vol. 12, p. 1399464, 2024.
[http://dx.doi.org/10.3389/fenrg.2024.1399464]

[59] S. Hamad Khaleefah, S.A. Mostafa, S.S. Gunasekaran, U. Farooq Khattak, M. Ahmed Jubair, and R. Afyenni, "Optimizing smart power grid stability based on the prediction of a deep learning model", *JOIV : International Journal on Informatics Visualization,* vol. 8, no. 3, p. 1091, 2024.
[http://dx.doi.org/10.62527/joiv.8.2.2758]

[60] R. Derakhshani, L. Lankof, A. GhasemiNejad, and M. Zaresefat, "Artificial intelligence-driven assessment of salt caverns for underground hydrogen storage in Poland", *Sci. Rep.,* vol. 14, no. 1, p. 14246, 2024.
[http://dx.doi.org/10.1038/s41598-024-64020-9] [PMID: 38902291]

[61] G. Wang, Z. Luo, H.G. Desta, M. Chen, Y. Dong, and B. Lin, "AI-driven development of high-performance solid-state hydrogen storage", *Energy Reviews,* no. Mar, p. 100106, 2024.

[62] M. Nachtane, "An overview of the recent advances in composite materials and artificial intelligence for hydrogen storage vessels design", MDPI , Mar. 2023.
[http://dx.doi.org/10.3390/jcs7030119]

[63] K. Katterbauer, A. Qasim, A. Marsala, and A. Yousef, A data driven artificial intelligence framework for hydrogen production optimization in waterflooded hydrocarbon reservoir.*Day 4 Thu, November 18, 2021.* SPE, 2021.

[64] Y. Cao, H.A. Dhahad, S.G. Zare, N. Farouk, A.E. Anqi, A. Issakhov, and A. Raise, "Potential application of metal-organic frameworks (MOFs) for hydrogen storage: Simulation by artificial intelligent techniques", *Int. J. Hydrogen Energy,* vol. 46, no. 73, pp. 36336-36347, 2021.
[http://dx.doi.org/10.1016/j.ijhydene.2021.08.167]

[65] L. Wang, S. Feng, C. Zhang, X. Zhang, X. Liu, H. Gao, Z. Liu, R. Li, J. Wang, and X. Jin, "Artificial intelligence and high-throughput computational workflows empowering the fast screening of metal–organic frameworks for hydrogen storage", *ACS Appl. Mater. Interfaces,* vol. 16, no. 28, pp. 36444-36452, 2024.
[http://dx.doi.org/10.1021/acsami.4c06416] [PMID: 38963298]

[66] X. Geng, M. Zhu, and X. Che, "Optimized dispatching method of new energy hydrogen production power grid based on artificial intelligence", *International Conference on Machine Intelligence and Digital Applications,* ACM: New York, NY, USA, pp. 406-410, 2024.

[http://dx.doi.org/10.1145/3662739.3669987]

[67] H. Alaa Elden Abdel Sadek Gaffar, *The Role of Artificial Intelligence in Enhancing the Development of Sustainable Clean Hydrogen Industries: A Case Study of Scatec ASA in Egypt.* vol. 16, no. 1, pp. 302–332, Jan. 2025.
[http://dx.doi.org/10.21608/jces.2025.419473]

[68] K. Katterbauer, A. Al Shehri, A. Qasim, and A. Yousif, "Sustainable hydrogen production utilizing artificial intelligence – a McKee reservoir study", *84th EAGE Annual Conference & Exhibition,* European Association of Geoscientists & Engineers, pp. 1-5, 2023.
[http://dx.doi.org/10.3997/2214-4609.202310062]

[69] Q. Qerimi, and B.S. Sergi, "The case for global regulation of carbon capture and storage and artificial intelligence for climate change", *Int. J. Greenh. Gas Control,* vol. 120, p. 103757, 2022.
[http://dx.doi.org/10.1016/j.ijggc.2022.103757]

[70] K. Aliyon, F. Rajaee, and J. Ritvanen, "Use of artificial intelligence in reducing energy costs of a post-combustion carbon capture plant", *Energy,* vol. 278, p. 127834, 2023.
[http://dx.doi.org/10.1016/j.energy.2023.127834]

[71] X. Chen, X. Wu, and K.Y. Lee, "The mutual benefits of renewables and carbon capture: Achieved by an artificial intelligent scheduling strategy", *Energy Convers. Manage.,* vol. 233, p. 113856, 2021.
[http://dx.doi.org/10.1016/j.enconman.2021.113856]

[72] A. M. Nassef, "Improving CO2 absorption using artificial intelligence and modern optimization for a sustainable environment", *Sustainability (Switzerland),* vol. 15, no. 12, Jun. 2023.
[http://dx.doi.org/10.3390/su15129512]

[73] N. Sharma, U. Singh, and S.S. Mahapatra, "Prediction of cost and emission from Indian coal-fired power plants with CO2 capture and storage using artificial intelligence techniques", *Front. Energy,* vol. 13, no. 1, pp. 149-162, 2019.
[http://dx.doi.org/10.1007/s11708-017-0482-6]

[74] E. V. Kotov, "Carbon capture and storage optimization with machine learning using an ANN model", *E3S Web of Conferences,* vol. 588, p. 01003, Nov. 2024.
[http://dx.doi.org/10.1051/e3sconf/202458801003]

[75] P.K. Patro, A. Acquaye, R. Jayaraman, and K. Salah, "Blockchain, IoT, and AI-based framework for traceability in carbon capture utilization storage (CCUS) supply chain", *Proceedings of the 2024 6th Blockchain and Internet of Things Conference,* ACM: New York, NY, USA, pp. 67-73, 2024.
[http://dx.doi.org/10.1145/3688225.3688234]

[76] J. Sabeena, "Enhancing carbon capture, utilization, and storage (CCUS) through AI-enabled CNN and bayesian networks", *International Conference on Sustainable Communication Networks and Application, ICSCNA 2023 - Proceedings,* Institute of Electrical and Electronics Engineers Inc., pp. 1547-1551, 2023.
[http://dx.doi.org/10.1109/ICSCNA58489.2023.10370286]

[77] B. Chennakrishnan, A. Kumar, and R. Singh, "Using artificial intelligence to evaluate uncertainty for optimizing CCUS", *Fifth EAGE Global Energy Transition Conference & Exhibition (GET 2024),* European Association of Geoscientists & Engineers, pp. 1-5, 2024.
[http://dx.doi.org/10.3997/2214-4609.202421241]

[78] K. Javanroodi, A. T. D. Perera, T. Hong, and V. M. Nik, *Designing climate resilient energy systems in complex urban areas considering urban morphology: A technical review,* 2023.
[http://dx.doi.org/10.1016/j.adapen.2023.100155]

[79] M. H. U. Khan, "Applications of artificial intelligence in climate-resilient smart-crop breeding", MDPI, Oct. 2022.
[http://dx.doi.org/10.3390/ijms231911156]

[80] J. Nyangon, "Climate-proofing critical energy infrastructure: Smart grids, artificial intelligence, and

machine learning for power system resilience against extreme weather events", *J. Infrastruct. Syst.,* vol. 30, no. 1, p. 03124001, 2024.
[http://dx.doi.org/10.1061/JITSE4.ISENG-2375]

[81] S.C. Sakapaji, and J.J. Puthenkalam, "Harnessing AI for climate-resilient agriculture: Opportunities and challenges", *European Journal of Theoretical and Applied Sciences,* vol. 1, no. 6, pp. 1144-1158, 2023.
[http://dx.doi.org/10.59324/ejtas.2023.1(6).111]

[82] S. Singh, and M.K. Goyal, "Enhancing climate resilience in businesses: The role of artificial intelligence", *J. Clean. Prod.,* vol. 418, p. 138228, 2023.
[http://dx.doi.org/10.1016/j.jclepro.2023.138228]

[83] A. Bostani, *Adaptive energy management system for electric vehicle charging stations: Leveraging AI for real-time grid stabilization and efficiency. E3S Web of Conferences,* vol. 591, p. 04002, Nov. 2024.
[http://dx.doi.org/10.1051/e3sconf/202459104002]

[84] O.P. Malik, "Artificial intelligence techniques applied to adaptive power system stabilizer design".*In: 2006 IEEE Power Engineering Society General Meeting.* IEEE, 2006, pp. 1932-5517.
[http://dx.doi.org/10.1109/PES.2006.1709226]

[85] H. Alaa Elden Abdel Sadek Gaffar, "The role of artificial intelligence in enhancing the development of sustainable clean hydrogen industries: A case study of scatec ASA in Egypt", vol. 16, no. 1, pp. 302–332, Jan. 2025.
[http://dx.doi.org/10.21608/jces.2025.419473]

[86] K. Kwon, S. Lee, and S. Kim, "AI-based home energy management system considering energy efficiency and resident satisfaction", *IEEE Internet Things J.,* vol. 9, no. 2, pp. 1608-1621, 2022.
[http://dx.doi.org/10.1109/JIOT.2021.3104830]

[87] S. Afroosheh, K. Esapour, R. Khorram-Nia, and M. Karimi, "Reinforcement learning layout-based optimal energy management in smart home: AI-based approach", *IET Gener. Transm. Distrib.,* vol. 18, no. 15, pp. 2509-2520, 2024.
[http://dx.doi.org/10.1049/gtd2.13203]

[88] H.R.O. Rocha, I.H. Honorato, R. Fiorotti, W.C. Celeste, L.J. Silvestre, and J.A.L. Silva, "An artificial intelligence based scheduling algorithm for demand-side energy management in smart homes", *Appl. Energy,* vol. 282, p. 116145, 2021.
[http://dx.doi.org/10.1016/j.apenergy.2020.116145]

[89] H. Shareef, M.S. Ahmed, A. Mohamed, and E. Al Hassan, "Review on home energy management system considering demand responses, smart technologies, and intelligent controllers", *IEEE Access,* vol. 6, pp. 24498-24509, 2018.
[http://dx.doi.org/10.1109/ACCESS.2018.2831917]

[90] W. Hua, Y. Chen, M. Qadrdan, J. Jiang, H. Sun, and J. Wu, "Applications of blockchain and artificial intelligence technologies for enabling prosumers in smart grids: A review", Elsevier Ltd., Jun. 2022.
[http://dx.doi.org/10.1016/j.rser.2022.112308]

[91] A. Kumari, R. Gupta, S. Tanwar, and N. Kumar, "Blockchain and AI amalgamation for energy cloud management: Challenges, solutions, and future directions", *J. Parallel Distrib. Comput.,* vol. 143, pp. 148-166, 2020.
[http://dx.doi.org/10.1016/j.jpdc.2020.05.004]

[92] A. Esmat, M. de Vos, Y. Ghiassi-Farrokhfal, P. Palensky, and D. Epema, "A novel decentralized platform for peer-to-peer energy trading market with blockchain technology", *Appl. Energy,* vol. 282, p. 116123, 2021.
[http://dx.doi.org/10.1016/j.apenergy.2020.116123]

[93] G. Gao, C. Song, T.G.T.A. Bandara, M. Shen, F. Yang, W. Posdorfer, D. Tao, and Y. Wen, "FogChain: A blockchain-based peer-to-peer solar power trading system powered by fog AI", *IEEE Internet Things J.,* vol. 9, no. 7, pp. 5200-5215, 2022.

[http://dx.doi.org/10.1109/JIOT.2021.3109057]

[94] A. Boumaiza, and A. Sanfilippo, "AI for energy: A blockchain-based trading market", In: *IECON Proceedings (Industrial Electronics Conference),* IEEE Computer Society, pp. 2577-1647, Oct. 2022.

[95] J. Li, M. S. Herdem, J. Nathwani, and J. Z. Wen, "Methods and applications for Artificial Intelligence, Big Data, Internet of Things, and Blockchain in smart energy management", *Elsevier B.V.,* Jan. 2023. [http://dx.doi.org/10.1016/j.egyai.2022.100208]

[96] H. Shahinzadeh, S. Mohammadali Zanjani, J. Moradi, M.H. Fayaz-Dastgerdi, W. Yaici, and M. Benbouzid, "The transition toward merging big data analytics, IoT, and artificial intelligence with blockchain in transactive energy markets", *IEEE Global Energy Conference, GEC 2022,* Institute of Electrical and Electronics Engineers Inc., pp. 241-246, 2022. [http://dx.doi.org/10.1109/GEC55014.2022.9986604]

[97] L. Baklaga, "Synergizing AI and blockchain: Innovations in decentralized carbon markets for emission reduction through intelligent carbon credit trading", *Journal of Computer Science and Technology Studies,* vol. 6, no. 2, pp. 111-120, 2024. [http://dx.doi.org/10.32996/jcsts.2024.6.2.13]

[98] M. Zheng, H. Salim, T. Liu, R.A. Stewart, J. Lu, and S. Zhang, "Intelligence-assisted predesign for the sustainable recycling of lithium-ion batteries and beyond", *Energy Environ. Sci.,* vol. 14, no. 11, pp. 5801-5815, 2021. [http://dx.doi.org/10.1039/D1EE01812D]

[99] S. Ma, Q. Zhao, H. Wang, and X. Song, "Energy conservation and recycling transformation of clean energy heating based on artificial intelligence", *Int. J. Mater. Prod. Technol.,* vol. 67, no. 3/4, pp. 362-377, 2023. [http://dx.doi.org/10.1504/IJMPT.2023.136538]

[100] M. Fernandez, A. Faturahman, and N.A. Santoso, "Harnessing machine learning to optimize renewable energy utilization in waste recycling", *International Transactions on Education Technology (ITEE),* vol. 2, no. 2, pp. 173-182, 2024. [ITEE]. [http://dx.doi.org/10.33050/itee.v2i2.595]

[101] M. Johnson, A. Khatoon, and C. Fitzpatrick, "Application of AI and machine vision to improve battery detection and recovery in e-waste management", *2022 International Conference on Electrical, Computer, Communications and Mechatronics Engineering (ICECCME),* IEEE, pp. 1-6, 2022. [http://dx.doi.org/10.1109/ICECCME55909.2022.9988629]

[102] K.E. Bassey, A.R. Juliet, and A.O. Stephen, "AI-enhanced lifecycle assessment of renewable energy systems", *Engineering Science & Technology Journal,* vol. 5, no. 7, pp. 2082-2099, 2024. [http://dx.doi.org/10.51594/estj.v5i7.1254]

[103] K. Ukoba, K. O. Olatunji, E. Adeoye, T. C. Jen, and D. M. Madyira, "Optimizing renewable energy systems through artificial intelligence: Review and future prospects", *SAGE Publications Inc.,* Nov. 2024. [http://dx.doi.org/10.1177/0958305X241256293]

[104] J. Huang, and D.D. Koroteev, "Artificial intelligence for planning of energy and waste management", *Sustain. Energy Technol. Assess.,* vol. 47, p. 101426, 2021. [http://dx.doi.org/10.1016/j.seta.2021.101426]

[105] V. Melinda, T. Williams, J. Anderson, J.G. Davies, and C. Davis, "Enhancing waste-to-energy conversion efficiency and sustainability through advanced artificial intelligence integration", *International Transactions on Education Technology (ITEE),* vol. 2, no. 2, pp. 183-192, 2024. [ITEE]. [http://dx.doi.org/10.33050/itee.v2i2.597]

[106] D.S. Lee, S.T. Lee, Y.T. Chen, and P.Y. Su, "Artificial intelligence technique development for energy-efficient waste-to-energy: A case study of an incineration plant", *Case Stud. Therm. Eng.,* vol. 61, p. 105071, 2024. [http://dx.doi.org/10.1016/j.csite.2024.105071]

[107] J. Zhou, T. Shi, Q. Qian, C. He, and J. Ren, "Protocol for the design and accelerated optimization of a waste-to-energy system using AI tools", *STAR Protoc,* vol. 4, no. 4, Dec. 2023. [http://dx.doi.org/10.1016/j.xpro.2023.102685]

[108] T. Tabassum-Abbasi, T. Abbasi, P. Patnaik, B.M.J. Ali, and S.A. Abbasi, "Artificial intelligence–based optimization of a novel process for generating volatile fatty acid energy precursors from date palm waste", *Biomass Convers. Biorefin.,* vol. 14, no. 19, pp. 24583-24595, 2024. [http://dx.doi.org/10.1007/s13399-023-04812-7]

[109] S.R. Das, P.K. Ray, A.K. Sahoo, K.K. Singh, G. Dhiman, and A. Singh, "Artificial intelligence based grid connected inverters for power quality improvement in smart grid applications", *Comput. Electr. Eng.,* vol. 93, p. 107208, 2021. [http://dx.doi.org/10.1016/j.compeleceng.2021.107208]

[110] E. Esenogho, K. Djouani, and A.M. Kurien, "Integrating artificial intelligence internet of things and 5g for next-generation smartgrid: A survey of trends challenges and prospect", *IEEE Access,* vol. 10, pp. 4794-4831, 2022. [http://dx.doi.org/10.1109/ACCESS.2022.3140595]

[111] D.R. Chirra, "Secure data sharing in multi-cloud environments: A cryptographic framework for healthcare systems", *Revista De Inteligencia Artificial En Medicina,* vol. 15, no. 1, pp. 821-843, 2024. [AI for Medicine Health].

[112] S. Kaur, R. Kumar, K. Singh, and Y. Huang, "Leveraging artificial intelligence for enhanced sustainable energy management", *Journal of Sustainability for Energy,* vol. 3, no. 1, pp. 1-20, 2024. [http://dx.doi.org/10.56578/jse030101]

[113] Z. Fan, Z. Yan, and S. Wen, "Deep learning and artificial intelligence in sustainability: A review of SDGs, renewable energy, and environmental health", *Sustainability (Switzerland),* vol. 15, no. 18, Sep. 2023. [http://dx.doi.org/10.3390/su151813493]

[114] W. Shin, J. Han, and W. Rhee, "AI-assistance for predictive maintenance of renewable energy systems", *Energy,* vol. 221, p. 119775, 2021. [http://dx.doi.org/10.1016/j.energy.2021.119775]

[115] B.N. Alhasnawi, S.M.M. Almutoki, F.F.K. Hussain, A. Harrison, B. Bazooyar, M. Zanker, and V. Bureš, "A new methodology for reducing carbon emissions using multi-renewable energy systems and artificial intelligence", *Sustain Cities Soc.,* vol. 114, p. 105721, 2024. [http://dx.doi.org/10.1016/j.scs.2024.105721]

[116] F. Conte, F. D'Antoni, G. Natrella, and M. Merone, "A new hybrid AI optimal management method for renewable energy communities", *Energy and AI,* vol. 10, Nov. 2022. [http://dx.doi.org/10.1016/j.egyai.2022.100197]

[117] D. Shin, J. Lee, J. Son, Y. Yun, Y. Song, and J. Song, "Intelligent combustion control in waste-to-energy facilities: Enhancing efficiency and reducing emissions using AI and IoT", *Energies,* vol. 17, no. 18, p. 4634, 2024. [http://dx.doi.org/10.3390/en17184634]

[118] U. Soni, A. Roy, A. Verma, and V. Jain, *Forecasting municipal solid waste generation using artificial intelligence models - a case study in India,* 2019. [http://dx.doi.org/10.1007/s42452-018-0157-x]

[119] M.-L. How, and S.-M. Cheah, *Forging the future: Strategic approaches to quantum ai integration for industry transformation,* 2024. [http://dx.doi.org/10.3390/ai5010015]

CHAPTER 9

AI in Electrochemical Healthcare Devices

M.S. Sumitha[1] and **T.S Xavier**[1,*]

[1] *Centre for Advanced Materials Research, Department of Physics, Government College for Women, University of Kerala, Thiruvananthapuram, India*

Abstract: Artificial Intelligence (AI) is revolutionizing the design and application of electrochemical healthcare devices, enhancing their accuracy, efficacy, and customization. Traditionally used for diagnosis and monitoring, such as in glucose monitors and biosensors, these technologies are undergoing significant advancements driven by AI. Machine learning enables rapid processing of complex data from multiple sensors, improving decision-making, forecasting, and signal processing by reducing noise and enhancing sensitivity and precision. This ensures reliable outcomes and facilitates the identification of trends in patient data, accelerating disease detection and enabling personalized treatment protocols. When integrated with wearable electrochemical devices, AI algorithms enable continuous monitoring and real-time insights for patients and healthcare providers. AI-driven real-time data analysis further supports the development of adaptive systems capable of predicting and mitigating potential health risks before they escalate. Additionally, AI accelerates the innovation of electrochemical devices by simulating and optimizing electrochemical reactions, advancing material science and sensor design. Despite these benefits, challenges persist, including ensuring data privacy, interpreting complex AI models, addressing ethical concerns, and overcoming regulatory and integration barriers within healthcare systems. Over-reliance on large datasets and computational methods raises practical and ethical issues. Future efforts should focus on improving model transparency, establishing robust data governance frameworks, and fostering interdisciplinary collaboration to bridge technology and clinical practice. By addressing these challenges, the integration of AI with electrochemical healthcare devices has the potential to transform medical diagnostics and treatments, offering adaptable, patient-centric solutions while encouraging innovation and overcoming current limitations.

Keywords: Artificial Intelligence (AI), Biosensors, Cancer screening, Diagnostics, Early detection, Electrochemical devices, Glucose monitoring, Healthcare, Machine learning, Real-time detection.

* **Corresponding author Xavier T.S.**: Centre for Advanced Materials Research, Department of Physics, Government College for Women, University of Kerala, Thiruvananthapuram, India; E-mail: xavierkattukulam@gmail.com

Shreya Sharma, Peeyush Phogat, Ranjana Jha & Sukhvir Singh (Eds.)

INTRODUCTION TO ELECTROCHEMICAL HEALTHCARE DEVICES

Overview of Electrochemical Principles

Modern medical technology relies on electrochemical principles that enable accurate detection and monitoring of biological activity through the interaction of electrical energy and chemical reactions [1, 2]. Key components like electrodes, electrolytes, and transducers are essential, as they convert these electrochemical reactions into measurable electrical signals. Electrochemical technology has various applications in modern medicine, including gadgets like glucose monitors, wearable health trackers, implantable pacemakers, and neurostimulators [3, 4]. These systems are incredibly sensitive and specific in identifying crucial health markers. They work through processes such as oxidation-reduction reactions, ion exchange, and adsorption mechanisms to provide accurate and reliable readings. By harnessing these principles, modern medicine can offer advanced and precise diagnostic and monitoring tools that significantly improve patient care.

Electrochemical healthcare gadgets have improved their capabilities and influence through the use of Artificial Intelligence (AI) [5, 6]. Artificial intelligence algorithms have enhanced signal processing, enabled real-time data analysis, and diminished noise interference, thereby yielding diagnostic results that are more precise and dependable. Machine learning algorithms can discern complex patterns in electrochemical signals, enabling predictive analytics and early disease identification [7, 8]. AI is revolutionizing personalized healthcare through the automation of processes such as calibration and maintenance, in addition to offering treatment recommendations derived from data obtained from electrochemical sensors. The collaboration of electrochemical technology and artificial intelligence is initiating a new epoch of precision medicine. Through sophisticated algorithms, AI has enhanced signal processing, facilitated real-time data analysis, and reduced noise interference, resulting in diagnostic outcomes that are both exceptionally accurate and reliable.

While electrochemical devices powered by artificial intelligence hold incredible potential, their development continues to face several challenges. Major challenges include the necessity for resilient, biocompatible materials that are manageable, as well as the requirement to standardize manufacturing methods and efficiently handle extensive datasets [9]. Future progress will be achievable through breakthroughs in non-invasive monitoring devices, improved artificial intelligence algorithms, and hybrid sensing technologies [10, 11]. These technologies provide the potential to transform healthcare through their portability, sophisticated AI capabilities, and economic efficiency. They provide accessible, individualised care, instantaneous diagnostic capabilities, and a variety of supplementary services.

Current Applications in Healthcare

AI has significantly transformed the development and optimization of electrochemical devices in healthcare, particularly in diagnostics and therapeutics [12, 13]. A major breakthrough is the integration of AI with biosensors, enhancing the detection and monitoring of biomolecules. Electrochemical biosensors, powered by AI algorithms, can analyze complex datasets in real-time, enabling rapid and precise diagnostics for diseases such as diabetes, cancer, and infectious diseases [14]. AI-powered platforms can optimize electrode materials, boost sensor sensitivity, and refine signal processing, resulting in better performance and the miniaturization of point-of-care testing devices. AI-enabled glucometers and wearable electrochemical sensors offer continuous monitoring, making personalized and timely medical care possible.

One important application lies in drug delivery systems, where AI models predict and control the performance of electrochemical devices to achieve accurate and effective therapeutic outcomes. Smart electrochemical drug delivery systems utilize AI to adjust parameters like pH, voltage, and current, ensuring precise drug release based on patient-specific data [15]. Additionally, AI aids in designing advanced materials for these devices, such as nanostructured electrodes and biocompatible coatings, which enhance device functionality and longevity [16]. These innovations not only improve patient outcomes but also reduce healthcare costs by streamlining treatments and minimizing the need for invasive procedures [17]. The combination of AI and electrochemical technologies is reshaping healthcare by enabling the creation of smarter, more efficient, and reliable medical devices. Fig. (**1**) schematically represents applications of AI in various aspects of healthcare [18].

THE ROLE OF ARTIFICIAL INTELLIGENCE IN HEALTHCARE

Historical Perspectives

Innovative ideas, advanced technologies, and an expanding range of applications have driven the evolution of AI. Early philosophical explorations of the mind and cognition provided the computational reasoning foundation for AI. Claude Shannon, John McCarthy, and Marvin Minsky were among the pioneers who formally utilized the term "artificial intelligence" at the 1956 Dartmouth Conference to signify the aim of creating robots with cognitive capabilities akin to those of humans [19, 20]. The emergence of symbolic reasoning and early programming languages like LISP significantly contributed to the progression of AI during this period.

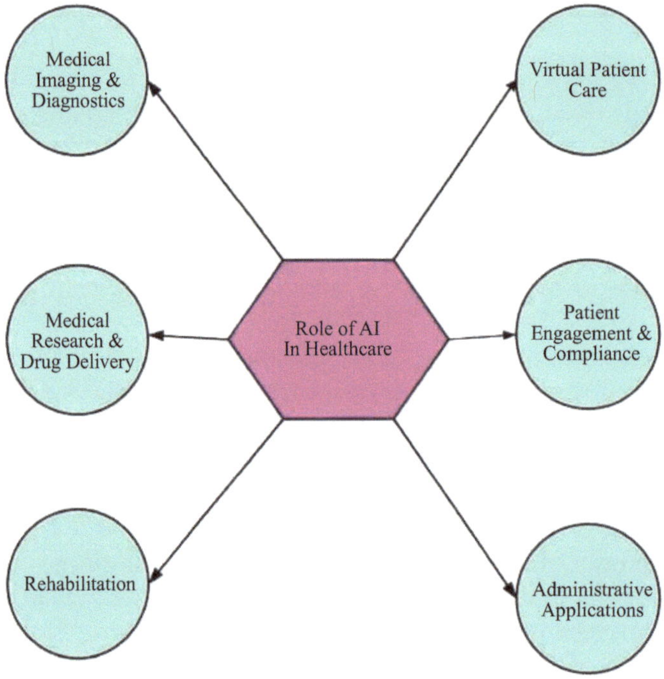

Fig. (1). Schematic illustration of various applications of AI in healthcare[Reprinted with permission from [18]. Copyright (2023) by the authors. Licensee MDPI, Basel, Switzerland.

The advancement of artificial intelligence (AI) has occurred in surges interspersed with phases of standstill, known as "AI winters," caused by both overzealous predictions and actual limitations in current technology [21, 22]. The advent of rule-based expert systems in the 1970s and 1980s demonstrated the early accomplishments of AI in domains like logistics and medical diagnostics [23]. The technology's restricted processing capacity and rigidity limited its additional applicability. The advent of machine learning in the 1990s was a notable progression, allowing AI systems to derive insights from data patterns rather than relying exclusively on predetermined rules [24, 25]. With advancements in processing power and the growing availability of large datasets, Artificial Intelligence (AI) is becoming an integral part of modern technology.

Evolution and Impact

The advancements in processing power, machine learning, and big data analytics have propelled the transformative emergence of AI in the healthcare industry.

MYCIN, an artificial intelligence system created in the 1970s for the identification of bacterial infections, was among the first rule-based systems employed for diagnosis and treatment planning [26, 27]. While these systems demonstrated the potential of AI, they were constrained by strict limitations and lacked the flexibility to adapt to new situations. The advent of machine learning in the 1990s marked a significant milestone, allowing AI systems to autonomously analyze intricate medical data and discern patterns [28 - 30]. During this decade, radiographic image identification systems and patient management predictive analytics frameworks underwent substantial developments. The integration of AI with EHRs has enhanced healthcare workflows, facilitating more individualized therapy [31, 32].

Artificial intelligence is currently influencing various sectors of healthcare, including diagnosis, treatment, drug development, and patient monitoring. Currently, deep learning algorithms surpass human experts in diagnosing diseases like cancer and cardiovascular conditions by analyzing medical images [33, 34]. AI-driven solutions improve drug discovery by identifying promising molecules and predicting therapeutic efficacy, hence reducing development delays and expenses. Patients can proficiently manage their chronic diseases with AI-enabled wearable devices and telemedicine systems that provide real-time health monitoring and predictive analytics [35, 36]. AI enhances healthcare accessibility and resilience by optimizing resource allocation and predicting illness outbreaks. It is set to transform medicine in the future years by enhancing outcomes, reducing expenses, and democratizing healthcare worldwide.

INTEGRATING AI INTO ELECTROCHEMICAL DEVICES

Technological Innovations-AI-Enhanced Imaging Tools and Predictive Analytics

The integration of AI models has become prevalent in radiology, enabling the rapid analysis of extensive medical images [37, 38]. AI can identify minute tumors in mammograms that human observers may overlook [39, 40]. These instruments not only accelerate the commencement of treatment but also enhance diagnostic accuracy. This domain is characterized by systems such as IBM Watson Health and Google's DeepMind [41, 42]. In predictive analytics, AI employs patient data (*e.g.*, electronic health records, genetic information) to evaluate the probability of diseases such as diabetes and cardiovascular disorders [43, 44]. Thus, healthcare professionals can transition from reactive to proactive care by employing preventative strategies. Fig. (**2**) schematically illustrates the AI-assisted personalized treatment and Table **1** depicts the applications of AI in electrochemical healthcare devices [45].

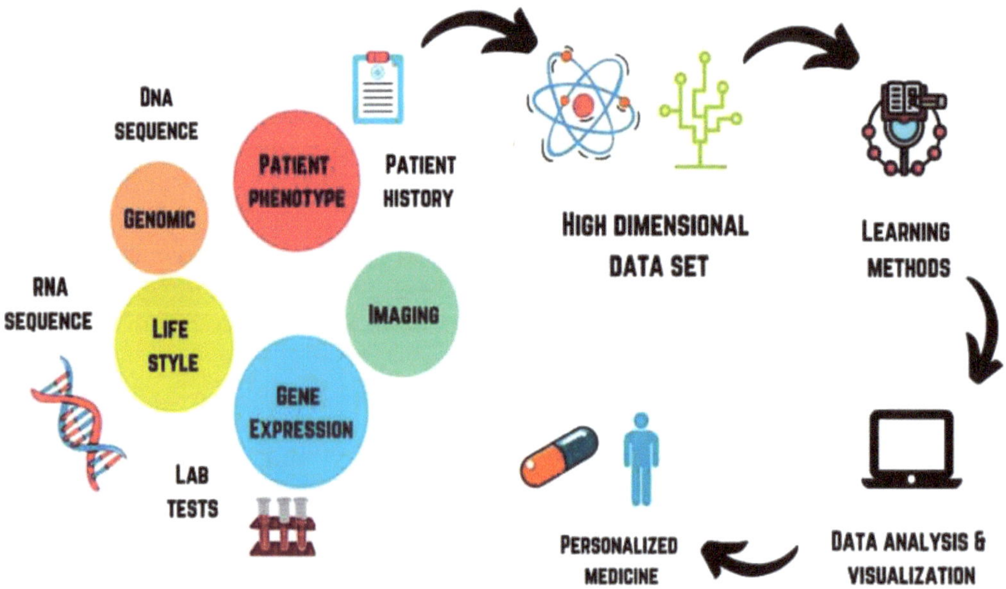

Fig. (2). Schematic illustration of AI-assisted personalized treatment. Reprinted with permission from S. K. Bhattamisra, P. Banerjee, P. Gupta, J. Mayuren, S. Patra, and M. Candasamy, "Artificial Intelligence in Pharmaceutical and Healthcare Research," Big Data and Cognitive Computing, volume 7, no. 1, 2023, doi: 10.3390/bdcc7010010. Copyright (2023) by the authors. Licensee MDPI, Basel, Switzerland.] [45]

Table 1. Applications of AI in electrochemical health devices.

Application	Description	AI Role	Examples	References
Disease Diagnosis	Early detection and diagnosis of diseases using biosensors.	Analyzing complex sensor data to detect anomalies.	Glucose monitors, cancer biomarkers.	[46 - 48]
Real-Time Monitoring	Continuous tracking of vital signs and health metrics through wearable devices.	Processing and visualizing real-time data streams.	Wearable ECG or glucose sensors.	[49, 50]
Predictive Healthcare	Forecasting potential health issues before symptoms escalate.	Predicting trends from historical and real-time data.	AI-driven preventive health systems.	[51, 52]
Device Development	Accelerating the design and optimization of novel sensors and materials.	Simulating and optimizing electrochemical reactions.	New electrochemical biosensors.	[53, 54]
Personalized Treatment	Tailoring treatment protocols based on patient-specific data.	Identifying correlations in patient datasets.	Drug response monitoring devices.	[55, 56]

Personalized Medicine- Precision Treatment and Drug Development

AI integrates diverse data sources, such as genetics, proteomics, and environmental factors, to develop precisely focused medicines [57, 58]. AI algorithms can identify the most effective chemotherapy medicines depending on a patient's genetic mutations [59, 60]. Traditional drug development is an extended procedure; however, artificial intelligence significantly expedites it by predicting molecular interactions with diseases [61, 62]. Companies like Insilico Medicine utilize AI to identify therapeutic possibilities, accelerating the transition from research to clinical trials [63, 64].

Telemedicine and Virtual Health Assistants- Chatbots, Virtual Assistants and 13Remote Monitoring

AI-driven platforms such as Babylon Health and Woebot offer round-the-clock support for non-urgent inquiries. These solutions alleviate the workload of healthcare providers while guaranteeing patients prompt access to information. AI-integrated wearables, such as Fitbits and Continuous Glucose Monitors (CGMs), provide real-time health data to healthcare professionals. These advanced devices, equipped with AI, notify both patients and doctors about potential health risks, like irregular heartbeats or dangerously low blood sugar, helping to catch critical changes early and prevent serious complications.

Surgical Robots and Automation-AI-Assisted Surgery

Robotic systems like the da Vinci Surgical System use advanced technology to enhance the precision of surgeries [65]. They help surgeons perform delicate, long procedures, such as minimally invasive heart surgeries, with greater accuracy by minimizing tremors [66]. The study by Bertelsen *et al.* reviews the current state of surgical robotics for spinal interventions, identifying 18 robots, including five commercially available systems and several research prototypes. Although spinal robotic surgery is still in its early stages, it holds significant potential for future advancements [67]. The article by Runciman *et al.* presents hydraulically actuated soft robotic actuators designed for Minimally Invasive Surgery (MIS), capable of precise open-loop positioning and significant force exertion. The actuators demonstrate repeatability with Root Mean Square Error (RMSE) values as low as 0.350 mm and hysteresis of up to 0.958 mm in various configurations. The system, which uses soft actuators that transition from low to high volume and stiffness, shows potential for use in MIS by offering flexibility, low-profile design, and controllability, as demonstrated by a successful circle tracing task [68].

Mental Health and Neurology=AI in Mental Health Care and Brain-computer Interfaces (BCIs)

Artificial intelligence systems are employed to evaluate language, tone, and facial expressions to detect indicators of mental health issues. Platforms such as Wysa provide therapy utilising Natural Language Processing (NLP) and cognitive behavioural methodologies [66]. Moreover, artificial intelligence-driven Brain-Computer Interfaces (BCIs) interpret neural impulses, allowing individuals with paralysis to operate prosthetic limbs or communicate through specialised devices [69]. As AI advances, these interfaces are increasingly dependable and customizable, enabling users to address their own needs more efficiently.

Disease Prediction and Epidemiology-Pandemic Management and Early Warning Systems

Throughout the COVID-19 pandemic, artificial intelligence was important in employing predictive models to pinpoint virus hotspots and optimize vaccination distribution [70]. Instruments such as BlueDot detected the outbreak weeks before the issuing of formal global alerts [71]. Through the analysis of data from diverse sources, such as social media and medical records, AI facilitated the prediction of disease epidemics, allowing for expedited interventions. AI forecasted dengue epidemics in South America by analyzing climate and population density patterns, facilitating early intervention and enhanced preparedness [72].

Health Record Management-Artificial Intelligence in Electronic Health Records (EHRs) and Data Analysis for Decision Support

The integration of AI into normal tasks such as medical coding and data entry diminishes the likelihood of errors. Advanced systems like Nuance's Dragon Medical One allow physicians to voice their reports, eliminating the necessity for human data entry [73]. AI utilizes patterns in data and Electronic Health Records (EHRs) to enhance clinical decision-making, including identifying potential drug interactions and suggesting diagnostic tests [73].

Patient Experience Enhancement-Personalized Patient Engagement and Enhanced Accessibility

Healthcare tools are made to fit the reading level and culture of each patient. This makes it easier for them to understand and follow medical advice. Assistive technologies such as speech-to-text and text-to-speech applications enhance accessibility for individuals with disabilities, hence fostering inclusion [74]. Apps like Seeing AI help people who are blind or visually impaired move around hospitals more freely, which makes it easier for them to get care [75].

METHODOLOGIES AND APPROACHES

Machine Learning (ML) Algorithms

Supervised Learning

These algorithms are trained on annotated datasets that exhibit defined input-output relationships [76]. Machine learning models are developed to assess electrochemical responses from glucose oxidase-based sensors in glucose monitoring, correlating these signals with blood glucose levels [77, 78]. Prevalent approaches include Support Vector Machines (SVMs) for detecting sensor outputs and decision trees for associating input data with certain health problems, such as diabetes or hyperglycemia [79, 80].

Unsupervised Learning

Unsupervised machine learning is employed to reveal latent patterns in electrochemical data without pre-existing classifications [81, 82]. Clustering algorithms, such as k-means, can categorize electrochemical responses into classifications (*e.g.*, normal *versus* pathological levels) based on their characteristics.

Reinforcement Learning

Reinforcement learning systems ascertain optimal actions *via* trial and error, influenced by rewards or punishments [83, 84]. In electrochemical drug delivery systems, reinforcement learning algorithms adjust the medication release rate according to real-time sensor data inputs.

Deep Learning Models

- ***Convolutional Neural Networks (CNNs):*** Impedance maps and various types of electrochemical imaging data are especially compatible with the spatial data analysis functionalities of Convolutional Neural Networks (CNNs) [85, 86]. By examining variations in impedance, they may identify precise areas of inflamed or infected tissue.
- ***Recurrent Neural Networks (RNNs):*** In the realm of sequential data, Recurrent Neural Networks (RNNs), especially Long Short-Term Memory (LSTM) networks, excel [87, 88]. Lactate and oxygen sensors integrated into wearable technology are components of continuous monitoring devices currently undergoing a time-series data analysis [88, 89].
- ***Autoencoders:*** These neural networks facilitate feature extraction and mitigate noise in intricate datasets. Autoencoders can extract essential features associated

with specific biomarkers from voltammetry data acquired from multi-analyte sensors [90].

Data Fusion Techniques and Predictive Modeling, and Anomaly Detection

- Data fusion is the integration of information from various sensors or biomarkers to construct a holistic health profile. Electrochemical data from a glucose sensor can be amalgamated with electrocardiogram (ECG) data to improve the understanding of the correlation between blood glucose levels and cardiovascular health [91, 92]. Techniques like Bayesian inference or neural network-based fusion ensure that the combined data provide more reliable diagnostic or therapeutic insights than individual sensors alone [93, 94].
- AI models predict health trends by analyzing historical data. For instance, predictive algorithms can anticipate glucose levels in the forthcoming hours, assisting diabetic patients in managing their food or medicine [95, 96]. Anomaly detection methods, such as isolation forests, recognize departures from predefined patterns in real time [97]. A sudden increase in lactate levels identified by a biosensor may signify tissue hypoxia, necessitating prompt medical intervention.

Electrochemical Signal Processing

- ***Noise Filtering:*** Electrochemical sensors frequently experience interference from external variables such as temperature, humidity, and competing ions. AI models, including wavelet transformations and Kalman filters, facilitate the elimination of noise from raw signals, ensuring precise measurements [98].
- ***Feature Extraction:*** Algorithms analyze cyclic voltammetry curves and other intricate electrochemical data to discover relevant biomarkers [99]. AI can enhance the distinction of attributes associated with glucose, uric acid, and cholesterol in multi-analyte detection [100, 101].

Edge AI for Wearable Devices

- Edge AI facilitates real-time data processing by deploying AI algorithms directly on wearable devices, eliminating the necessity for cloud access [102, 103]. Continuous glucose monitors employing artificial intelligence models can diminish delay by locally processing data and delivering prompt responses [104]. Devices are engineered for prolonged utilization without necessitating frequent battery replacements by utilizing energy-efficient technology, such as TinyM [105, 106].

Integration with Internet of Things (IoT), Biosensor Calibration, and Optimization

- Electrochemical devices facilitated by the Internet of Things (IoT) transmit data in real time to cloud platforms for sophisticated analysis [107, 108]. A wearable device tracks electrolytes and hydration, relaying information through a smartphone application [109, 110]. IoT networks enable AI to concurrently monitor and evaluate the health state of multiple patients in a medical setting by integrating diverse sensors with centralized systems [111, 112].
- For electrochemical biosensors to maintain their accuracy, calibration is a continuing activity. This process is now entirely automated due to AI. Models automatically adjust the sensitivity of the sensors in response to changes in environmental variables like pH or temperature [113, 114]. To increase the sensor's dependability and lifespan, a self-calibrating AI system might detect when it's drifting and immediately fix it [115, 116].

Hybrid Models

- The integration of artificial intelligence-based data analytics with physics-based electrochemical reaction simulations produces hybrid models [117, 118]. Glucose sensors that utilize hybrid models to evaluate real-time sensor data employ AI to simulate enzyme-substrate interactions [119]. Incorporating physical constraints and domain knowledge into AI systems improves predictive accuracy.

Personalized Health Management and Explainable AI (XAI)

- Advancements in artificial intelligence have enabled electrochemical devices to customize themselves for certain health needs [120, 121]. A hydration monitoring sensor worn by the user can modify its sensitivity based on varying activity levels and environmental conditions, such as an increase in the user's body temperature during physical exertion. Tailored AI input, including insulin pump dosage suggestions, enhances health outcomes and mitigates problems [122, 123].
- In electrochemical health devices, XAI guarantees that the decision-making processes of AI systems are transparent and comprehensible [124, 125]. An AI software that detects abnormal blood pH levels can correlate them with particular alterations in electrochemical signaling to improve the understanding of its predictions [126]. This depends on obtaining regulatory approval and fostering confidence among healthcare practitioners and patients.

APPLICATIONS

Diabetes Management and Glucose Monitoring

Continuous Glucose Monitors (CGMs) featuring AI capabilities, such as those manufactured by Abbott or Dexcom, can monitor blood glucose levels in real time [127]. To facilitate glycemic management, AI examines these parameters for patterns and trends. Machine learning algorithms can forecast variations in blood glucose levels by leveraging historical trends, dietary data, and physical activity metrics. These predictions prompt clients to implement strategies to avert potentially harmful fluctuations in glucose levels. AI technologies can improve safety for individuals with Type 1 diabetes by delivering real-time notifications to patients or caregivers regarding dangerously low glucose levels [128]. Insulin pumps integrated with continuous glucose monitors, powered by artificial intelligence, form a closed-loop system. These devices emulate pancreatic function by autonomously calculating and administering insulin amounts. AI evaluates variables including insulin sensitivity, physical activity, and carbohydrate consumption to provide accurate insulin dosages [129]. By analyzing daily patterns, AI systems can optimize insulin supply, granting patients improved control and reducing their burden. Fig. (**3**) schematically illustrates a smart glucose monitoring system for a diabetic patient [46].

AI algorithms can predict postprandial glucose levels based on the type and amount of food ingested [130]. As a result, individuals may modify their insulin dosages or food regimens as necessary. AI analyzes past glucose data to predict HbA1c trends, enabling proactive modifications to treatment procedures [131]. AI assesses the influence of stress, sleep, and exercise on glucose levels by integrating data from wearable sensors. Employ an AI-powered mobile application like MySugr or BlueStar to improve glycemic control with personalized food and activity suggestions [132]. Natural Language Processing (NLP) empowers virtual assistants to encourage patients to comply with their prescription regimens and adopt healthy lifestyle changes. The integration of CGM data with telemedicine systems enhances AI algorithms, hence advancing remote patient monitoring by healthcare practitioners [133]. AI analyzes glucose data patterns and generates concise summaries to aid clinicians in making informed decisions during virtual consultations. It examines data from several patients to discern trends and enhance treatment procedures for certain groups. Also, it improves the precision of non-invasive sensors through optical or bioimpedance techniques, making finger-prick testing redundant. For effective diabetes care, AI integrates glucose sensor data with other physiological factors such as heart rate [134]. The integration of AI models into wearable devices allows consumers to receive real-time input without reliance on internet connectivity. It improves the accessibility and engagement of diabetic applications by personalizing the user experience according to individual preferences. The identification of diabetes biomarkers by AI facilitates the creation of innovative medications aimed at these indicators [135]. AI can improve the efficacy of clinical trials for diabetic treatments by accurately selecting suitable individuals.

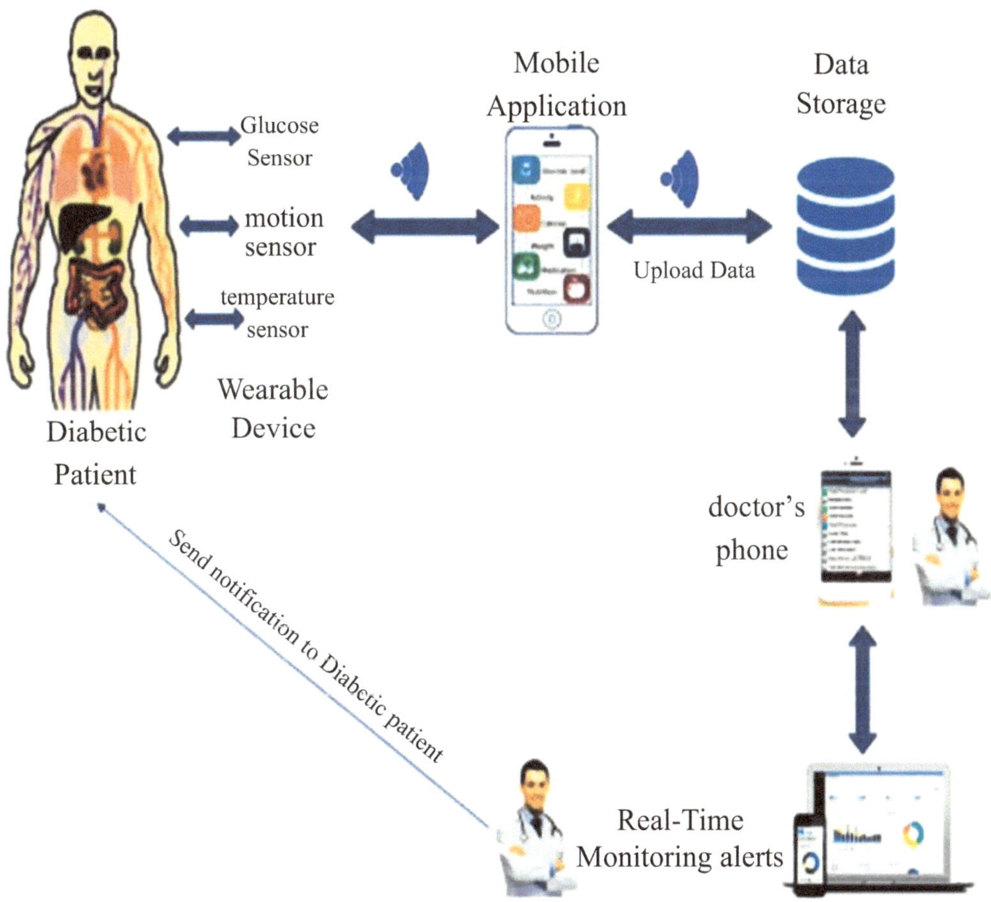

Fig. (3). Schematic illustration of a smart glucose monitoring system. Reprinted with permission from ref. [46]. Copyright (2020) by the authors. Licensee MDPI, Basel, Switzerland.

Electrochemical Sensors for Cardiac Health

Monitoring of cardiac health is being greatly improved by the combination of electrochemical sensors and AI. This progress is chiefly attributable to AI's capacity for non-invasive, real-time diagnoses, ongoing monitoring, and personalized therapy options. Electrochemical sensors integrated with AI can proficiently analyze data and detect biomarkers linked to cardiovascular illnesses, such as troponins, lactate, and cholesterol. Electrochemical sensors can identify specific cardiac biomarkers in biological fluids, like saliva, perspiration, or blood [136, 137]. Common biomarkers are essential for the diagnosis and monitoring of various health disorders. Troponin is an essential biomarker utilized for the identification of myocardial infarction, offering critical insights into cardiac damage [138]. Lactate levels are frequently measured to evaluate tissue oxygenation and heart strain, acting as a marker of physiological discomfort or metabolic dysregulation [139]. Cholesterol levels and LDL/HDL ratios are established indicators of cardiovascular disease risk, providing insights into lipid metabolism and the possible development of atherosclerosis [140]. These biomarkers jointly empower healthcare providers to make informed clinical decisions and enhance patient management techniques.

Sensors employ electrochemical methods, such as voltammetry, amperometry, and impedance spectroscopy, to quantify biomarker concentrations [141]. Ideal for subtle, continuous surveillance when utilized as a smartwatch or a patch. AI analyses unrefined sensor data, eliminating noise to enhance data precision. Artificial intelligence can identify arrhythmias and ischaemia by evaluating patterns in electrochemical data. Models can predict the likelihood of future cardiac events by analyzing trends in biomarker levels and physiological data. AI-powered wearable electrochemical sensors incessantly track biomarkers, such as potassium and lactate, notifying users of possible issues like heart failure or arrhythmias. When critical thresholds are surpassed, AI systems alert users and healthcare professionals to facilitate a timely response. It can enhance diagnosis accuracy by amalgamating data from electrochemical sensors with additional monitoring techniques, such as electrocardiograms or pulse oximetry [142]. Myocardial infarction is strongly indicated by alterations in troponin levels alongside abnormal ECG patterns. A detailed cardiovascular risk profile is produced by a combination of sensors that track glucose, lactate, and cholesterol levels, alongside artificial intelligence to identify correlations. Fig. (**4**) schematically illustrates the AI-assisted early diagnosis of ECG arrhythmia in the healthcare system [49].

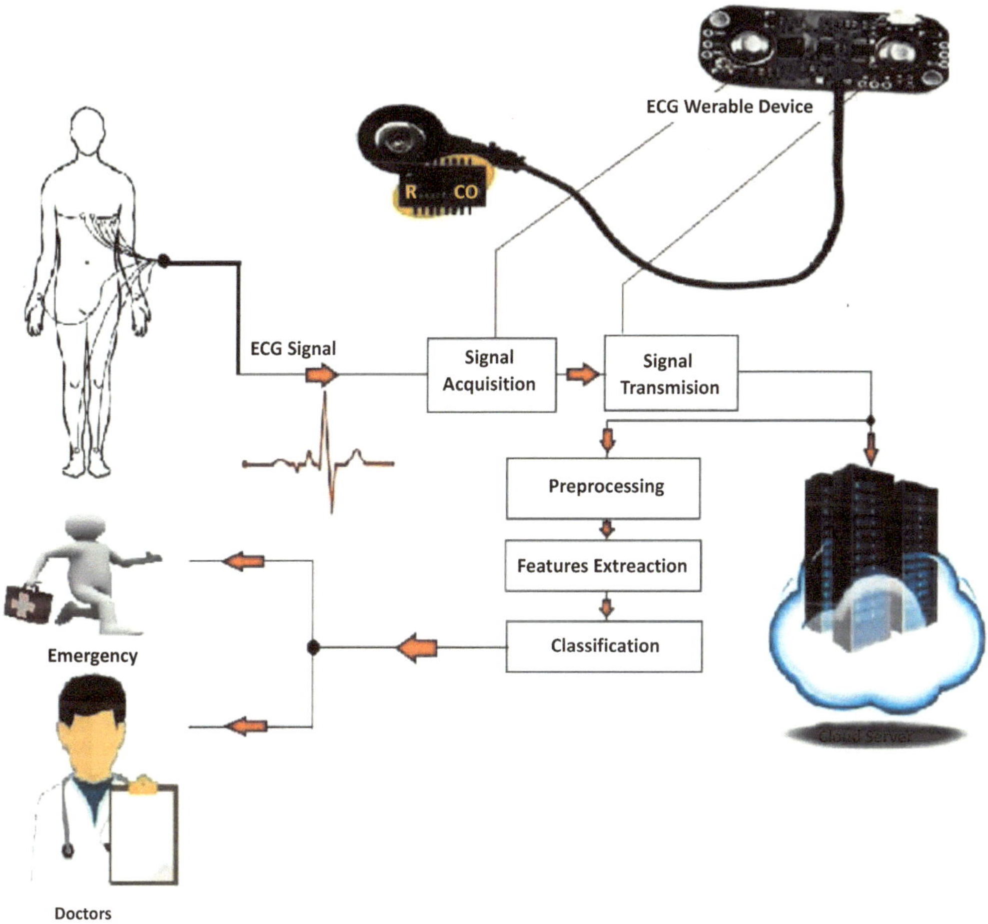

Fig. (4). Schematic illustration of AI-assisted early detection of cardiac healthcare system [Reprinted with permission from [49]. Copyright (2023) by the authors. Licensee MDPI, Basel, Switzerland.

In emergencies, portable equipment with electrochemical sensors can swiftly evaluate cardiac biomarkers, such as troponin levels. Artificial intelligence-driven algorithms can rapidly analyze POCT data, enabling physicians to manage cardiac episodes more effectively. AI utilizes data from electrochemical sensors and individual health profiles to generate treatment and lifestyle suggestions. AI employs real-time data to adjust treatment protocols, whereas electrochemical sensors evaluate the impact of cardiac medications, including statins [143]. AI techniques, including wavelet transforms and Kalman filters, mitigate signal aberrations and ensure precise electrochemical measurements. Machine learning models are employed to analyze complex voltammetry or impedance data, enhancing the precision of biomarker discovery by identifying critical characteristics. Pacemakers and defibrillators employ electrochemical sensors to evaluate cardiac biomarkers and battery longevity. AI may predict when a gadget malfunctions or requires maintenance, ensuring uninterrupted performance. An alternative to blood testing that is non-invasive, utilizing electrochemical sensors to identify cardiac biomarkers in sweat [144]. AI improves signal processing to distinguish biomarkers from non-biomarkers. The use of AI-powered saliva sensors represents a suitable non-invasive method for monitoring cardiac biomarkers [145, 146]. To improve public health initiatives, AI collects data from electrochemical sensors and identifies trends in cardiovascular health among populations. It augments research by utilizing sensor data to evaluate the impact of cardiovascular drugs in clinical trials.

DATA ANALYTICS AND MACHINE LEARNING IN ELECTROCHEMICAL DEVICES

Sensor measurements are crucial for electrochemical devices to get data. Sensors provide real-time monitoring of parameters including temperature, pressure, current, and voltage in systems such as supercapacitors, fuel cells, and batteries. Techniques like as impedance spectroscopy, potentiometry, and amperometry are commonly utilized in these studies because they offer continuous and accurate data, essential for system optimization and performance evaluation [147]. Electrochemical measurements are an essential aspect of data collecting, in conjunction with sensor data. Data obtained from chronoamperometry, chronopotentiometry, Electrochemical Impedance Spectroscopy (EIS), and Cyclic Voltammetry (CV) clarify charge/discharge cycles, reaction kinetics, and diverse electrochemical characteristics. This data is crucial for comprehending the functionality and effectiveness of devices.

In the evaluation of electrochemical devices, environmental data is crucial [148]. The device's performance can be significantly affected by factors such as humidity, temperature, and air pressure. Through the analysis of these data and the correlation of environmental variables with device performance, researchers can improve the development of systems that demonstrate reliable functioning in varied situations. The examination of electrochemical reaction behavior requires kinetic data and impedance spectroscopy. The progress of predictive models and the improvement of device designs rely on these observations, as they clarify reaction mechanisms and material properties. When analyzed by machine learning algorithms, this data can reveal previously overlooked tendencies, promoting data-driven progress in electrochemical technology [149]. To promote electrochemical device research, guarantee reliable performance, and propel future innovations in sensor and energy storage technologies, it is crucial to gather and manage this varied information.

Machine Learning Algorithms and Predictive Models

ML is transforming the healthcare sector by facilitating more precise diagnoses, enhanced treatment strategies, and individualized medicine. Integrating predictive models and machine learning algorithms into healthcare systems improves patient outcomes by enabling early diagnosis, risk assessment, decision-making, and integration [150]. ML algorithms can analyze medical imaging, genetic data, or patient records to aid in the diagnosis of diseases, including cancer, diabetes, cardiovascular issues, and neurological conditions [151]. Machine learning enhances proactive healthcare management by forecasting disease progression, patient outcomes, and the likelihood of developing specific illnesses. For example, it can be used to assess the probability of postoperative readmission or the development of chronic diseases like diabetes. Machine learning can improve medication effectiveness and minimize bad effects by evaluating patient data, including genetic information, and tailoring treatment strategies for individual patients [152]. Pharmacogenomics uses machine learning to forecast the interaction between a person's genetic makeup and a pharmaceutical agent.

Machine learning models can aid healthcare providers in making evidence-based decisions concerning diagnosis, treatment, and patient management. Machine learning algorithms can assess a patient's symptoms and medical history to propose possible diagnoses and treatment alternatives. Medical image analysis frequently uses machine learning, especially deep learning, to diagnose conditions such as cancers, fractures, or neurological diseases. Convolutional Neural Networks (CNNs) are employed to detect patterns in X-rays, MRIs, and CT scans for diagnosing diseases such as lung cancer and brain tumors [153]. Machine learning can examine large information included in electronic health records to discern trends, risk factors, and appropriate treatments. Early intervention in chronic diseases can be enhanced by identifying high-risk patients through historical data analysis. Machine learning algorithms are utilized to determine the most effective treatment alternatives based on data from clinical trials, patient results, and medical literature. Fig. (**5**) schematically illustrates some of the AI learning models/tools used in the pharmaceutical industry [119].

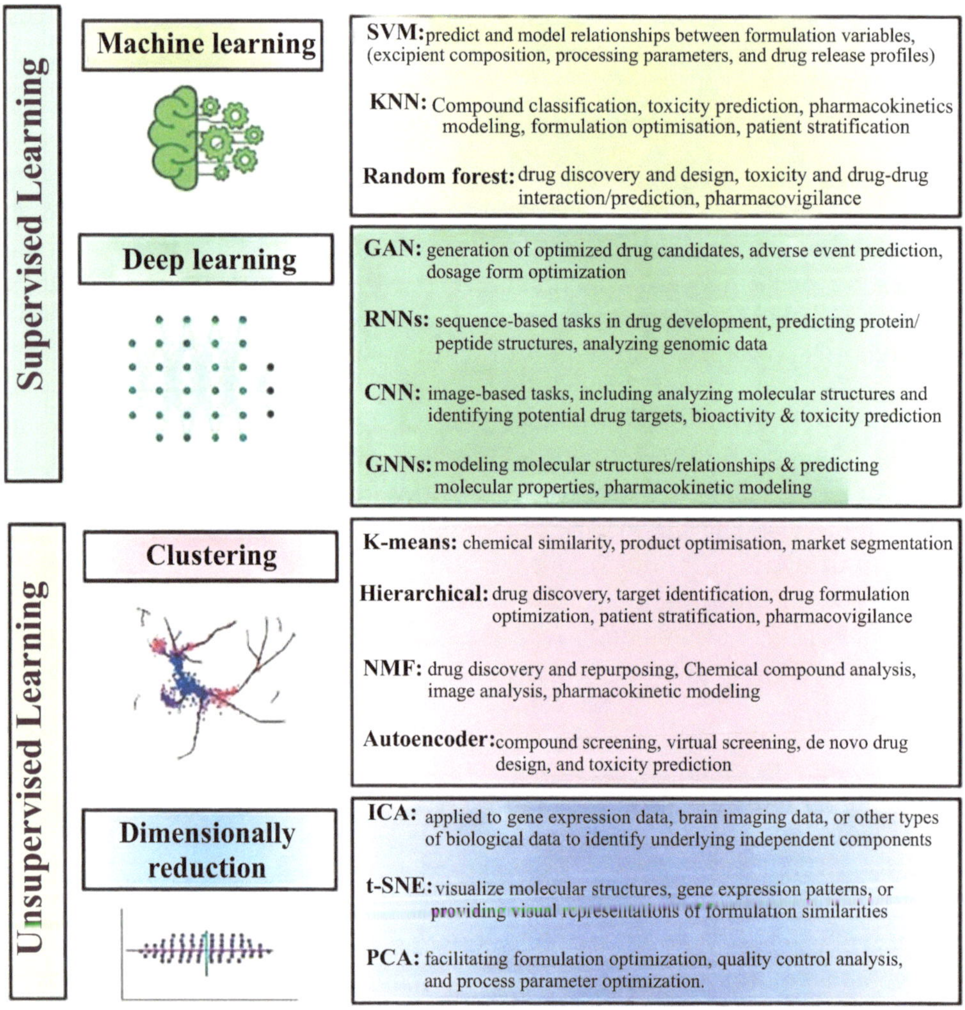

Fig. (5). Different AI models/Tools used for pharmaceutical applications [Reprinted with permission from [119]. Copyright (2023) by the authors. Licensee MDPI, Basel, Switzerland.

Common Machine Learning Algorithms Used in Healthcare

Various areas in healthcare data analysis have extensively employed ML algorithms, enhancing decision-making and producing significant results. The healthcare sector often employs supervised learning algorithms for diagnostic and prognostic applications. Linear Regression is commonly employed to predict continuous variables, such as illness risk scores or hospital stay durations [154]. In binary classification tasks, such as forecasting a patient's likelihood of developing a specific condition like heart disease, Logistic Regression proves to be highly effective [155, 156]. Medical image analysis and disease diagnosis utilizing patient data demonstrate classification tasks that effectively employ Support Vector Machines (SVM) [157]. Random Forest, utilized for disease diagnosis and prognosis, is an algorithm appropriate for both classification and regression tasks [158]. Naive Bayes is a probabilistic classifier commonly utilized for risk prediction tasks, such as assessing the likelihood of diabetes onset [159]. K-Nearest Neighbors (K-NN) assesses disease risk by juxtaposing patients with historical data. K-NN is a commonly utilized method in this domain [160]. Unsupervised learning is a technique wherein algorithms aim to identify relationships and patterns within unlabeled data. K-Means Clustering is essential for defining sickness types and formulating tailored treatments by grouping individuals with similar traits [161]. Epidemiological investigations occasionally utilize Hierarchical grouping, an effective technique for categorizing patients or symptoms [162]. Methods such as Principal Component Analysis (PCA) enhance the visualization and feature extraction of complex healthcare data [163]. Autoencoders, a neural network architecture, are employed for anomaly detection, including the recognition of anomalous test findings that may indicate potential health concerns [164].

In time-series prediction tasks, such as monitoring physiological data like heart rate or tracking disease progression, Recurrent Neural Networks (RNNs) and Long Short-Term Memory (LSTM) models have significant efficacy [165]. Generative Adversarial Networks (GANs) can generate synthetic medical pictures for model training, data augmentation, or situations with constrained datasets [166]. In customized medicine, Deep Reinforcement Learning is utilized as a method for systems to ascertain suitable treatment options for patients based on their interactions and collected data [167]. Ensemble learning algorithms, which integrate many models to enhance predictive accuracy, encompass boosting and bagging techniques [168]. Predicting patient outcomes or illness classifications is a prevalent application of algorithms such as AdaBoost and Gradient Boosting [169]. In the domain of imbalanced and high-dimensional healthcare datasets, especially those utilized for predicting disease risks or patient outcomes, the extremely efficient boosting method XGBoost exhibits outstanding results [170].

Predictive modeling in healthcare employs historical data to forecast future outcomes, enabling both preventive and personalized treatment. Risk prediction models evaluate the likelihood of disease onset, such as diabetes, cancer, cardiovascular disease, or heart failure, by analyzing a patient's demographics, lifestyle, and medical history. Models for assessing heart attack risk incorporate variables such as cholesterol levels, blood pressure, smoking habits, and familial history. Survival analysis methods, including Cox proportional hazards models and Kaplan-Meier survival curves, are utilized to predict patient survival times, specifically the anticipated lifespan of cancer patients receiving treatment [171]. Likewise, for chronic conditions like Chronic Obstructive Pulmonary Disease (COPD) or heart failure, readmission prediction models assess the probability of a patient's rehospitalization after release [172].

Data Privacy and Security Measures for AI in Electrochemical Healthcare Devices

Protecting sensitive medical data acquired by electrochemical devices requires stringent data privacy and security protocols. Data encryption is an essential mechanism for safeguarding the confidentiality and integrity of information [173]. Data must be encrypted both at rest on devices or servers and during transmission between devices, servers, and cloud platforms. To avert misuse or illegal access during transmission, data sent from a wearable electrochemical sensor to a cloud server may be encrypted [174]. Access control and authentication are essential for regulating access to private medical records. To guarantee that only authorized personnel, such as physicians and patients, can access or alter patient records, advanced security measures, including Role-Based Access Control (RBAC) and Multi-Factor Authentication (MFA), are employed [175]. Secure login protocols, encompassing PINs and biometric identification, provide additional safeguards [176]. Robust authentication mechanisms must be implemented to ensure that only authorized individuals can access medical data stored within an implantable electrochemical device.

Data anonymization and pseudonymization are efficacious techniques for protecting patient privacy during data sharing for research or other purposes [177, 178]. To illustrate the claim, participants' identities can be protected in clinical research by employing pseudonymized data from glucose monitoring devices. Secure Sockets Layer (SSL) and Transport Layer Security (TLS) are critical technologies for safeguarding transmission security and thwarting data interception [179]. To preserve patient confidentiality and data integrity, data from cardiac electrochemical devices, including pacemakers, can be securely sent to a hospital's monitoring system using TLS encryption. Federated learning and privacy-preserving artificial intelligence are two approaches that augment data privacy [180]. Federated learning guarantees that secure patient data is retained on the device, enabling local training of AI models. This approach reduces data exposure and diminishes privacy risks. For instance, local electrochemical devices utilize AI algorithms to anticipate the development of diabetic crises while preserving the anonymity of people's health records.

Blockchain technology provides a transparent and dependable method for preserving the accuracy and integrity of medical records [181]. Blockchain guarantees immutable records by establishing a permanent trail of data transfers and transactions. An application example is the secure recording of glucose level data *via* electrochemical sensors utilizing blockchain technology. This enables dependable audits and prevents unauthorized alterations. Although security protocols are crucial, the interpretability of healthcare AI models holds more significance. The implementation of explainable AI (XAI) tools clarifies the reasoning behind AI-generated judgments for patients and physicians alike [182]. As a result, confidence is bolstered, and decisions are founded on reliable, intelligible information. For instance, an AI model employing data from wearable sensors to predict hypoglycemia episodes should clearly specify which sensor values were critical in making that forecast. To uphold stringent privacy and security requirements, compliance with statutory frameworks such as HIPAA in the United States, GDPR in Europe, and CCPA in California is vital [183, 184]. Acquiring patients' informed consent, limiting access to their data, and protecting their right to data deletion are all requirements established by these frameworks. Healthcare workers must adhere to HIPAA regulations while collecting and managing patient data using wearable electrochemical devices for glucose monitoring.

Implementing these measures will create a strong platform for the integration of AI in electrochemical healthcare devices, protecting patient privacy, data integrity, and safety while promoting innovation.

SUSTAINABLE DEVELOPMENT GOALS (SDGs)

As part of the 2030 Agenda, UN Secretary-General Ban Ki-moon set 17 worldwide sustainable development targets in 2015 [185]. The all-encompassing framework addresses human beings' greatest challenges—economic growth, poverty, inequality, health, education, and environmental sustainability, among others. Every goal defines methods and targets to enable governments and businesses to build a fairer, inclusive, and sustainable society. Emphasizing interconnection, the Sustainable Development Goals demonstrate how progress in one area may drive expansion in others. Including AI-integrated electrochemical biosensors, the Sustainable Development Goals (SDGs) assist in evaluating and enhancing the social effects of healthcare technology development [186]. Including these technologies in the SDGs guarantees that technical development helps people and the environment by increasing global relevance and policy coherence.

HISTORICAL EVOLUTION AND SDG ALIGNMENT OF AI IN ELECTROCHEMICAL HEALTHCARE DEVICES

Historical Progression of Electrochemical Healthcare Devices

The journey of electrochemical healthcare devices dates back to the 1960s with the invention of the first enzyme-based glucose biosensor by Leland Clark. Over the decades, these devices have evolved significantly in terms of sensitivity, selectivity, and real-time functionality. Key historical milestones include:

- 1970s–1980s: Emergence of potentiometric and amperometric biosensors for clinical diagnostics.
- 1990s–2000s: Miniaturization of sensors, development of disposable test strips, and integration with microelectronics.
- 2010s: Introduction of wearable electrochemical sensors, enabling continuous and non-invasive monitoring.
- 2020s–Present: Convergence with Artificial Intelligence (AI), allowing predictive analytics, pattern recognition, anomaly detection, and real-time health decision-making through machine learning and deep learning algorithms.

The integration of AI with electrochemical sensors marks a transformative step in personalized medicine, especially in preventive healthcare and chronic disease management.

Impact Mapping to Sustainable Development Goals (SDGs)

The current wave of innovations in AI-integrated electrochemical healthcare devices resonates profoundly with the United Nations' Sustainable Development Goals (SDGs). These innovations not only drive scientific progress but also promote inclusivity, sustainability, and equity in healthcare. Table **2** is an analytical overview linking this technology to specific SDG targets.

Table 2. Alignment of AI-Driven Electrochemical Healthcare Devices with UN Sustainable Development Goals (SDGs).

SDG Goal	Goal Description	Relevance to AI in Electrochemical Healthcare Devices	Key Contributions	References
SDG 3: Good Health and Well-being	Ensure healthy lives and promote well-being for all at all ages	AI-enhanced diagnostics and real-time monitoring of biomarkers using electrochemical sensors	Early disease detection, personalized medicine, remote health monitoring	[187, 188]

(Table 2) cont.....

SDG Goal	Goal Description	Relevance to AI in Electrochemical Healthcare Devices	Key Contributions	References
SDG 9: Industry, Innovation and Infrastructure	Build resilient infrastructure, promote sustainable industrialization and foster innovation	Integration of AI with sensor technology promotes innovation in medical diagnostics	Development of smart, portable, and low-cost diagnostic tools	[189, 190]
SDG 12: Responsible Consumption and Production	Ensure sustainable consumption and production patterns	Reusable and eco-friendly electrochemical sensors reduce medical waste	Sustainable materials, AI-based lifecycle optimization	[191, 192]
SDG 17: Partnerships for the Goals	Strengthen the means of implementation and revitalize the global partnership for sustainable development	Cross-disciplinary research and international collaborations in AI and healthcare	Promotes global knowledge-sharing, capacity building, and scalable healthcare models	[193, 194]

Policy and Global Health Implications

The convergence of AI and electrochemical sensing technologies offers numerous implications for policy, global health equity, and sustainable development:

- Healthcare Access in Low-Resource Settings: AI-empowered electrochemical diagnostics eliminate the need for sophisticated infrastructure, enabling community-level health interventions and diagnostics.
- Pandemic Response and Disease Surveillance: Portable biosensors integrated with AI algorithms can aid in rapid screening during outbreaks and monitor disease spread with high accuracy.
- Maternal and Neonatal Care: Continuous monitoring of vital biomarkers using wearable biosensors ensures safer pregnancies and early intervention in neonatal complications, supporting maternal health targets under SDG 3.
- Policy Innovation: These devices call for new frameworks in health data governance, privacy, ethical AI use, and public health funding strategies.

The evolution of AI in electrochemical healthcare devices exemplifies how cutting-edge technology can serve humanity's most urgent health and sustainability needs. A clear alignment with multiple SDGs underlines the potential of this field not just for scientific discovery, but for global transformation—making healthcare smarter, more sustainable, and universally accessible. Real-life examples of AI in electrochemical healthcare devices supporting SDGs are listed in Table **3**.

Table 3. Real-Life examples of ai in electrochemical healthcare devices supporting SDGs.

SDG Goal	Example/Project	Device or Application	Description and Impact	Country/Organization
SDG 3	FreeStyle Libre with AI AI-based Electrochemical Breath Analyzer AI-integrated Multiplex Biosensor	Wearable glucose monitor Lung cancer detection device Multi-cancer detection	Continuously monitors glucose levels with predictive AI to warn users about hypo/hyperglycemia, enhancing diabetes management. Uses AI to analyze VOCs in breath samples *via* electrochemical reactions for early-stage cancer detection. Detects multiple cancer biomarkers simultaneously with AI-powered interpretation of electrochemical signals.	Abbott, USA Owlstone Medical, UK UCLA & Stanford University, USA
SDG 9	COVID-19 Electrochemical AI Sensor AI-enabled Wearable Sweat Sensor BioMind AI Platform	Rapid diagnostic biosensor Fitness and health monitoring Diagnostic imaging and sensor integration	AI algorithms combined with electrochemical detection for ultra-fast, low-cost COVID testing. Tracks electrolyte imbalance, hydration, and fatigue levels during workouts using AI and sweat analysis. Combines sensor data with imaging analytics for neurological disorder diagnosis.	GNA Biosolutions, Germany Northwestern University, USA BioMind, Singapore
SDG 12	Graphene-based Biodegradable Sensors Paper-based Electrochemical AI Sensor	Sustainable health monitoring devices Early disease diagnosis	Developed with eco-friendly materials (*e.g.*, cellulose, chitosan); reusable and recyclable biosensors integrated with AI. Disposable yet sustainable diagnostic tool made from paper and carbon ink, integrated with AI for decision support.	IIT Delhi, India University of Cambridge, UK

(Table 3) cont.....

SDG Goal	Example/Project	Device or Application	Description and Impact	Country/Organization
SDG 17	Global AI4H Initiative (WHO) AI-Biosensor for TB Detection Smart Health Diagnostics for Maternal Care	AI for Health regulatory framework Point-of-care device for Low and Middle Income Countries AI + biosensor wearables	Collaborates with governments and academia to standardize and deploy AI-integrated health sensors globally. AI-enhanced portable electrochemical biosensor for rapid tuberculosis screening in underserved areas. Real-time monitoring of pregnant women's vitals in rural settings and supports early intervention.	WHO, PATH, FIND FIND & African Health Ministries University of Toronto & WHO

Challenges and Ethical Considerations: Data Privacy and Security in Electrochemical Healthcare Devices

The integration of electrochemical devices with AI has revolutionized healthcare by improving patient care and refining medicinal therapies. Wearable biosensors, implantable systems, and electrochemical sensors continuously gather and analyze essential data for monitoring blood glucose or electrolytes [195]. This integration presents considerable issues with data privacy and security. Safeguarding sensitive patient information, device performance metrics, and health indicators from illegal access or exploitation is essential for preserving confidence and ensuring patient safety.

Types of Data Collected by Electrochemical Devices

Protecting the sensitive data gathered by electrochemical devices employed in healthcare is essential. Collecting biometric data, such as blood pressure, oxygen saturation, glucose levels, and heart rate, is a routine practice. An example is the continuous monitoring of glucose levels in diabetic patients with wearable electrochemical sensors. Implantable or wearable devices are commonly utilized to collect physiological data, including ion concentrations (*e.g.*, sodium, potassium) and pH values [196]. An electrochemical sensor that quantifies pH levels in individuals with renal illness is one such instance. To achieve the most accurate measurements, certain devices also record environmental data, including ambient temperature, humidity, and the user's precise position. A wearable glucose monitor may leverage ambient data to improve accuracy in various environments. Furthermore, Electronic Health Records (EHRs) frequently associate electrochemical devices with personal health information, including medical history, health status, and prescription usage [197]. An excellent case is a cardiac implant that monitors a patient's heart rate and associates that data with their medical history.

Key Privacy and Security Concerns

When handling sensitive healthcare data, there are serious dangers of privacy invasion, medical record misuse, and personal information theft [198]. Data breaches provide a significant threat, as hackers may potentially reveal critical information through electrochemical device assaults [150]. The information from a wearable glucose monitor may be compromised or used by a malicious organization, impacting healthcare decisions. Inadequate or defective security measures to safeguard against unauthorized access to the AI models of these devices may jeopardize patient confidentiality. Healthcare professionals or unauthorized individuals may access data. Due to the potential for compromised data from devices like glucose monitors to result in erroneous treatment decisions by physicians—which jeopardizes patient safety—it is essential to maintain data integrity. Additionally, specific electrochemical devices transmit data to cloud platforms for analysis and storage through third-party data sharing [199]. Enhanced regulation of these platforms is essential to avert the exploitation of personal data. Patient data may be unintentionally compromised in the event of a security breach inside a cloud-based storage system utilized for data from electrochemical devices. Table **4** gives a brief summary of challenges in AI Integration with electrochemical Devices.

Table 4. Brief summary of challenges in AI integration with electrochemical devices.

Field of Application	Key Benefits	Role of AI in Enhancing Outcomes
Data Privacy	Protecting sensitive patient data during collection and analysis.	Implementing robust encryption and anonymization techniques.
Complexity of AI Models	Difficulty in interpreting black-box models used in healthcare devices.	Developing explainable AI (XAI) frameworks for transparency.
Ethical Concerns	Addressing biases in AI models and ensuring equitable healthcare access.	Regular audits of AI models for bias and adherence to ethical standards.
Regulatory Barriers	Meeting regulatory standards and gaining approval for AI-driven devices.	Working closely with regulatory bodies to establish clear guidelines for AI integration.
Resource Dependence	Reliance on large datasets and high computational power for effective AI functionality.	Optimizing algorithms to work with smaller datasets and leveraging cloud-based solutions.
Integration with Healthcare	Incorporating AI into existing healthcare infrastructure and workflows.	Creating seamless interfaces and ensuring compatibility with current systems.

REGULATORY APPROVALS AND COMPLIANCE STANDARDS

To ensure safety, efficacy, and clinical reliability, AI-powered medical devices must undergo stringent regulatory approval before being introduced to the market. Two of the most prominent regulatory pathways include the U.S. Food and Drug Administration (FDA) and the European Medicines Agency (EMA) in coordination with Notified Bodies. In the United States, devices must receive FDA clearance through pathways such as 510(k), *De Novo* classification, or Premarket Approval (PMA), each requiring robust clinical validation, algorithm transparency, and provisions for post-market surveillance [200, 201]. In the European Union, the CE Mark (Conformité Européenne) is granted based on compliance with the Medical Device Regulation (MDR), encompassing safety, performance, and detailed risk analysis [202 - 204]. Other national regulatory agencies—such as the Medicines and Healthcare products Regulatory Agency (MHRA) in the UK, the Pharmaceuticals and Medical Devices Agency (PMDA) in Japan, Health Canada, and the Central Drugs Standard Control Organization (CDSCO) in India—are also integrating AI-specific regulatory frameworks [205, 206]. On a global scale, the World Health Organization's AI for Health (AI4H) initiative is actively working to develop benchmarking tools aimed at regulatory harmonization across countries [207]. AI/ML-based medical devices present unique challenges, including algorithm drift, inherent bias, explainability of decisions, and real-time performance reliability. In response, regulatory bodies are shifting from traditional static approval models to more adaptive regulatory pathways that permit safe and validated algorithm updates after the initial market approval.

Challenges in Commercialization

While innovation in AI-biosensor technology is progressing rapidly, scaling these devices from the laboratory to the market presents several complex challenges. One major hurdle is scalability—devices that perform reliably in controlled lab environments often encounter performance issues when exposed to real-world variabilities such as changes in temperature, humidity, and user handling. Interoperability is another significant barrier; successful integration with existing health information technologies like Electronic Health Records (EHRs), telemedicine platforms, and other diagnostic tools requires adherence to standardized protocols and interface compatibility [208]. Additionally, reimbursement and payment models remain underdeveloped in many national healthcare systems, as formal policies to cover AI-integrated biosensors are still under development. The time to market is also considerable, with device development and approval processes typically spanning 3 to 7 years due to the need for rigorous clinical trials, iterative regulatory feedback, and sustained funding. Furthermore, since these devices often process sensitive patient data, strict compliance with global data protection regulations such as the General Data Protection Regulation (GDPR) and the Health Insurance Portability and Accountability Act (HIPAA) is essential to ensure privacy and security [209, 210].

Funding Sources and Innovation Ecosystem

To bridge the so-called "valley of death" between research and commercialization, a diverse array of funding pathways has emerged to support the development of AI in electrochemical healthcare. Venture capital plays a pivotal role, with companies like AliveCor, Butterfly Network, and Tempus securing hundreds of millions of dollars in investment to advance AI-driven biosensor technologies [211, 212]. Many of these startups originate from academic spin-offs or biotech incubators, leveraging cutting-edge research and entrepreneurial ecosystems. In parallel, government grants and public-private partnerships are vital sources of support. Institutions such as the National Institutes of Health (NIH) in the U.S., Horizon Europe, the Biotechnology Industry Research Assistance Council (BIRAC) in India, and Innovate UK offer seed and scale-up funding for innovative health technologies. Additionally, initiatives like BARDA Ventures (USA) and the Innovative Medicines Initiative (IMI) in the EU focus on de-risking high-impact, early-stage medical innovations. On a global scale, organizations such as the Bill & Melinda Gates Foundation, PATH, and the Wellcome Trust are instrumental in funding AI-powered diagnostic tools targeted at improving healthcare access and outcomes in Low- and Middle-Income Countries (LMICs) [213, 214].

POLICY FRAMEWORKS, INDUSTRY RELEVANCE, AND COMMERCIALIZATION OF AI-POWERED ELECTROCHEMICAL HEALTHCARE DEVICES

Policy Frameworks: Global Governance of AI in Medical Devices

To responsibly accelerate the adoption of AI in healthcare devices, it is essential to establish robust policy and regulatory frameworks that strike a balance between innovation, safety, equity, and ethical standards. International and regional policies are evolving to address the unique challenges posed by AI technologies. The World Health Organization's AI for Health (AI4H) initiative, for instance, aims to create a global benchmarking framework for AI-powered medical tools while emphasizing equitable deployment in LMICs. In Europe, the Medical Device Regulation (MDR) mandates stringent requirements such as post-market surveillance, explainability of AI algorithms, comprehensive risk classification, and mechanisms for real-time software updates. The U.S. FDA's Digital Health Innovation Action Plan advocates a Total Product Lifecycle (TPLC) approach for

AI/ML-based medical software, emphasizing continuous real-world performance evaluation [215]. On a broader scale, the OECD AI Principles support the development of trustworthy AI by promoting values like transparency, inclusiveness, accountability, and robustness [216]. Similarly, UNESCO's AI Ethics Framework encourages the fair, inclusive, and environmentally sustainable application of AI in public health contexts. These evolving frameworks recognize the dynamic and adaptive nature of AI algorithms, necessitating agile, iterative, and interdisciplinary oversight strategies that can evolve in tandem with technological progress.

Industry Relevance: AI-Electrochemical Devices in the Global Health Economy

The rise of AI-integrated electrochemical healthcare technologies signifies a paradigm shift in medical diagnostics and monitoring. Their relevance extends across domains:

- ***Personalized Healthcare***

AI-biosensors enable real-time tracking of biomarkers, leading to personalized diagnosis and drug response monitoring. Example: Wearable sweat sensors predicting electrolyte imbalance in athletes or cardiac patients.

- ***Global Health & Disease Surveillance***

AI-driven biosensors are crucial in epidemic preparedness, especially in rural or resource-limited settings. Example: Portable COVID-19 electrochemical AI diagnostics deployed in Africa and Southeast Asia.

- ***Industrial and Pharmaceutical R&D***

Pharmaceutical companies integrate AI-biosensors for point-of-care clinical trials, reducing cost and improving speed.

- ***Circular and Green Economy Integration***

Devices increasingly use biodegradable substrates and eco-friendly materials, aligning with SDG 12. AI optimizes sensor use, predictive maintenance, and device reuse, minimizing e-waste.

Commercialization Pathways: From Innovation to Market Adoption

The deployment of AI-powered electrochemical healthcare devices faces several critical challenges across regulatory, infrastructural, technical, and social domains. Regulatory delays are a significant barrier, as AI and Machine Learning (ML) technologies often require adaptive validation mechanisms that current frameworks are not fully equipped to handle. The absence of harmonized global standards exacerbates this issue—AI-based glucose monitors, for example, may require separate validations in each country, delaying international rollout. Infrastructure gaps, particularly in LMICs, also hinder adoption. Inadequate digital connectivity, unreliable electricity, and the lack of supportive technologies such as 4G/5G networks compromise the real-time functionality of AI diagnostics [217]. On the technical side, data interoperability presents another hurdle, as many AI devices are not compatible with existing hospital IT ecosystems such as Electronic Health Records (EHRs) and Picture Archiving and Communication Systems (PACS), due to a lack of standard Application Programming Interfaces (APIs) and data exchange protocols. Moreover, pricing and reimbursement issues remain unresolved in many regions—AI-enabled biosensors are frequently classified as experimental, resulting in limited insurance coverage or public healthcare support. Lastly, public trust and digital literacy are essential for meaningful integration. Patients and healthcare providers alike must be able to understand, trust, and effectively engage with AI-driven decisions, but concerns about algorithmic bias, transparency, and explainability can create hesitancy and resistance to adoption [218]. Addressing these multifaceted challenges is key to unlocking the full potential of AI in healthcare.

CHALLENGES AND FUTURE DIRECTIONS IN ELECTROCHEMICAL HEALTHCARE DEVICES

As electrochemical devices in healthcare increasingly integrate with the Internet of Things (IoT), escalating cybersecurity concerns present substantial challenges [219]. These devices frequently retain and convey important patient data, rendering them appealing targets for assailants. The complexity of cyber attacks requires ongoing adjustments to encryption techniques, firewalls, and threat detection systems. Future developments should prioritize the enhancement of more resilient Intrusion Detection Systems (IDS) and real-time monitoring technologies that can identify and mitigate cybersecurity threats aimed against electrochemical devices [220, 221]. These procedures are crucial for protecting patient data and ensuring the integrity of device performance.

A significant issue exists in reconciling privacy with data utilization. AI models included in electrochemical healthcare devices necessitate substantial data availability for efficient training and precise forecasts. Nonetheless, safeguarding data privacy is crucial for preserving patient trust and adhering to regulatory mandates. Achieving this equilibrium is a multifaceted challenge. Future developments may integrate several privacy techniques, enabling AI models to extract insights from aggregated data without directly accessing individual patient information. These measures can mitigate privacy threats while fostering effective AI-driven advancements in healthcare [222].

Cross-border data protection introduces an additional layer of complication. Numerous healthcare organizations utilize cloud-based systems for the storage and processing of patient data, frequently across multiple countries [223]. This may result in difficulties in complying with diverse data privacy laws and regulatory mandates. Healthcare providers and manufacturers of electrochemical devices must adhere to international legislation for cross-border data sharing to mitigate these issues [224]. Implementing standardised protocols and secure mechanisms for data sharing can enhance international collaboration while safeguarding patients' confidential information. Addressing these problems would facilitate the integration of electrochemical devices with advanced technology, guaranteeing healthcare solutions that are secure, efficient, and universally accessible.

CONCLUSION

New electrochemical health equipment has allowed for more accurate diagnosis, faster treatments, and individualized care. The healthcare sector will benefit significantly from this enhancement. By collecting vital signs and analyzing them with state-of-the-art technology, implanted monitors and wearable sensors can improve predictive analytics, reducing health risks and enabling early sickness detection. Among the chronic diseases, these devices are absolutely vital for managing diabetes, heart disease, and renal disease. Deep learning and federated learning, among other methods, have made it possible to do complex and safe analyses of big databases. Protecting private health data, making honest and open decisions, and handling moral conundrums such as algorithmic discrimination and data ownership remain difficult, nevertheless. Resolving these problems will call for both future deployment of differential privacy and blockchain technologies as well as international collaboration. By eliminating these obstacles, these integrated technologies have the capacity to totally revolutionize healthcare, improving diagnosis, treatment effectiveness, and resource economy.

ACKNOWLEDGMENTS

The authors acknowledge the Centralized Common Instrumentation Centre (CCIF), Kerala Government Project Performance Linked Encouragement for Academic Studies (PLEASE), Government College for Women, Thiruvananthapuram, University of Kerala, and DST-FIST for the execution of this work.

REFERENCES

[1] D. Grieshaber, R. MacKenzie, J. Vörös, and E. Reimhult, "Electrochemical biosensors - sensor principles and architectures", *Sensors (Basel),* vol. 8, no. 3, pp. 1400-1458, 2008. [http://dx.doi.org/10.3390/s80314000] [PMID: 27879772]

[2] J. Kirsch, C. Siltanen, Q. Zhou, A. Revzin, and A. Simonian, "Biosensor technology: recent advances in threat agent detection and medicine", *Chem. Soc. Rev.,* vol. 42, no. 22, pp. 8733-8768, 2013. [http://dx.doi.org/10.1039/c3cs60141b] [PMID: 23852443]

[3] S. Mukherjee, S. Suleman, R. Pilloton, J. Narang, and K. Rani, "State of the art in smart portable, wearable, ingestible and implantable devices for health status monitoring and disease management", *Sensors (Basel),* vol. 22, no. 11, p. 4228, 2022. [http://dx.doi.org/10.3390/s22114228] [PMID: 35684847]

[4] M.M.H. Shuvo, T. Titirsha, N. Amin, and S.K. Islam, "Energy harvesting in implantable and wearable medical devices for enduring precision healthcare", *Energies,* vol. 15, no. 20, p. 7495, 2022. [http://dx.doi.org/10.3390/en15207495]

[5] S.N.A.B.M. Nashruddin, F.H.M. Salleh, R.M. Yunus, and H.B. Zaman, "Artificial intelligence−powered electrochemical sensor: Recent advances, challenges, and prospects", *Heliyon,* vol. 10, no. 18, p. e37964, 2024. [http://dx.doi.org/10.1016/j.heliyon.2024.e37964] [PMID: 39328566]

[6] P. Manickam, S.A. Mariappan, S.M. Murugesan, S. Hansda, A. Kaushik, R. Shinde, and S.P. Thipperudraswamy, "Artificial intelligence (AI) and internet of medical things (IoMT) assisted biomedical systems for intelligent healthcare", *Biosensors (Basel),* vol. 12, no. 8, p. 562, 2022. [http://dx.doi.org/10.3390/bios12080562] [PMID: 35892459]

[7] K. Murugan, K. Gopalakrishnan, K. Sakthivel, S. Subramanian, I-C. Li, Y-Y. Lee, T-W. Chiu, and G-P. Chang-Chien, "Review—machine learning-driven advances in electrochemical sensing: A horizon scan", *J. Electrochem. Soc.,* vol. 171, no. 9, p. 097503, 2024. [http://dx.doi.org/10.1149/1945-7111/ad6b4a]

[8] F. Haghayegh, A. Norouziazad, E. Haghani, A.A. Feygin, R.H. Rahimi, H.A. Ghavamabadi, D. Sadighbayan, F. Madhoun, M. Papagelis, T. Felfeli, and R. Salahandish, "Revolutionary point-of-care wearable diagnostics for early disease detection and biomarker discovery through intelligent technologies", *Adv. Sci. (Weinh.),* vol. 11, no. 36, p. 2400595, 2024. [http://dx.doi.org/10.1002/advs.202400595] [PMID: 38958517]

[9] Y.A. Qadri, A. Nauman, Y.B. Zikria, A.V. Vasilakos, and S.W. Kim, "The future of healthcare internet of things: A survey of emerging technologies", *IEEE Commun. Surv. Tutor.,* vol. 22, no. 2, pp. 1121-1167, 2020. [http://dx.doi.org/10.1109/COMST.2020.2973314]

[10] N.L. Kazanskiy, S.N. Khonina, and M.A. Butt, "A review on flexible wearables – Recent developments in non-invasive continuous health monitoring", *Sens. Actuators A Phys.,* vol. 366, p. 114993, 2024. [http://dx.doi.org/10.1016/j.sna.2023.114993]

[11] C. Wang, T. He, H. Zhou, Z. Zhang, and C. Lee, "Artificial intelligence enhanced sensors - enabling technologies to next-generation healthcare and biomedical platform", *Bioelectron. Med.,* vol. 9, no. 1, p. 17, 2023. [http://dx.doi.org/10.1186/s42234-023-00118-1] [PMID: 37528436]

[12] T. Wasilewski, W. Kamysz, and J. Gębicki, "AI-assisted detection of biomarkers by sensors and biosensors for early diagnosis and monitoring", *Biosensors,* vol. 14, no. 7, p. 356, 2024. [http://dx.doi.org/10.3390/bios14070356]

[13] R. Vashistha, A.K. Dangi, A. Kumar, D. Chhabra, and P. Shukla, "Futuristic biosensors for cardiac health care: an artificial intelligence approach", *3 Biotech,* vol. 8, no. 8, p. 358, 2018. [http://dx.doi.org/10.1007/s13205-018-1368-y]

[14] S. Dave, A. Dave, S. Radhakrishnan, J. Das, and S. Dave, "Biosensors for healthcare: an artificial intelligence approach."*Biosensors for Emerging and Re-Emerging Infectious Diseases.,* J. Das, S. Dave, S. Radhakrishnan, P. Mohanty, Eds., Academic Press, 2022, pp. 365-383. [http://dx.doi.org/10.1016/B978-0-323-88464-8.00008-7]

[15] R. Sharma, D. Singh, P. Gaur, and D. Joshi, "Intelligent automated drug administration and therapy: future of healthcare", *Drug Deliv. Transl. Res.,* vol. 11, no. 5, pp. 1878-1902, 2021. [http://dx.doi.org/10.1007/s13346-020-00876-4] [PMID: 33447941]

[16] P. Hassanzadeh, F. Atyabi, and R. Dinarvand, "The significance of artificial intelligence in drug delivery system design", *Adv. Drug Deliv. Rev.,* vol. 151-152, pp. 169-190, 2019. [http://dx.doi.org/10.1016/j.addr.2019.05.001] [PMID: 31071378]

[17] A. Awad, S.J. Trenfield, T.D. Pollard, J.J. Ong, M. Elbadawi, L.E. McCoubrey, A. Goyanes, S. Gaisford, and A.W. Basit, "Connected healthcare: Improving patient care using digital health technologies", *Adv. Drug Deliv. Rev.,* vol. 178, p. 113958, 2021. [http://dx.doi.org/10.1016/j.addr.2021.113958] [PMID: 34478781]

[18] A. Al Kuwaiti, K. Nazer, A. Al-Reedy, S. Al-Shehri, A. Al-Muhanna, A.V. Subbarayalu, D. Al Muhanna, and F.A. Al-Muhanna, "A review of the role of artificial intelligence in healthcare", *J. Pers. Med.,* vol. 13, no. 6, p. 951, 2023. [http://dx.doi.org/10.3390/jpm13060951] [PMID: 37373940]

[19] V. Rajaraman, "JohnMcCarthy — Father of artificial intelligence", *Resonance,* vol. 19, no. 3, pp. 198-207, 2014. [http://dx.doi.org/10.1007/s12045-014-0027-9]

[20] P. Marquis, O. Papini, and H. Prade, "Elements for a history of artificial intelligence" In: *A Guided Tour of Artificial Intelligence Research: Volume I: Knowledge Representation, Reasoning and Learning,* P. Marquis, O. Papini, and H. Prade, Eds., Cham: Springer International Publishing, 2020, pp. 1–43. [http://dx.doi.org/10.1007/978-3-030-06164-7_1]

[21] B. Dellot, and F. Wallace-Stephens, *The age of automation artificial intelligence, robotics and the future of low-skilled work,* 2017.

[22] E. Shellshear, M. Tremeer, and C. Bean, "Machine learning, deep learning and neural networks."*Artificial Intelligence in Medicine: Applications, Limitations and Future Directions.,* M. Raz, T.C. Nguyen, E. Loh, Eds., Springer Nature Singapore: Singapore, 2022, pp. 35-75. [http://dx.doi.org/10.1007/978-981-19-1223-8_3]

[23] J. Yanase, and E. Triantaphyllou, "A systematic survey of computer-aided diagnosis in medicine: Past and present developments", *Expert Syst. Appl.,* vol. 138, p. 112821, 2019. [http://dx.doi.org/10.1016/j.eswa.2019.112821]

[24] S. Raschka, J. Patterson, and C. Nolet, "Machine learning in python: main developments and technology trends in data science, machine learning, and artificial intelligence", *Information (Basel),* vol. 11, no. 4, p. 193, 2020. [http://dx.doi.org/10.3390/info11040193]

[25] R. Confalonieri, L. Coba, B. Wagner, and T.R. Besold, "A historical perspective of explainable Artificial Intelligence", *Wiley Interdiscip. Rev. Data Min. Knowl. Discov.,* vol. 11, no. 1, p. e1391, 2021. [http://dx.doi.org/10.1002/widm.1391]

[26] K. Orhan, and H. Amasya, "Artificial intelligence from medicine to dentistry."*Artificial Intelligence in Dentistry.,* K. Orhan, R. Jagtap, Eds., Springer International Publishing: Cham, 2023, pp. 33-42. [http://dx.doi.org/10.1007/978-3-031-43827-1_3]

[27] S.M. Anwar, "Expert systems for interpretable decisions in the clinical domain" In: *AI in Clinical Medicine,* 2023, pp. 66–72.

[http://dx.doi.org/10.1002/9781119790686.ch7]

[28] E. Seeram, and V. Kanade, "AI Fundamentals."*Artificial intelligence in medical imaging technology: An introduction.,* E. Seeram, V. Kanade, Eds., Springer Nature Switzerland: Cham, 2024, pp. 17-34. [http://dx.doi.org/10.1007/978-3-031-64049-0_2]

[29] O. Kubassova, F. Shaikh, C. Melus, and M. Mahler, "History, current status, and future directions of artificial intelligence."*Precision Medicine and Artificial Intelligence.,* M. Mahler, Ed., Academic Press, 2021, pp. 1-38. [http://dx.doi.org/10.1016/B978-0-12-820239-5.00002-4]

[30] Z. Shao, R. Zhao, S. Yuan, M. Ding, and Y. Wang, "Tracing the evolution of AI in the past decade and forecasting the emerging trends", *Expert Syst. Appl.,* vol. 209, p. 118221, 2022. [http://dx.doi.org/10.1016/j.eswa.2022.118221]

[31] S. Zeb, N. Fnu, N. Abbasi, and M. Fahad, "AI in healthcare: Revolutionizing diagnosis and therapy", *International Journal of Multidisciplinary Sciences and Arts,* vol. 3, no. 3, pp. 118-128, 2024. [http://dx.doi.org/10.47709/ijmdsa.v3i3.4546]

[32] Abbasi, Nasrullah, "AI in Healthcare: Integrating advanced technologies with traditional practices for enhanced patient care". BULLET : Jurnal Multidisiplin Ilmu, vol. 2, no. 3, 2023, pp. 546-556.

[33] A. Nazir, A. Hussain, M. Singh, and A. Assad, *"Deep learning in medicine: advancing healthcare with intelligent solutions and the future of holography imaging in early diagnosis".* Multimed Tools Appl, 2024. [http://dx.doi.org/10.1007/s11042-024-19694-8]

[34] S. Tuli, N. Basumatary, S.S. Gill, M. Kahani, R.C. Arya, G.S. Wander, and R. Buyya, "HealthFog: An ensemble deep learning based smart healthcare system for automatic diagnosis of heart diseases in integrated IoT and fog computing environments", *Future Gener. Comput. Syst.,* vol. 104, pp. 187-200, 2020. [http://dx.doi.org/10.1016/j.future.2019.10.043]

[35] D.K. Murala, S.K. Panda, and S.P. Dash, "MedMetaverse: Medical care of chronic disease patients and managing data using artificial intelligence, blockchain, and wearable devices state-of-the-art methodology", *IEEE Access,* vol. 11, pp. 138954-138985, 2023. [http://dx.doi.org/10.1109/ACCESS.2023.3340791]

[36] T.B. Marvasti, Y. Gao, K.R. Murray, S. Hershman, C. McIntosh, and Y. Moayedi, "Unlocking tomorrow's health care: Expanding the clinical scope of wearables by applying artificial intelligence", *Can. J. Cardiol.,* vol. 40, no. 10, pp. 1934-1945, 2024. [http://dx.doi.org/10.1016/j.cjca.2024.07.009] [PMID: 39025363]

[37] R. Najjar, "Redefining radiology: A review of artificial intelligence integration in medical imaging", *Diagnostics (Basel),* vol. 13, no. 17, p. 2760, 2023. [http://dx.doi.org/10.3390/diagnostics13172760] [PMID: 37685300]

[38] M. Tsuneki, "Deep learning models in medical image analysis", *J. Oral Biosci./ JAOB, Jpn. Assoc. Oral Biol.,* vol. 64, no. 3, pp. 312-320, 2022. [http://dx.doi.org/10.1016/j.job.2022.03.003] [PMID: 35306172]

[39] S. Astley, I. Hutt, P. Miller, P. Rose, C. Taylor, C. Boggis, S. Adamson, T. Valentine, J. Davies, and J. Armstrong, "Automation in mammography: Computer vision and human perception", *Int. J. Pattern Recognit. Artif. Intell.,* vol. 7, no. 6, pp. 1313-1338, 1993. [http://dx.doi.org/10.1142/S0218001493000649]

[40] Z. Jiang, Z. Gandomkar, P.D. Trieu, S.T. Taba, M.L. Barron, and S.J. Lewis, "AI for interpreting screening mammograms: implications for missed cancer in double reading practices and challenging-to-locate lesions", *Sci. Rep.,* vol. 14, no. 1, p. 11893, 2024. [http://dx.doi.org/10.1038/s41598-024-62324-4] [PMID: 38789575]

[41] D. Kim, and Y. Yoo, *Association for information systems association for information systems AIS*

electronic library (AISeL) AIS electronic library (AISeL) AI as a floating signifier and the destabilization of categorical AI as a floating signifier and the destabilization of categorical meaning: Healthcare AI and IBM watson meaning: Healthcare AI and IBM watson, 2024.https://aisel.aisnet.org/icis2024/aiinbus/aiinbus/1

[42] S. Zeb, N. Fnu, N. Abbasi, and M.U. Qayyum, "BULLET: Jurnal multidisiplin ilmu transforming healthcare: Artificial intelligence's place in contemporary medicine. 2024",

[43] M. Subramanian, A. Wojtusciszyn, L. Favre, S. Boughorbel, J. Shan, K.B. Letaief, N. Pitteloud, and L. Chouchane, "Precision medicine in the era of artificial intelligence: implications in chronic disease management", *J. Transl. Med.,* vol. 18, no. 1, p. 472, 2020. [http://dx.doi.org/10.1186/s12967-020-02658-5] [PMID: 33298113]

[44] Z. Ahmed, K. Mohamed, S. Zeeshan, and X. Dong, "Artificial intelligence with multi-functional machine learning platform development for better healthcare and precision medicine", *Database (Oxford),* vol. 2020, p. baaa010, 2020. [http://dx.doi.org/10.1093/database/baaa010] [PMID: 32185396]

[45] S.K. Bhattamisra, P. Banerjee, P. Gupta, J. Mayuren, S. Patra, and M. Candasamy, "Artificial intelligence in pharmaceutical and healthcare research", *Big Data and Cognitive Computing,* vol. 7, no. 1, p. 10, 2023. [http://dx.doi.org/10.3390/bdcc7010010]

[46] A. Rghioui, J. Lloret, M. Harane, and A. Oumnad, "A smart glucose monitoring system for diabetic patient", *Electronics (Basel),* vol. 9, no. 4, p. 678, 2020. [http://dx.doi.org/10.3390/electronics9040678]

[47] A.Y. Ng, C.J.G. Oberije, É. Ambrózay, E. Szabó, O. Serfőző, E. Karpati, G. Fox, B. Glocker, E.A. Morris, G. Forrai, and P.D. Kecskemethy, "Prospective implementation of AI-assisted screen reading to improve early detection of breast cancer", *Nat. Med.,* vol. 29, no. 12, pp. 3044-3049, 2023. [http://dx.doi.org/10.1038/s41591-023-02625-9] [PMID: 37973948]

[48] H. Xu, R.S.Y. Tang, T.Y.T. Lam, G. Zhao, J.Y.W. Lau, Y. Liu, Q. Wu, L. Rong, W. Xu, X. Li, S.H. Wong, S. Cai, J. Wang, G. Liu, T. Ma, X. Liang, J.W.Y. Mak, H. Xu, P. Yuan, T. Cao, F. Li, Z. Ye, Z. Shutian, and J.J.Y. Sung, "Artificial intelligence–assisted colonoscopy for colorectal cancer screening: A multicenter randomized controlled trial", *Clin. Gastroenterol. Hepatol.,* vol. 21, no. 2, pp. 337-346.e3, 2023. [http://dx.doi.org/10.1016/j.cgh.2022.07.006] [PMID: 35863686]

[49] M. Hassaballah, Y.M. Wazery, I.E. Ibrahim, and A. Farag, "ECG heartbeat classification using machine learning and metaheuristic optimization for smart healthcare systems", *Bioengineering (Basel),* vol. 10, no. 4, p. 429, 2023. [http://dx.doi.org/10.3390/bioengineering10040429] [PMID: 37106616]

[50] R.A. Vigersky, S.J. Fonda, M. Chellappa, M.S. Walker, and N.M. Ehrhardt, "Short- and long-term effects of real-time continuous glucose monitoring in patients with type 2 diabetes", *Diabetes Care,* vol. 35, no. 1, pp. 32-38, 2012. [http://dx.doi.org/10.2337/dc11-1438] [PMID: 22100963]

[51] B.P. Kasaraneni, *Distributed learning and broad applications in scientific research advanced ai techniques for predictive maintenance in health insurance: Models.* Applications, and Real-World Case Studies, 2019.

[52] S. Mulukuntla, and M. Gaddam, "Data-driven healthcare: Trends in machine learning and AI for disease prediction and prevention", *ESP J Eng Technol Adv,* vol. 1, no. 1, pp. 2583-2646, 2021. [http://dx.doi.org/10.56472/25832646/JETA-V1I1P106]

[53] Y. Zhao, X. Wang, T. Sun, P. Shan, Z. Zhan, Z. Zhao, Y. Jiang, M. Qu, Q. Lv, Y. Wang, P. Liu, and S. Chen, "Artificial intelligence-driven electrochemical immunosensing biochips in multi-component detection", *Biomicrofluidics,* vol. 17, no. 4, p. 041301, 2023. [http://dx.doi.org/10.1063/5.0160808] [PMID: 37614678]

[54] E. Voitechovič, and R. Pauliukaite, "Electrochemical multisensor systems and arrays in the era of artificial intelligence", *Curr. Opin. Electrochem.,* vol. 42, p. 101411, 2023. [http://dx.doi.org/10.1016/j.coelec.2023.101411]

[55] Y. Ding, J. Chen, Q. Wu, B. Fang, W. Ji, X. Li, C. Yu, X. Wang, X. Cheng, H-D. Yu, Z. Hu, K. Uvdal, P. Li, L. Li, and W. Huang, "Artificial intelligence-assisted point-of-care testing system for ultrafast and quantitative detection of drug-resistant bacteria", *SmartMat,* vol. 5, no. 3, p. e1214, 2024. [http://dx.doi.org/10.1002/smm2.1214]

[56] J. Naguib, *AI-assisted genotype analysis of hepatitis viruses: A systematic review on precision therapy and sequencing innovations.*.www.ijfmr.com

[57] S. Quazi, "Artificial intelligence and machine learning in precision and genomic medicine", *Med. Oncol.,* vol. 39, no. 8, p. 120, 2022. [http://dx.doi.org/10.1007/s12032-022-01711-1] [PMID: 35704152]

[58] J. Xu, P. Yang, S. Xue, B. Sharma, M. Sanchez-Martin, F. Wang, K.A. Beaty, E. Dehan, and B. Parikh, "Translating cancer genomics into precision medicine with artificial intelligence: applications, challenges and future perspectives", *Hum. Genet.,* vol. 138, no. 2, pp. 109-124, 2019. [http://dx.doi.org/10.1007/s00439-019-01970-5] [PMID: 30671672]

[59] Z. Dlamini, F.Z. Francies, R. Hull, and R. Marima, "Artificial intelligence (AI) and big data in cancer and precision oncology", *Comput. Struct. Biotechnol. J.,* vol. 18, pp. 2300-2311, 2020. [http://dx.doi.org/10.1016/j.csbj.2020.08.019] [PMID: 32994889]

[60] B. Bhinder, C. Gilvary, N.S. Madhukar, and O. Elemento, "Artificial intelligence in cancer research and precision medicine", *Cancer Discov.,* vol. 11, no. 4, pp. 900-915, 2021. [http://dx.doi.org/10.1158/2159-8290.CD-21-0090] [PMID: 33811123]

[61] R. Gupta, D. Srivastava, M. Sahu, S. Tiwari, R.K. Ambasta, and P. Kumar, "Artificial intelligence to deep learning: machine intelligence approach for drug discovery", *Mol. Divers.,* vol. 25, no. 3, pp. 1315-1360, 2021. [http://dx.doi.org/10.1007/s11030-021-10217-3] [PMID: 33844136]

[62] P.C. Tiwari, R. Pal, M.J. Chaudhary, and R. Nath, "Artificial intelligence revolutionizing drug development: Exploring opportunities and challenges", *Drug Dev. Res.,* vol. 84, no. 8, pp. 1652-1663, 2023. [http://dx.doi.org/10.1002/ddr.22115] [PMID: 37712494]

[63] F. Pappalardo, G. Russo, F.M. Tshinanu, and M. Viceconti, "*In silico* clinical trials: concepts and early adoptions", *Brief. Bioinform.,* vol. 20, no. 5, pp. 1699-1708, 2019. [http://dx.doi.org/10.1093/bib/bby043] [PMID: 29868882]

[64] F. Boniolo, E. Dorigatti, A.J. Ohnmacht, D. Saur, B. Schubert, and M.P. Menden, "Artificial intelligence in early drug discovery enabling precision medicine", *Expert Opin. Drug Discov.,* vol. 16, no. 9, pp. 991-1007, 2021. [http://dx.doi.org/10.1080/17460441.2021.1918096] [PMID: 34075855]

[65] B.S. Peters, P.R. Armijo, C. Krause, S.A. Choudhury, and D. Oleynikov, "Review of emerging surgical robotic technology", *Surg. Endosc.,* vol. 32, no. 4, pp. 1636-1655, 2018. [http://dx.doi.org/10.1007/s00464-018-6079-2] [PMID: 29442240]

[66] C.D. Spyropoulos, "AI planning and scheduling in the medical hospital environment", *Artif. Intell. Med.,* vol. 20, no. 2, pp. 101-111, 2000. [http://dx.doi.org/10.1016/S0933-3657(00)00059-2] [PMID: 10936748]

[67] A. Bertelsen, J. Melo, E. Sánchez, and D. Borro, "A review of surgical robots for spinal interventions", *Int. J. Med. Robot.,* vol. 9, no. 4, pp. 407-422, 2013. [http://dx.doi.org/10.1002/rcs.1469] [PMID: 23239581]

[68] M. Runciman, J. Avery, A. Darzi, and G. Mylonas, "Open loop position control of soft hydraulic actuators for minimally invasive surgery", *Appl. Sci. (Basel),* vol. 11, no. 16, p. 7391, 2021.

[http://dx.doi.org/10.3390/app11167391]

[69] N. Danias, and A. Koukopoulos, *Neuralink technology and superego functions: The case of China's social credit system.*.https://orcid.org/0000-0003-0678-5630

[70] G. Arora, J. Joshi, R.S. Mandal, N. Shrivastava, R. Virmani, and T. Sethi, "Artificial intelligence in surveillance, diagnosis, drug discovery and vaccine development against COVID-19", *Pathogens,* vol. 10, no. 8, p. 1048, 2021. [http://dx.doi.org/10.3390/pathogens10081048] [PMID: 34451513]

[71] L. Zhang, W. Guo, and C. Lv, "Modern technologies and solutions to enhance surveillance and response systems for emerging zoonotic diseases", *Science in One Health,* vol. 3, p. 100061, 2024. [http://dx.doi.org/10.1016/j.soh.2023.100061] [PMID: 39077381]

[72] K. Tallam, and M.P. Quang, "Applications of artificial intelligence in predicting dengue outbreaks in the face of climate change: a case study along coastal India, 2023", [http://dx.doi.org/10.1101/2023.01.18.23284134]

[73] J. Lorkowski, and M. Malinowska, "The future of medical documentation - Review of selected literature", *Preprints*. 2020. [http://dx.doi.org/10.20944/preprints202005.0350.v1]

[74] L. Orynbay, B. Razakhova, P. Peer, B. Meden, and Ž. Emeršič, "Recent advances in synthesis and interaction of speech, text, and vision", *Electronics (Basel),* vol. 13, no. 9, p. 1726, 2024. [http://dx.doi.org/10.3390/electronics13091726]

[75] S. Real, and A. Araujo, "Navigation systems for the blind and visually impaired: Past work, challenges, and open problems", *Sensors (Basel),* vol. 19, no. 15, p. 3404, 2019. [http://dx.doi.org/10.3390/s19153404] [PMID: 31382536]

[76] P. Cunningham, M. Cord, and S.J. Delany, "Supervised learning."*Machine learning techniques for multimedia: Case studies on organization and retrieval.,* M. Cord, P. Cunningham, Eds., Springer Berlin Heidelberg: Berlin, Heidelberg, 2008, pp. 21-49. [http://dx.doi.org/10.1007/978-3-540-75171-7_2]

[77] T. Saha, R. Del Caño, K. Mahato, E. De la Paz, C. Chen, S. Ding, L. Yin, and J. Wang, "Wearable electrochemical glucose sensors in diabetes management: A comprehensive review", *Chem. Rev.,* vol. 123, no. 12, pp. 7854-7889, 2023. [http://dx.doi.org/10.1021/acs.chemrev.3c00078] [PMID: 37253224]

[78] M.H. Hassan, C. Vyas, B. Grieve, and P. Bartolo, "Recent advances in enzymatic and non-enzymatic electrochemical glucose sensing", *Sensors (Basel),* vol. 21, no. 14, p. 4672, 2021. [http://dx.doi.org/10.3390/s21144672] [PMID: 34300412]

[79] U.M. Butt, S. Letchmunan, M. Ali, F.H. Hassan, A. Baqir, and H.H.R. Sherazi, "Machine learning based diabetes classification and prediction for healthcare applications", *J. Healthc. Eng.,* vol. 2021, no. 1, pp. 1-17, 2021. [http://dx.doi.org/10.1155/2021/9930985] [PMID: 34631003]

[80] M.A. Makroum, M. Adda, A. Bouzouane, and H. Ibrahim, "Machine learning and smart devices for diabetes management: Systematic review", *Sensors (Basel),* vol. 22, no. 5, p. 1843, 2022. [http://dx.doi.org/10.3390/s22051843] [PMID: 35270989]

[81] H. He, Y. Wang, Y. Qi, Z. Xu, Y. Li, and Y. Wang, "From prediction to design: Recent advances in machine learning for the study of 2D materials", *Nano Energy,* vol. 118, p. 108965, 2023. [http://dx.doi.org/10.1016/j.nanoen.2023.108965]

[82] J. Zhao, X. Han, M. Ouyang, and A.F. Burke, "Specialized deep neural networks for battery health prognostics: Opportunities and challenges", *Journal of Energy Chemistry,* vol. 87, pp. 416-438, 2023. [http://dx.doi.org/10.1016/j.jechem.2023.08.047]

[83] A.G. Barto, "Reinforcement learning."*Neural Systems for Control.,* O. Omidvar, D.L. Elliott, Eds., Academic Press: San Diego, 1997, pp. 7-30.

[http://dx.doi.org/10.1016/B978-012526430-3/50003-9]

[84] Optimizing Decision-Making with AI-Enhanced Support Systems: Leveraging Reinforcement Learning and Bayesian Networks. (2020). International Journal of AI and ML, 1(2). https://www.cognitivecomputingjournal.com/index.php/IJAIML-V1/article/view/59

[85] Y. Sung, H-J. Jeon, D. Kim, M-S. Kim, J. Choi, H.R. Jo, J. Oh, O-J. Lee, and H.G. Lim, "Internal pipe corrosion assessment method in water distribution system using ultrasound and convolutional neural networks", *npj Clean Water,* vol. 7, no. 1, p. 63, 2024. [http://dx.doi.org/10.1038/s41545-024-00358-x]

[86] S. Zhou, B. Chen, E.S. Fu, and H. Yan, "Computer vision meets microfluidics: a label-free method for high-throughput cell analysis", *Microsyst. Nanoeng.,* vol. 9, no. 1, p. 116, 2023. [http://dx.doi.org/10.1038/s41378-023-00562-8] [PMID: 37744264]

[87] A.M. Pattanayak, A. Swetapadma, and B. Sahoo, "Exploring different dynamics of recurrent neural network methods for stock market prediction - A comparative study", *Appl. Artif. Intell.,* vol. 38, no. 1, p. 2371706, 2024. [http://dx.doi.org/10.1080/08839514.2024.2371706]

[88] M. Abotaleb, and P.K. Dutta, "Optimizing long short-term memory networks for univariate time series forecasting: a comprehensive guide."*Non-Linear Optimization Strategies with Artificial Intelligence.,* R. Bhardwaj, P.K. Dutta, P. Raj, A. Kumar, K. Saini, A.G. Briones, M.K.A. Kaabar, Eds., De Gruyter: Berlin, Boston, 2024, pp. 427-442. [http://dx.doi.org/10.1515/9783111331133-020]

[89] Y. He, P. Huang, W. Hong, Q. Luo, L. Li, and K.L. Tsui, "In-depth insights into the application of recurrent neural networks (RNNs) in traffic prediction: A comprehensive review", *Algorithms,* vol. 17, no. 9, p. 398, 2024. [http://dx.doi.org/10.3390/a17090398]

[90] X. Li, H. Zhu, B. Gu, C. Yao, Y. Gu, W. Xu, J. Zhang, J. He, X. Liu, and D. Li, Advancing intelligent organ-on-a-chip systems with comprehensive *in situ* Bioanalysis., *Adv. Mater.,* vol. 36, no. 18, p. 2305268, 2024. [http://dx.doi.org/10.1002/adma.202305268] [PMID: 37688520]

[91] B. Khan, Z. Riaz, R.S. Ahmad, and B.L. Khoo, "Advancements in wearable sensors for cardiovascular disease detection for health monitoring", *Mater. Sci. Eng. Rep.,* vol. 159, p. 100804, 2024. [http://dx.doi.org/10.1016/j.mser.2024.100804]

[92] Y. Zhang, X.T. Zheng, X. Zhang, J. Pan, and A.V.Y. Thean, "Hybrid integration of wearable devices for physiological monitoring", *Chem. Rev.,* vol. 124, no. 18, pp. 10386-10434, 2024. [http://dx.doi.org/10.1021/acs.chemrev.3c00471] [PMID: 39189683]

[93] X. Xu, J. Li, Z. Zhu, L. Zhao, H. Wang, C. Song, Y. Chen, Q. Zhao, J. Yang, and Y. Pei, "A comprehensive review on synergy of multi-modal data and AI technologies in medical diagnosis", *Bioengineering (Basel),* vol. 11, no. 3, p. 219, 2024. [http://dx.doi.org/10.3390/bioengineering11030219] [PMID: 38534493]

[94] J. Duan, J. Xiong, Y. Li, and W. Ding, "Deep learning based multimodal biomedical data fusion: An overview and comparative review", *Inf. Fusion,* vol. 112, p. 102536, 2024. [http://dx.doi.org/10.1016/j.inffus.2024.102536]

[95] K. Plis, R. Bunescu, C. Marling, J. Shubrook, and F. Schwartz, *A machine learning approach to predicting blood glucose levels for diabetes management.*.www.aaai.org

[96] M. Vettoretti, G. Cappon, A. Facchinetti, and G. Sparacino, "Advanced diabetes management using artificial intelligence and continuous glucose monitoring sensors", *Sensors (Basel),* vol. 20, no. 14, p. 3870, 2020. [http://dx.doi.org/10.3390/s20143870] [PMID: 32664432]

[97] S.G. Kumar, S.J. Corrado, T.G. Puranik, and D.N. Mavris, "Application of isolation forest for

detection of energy anomalies in ads-b trajectory data", In: *AIAA SCITECH 2022 Forum,* in AIAA SciTech Forum., American Institute of Aeronautics and Astronautics, 2021. [http://dx.doi.org/10.2514/6.2022-2441]

[98] C. Song, and L. Yao, "Application of artificial intelligence based on synchrosqueezed wavelet transform and improved deep extreme learning machine in water quality prediction", *Environ. Sci. Pollut. Res. Int.,* vol. 29, no. 25, pp. 38066-38082, 2022. [http://dx.doi.org/10.1007/s11356-022-18757-3] [PMID: 35067886]

[99] K. Sinha, Z. Uddin, H.I. Kawsar, S. Islam, M.J. Deen, and M.M.R. Howlader, "Analyzing chronic disease biomarkers using electrochemical sensors and artificial neural networks", *Trends Analyt. Chem.,* vol. 158, p. 116861, 2023. [http://dx.doi.org/10.1016/j.trac.2022.116861]

[100] S.S. Arya, S.B. Dias, H.F. Jelinek, L.J. Hadjileontiadis, and A.M. Pappa, "The convergence of traditional and digital biomarkers through AI-assisted biosensing: A new era in translational diagnostics?", *Biosens. Bioelectron.,* vol. 235, p. 115387, 2023. [http://dx.doi.org/10.1016/j.bios.2023.115387] [PMID: 37229842]

[101] L.C. Malucelli, "Analytical accuracy and clinical agreement of a novel internet of things and ai-based point-of-care testing laboratory", *medRxiv,* p. 2021.10.29.21264864. [http://dx.doi.org/10.1101/2021.10.29.21264864]

[102] A.T. Shumba, T. Montanaro, I. Sergi, L. Fachechi, M. De Vittorio, and L. Patrono, "Leveraging IoT-aware technologies and AI Techniques for real-time critical healthcare applications", *Sensors (Basel),* vol. 22, no. 19, p. 7675, 2022. [http://dx.doi.org/10.3390/s22197675] [PMID: 36236773]

[103] L. Sun, X. Jiang, H. Ren, and Y. Guo, "Edge-cloud computing and artificial intelligence in internet of medical things: architecture, technology and application", *IEEE Access,* vol. 8, pp. 101079-101092, 2020. [http://dx.doi.org/10.1109/ACCESS.2020.2997831]

[104] E. Chen, S. Prakash, V. Janapa Reddi, D. Kim, and P. Rajpurkar, "A framework for integrating artificial intelligence for clinical care with continuous therapeutic monitoring", *Nat. Biomed. Eng.,* vol. 9, no. 4, pp. 445-454, 2023. [http://dx.doi.org/10.1038/s41551-023-01115-0] [PMID: 37932379]

[105] A. Sabovic, M. Aernouts, D. Subotic, J. Fontaine, E. De Poorter, and J. Famaey, "Towards energy-aware tinyML on battery-less IoT devices", *Internet of Things,* vol. 22, p. 100736, 2023. [http://dx.doi.org/10.1016/j.iot.2023.100736]

[106] R. Kallimani, K. Pai, P. Raghuwanshi, S. Iyer, and O.L.A. López, "TinyML: Tools, applications, challenges, and future research directions", *Multimedia Tools Appl.,* vol. 83, no. 10, pp. 29015-29045, 2023. [http://dx.doi.org/10.1007/s11042-023-16740-9]

[107] S. Dhamal Bharati Vidyapeeth, J. Thorat Bharati Vidyapeeth, V. Dhamal, S.V. Dhamal, and J.C. Thorat, *IOT applications in analytical chemistry: real-time monitoring and sensing chapter-5 iot applications in analytical chemistry: real-time monitoring and sensing.* 2023. https://www.researchgate.net/publication/373862751

[108] M. Mayer, and A.J. Baeumner, "A megatrend challenging analytical chemistry: Biosensor and chemosensor concepts ready for the internet of things", *Chem. Rev.,* vol. 119, no. 13, pp. 7996-8027, 2019. [http://dx.doi.org/10.1021/acs.chemrev.8b00719] [PMID: 31070892]

[109] C. Legner, U. Kalwa, V. Patel, A. Chesmore, and S. Pandey, "Sweat sensing in the smart wearables era: Towards integrative, multifunctional and body-compliant perspiration analysis", *Sens. Actuators A Phys.,* vol. 296, pp. 200-221, 2019. [http://dx.doi.org/10.1016/j.sna.2019.07.020]

[110] W. Gao, S. Emaminejad, H.Y.Y. Nyein, S. Challa, K. Chen, A. Peck, H.M. Fahad, H. Ota, H. Shiraki, D. Kiriya, D.H. Lien, G.A. Brooks, R.W. Davis, and A. Javey, Fully integrated wearable sensor arrays for multiplexed *in situ* perspiration analysis., *Nature,* vol. 529, no. 7587, pp. 509-514, 2016. [http://dx.doi.org/10.1038/nature16521] [PMID: 26819044]

[111] M. Alshamrani, "IoT and artificial intelligence implementations for remote healthcare monitoring systems: A survey", *J King Saud Univ Comput Inf Sci,* vol. 34, no. 8, pp. 4687-4701, 2022. [http://dx.doi.org/10.1016/j.jksuci.2021.06.005]

[112] R. Dwivedi, D. Mehrotra, and S. Chandra, "Potential of internet of medical things (IoMT) applications in building a smart healthcare system: A systematic review", *J. Oral Biol. Craniofac. Res.,* vol. 12, no. 2, pp. 302-318, 2022. [http://dx.doi.org/10.1016/j.jobcr.2021.11.010] [PMID: 34926140]

[113] Z. Zhou, T. Xu, and X. Zhang, "Empowerment of AI algorithms in biochemical sensors", *Trends Analyt. Chem.,* vol. 173, p. 117613, 2024. [http://dx.doi.org/10.1016/j.trac.2024.117613]

[114] Y. Wu, A. AL-Huqail, Z.A. Farhan, T. Alkhalifah, F. Alturise, and H.E. Ali, "Enhanced artificial intelligence for electrochemical sensors in monitoring and removing of azo dyes and food colorant substances", *Food Chem. Toxicol.,* vol. 169, p. 113398, 2022. [http://dx.doi.org/10.1016/j.fct.2022.113398] [PMID: 36096291]

[115] R. Ahmad, B. Rinner, R. Wazirali, S.K.M. Abujayyab, and R. Almajalid, "Two-level sensor self-calibration based on interpolation and autoregression for low-cost wireless sensor networks", *IEEE Sens. J.,* vol. 23, no. 20, pp. 25242-25253, 2023. [http://dx.doi.org/10.1109/JSEN.2023.3309759]

[116] A. Asilian, and S.M. Zanjani, "Application of levenberg-marquardt backpropagation algorithm in artificial neural network for self-calibration of deflection type wheatstone bridge circuit in CO electrochemical gas sensor", *Majlesi Journal of Electrical Engineering,* vol. 18, no. 1, pp. 21-32, 2024. [http://dx.doi.org/10.30486/mjee.2023.1988651.1157]

[117] H. Sorouri, A. Oshnoei, Y. Che, and R. Teodorescu, "A comprehensive review of hybrid battery state of charge estimation: Exploring physics-aware AI-based approaches", *J. Energy Storage,* vol. 100, p. 113604, 2024. [http://dx.doi.org/10.1016/j.est.2024.113604]

[118] M. Borah, Q. Wang, S. Moura, D.U. Sauer, and W. Li, "Synergizing physics and machine learning for advanced battery management", *Commun. Eng.,* vol. 3, no. 1, p. 134, 2024. [http://dx.doi.org/10.1038/s44172-024-00273-6] [PMID: 39300192]

[119] L.K. Vora, A.D. Gholap, K. Jetha, R.R.S. Thakur, H.K. Solanki, and V.P. Chavda, "Artificial intelligence in pharmaceutical technology and drug delivery design", *Pharmaceutics,* vol. 15, no. 7, p. 1916, 2023. [http://dx.doi.org/10.3390/pharmaceutics15071916] [PMID: 37514102]

[120] L. Zheng, M. Cao, Y. Du, Q. Liu, M.Y. Emran, A. Kotb, M. Sun, C.B. Ma, and M. Zhou, "Artificial enzyme innovations in electrochemical devices: advancing wearable and portable sensing technologies", *Nanoscale,* vol. 16, no. 1, pp. 44-60, 2023. [http://dx.doi.org/10.1039/D3NR05728C] [PMID: 38053393]

[121] M.A. Mujawar, H. Gohel, S.K. Bhardwaj, S. Srinivasan, N. Hickman, and A. Kaushik, "Nano-enabled biosensing systems for intelligent healthcare: towards COVID-19 management", *Mater. Today Chem.,* vol. 17, p. 100306, 2020. [http://dx.doi.org/10.1016/j.mtchem.2020.100306] [PMID: 32835155]

[122] P.G. Jacobs, P. Herrero, A. Facchinetti, J. Vehi, B. Kovatchev, M.D. Breton, A. Cinar, K.S. Nikita, F.J. Doyle, J. Bondia, T. Battelino, J.R. Castle, K. Zarkogianni, R. Narayan, and C. Mosquera-Lopez, "Artificial intelligence and machine learning for improving glycemic control in diabetes: Best practices, pitfalls, and opportunities", *IEEE Rev. Biomed. Eng.,* vol. 17, pp. 19-41, 2024.

[http://dx.doi.org/10.1109/RBME.2023.3331297] [PMID: 37943654]

[123] M. Eghbali-Zarch, and S. Masoud, "Application of machine learning in affordable and accessible insulin management for type 1 and 2 diabetes: A comprehensive review", *Artif. Intell. Med.,* vol. 151, p. 102868, 2024.
[http://dx.doi.org/10.1016/j.artmed.2024.102868] [PMID: 38632030]

[124] J. Zhao, X. Qu, Y. Wu, M. Fowler, and A.F. Burke, "Artificial intelligence-driven real-world battery diagnostics", *Energy and AI,* vol. 18, p. 100419, 2024.
[http://dx.doi.org/10.1016/j.egyai.2024.100419]

[125] R. Qureshi, M. Irfan, H. Ali, A. Khan, A.S. Nittala, S. Ali, A. Shah, T.M. Gondal, F. Sadak, Z. Shah, M.U. Hadi, S. Khan, Q. Al-Tashi, J. Wu, A. Bermak, and T. Alam, "Artificial intelligence and biosensors in healthcare and its clinical relevance: A review", *IEEE Access,* vol. 11, pp. 61600-61620, 2023.
[http://dx.doi.org/10.1109/ACCESS.2023.3285596]

[126] D. Prakashan, A. Kaushik, and S. Gandhi, "Smart sensors and wound dressings: Artificial intelligence-supported chronic skin monitoring – A review", *Chem. Eng. J.,* vol. 497, p. 154371, 2024.
[http://dx.doi.org/10.1016/j.cej.2024.154371]

[127] S.K. Garg, and H.K. Akturk, "The future of continuous glucose monitoring", *Diabetes Technol. Ther.,* vol. 19, no. S3, pp. S-1-S-2, 2017.
[http://dx.doi.org/10.1089/dia.2017.0097] [PMID: 28585872]

[128] I. Rodríguez-Rodríguez, M. Campo-Valera, and J.V. Rodríguez, "Forecasting glycaemia for type 1 diabetes mellitus patients by means of IoMT devices", *Internet of Things,* vol. 24, p. 100945, 2023.
[http://dx.doi.org/10.1016/j.iot.2023.100945]

[129] I. Contreras, and J. Vehi, "Artificial intelligence for diabetes management and decision support: Literature review", *J. Med. Internet Res.,* vol. 20, no. 5, p. e10775, 2018.
[http://dx.doi.org/10.2196/10775] [PMID: 29848472]

[130] E.A. Pustozerov, A.S. Tkachuk, E.A. Vasukova, A.D. Anopova, M.A. Kokina, I.V. Gorelova, T.M. Pervunina, E.N. Grineva, and P.V. Popova, "Machine learning approach for postprandial blood glucose prediction in gestational diabetes mellitus", *IEEE Access,* vol. 8, pp. 219308-219321, 2020.
[http://dx.doi.org/10.1109/ACCESS.2020.3042483]

[131] Z. Jahangir, H. Qureshi, and J. Naguib, *From data to decisions: The AI revolution in diabetes care.* 2023. https://www.researchgate.net/publication/383359865

[132] M. Shomali, P. Mora, G. Aleppo, M. Peeples, A. Kumbara, J. MacLeod, and A. Iyer, "The critical elements of digital health in diabetes and cardiometabolic care", *Front. Endocrinol. (Lausanne),* vol. 15, p. 1469471, 2024.
[http://dx.doi.org/10.3389/fendo.2024.1469471] [PMID: 39351525]

[133] Z. Jeddi, and A. Bohr, "Remote patient monitoring using artificial intelligence."*Artificial Intelligence in Healthcare.,* A. Bohr, K. Memarzadeh, Eds., Academic Press, 2020, pp. 203-234.
[http://dx.doi.org/10.1016/B978-0-12-818438-7.00009-5]

[134] A. Ahmed, S. Aziz, A. Abd-alrazaq, F. Farooq, M. Househ, and J. Sheikh, "the effectiveness of wearable devices using artificial intelligence for blood glucose level forecasting or prediction: Systematic review", *J. Med. Internet Res.,* vol. 25, p. e40259, 2023.
[http://dx.doi.org/10.2196/40259] [PMID: 36917147]

[135] T. Addissouky, M. Ali, I.E.T. El Sayed, and Y. Wang, "Revolutionary innovations in diabetes research: From biomarkers to genomic medicine", *Iran J Diabetes Obes,* Dec 2023.
[http://dx.doi.org/10.18502/ijdo.v15i4.14556]

[136] V. Mani, T. Beduk, W. Khushaim, A.E. Ceylan, S. Timur, O.S. Wolfbeis, and K.N. Salama, "Electrochemical sensors targeting salivary biomarkers: A comprehensive review", *Trends Analyt. Chem.,* vol. 135, p. 116164, 2021.

[http://dx.doi.org/10.1016/j.trac.2020.116164]

[137] A.J. Steckl, and P. Ray, "Stress biomarkers in biological fluids and their point-of-use detection", *ACS Sens.,* vol. 3, no. 10, pp. 2025-2044, 2018. [http://dx.doi.org/10.1021/acssensors.8b00726] [PMID: 30264989]

[138] M.F.M. Fathil, M.K. Md Arshad, S.C. Gopinath, U. Hashim, R. Adzhri, R.M. Ayub, A.R. Ruslinda, M. Nuzaihan M N, A.H. Azman, M. Zaki, and T.H. Tang, "Diagnostics on acute myocardial infarction: Cardiac troponin biomarkers", *Biosens. Bioelectron.,* vol. 70, pp. 209-220, 2015. [http://dx.doi.org/10.1016/j.bios.2015.03.037] [PMID: 25841117]

[139] Ø. Fluge, O. Mella, O. Bruland, K. Risa, S.E. Dyrstad, K. Alme, I.G. Rekeland, D. Sapkota, G.V. Røsland, A. Fosså, I. Ktoridou-Valen, S. Lunde, K. Sørland, K. Lien, I. Herder, H. Thürmer, M.E. Gotaas, K.A. Baranowska, L.M.L.J. Bohnen, C. Schäfer, A. McCann, K. Sommerfelt, L. Helgeland, P.M. Ueland, O. Dahl, and K.J. Tronstad, "Metabolic profiling indicates impaired pyruvate dehydrogenase function in myalgic encephalopathy/chronic fatigue syndrome", *JCI Insight,* vol. 1, no. 21, p. e89376, 2016. [http://dx.doi.org/10.1172/jci.insight.89376] [PMID: 28018972]

[140] R.K. Upadhyay, "Emerging risk biomarkers in cardiovascular diseases and disorders", *J. Lipids,* vol. 2015, no. 1, pp. 1-50, 2015. [http://dx.doi.org/10.1155/2015/971453] [PMID: 25949827]

[141] S. Manoharan Nair Sudha Kumari, and X. Thankappan Suryabai, "Sensing the future—frontiers in biosensors: Exploring classifications, principles, and recent advances", *ACS Omega,* vol. 9, no. 50, pp. 48918-48987, 2024. [http://dx.doi.org/10.1021/acsomega.4c07991] [PMID: 39713646]

[142] C. Krittanawong, A.J. Rogers, K.W. Johnson, Z. Wang, M.P. Turakhia, J.L. Halperin, and S.M. Narayan, "Integration of novel monitoring devices with machine learning technology for scalable cardiovascular management", *Nat. Rev. Cardiol.,* vol. 18, no. 2, pp. 75-91, 2021. [http://dx.doi.org/10.1038/s41569-020-00445-9] [PMID: 33037325]

[143] K.R. King, L.P. Grazette, D.N. Paltoo, J.T. McDevitt, S.K. Sia, P.M. Barrett, F.S. Apple, P.A. Gurbel, R. Weissleder, H. Leeds, E.J. Iturriaga, A.K. Rao, B. Adhikari, P. Desvigne-Nickens, Z.S. Galis, and P. Libby, "Point-of-care technologies for precision cardiovascular care and clinical research", *JACC Basic Transl. Sci.,* vol. 1, no. 1-2, pp. 73-86, 2016. [http://dx.doi.org/10.1016/j.jacbts.2016.01.008] [PMID: 26977455]

[144] J. Wei, X. Zhang, S.M. Mugo, and Q. Zhang, "A portable sweat sensor based on carbon quantum dots for multiplex detection of cardiovascular health biomarkers", *Anal. Chem.,* vol. 94, no. 37, pp. 12772-12780, 2022. [http://dx.doi.org/10.1021/acs.analchem.2c02587] [PMID: 36066349]

[145] F.G. Bellagambi, A. Baraket, A. Longo, M. Vatteroni, N. Zine, J. Bausells, R. Fuoco, F. Di Francesco, P. Salvo, G.S. Karanasiou, D.I. Fotiadis, A. Menciassi, and A. Errachid, "Electrochemical biosensor platform for TNF-α cytokines detection in both artificial and human saliva: Heart failure", *Sens. Actuators B Chem.,* vol. 251, pp. 1026-1033, 2017. [http://dx.doi.org/10.1016/j.snb.2017.05.169]

[146] E.E. Tripoliti, P. Ioannidou, P. Toumpaniaris, A. Rammos, D. Pacitto, J.C. Lourme, Y. Goletsis, K.K. Naka, A. Errachid, and D.I. Fotiadis, "Point-of-care testing devices for heart failure analyzing blood and saliva samples", *IEEE Rev. Biomed. Eng.,* vol. 13, pp. 17-31, 2020. [http://dx.doi.org/10.1109/RBME.2019.2905730] [PMID: 30892234]

[147] M.S. Sumitha, and T.S. Xavier, "Recent advances in electrochemical biosensors – A brief review", *Hybrid Advances,* vol. 2, p. 100023, 2023. [http://dx.doi.org/10.1016/j.hybadv.2023.100023]

[148] G. Hanrahan, D.G. Patil, and J. Wang, "Electrochemical sensors for environmental monitoring: design, development and applications", *J. Environ. Monit.,* vol. 6, no. 8, pp. 657-664, 2004.

[http://dx.doi.org/10.1039/b403975k] [PMID: 15292947]

[149] X. Shi, G. Zhang, Y. Lu, and H. Pang, "Applications of machine learning in electrochemistry", *Renewables,* vol. 1, no. 6, pp. 668-693, 2023. [http://dx.doi.org/10.31635/renewables.023.202300039]

[150] L. Ayala, *Cybersecurity for Hospitals and Healthcare Facilities.* Apress, 2016. [http://dx.doi.org/10.1007/978-1-4842-2155-6]

[151] P. Singh, N. Singh, K.K. Singh, and A. Singh, "Diagnosing of disease using machine learning."*Machine Learning and the Internet of Medical Things in Healthcare.,* K.K. Singh, M. Elhoseny, A. Singh, A.A. Elngar, Eds., Academic Press, 2021, pp. 89-111. [http://dx.doi.org/10.1016/B978-0-12-821229-5.00003-3]

[152] K.J. Prabhod, The Role of Machine Learning in Genomic Medicine: Advancements in Disease Prediction and Treatment. Journal of Deep Learning in Genomic Data Analysis, 2022, vol. 2, no. 1, p. 1–52. https://thelifescience.org/index.php/jdlgda/article/view/24

[153] D.R. Sarvamangala, and R.V. Kulkarni, "Convolutional neural networks in medical image understanding: a survey", *Evol. Intell.,* vol. 15, no. 1, pp. 1-22, 2022. [http://dx.doi.org/10.1007/s12065-020-00540-3] [PMID: 33425040]

[154] M.G. Seneff, J.E. Zimmerman, W.A. Knaus, D.P. Wagner, and E.A. Draper, "Predicting the duration of mechanical ventilation. The importance of disease and patient characteristics", *Chest,* vol. 110, no. 2, pp. 469-479, 1996. [http://dx.doi.org/10.1378/chest.110.2.469] [PMID: 8697853]

[155] S. Mohan, C. Thirumalai, and G. Srivastava, "Effective heart disease prediction using hybrid machine learning techniques", *IEEE Access,* vol. 7, pp. 81542-81554, 2019. [http://dx.doi.org/10.1109/ACCESS.2019.2923707]

[156] C.M. Bhatt, P. Patel, T. Ghetia, and P.L. Mazzeo, "Effective heart disease prediction using machine learning techniques", *Algorithms,* vol. 16, no. 2, p. 88, 2023. [http://dx.doi.org/10.3390/a16020088]

[157] M.M. Rahman, B.C. Desai, and P. Bhattacharya, "Medical image retrieval with probabilistic multi-class support vector machine classifiers and adaptive similarity fusion", *Comput. Med. Imaging Graph.,* vol. 32, no. 2, pp. 95-108, 2008. [http://dx.doi.org/10.1016/j.compmedimag.2007.10.001] [PMID: 18037271]

[158] P. Palimkar, R.N. Shaw, and A. Ghosh, "Machine learning technique to prognosis diabetes disease: random forest classifier approach."*Advanced Computing and Intelligent Technologies.,* M. Bianchini, V. Piuri, S. Das, R.N. Shaw, Eds., Springer Singapore: Singapore, 2022, pp. 219-244. [http://dx.doi.org/10.1007/978-981-16-2164-2_19]

[159] A.Z. Arrayyan, H. Setiawan, and K.T. Putra, "Naive bayes for diabetes prediction: Developing a classification model for risk identification in specific populations", *Semesta Teknika,* vol. 27, no. 1, pp. 28-36, 2024. [http://dx.doi.org/10.18196/st.v27i1.21008]

[160] S. Bijari, S. Sayfollahi, S. Mardokh-Rouhani, S. Bijari, S. Moradian, Z. Zahiri, and S.M. Rezaeijo, "Radiomics and deep features: Robust classification of brain hemorrhages and reproducibility analysis using a 3D autoencoder neural network", *Bioengineering (Basel),* vol. 11, no. 7, p. 643, 2024. [http://dx.doi.org/10.3390/bioengineering11070643] [PMID: 39061725]

[161] R.W. Grant, J. McCloskey, M. Hatfield, C. Uratsu, J.D. Ralston, E. Bayliss, and C.J. Kennedy, "Use of latent class analysis and k-means clustering to identify complex patient profiles", *JAMA Netw. Open,* vol. 3, no. 12, pp. e2029068-e2029068, 2020. [http://dx.doi.org/10.1001/jamanetworkopen.2020.29068] [PMID: 33306116]

[162] C.G. Victora, S.R. Huttly, S.C. Fuchs, and M.T. Olinto, "The role of conceptual frameworks in epidemiological analysis: a hierarchical approach", *Int. J. Epidemiol.,* vol. 26, no. 1, pp. 224-227,

1997.
[http://dx.doi.org/10.1093/ije/26.1.224] [PMID: 9126524]

[163] A. Rehman, S. Naz, and I. Razzak, "Leveraging big data analytics in healthcare enhancement: trends, challenges and opportunities", *Multimedia Syst.,* vol. 28, no. 4, pp. 1339-1371, 2022.
[http://dx.doi.org/10.1007/s00530-020-00736-8]

[164] F. Esmaeili, E. Cassie, H.P.T. Nguyen, N.O.V. Plank, C.P. Unsworth, and A. Wang, "Anomaly detection for sensor signals utilizing deep learning autoencoder-based neural networks", *Bioengineering (Basel),* vol. 10, no. 4, p. 405, 2023.
[http://dx.doi.org/10.3390/bioengineering10040405] [PMID: 37106591]

[165] S. Mao, and E. Sejdić, "A review of recurrent neural network-based methods in computational physiology", *IEEE Trans. Neural Netw. Learn. Syst.,* vol. 34, no. 10, pp. 6983-7003, 2023.
[http://dx.doi.org/10.1109/TNNLS.2022.3145365] [PMID: 35130174]

[166] Y. Chen, X.H. Yang, Z. Wei, A.A. Heidari, N. Zheng, Z. Li, H. Chen, H. Hu, Q. Zhou, and Q. Guan, "Generative adversarial networks in medical image augmentation: A review", *Comput. Biol. Med.,* vol. 144, p. 105382, 2022.
[http://dx.doi.org/10.1016/j.compbiomed.2022.105382] [PMID: 35276550]

[167] A. Coronato, M. Naeem, G. De Pietro, and G. Paragliola, "Reinforcement learning for intelligent healthcare applications: A survey", *Artif. Intell. Med.,* vol. 109, p. 101964, 2020.
[http://dx.doi.org/10.1016/j.artmed.2020.101964] [PMID: 34756216]

[168] N. Rane, S.P. Choudhary, and J. Rane, "Ensemble deep learning and machine learning: applications, opportunities, challenges, and future directions", *Studies in Medical and Health Sciences,* vol. 1, no. 2, pp. 18-41, 2024.
[http://dx.doi.org/10.48185/smhs.v1i2.1225]

[169] M. Soui, N. Mansouri, R. Alhamad, M. Kessentini, and K. Ghedira, "NSGA-II as feature selection technique and AdaBoost classifier for COVID-19 prediction using patient's symptoms", *Nonlinear Dyn.,* vol. 106, no. 2, pp. 1453-1475, 2021.
[http://dx.doi.org/10.1007/s11071-021-06504-1] [PMID: 34025034]

[170] T. Kavzoglu, and A. Teke, "Predictive performances of ensemble machine learning algorithms in landslide susceptibility mapping using random forest, extreme gradient boosting (XGBoost) and natural gradient boosting (NGBoost)", *Arab. J. Sci. Eng.,* vol. 47, no. 6, pp. 7367-7385, 2022.
[http://dx.doi.org/10.1007/s13369-022-06560-8]

[171] P.I. Adamu, M.O. Adamu, H.I. Okagbue, L. Opoola, and S.A. Bishop, "Survival analysis of cancer patients in north eastern Nigeria from 2004 – 2017 – A kaplan - meier method", *Open Access Maced. J. Med. Sci.,* vol. 7, no. 4, pp. 642-649, 2019.
[http://dx.doi.org/10.3889/oamjms.2019.109] [PMID: 30894929]

[172] P. Almagro, B. Barreiro, A. Ochoa de Echagüen, S. Quintana, M. Rodríguez Carballeira, J.L. Heredia, and J. Garau, "Risk factors for hospital readmission in patients with chronic obstructive pulmonary disease", *Respiration,* vol. 73, no. 3, pp. 311-317, 2006.
[http://dx.doi.org/10.1159/000088092] [PMID: 16155352]

[173] S. Bellamkonda, *Securing data with encryption: A comprehensive guide 'Securing data with encryption: A comprehensive guide,',* 2019.https://www.researchgate.net/publication/385624069

[174] R. Uddin, and I. Koo, Real-time remote patient monitoring: A review of biosensors integrated with multi-Hop IoT systems *via* Cloud Connectivity., *Appl. Sci. (Basel),* vol. 14, no. 5, p. 1876, 2024.
[http://dx.doi.org/10.3390/app14051876]

[175] S. Satish, H. Gonaygunta, K. Meduri, and M.H. Maturi, A comprehensive analysis of security and privacy concerns in healthcare applications of fog computing. *International Numeric Journal of Machine Learning and Robots*, vol. 6, no. 6, 1-25, 2022. https://injmr.com/index.php/fewfewf/article/view/84

[176] M.I. Zulfiqar, and I. Younis, "Enhanced security paradigms: Converging IoT and biometrics for advanced locker protection", *IEEE Internet Things J.,* vol. 11, no. 20, pp. 33811-33819, 2024. [http://dx.doi.org/10.1109/JIOT.2024.3432282]

[177] I. Basdekis, "Pseudonymisation in the context of GDPR-compliant medical research", In: *2023 19th International Conference on the Design of Reliable Communication Networks (DRCN),* 2023, pp. 1–6. [http://dx.doi.org/10.1109/DRCN57075.2023.10108370]

[178] I. Makhdoom, M. Abolhasan, J. Lipman, N. Shariati, D. Franklin, and M. Piccardi, "Securing personally identifiable information: A survey of SOTA techniques, and a way forward", *IEEE Access,* vol. 12, pp. 116740-116770, 2024. [http://dx.doi.org/10.1109/ACCESS.2024.3447017]

[179] M. Papoutsakis, K. Fysarakis, G. Spanoudakis, S. Ioannidis, and K. Koloutsou, "Towards a collection of security and privacy patterns", *Appl. Sci. (Basel),* vol. 11, no. 4, p. 1396, 2021. [http://dx.doi.org/10.3390/app11041396]

[180] V. Kumar, R. Vangoor, A. K. Reddy, and C. S. Ravi, "Distributed learning and broad applications in scientific research", 2019.

[181] Y.Y. Ghadi, T. Mazhar, T. Shahzad, M. Amir khan, A. Abd-Alrazaq, A. Ahmed, and H. Hamam, "The role of blockchain to secure internet of medical things", *Sci. Rep.,* vol. 14, no. 1, p. 18422, 2024. [http://dx.doi.org/10.1038/s41598-024-68529-x] [PMID: 39117650]

[182] N. Rane, S. Choudhary, and J. Rane, "Explainable artificial intelligence (XAI) in healthcare: Interpretable models for clinical decision support", *SSRN,* 2023. [http://dx.doi.org/10.2139/ssrn.4637897]

[183] D. Sargiotis, "Legal and regulatory considerations in data governance."*Data Governance: A Guide.,* D. Sargiotis, Ed., Springer Nature Switzerland: Cham, 2024, pp. 445-466. [http://dx.doi.org/10.1007/978-3-031-67268-2_15]

[184] P. Mulgund, B.P. Mulgund, R. Sharman, and R. Singh, "The implications of the California Consumer Privacy Act (CCPA) on healthcare organizations: Lessons learned from early compliance experiences", *Health Policy Technol.,* vol. 10, no. 3, p. 100543, 2021. [http://dx.doi.org/10.1016/j.hlpt.2021.100543]

[185] Q. Wang, Z.H. Ren, W.M. Zhao, L. Wang, X. Yan, A. Zhu, F. Qiu, and K.K. Zhang, "Research advances on surface plasmon resonance biosensors", *Nanoscale,* vol. 14, no. 3, pp. 564-591, 2022. [http://dx.doi.org/10.1039/D1NR05400G] [PMID: 34940766]

[186] I. Adamopoulos, A. Valamontes, J. Karantonis, N. Syrou, I. Damikouka, and G. Dounias, "The impact of PFAS on the public health and safety of future food supply in Europe: Challenges and AI technologies solutions of environmental sustainability", 2025.

[187] N.C. Upreti, V. Singh, and N. Nagpal, *Towards a healthier future: The transformative role of AI in promoting good health and well-being (SDG-3),* 2023.https://dblp.org/pid/64/5313-1.html

[188] https://www.un.org/sustainabledevelopment/health/

[189] S. Kufeoglu, *SDG-9: Industry.* Innovation and infrastructure, 2022, pp. 349-369. [http://dx.doi.org/10.1007/978-3-031-07127-0_11]

[190] https://www.un.org/sustainabledevelopment/infrastructure-industrialization/

[191] https://www.unep.org/topics/sustainable-development-goals/why-do-sustainable-development-goals-matter/goal-12

[192] F. Arduini, L. Micheli, V. Scognamiglio, V. Mazzaracchio, and D. Moscone, "Sustainable materials for the design of forefront printed (bio)sensors applied in agrifood sector", *Trends Analyt. Chem.,* vol. 128, p. 115909, 2020. [http://dx.doi.org/10.1016/j.trac.2020.115909]

[193] https://www.un.org/sustainabledevelopment/globalpartnerships/

[194] C.N. Ugwu, "Sustainable development goals (SDGs) and resilient healthcare systems: Addressing medicine and public health challenges in conflict zones," Medicine, vol. 104, no. 7, 2025, [Online]. Available: https://journals.lww.com/md-journal/fulltext/2025/02140/sustainable_development_goals__sdgs__and_resilient.8.aspx [http://dx.doi.org/10.1097/MD.0000000000041535]

[195] H. Teymourian, A. Barfidokht, and J. Wang, "Electrochemical glucose sensors in diabetes management: an updated review (2010–2020)", *Chem. Soc. Rev.,* vol. 49, no. 21, pp. 7671-7709, 2020. [http://dx.doi.org/10.1039/D0CS00304B] [PMID: 33020790]

[196] J.R. Sempionatto, I. Jeerapan, S. Krishnan, and J. Wang, "Wearable chemical sensors: Emerging systems for on-body analytical chemistry", *Anal. Chem.,* vol. 92, no. 1, pp. 378-396, 2020. [http://dx.doi.org/10.1021/acs.analchem.9b04668] [PMID: 31626731]

[197] Christiana Adeyemi, Bisola Oluwafadekemi Adegoke, and Tolulope Odugbose, "The impact of healthcare information technology on reducing medication errors: A review of recent advances", *Int J Front Med Surg Res,* vol. 5, no. 2, pp. 20-29, 2024. [http://dx.doi.org/10.53294/ijfmsr.2024.5.2.0034]

[198] K. Abouelmehdi, A. Beni-Hessane, and H. Khaloufi, "Big healthcare data: preserving security and privacy", *J. Big Data,* vol. 5, no. 1, p. 1, 2018. [http://dx.doi.org/10.1186/s40537-017-0110-7]

[199] Y. Liu, L. Zhang, Y. Yang, L. Zhou, L. Ren, F. Wang, R. Liu, Z. Pang, and M.J. Deen, "A novel cloud-based framework for the elderly healthcare services using digital twin", *IEEE Access,* vol. 7, pp. 49088-49101, 2019. [http://dx.doi.org/10.1109/ACCESS.2019.2909828]

[200] K. Chen, T.P. Lim, J.S.P. Yuen, H. Ho, and D.G. Murphy, "Regulatory considerations for new drugs and devices."*Translational Urology.,* A.E.M. Eltorai, A. Arab, A. Atala, M.M. Siddiqui, Eds., Academic Press, 2025, pp. 293-299. [http://dx.doi.org/10.1016/B978-0-323-90186-4.00060-2]

[201] S.J. Rimpi, S.J. Verma, Pinky, and A. Baldi, "Evidence-based recommendations for comprehensive regulatory guidelines in medical devices: the imperative for global harmonization", *Naunyn Schmiedebergs Arch. Pharmacol.,* vol. 398, no. 7, pp. 7697-7711, 2025. [http://dx.doi.org/10.1007/s00210-025-03843-3] [PMID: 39907781]

[202] R. V. Allison, "Ensuring patient safety: navigating eu mdr compliance and global policy in healthcare", 2024.

[203] https://www.um.edu.mt/library/oar/handle/123456789/72711

[204] D. Claire, and E. Almojero, *Risks in medical device vigilance,* 2023. https://www.um.edu.mt/library/oar/handle/123456789/115854

[205] FG-AI4H - Focus Group on Artificial Intelligence for Health. (n.d.). Retrieved November 22, 2025, from https://www.itu.int/pub/T-FG-AI4H

[206] J. Morley, E. Hine, H. Roberts, R. Sirbu, H. Ashrafian, C. Blease, M. Boyd, J.L. Chen, A.D.P. Chiavegatto Filho, E. Coiera, I.G. Cohen, A. Fiske, N. Jayakumar, A. Kerasidou, F. Mandreoli, M.D. McCradden, S. Namuganza, E.O. Nsoesie, R.B. Parikh, S. Reddy, J. Sedlakova, T. Sunbul, S. van Baalen, H. van Kolfschooten, and L. Floridi, "Global health in the age of AI", *Charting a Course for Ethical Implementation and Societal Benefit,* no. Apr, 2025. [http://dx.doi.org/10.2139/ssrn.5217060]

[207] Kijewski S, Ronchi E, Vayena E. International organisations and the global governance of AI in health. In: Solaiman B, Cohen IG, editors. Research Handbook on Health, AI and the Law. Cheltenham, UK: Edward Elgar Publishing Ltd; 2024 Jul 16. Chapter 15. Available from: https://www.ncbi.nlm.nih.gov/books/NBK613223/ 10.4337/9781802205657.ch15

[208] F.A. Reegu, H. Abas, Y. Gulzar, Q. Xin, A.A. Alwan, A. Jabbari, R.G. Sonkamble, and R.A. Dziyauddin, "Blockchain-based framework for interoperable electronic health records for an improved healthcare system", *Sustainability (Basel),* vol. 15, no. 8, p. 6337, 2023. [http://dx.doi.org/10.3390/su15086337]

[209] A. Schmidt, "Regulatory challenges in healthcare IT: ensuring compliance with HIPAA and GDPR," Academic Journal of Science and Technology, vol. 3, no. 1, pp. 1−7-1−7, Oct. 2020, Accessed: May 11, 2025. [Online]. Available: https://acadexpinnara.com/index.php/ajst/article/ view/82

[210] E. Isibor, "Regulation of healthcare data security: Legal obligations in a digital age", 2024. [http://dx.doi.org/10.2139/ssrn.4957244]

[211] S. Brayne, S. Mckellar, K. Tzafestas, and R. Georghiou, *Artificial intelligence in the life sciences & patent analytics: Market developments and intellectual property landscape,* 2018.www.ip-pragmatics.com

[212] https://www.butterflynetwork.com/press-releases/fda-clearance-butterfly-auto-b-lines-ai-tool?srsltid=AfmBOooDnAzdrFUfLB-bN6d_oIObeXIVMDFAp6KClI_NL76fJi0riePY

[213] J. Shaffer, A. Alenichev, and M.C. Faure, "The gates foundation's new AI initiative: attempting to leapfrog global health inequalities?", *BMJ Glob. Health,* vol. 8, no. 11, p. e013874, 2023. [http://dx.doi.org/10.1136/bmjgh-2023-013874] [PMID: 37923320]

[214] "Novo nordisk foundation, wellcome, and the bill & melinda gates foundation join forces to accelerate global health equity and impact", *Gates Foundation,* 2024. https://www.gatesfoundation.org/ideas/media-center/press-releases/2024/05/novo-nordisk-wellcome-health

[215] "A complete guide to the FDA's AI/ML guidance for medical devices", *Ketryx.* https://www.ketryx.com/blog/a-complete-guide-to-the-fdas-ai-ml-guidance-for-medical-devices

[216] "AI principles overview", *OECD.AI.*https://oecd.ai/en/ai-principles

[217] M. Pons, E. Valenzuela, B. Rodríguez, J.A. Nolazco-Flores, and C. Del-Valle-Soto, "Utilization of 5G technologies in IoT applications: Current limitations by interference and network optimization difficulties—a review", *Sensors,* vol. 23, no. 8, p. 3876, 2023. [http://dx.doi.org/10.3390/S23083876]

[218] T.P. Quinn, M. Senadeera, S. Jacobs, S. Coghlan, and V. Le, "Trust and medical AI: the challenges we face and the expertise needed to overcome them", *J. Am. Med. Inform. Assoc.,* vol. 28, no. 4, pp. 890-894, 2021. [http://dx.doi.org/10.1093/jamia/ocaa268] [PMID: 33340404]

[219] Z.N. Aghdam, A.M. Rahmani, and M. Hosseinzadeh, "The role of the internet of things in healthcare. Future trends and challenges", *Comput. Methods Programs Biomed.,* vol. 199, p. 105903, 2021. [http://dx.doi.org/10.1016/j.cmpb.2020.105903] [PMID: 33348073]

[220] H. Nandanwar, and R. Katarya, "Deep learning enabled intrusion detection system for industrial IOT environment", *Expert Syst. Appl.,* vol. 249, p. 123808, 2024. [http://dx.doi.org/10.1016/j.eswa.2024.123808]

[221] T. Batiha, M. Prauzek, and P. Krömer, "Intrusion detection in wireless sensor networks by an ensemble of artificial neural networks."*Intelligent Decision Technologies 2019.,* I. Czarnowski, R.J. Howlett, L.C. Jain, Eds., Springer Singapore: Singapore, 2020, pp. 323-333. [http://dx.doi.org/10.1007/978-981-13-8311-3_28]

[222] S.M. Williamson, and V. Prybutok, "Balancing privacy and progress: A review of privacy challenges, systemic oversight, and patient perceptions in AI-driven healthcare", *Appl. Sci. (Basel),* vol. 14, no. 2, p. 675, 2024. [http://dx.doi.org/10.3390/app14020675]

[223] L. Rajabion, A.A. Shaltooki, M. Taghikhah, A. Ghasemi, and A. Badfar, "Healthcare big data processing mechanisms: The role of cloud computing", *Int. J. Inf. Manage.,* vol. 49, pp. 271-289,

2019.
[http://dx.doi.org/10.1016/j.ijinfomgt.2019.05.017]

[224] Bincoletto G. Data protection issues in cross-border interoperability of Electronic Health Record systems within the European Union. Data & Policy. 2020;2:e3.

SUBJECT INDEX

A

B

C

D

E

Shreya Sharma, Peeyush Phogat, Ranjana Jha & Sukhvir Singh (Eds.)

R

S

T

U

V

W

www.ingramcontent.com/pod-product-compliance
Ingram Content Group UK Ltd.
Pitfield, Milton Keynes, MK11 3LW, UK
UKHW060011051026
15591UKWH00002B/148
* 9 7 9 8 8 9 8 8 1 1 8 8 4 *